# Contents

# Acknowledgments

Thanks are due to the following: Barbara Abrash, Tony Bennett, Sarah Berry, Geoff Bishop, Sarah Boston, Elizabeth Botta, Barbara Browning, Scott Bukatman, Ed Buscombe, Mary Byers, Jo Clifford, Stuart Cunningham, John Darling, Jonathan Dawson, Jane Gaines, Jane Gallop, Faye Ginsburg, Mitzi Goldman, Lawrence Grossberg, Petra Harris, John Hartley, May Joseph, Noel King, Micah Kleit, Linda Chiu-han Lai, Tomás López-Pumarejo, Alan Mansfield, Monica Marciczkiewicz, Randy Martin, Rick Maxwell, Tony May, Anne McClintock, Alec McHoul, Jim McKay, Patricia Mellencamp, Jeff Moen, Jennifer Moore, Meaghan Morris, Erika Muhammad, Brendon Murley, Fred Myers, Vinicius Navarro, Rob Nixon, Tom O'Regan, Peggy Phelan, Helen Pringle, Robyn Quin, Michael Real, Paula Real, Michael Renov, Trish Rosen, Andrew Ross, Judy Selhorst, Michael J. Shapiro, Ella Shohat, Paul Smith, Bob Stam, Jon Stratton, Ken Sweeney, Stephanie Tchan, Jennifer Wicke, Josephine Wilson, Peter Winn, Frederick Wiseman, Kathleen Woodward, George Yúdice, and all the people at the University of Minnesota Press. In their many ways, these people contributed to the production of this book.

Acknowledgment is due to those organizations and individuals who kindly permitted me to reproduce illustrative material: Cyril Ayris, Annabel Blay, *HQ Magazine*, Kristine Larsen, Elaine Morgan, Queensland Newspapers Pty. Ltd., Rick Robertson, Danny Tisdale, the Upjohn Company, and Frederick Wiseman. I also wish to thank the following for invitations to deliver addresses that have gone on to appear in chapter form: the Columbia Seminar at the Museum of Modern Art, New York; the Center for Twentieth Century Studies at the University of Wisconsin-Milwaukee; the Eastern Comparative Literature Conference in Honor of Edward W. Said; the Rockefeller Center for Media, Culture, and History at New York University; NYU's Comparative Literature Graduate Student conference; and the Australian Teachers of the Media. Various other forums were good spaces to test out ideas: Visible Evidence, the Marxist Literary Group Institute on Culture and Society, and the International Communication Association. Parts of the manuscript appeared in earlier versions in *Continuum*, *South East Asian Journal of Social Science*, *Social Text*, *Metro*, *Queensland Images*, *Filmnews*, *Culture and Policy*, *Southern Review*, and *Cultural Studies*.

Special thanks to seven people: Caitlin and Sarah—inspirations—and May, Fred, Bob, Andrew, and Faye, for showing me what collegial, companionly work can be.

PART

**I**     *Summations*

# Introduction:
# Daguerrotropes and Such

*In those days [1953] a Yale faculty member who owned a television set lived dangerously. In the midst of an academic community, he lived in sin. Nevertheless, in an act of defiance, we put our television set in the living room instead of the basement or the garage where most of the faculty kept theirs, and we weathered the disapprobation of colleagues who did not own or would not admit to owning this fascinating but forbidden instrument.*
::    Silber 113

*"You write for the radio, don't you?" — Tony*
*"No, television; for my sins." — Mark*
::    *Dial M for Murder*, Alfred Hitchcock, 1954

*Herodotus's* Histories *is the first great prose work in European literature.*
::    blurb for 1974 Penguin Classics edition

*There is slowly emerging a tepid, flaccid Middlebrow Culture that threatens to engulf everything in its spreading ooze.*
::    Macdonald 173

*My hope is my books become true after they have been written — not before.*
::    Foucault "Conversation" 5

Baltimore, 1913. An electric sign spells out "TRUTH" in letters ten feet high at a meeting of the National Association of Advertisers. The meeting produces the "Baltimore Truth Declaration," a code of conduct that specifies and denounces misleading advertising. This commitment to truth as a productive force and a banner for the industries of persuasion was two-sided. It combined an internal uncertainty—what constituted "the true" in a rapidly changing world characterized by competing definitions of need and agency—with an external anxiety: the state might intervene in the association's business through unwelcome regulation (Lears 20). That shift, between self-governance and public governance of the popular, under the sign of the political technology of truth, is the subject matter of this book. A technology is a popularly held logic, and a truth is an accepted fact. Their combination here with the political is intended to signify the abstraction of logic, the qualifier of struggle, and the genitive of reality. Without technology, there is no truth: it has no verb. People may "lie," but they cannot "true." When these technologies congeal to forge loyalty to the sovereign state through custom or art, they do so through the cultural citizen, who steps, sits, and shits outside the formalities of the Constitution, a citizen in need of daily maintenance through lore as much as its homonym. This technologization is not always the outcome of an overarching plan or system on the part of the state; hence a pursuit of the popular. That pursuit attempts to rein in and control folk and commercial cultures when they produce limit cases for cultural capitalism: gender and pornography, localism and internationalism, intellectualism and populism, multiculturalism and unitariness, for example. This book is agnostic about any absolute explanation underpinning the production of such truths through falsification or demystification. Instead, *Technologies of Truth* goes in search of moments when the popular and the civic brush up against one another to see where truth appears in community, commerce, and government. This is not "the affirmation of an irrational history," but "a real and intelligible history . . . of collective rational experiences," knowable through "quite precise and identifiable rules" that constitute a knowing subject, a known object, and their interaction (Lynch and Bogen 25; Foucault *Remarks* 63–64).

I shall return to the question of truth in the conclusion and elaborate an intersemiotic system of confirmation and contradiction. But I wish to signal now that this project does not supplant misrecognition by identifying "errors or illusions, shaded representations—in short, everything that impedes the formation of true discourses." Enough energy has been devoted to this "economy of untruth" and its accompanying commentary (Foucault "End" 147). In ancient, medieval, and modern philosophy, the possibility of truth is clear. Knowing what is true is not easy, but it is unquestionably desirable. Once "modernity" associates *itself* with the truth and justifies imperialism, class societies, Stalinism, gender inequality, racist science, and Nazism, the very idea of truth as a transcendent possibility comes into question. "True" statements become positional, contingent on the space, time, and language in which they are made and heard. So analytic philosophy, hardly an accomplice of poststructuralism, must cling to microscopic, artificial, controllable examples to make its point (Malpas 288, 292, 294). In that context, rather than establishing *what* is true, I want to see *how* truth is established.

The extension through societies of the capacity to read has as its corollary the possibility of a public beyond a group of people physically gathered together. That public is formed and reformed on a routine basis through technologies of truth—popular logics for establishing fact. I am using the concept of technology in a double sense, referring to popular logics as defined above and their embodiment in communicative forms. The multiplication of such technologies over this century has seen the means and sites of truth production themselves increase: more and more popular logics, forms of communicating them, and places for doing so. Radio, for example, has developed genres and themes for stations to organize their audiences, increased transmission and reproduction, and mobilized new spaces of reception, such as the beach and workplace. It has displaced the newspaper's monopoly over time—but limited spatial reach—through a mix of temporal continuity and a less measurable and contained dominion over space. For its part, the telephone made commercial, political, and private relationships both personal and instantaneously intersubjective. In France, its appearance in the 1870s marked a dialogic moment in the country's communications history. Reciprocity and accessibility were distinctively earmarked as never before, as what had been exclusively governmental and scientific instruments became public property (Innis 60; Attali and Stourdze 97–98).

In 1842, three years after daguerreotype images were announced, Congress endorsed them as a means of drawing the boundary between Canada and Maine. Samuel Morse had already told the National Academy of Design that photographs seemed to be "painted by Nature's self," not "copies of nature, but portions of nature herself." The word *daguerreotype* came to represent an unmediated truth that could assist in the mutual accreditation of aesthetic discourse and official culture as sources of realism (Czitrom 3–4). Its aura of rigorous honesty was quickly appropriated by newspapers to describe their overall enterprise, and continues to be so (*Pravda* as a title, or "newspaper of record" as a refrain). Audiovisual culture began to define governmental and Fourth Estate activities in a complex of space, time, and truth I am calling a *daguerrotrope*.

The nineteenth century also saw the appearance of sex and crime journalism in the United States through the penny paper, which derived its legitimacy from popularity, as opposed to a notion of the social function of news. The advent of telegraphy at this time enabled a massive increase in the velocity of information flowing across the United States, meeting the style and content needs of such texts perfectly—journalism could be less deliberative and more instantaneous. This drew critiques of the shift from public affairs to popular minutiae. As the telegraph became connected with the new dissociabilities and insensitivities of modern life, its permissive connection to the production and circulation of truth was brought into question, singled out because a fast relay of market sensitivities disturbed business operators. Cable's capacity to produce truth before breakfast was accused of exhausting newspaper readers' emotional energies at the wrong time of day. Neurological experts attributed their increased business to this and to such factors as the expansion of steam, periodical literature, science, and the education of women. The telegraph's presence in saloons enabled a huge expansion in working-class betting on sporting events. The telegraph's generic messages of goodwill became highly marketable and standardized, the prospect of individual marks—seemingly enhanced through popular education—devastated by the very industrialization that had produced it (Gross et al. 3–4; Czitrom 15, 19–21; Lever and Wheeler 127; Commager 419–20). This had major implications for the management of the population. Commercially determined industrialization and governmentally determined education were frequently uncomfortable with one another. Each pursued the popular for what could be divergent ends: monetary gain and civic conduct.

Industry, science, and the body were joined in a complex of power and knowledge as never before. The expansion of rail travel was a critical site for the emergence of new relations of space and power. Up to the 1850s, the human railway body had not been subjected to a medical gaze. Workers and passengers were soon pathologized, however, as speed, jolts, and noise were found to produce pain, anxiety, and poor verbal communication. "Railway spine" and "brain" were on their way. By the turn of the century, these complexes had been comprehensively theorized, as bodies succumbed to the stress supposedly produced by mechanical reconfigurations of time and space. With science becoming applied and transportation businesses referring to middle-class travelers as packages, the left noted a transformation of workers into commodities (Schivelbusch 113–14, 118, 136, 121, 145).

The steam engine revolutionized the speed of printing as well as travel. Nineteenth-century America and Europe saw spirited debate over whether the new popular genres such as newspapers, crime stories, and novels would breed anarchic readers lacking respect for the traditionally literate classes. The mass media posed a threat to established elites by enabling working people to become independently informed and distracted from their one true path of servitude. (Of course, the new commercialism was experienced across classes. As Jennifer Wicke has illustrated, the rise of "social reading" in the nineteenth century was intimately connected to the nexus of advertising and the novel, in both its popular and high-culture varieties.) It was feared this *Leserevolution* would produce chaotic, permissive practices of reading in place of the continuing study of a few important hermeneutic texts. Such concerns drove Edward Salmon to investigate young British girls' reading habits in the 1880s. Entering "houses of the poor" in search of "the effect on the maiden mind of the trash the maiden buys," he found "dislike of manual work," a lazy "love of freedom" brought on by exposure to "penny fictions" (C. Davidson 14–16; Salmon quoted in M. Barker 11).

The railways offered motion and excitement to early cinema: the Lumière brothers' *L'Arrivée d'un Train en Gare* had 1895 French audiences bobbing and weaving as the train approached the station, and the following year marked the commencement (unbroken since) of footage recording passengers arriving at Australia's Melbourne Cup horse race. Whereas the daguerreotype offered truth, when the next apparatus of vision appeared, it added to the panic from electrified transport and printed communication. By 1913, date of the "Baltimore Truth Declaration," newsreels and long-form narrative cinema had synchronized with neurology and moralism. The *Times* of London feared that the moving image's "new form of excitement . . . massacres, horrible catastrophes, motor-car smashes, [and] public hangings" would appeal to the "greedy eyes" of children, rendering them immune to the affect right-minded youth ought to experience on exposure to such horrors. But there was a counterdiscourse. D. W. Griffith defended *The Birth of a Nation* (1915) against accusations of racism through a revealing mixture of truth and/as distraction: previously restricted access to "the truths of history" policed by the university system would be broken down by cinema, even as it brought "diversion to the masses." Woodrow Wilson called the film "writing history with lightning" (*Times* quoted in M. Barker 11; Griffith quoted in Gross et al. 31; Wilson quoted in Haskell).

Moral decay as a characteristic of popular culture and truth as a means of building citizens form a nexus, ever present but rarely discussed so straightforwardly. By the 1920s, the spread of the car and the radio through North America were thought to have produced a technical and moral deskilling of the workforce, with ease and automation displacing thrift and responsibility, and emotions experienced through simulation. The evidence lay in women's use of cosmetics and men's taste for action-adventure films. By 1940, the telephone had been made responsible for the abolition of loneliness, the emergence of the city, the decline of the country, the prospect of the skyscraper, the democratization of everyday life, and the destruction of the American family. And broadcasting was even more frightening and promising, more contagious and withering, than the essentially private life of reading and talking (Commager 420; Neuman 16; Hartley *Tele-ology* 113).

Contorted connections of danger and value continue to determine discussion of the popular. Whereas electronic mail is hailed as a renewal of epistolary culture *and* a democratization of salon conversation, fiber optics and accelerated communication also threaten written signs, as economies of scale make digital video and audio equipment standard for personal computers. This new anonymity is likened to the chaotic publishing conditions of the French Revolution, when the expression of ideas left no signature. Such moments await legislation to identify thoughts with their authors. The arrival of the state on the scene marks a medium's power, when it has induced sufficient moral panic or potential for profit to generate regulation. These popular technologies have combined commerce, discipline, power, and knowledge under the sign of truth. Radical aspiration and conservative anxiety meet in utopic and dystopic projections that take commercial, governmental, and theoretical flight. Returning to the telegraph, we recall that this boon to instantaneous journalism was at first regarded as dangerously libertarian in its implications for individual communication, a threat to the domination of newspapers. Newspaper owners responded by forming the Associated Press. In a repeat move a century later, AP began to use the World Wide Web to distribute material (Markoff "Rise" and "If Medium"). Inventions that might loosen corporate control of information as a commodity are soon redisposed by oligopolistic organization and the laws of property.

Consider a seemingly quite different question, but one related to the connection of truth to popular culture: how to explain changes in the management of the American infant. Between the 1940s and 1960s, manuals on domestic pediatrics moved from chilly antihumanist accounts of the young child as a machine that should be handled only when broken, to warm, cuddly endorsements of spontaneous physical affection as a critical source of bonding and growth for baby and parent. This epistemological shift was part of a broad spectrum of social and intellectual changes, neither linear nor consistent, that produced correspondences and noncorrespondences among academic, popular, and public health fashions. Anthony Synnott references the alternately contradictory, separate, and isomorphic influences on such developments of "Freudian theory, psycho-therapy, primate research and anthropology . . . the Hippy movement, sensitivity training, somatopsychic theory, existentialist philosophy and, especially, the women's movement" (161).

We can discern similarly complex workings of truth in the life of a book once called *Schindler's Ark* (Thomas Keneally). It won the Booker Prize as Novel of the Year in 1982, became controversial for its success in that competition (was this fiction?), and then underwent a name change to suit North American sensibilities, laying the basis for Steven Spielberg's *Schindler's List* (1993), which won Academy Awards as fiction film of the year and became the source of enormous international debate (was this history?). Prior to publication, advertisements had referred to *Schindler's Ark* as, variously, "fiction," a "non-fiction novel," and, eventually, "fiction-with-an-Author's Note" (advertisements quoted in Quartermaine 62). So here we have a novel, based on fact, that drew intense criticism for lacking any imaginative wellspring after being endorsed as fiction book of the year, that offered truth and imagination to a further popular transformation.

To establish how that happened, we might benefit from looking at Keneally's "Author's Note" accompanying the text. Interviews with fifty survivors from seven countries provided the basis for his work, along with location trips and discussions with Schindler's associates. Keneally pre-empts criticism of the result like this:

> To use the texture and devices of a novel to tell a true story is a course that has frequently been followed in modern writing. It is the one I choose to follow here — both because the novelist's craft is the only one I can lay claim to, and because the novel's techniques seem suited for a character of such ambiguity and magnitude as Oskar. I have attempted, however, to avoid all fiction, since fiction would debase the record. (10)

Elsewhere, he refers to the book as "real science fiction which happened in the past." Had the Holocaust not happened, it would read like futuristic horror. Some critics denounced the book as "nonsense and an insult to fiction writers." Others claimed Keneally had greatly advanced "the cause of the documentary novel." The film drew similar criticism, notably in France. Much had been made there of Claude Lanzmann's *Shoah* (1985), a documentary about the Holocaust that used recorded memories of survivors, a performative point about the inability of Nazism to obliterate a people and their history and a generic one about "entertainment" politics and Holocaust reconstructions. Lanzmann derided Spielberg's attempt on the ground that it was not feasible to treat this subject matter fictively. But

Jeffrey Katzenberg, then head of Walt Disney Studios, said *Schindler's List* would "bring peace on earth, good will to men" and "set the course of world affairs." For one group of critics, it represented what should never be shown in fictive form, as a continuity-system narrative dominated by performance norms. To another group, shooting on location in Poland, incorporating footage of survivors together with the actors who portrayed them, and the sheer force of a major Spielberg event made the Holocaust real to generations who had no direct referent, with handheld camera techniques re-creating the discomfort of the characters for spectators. Audience response added to the confusion. In Germany, attempts were made to generate a class of heroes hidden from history who had fought the Nazis from within, the Lübeck synagogue was set alight—the first such attack since the Nazi era—and revisionist denials of the Holocaust continued. Some African American students laughed during a high school screening, which generated discussion of black-Jewish relations in 1990s America. And in Malaysia, the film was banned as propaganda (critics quoted in Quartermaine 61, 72; Gellately 475–76; Niney; Katzenberg quoted in D. Fogel 315; Manchel 86–87; Hartman 127; Wildt 245; Montgomery; Hansen 295; Niven 167–68, 173–75, 180; Weissman 293).

A seeming oxymoron—a novel that denied fiction—had disarticulated genre from content, generating controversies over truth that mounted with the increased popularity and fame of the book and multiplied following its transmogrification into one of the most feted films of the decade. To comprehend such shifts, we have to see where and how different systems of knowledge intersect and diverge: writing and reading character; generic boundaries; textual and commercial transitions among memory, interview, novelization, script, film production, and reception; the politics of Booker and Academy Award processes; and the status of two authors (one an Irish Australian high-to-middlebrow novelist, the other a Jewish American populist director) becoming, respectively, newly famous and newly serious. These dramatic shifts, across time, space, genre, and uptake, encompass the complexity of the popular and its proclivity for making truths.

The permissiveness of the popular poses problems whenever information is communicable beyond personal interaction. The very social, public, and political nature to such circulation has generally been theorized in cultural-capitalist states by three forms of knowledge: the aesthetic, the psychological, and the economic. Aesthetic discourse labels imagination and routine, distinguishing quality from dross. Psy-discourse identifies development and retardation, separating improvement and danger. Economic discourse measures popularity and elitism, delineating competition and distortion. The longevity and applicability of these systems of thought has given them occasionally overlapping, occasionally conflictual dominance in criticism and public policy. They have exercised great power over the inclusion or exclusion of cultural products in the registers of art, public safety, and mass distribution. All three have regulated popular culture, through textual canons, state intervention, and profit plans: the popular pursued as a contest for the cultural citizen.

As noted above, the domains do merge. Much art and cinema appreciation is concerned with perceptual and Freudian psy-complexes, and psychology gained early-childhood experiences in the aesthetics wing of philosophy. Commercial and cultural goods—plus the role of the state, criticism, and business in policing their relations—inhabit zones that stretch across these discourses. Their jurisdiction of different compartments of cultural existence has been fairly solid. There is a sociology of art and literature, and anthropology is clearly critical to First World appropriation of other cultures, but the split trinity is able to draw from and move into these areas without becoming beholden to them.

The global industrialization of popular culture over the past seventy years has been both providential and baleful for the operation of these discourses. It offers aesthetics a bad object against which materials can be contrasted, licensing textual analysis as a civilizing agent of education. For the psy-complexes, both lounge-based psychoanalysis and laboratory-based psychology, popular culture is an opportunity to uncover collective and individual weakness and strength, for the purposes of either cultural mapping and resistance or policy enumeration and advice. For marginalist economics, comparative advantage, opposition to cultural protection, and a trade-in-services discourse are applied to the popular to gain academic, governmental, and business rent. In each case, the internationalism of entertainment has strengthened the efforts of these discourses to assert their explanatory power while diminishing their statutes of limitation on space, time, and power.

I try in this book to imagine popular culture without being in thrall to the dominant strands of aesthetics, psychology, *or* neoclassical economics, but to observe them as knowledge effects. In other words, I seek to understand forms of media communication in everyday life without condemning or praising through the critical vocabulary associated with textual analysis, human interiority, or imaginary markets. At the same time, away from this somewhat intramural academic concern, I address some crucial issues in contemporary culture. This is a work of cultural studies, but it veers away from many of the standard methods and objects of that field and toward other, perhaps less fashionable, concerns: sports and magazines (not dance music and resistance), documentary and the museum (not feature film and the apparatus), TV citizenship education (not soap operas and unruly viewers), the new international division of cultural labor (not postcolonial autobiography), and masculinity and the law (not critique and confession). I concentrate on the intersection of textual, social, and economic forms of knowledge with the popular under the sign of government. I do not attempt a populist "inversion" that valorizes the spectacular or oppositional over the mundane and ordinary (Frow *Cultural* 6–7; Bourdieu *In Other* 150–55).

The book is divided in two. After a general overview of terminology in this introduction, I examine the field of cultural studies and debates over cultural policy studies in chapters 1 and 2. This picks up on some issues I enumerate in *The Well-Tempered Self*, but I am more concerned here with identifying texts, genres, and systems of interpretation that represent conflicts in contemporary culture. The second half applies those systems of interpretation at four sites, ranging across a variety of media, genres, and problems. Magazines, TV, film, and museums are the media; photojournalism, drama, documentary film, and tourism are the genres; and the cultural problems are masculinity, nationalism, citizenship, and incarceration.

The tensions that unify my concern are best described in Michel Foucault's concept of governmentality, elaborated below. He uses the term to explain "the way in which the modern state began to worry about individuals." This helps to account for a paradox, that even as Revolutionary France was embarking on a regime of slaughter, public health campaigns were under way. This was the ongoing Janus-faced "game between death and life" the state constructs for itself ("Conversation" 4). I deploy governmentality to understand three key concepts: textuality, population, and policy. The aim is to provide a radical critique of how culture and power function, from a fictocritical angle. Fictocriticism emerges at the point where theory tells tales, where it is itself revealed as a narrative. Uncovering this narrativization displaces "why" questions with "how" questions: How did I get here, which traces can I uncover, and what do they tell me about roads left untraveled? Subjectivity is both produced through writing and research *and* assigned an originary function, but each status is conditional. Fictocriticism moves along a track of (dis)alignment among feature journalism, academic theory, confessional narration, and the postmodern. As such, it is marked by publishing house and genre, the fraction of a culture industry that sustains it. The result is multiperspectival but also partial, a book of opinion that presents unresolved contortions and problems:

I am fully aware that I have never written anything other than fictions. For all that, I would not want to say that they are outside truth. It seems possible to me to make fiction work within truth, to induce truth effects within a fictional discourse, and in some way make the discourse of truth arouse, "fabricate" something which does not as yet exist, thus "fiction" something. One "fictions" history starting from a political reality that renders it true, one "fictions" a politics that doesn't as yet exist starting from an historical truth. (Foucault "Interview" 74–75)

*Technologies of Truth* is concerned with texts, audiences, and institutions. The book is "close to the center of 'television theory' (in a post-structuralist universe, an increasingly marooned assembly of ideas, stuck with the awkwardness of being at once more 'social' than cinema studies, more 'aesthetic' than media sociology, yet lacking the critical mass to break free of dependency on both)" (Corner 97). In each chapter, there is more than one genre, more than one text, and more than one approach to the specified problem, in keeping with a basic methodological point: the need to bring together forms of knowledge traditionally kept apart in the safe houses of social science versus the humanities. I do this in the spirit of Lawrence Grossberg's call for cultural studies to focus equally on production, text, and reception, to understand the micropolitics of a broad contextual map ("Can" 93).

There is an intentional irony here. Earlier I pronounced on the unhappy condition produced by a split triumvirate of text, psyche, and economy. My next move is to reinstate signs derived from these discourses: "genre" seems impeccably aesthetic, "audience" and "nation" are the bequest of moral panics from the Payne studies and before, and "modernity" and its "post" are, inter alia, developmentalist economic categories. This book does not lie outside these discourses, immune to them. And this is a performative point: narration may be secondary to the content it must express, but empirical events are themselves publicly known *exclusively in the form of stories* (H. White 28). The next—and most useful—move is surely to recombine the elements of these discourses, to work with a concept of genre, for example, as simultaneously textual, economic, and social. It will be my contention that these concepts and their parental human sciences are technologies of governance, systems of ordering conduct. The texts we read, the ways we read them, and the uses we make of those readings are produced by converging and diverging procedures that *govern* us but are susceptible to—in fact, constitutively composed of—contradiction. Their multiple perspectives on the person both enforce and weaken the disciplinary procedures of cultural capitalism. Meaning, self, and money are forced up against one another in the arts of state.

## Governmentality

Governmentality

> *Maybe what is really important for our modernity — that is, for our present — is not so much the étatisation of society, as the "governmentalization" of the state.*
> :: Foucault "Governmentality" 103

The significance of Foucault's "Governmentality" essay — and its potential value to cultural studies — is plain from the debate over cultural policy studies detailed in chapter 2. Foucault does not merely offer a history and a specification of institutional sovereignty in this paper. He models the analysis that I identify in chapter 1 as missing from contemporary cultural studies, providing a mode of narration and a typological network that sets the tone for what I have sought to achieve in the remainder of this volume. And he does so in an ironized mode, in keeping with his title's origin in Roland Barthes's *Mythologies* from twenty years earlier, when Barthes coined the term *governmentality* to describe variations in market prices and responses from the state (130).

"Governmentality" finds Foucault staring at a foundational reading of Western political science, Machiavelli's *The Prince*. He ponders the calumny, joviality, and esteem that have greeted this little book over the four hundred years it has made people think. Broadening his inquiries to other policy primers, he identifies a series of problems addressed at different moments in European economic and political organization. Five questions continue to be posed across the sixteenth century: "How to govern oneself, how to be governed, how to govern others, by whom the people will accept being governed, how to become the best possible governor." These issues arise as twin processes: the displacement of feudalism by the sovereign state, and the similarly conflictual Reformation and its counters. Daily economic and spiritual government are up for redefinition. While the state emerges as a centralizing tendency that seeks to normalize itself and others, a devolved religious authority is producing a void through ecclesiastical conflicts. Critics of *The Prince* and its neighbors respond to this lack of order by denying the sovereign a divine right of rule. The doctrine of transcendence has fallen into crisis, with the prince now a manager rather than the embodiment of immanent rule (Foucault "Governmentality" 87–90).

Governing comes to be described by a double movement. First, fitness to govern oneself models and develops the ability to govern others. These capacities are learned from guides on how to rule. This upward movement, whereby the sovereign masters self-governance, has its running partner. A second, downward movement translates these doctrines into household management, or *economy*. The autarkic autarch runs the state, which then recycles its own history as a model to be emulated at the level of the family, which in turn influences conduct away from the home. This backward and forward motion of public and private comes to be known as the *police*. Pedagogy extrapolates from the prince's self-knowledge to the rule of others, and policing transfers this motion into the head of the household and back onto the street. The sovereign has discovered how to run his life, and treats his dominions according to these lessons. The father learns how to run his family like a principality and train his minions to carry their docility and industry into the social sphere (91–92). Put another way, we might see this as the economization of government, a complex movement between self and society.

With the upheavals of the seventeenth century, such as the Thirty Years' War and rural and urban revolt, the conditions for implementing new modes of social organization arise. In eighteenth-century Europe, the definitional field of "the economy" begins to spread beyond the domestic sphere. Modernity emerges. What had been a managerial invention dedicated to forming correct conduct transforms itself into truth, a description of the social field. By now the government of *territory* is secondary to the government of *things* and the social relations among them. Government is conceived and actualized, then, in terms of climate, disease, industry, finance, custom, and disaster. It is, literally, a concern with life and death and what can be calculated/managed between them. Wealth and health become goals, to be attained through the disposition of capacities across the population: "biological existence was reflected in political existence" through the work of "bio-power." Bio-power "brought life and its mechanisms into the realm of explicit calculations, making knowledge-power an agent for transforming human life." Bodies become identified with politics, because managing them is part of running the country. For Foucault, "a society's 'threshold of modernity' has been reached when the life of the species is wagered on its own political strategies" ("Governmentality" 97, 92–95, and *History* 143).

The foundations of classical political economy are generally associated with a libertarian championing of the market. But as Michael J. Shapiro's study of Adam Smith has shown, the very founder of the discourse theorized sovereignty beyond the exhibition and maintenance of loyalty, and into the management of "flows of exchange within the social domain": it was politics that centered productivity in place of monarchy (*Reading "Adam Smith"* 11). Foucault sees both the physiocrats and Smith as con-

cerned with the transformation of sovereignty from legitimacy to technique: "what is free, what has to be free, and what has to be regulated,"
with crime and health key sites for playing out this knowledge in the public
realm ("Problematics" 124–25). When the British Parliament enacts legislation requiring smallpox vaccinations for all children in 1853, this is simultaneously a landmark in the uptake of medical knowledge and in public regulation of the body politic. Science and government combine in new
environmental-legal relations, under the sign of civic management and
economic productivity. Two years later, Achille Guillard invents "demography," merging "political arithmetic" and "political and natural observations," which had been on the rise since the first population inquiries
in seventeenth-century Britain. The new knowledge codifies five projects:
reproduction, aging, migration, public health, and ecology (Synnott 26;
A. Fogel 312–13).

The critical shift here is away from an autotelic accumulation of
power by the sovereign and toward the dispersal of power into the population. The center invests people with the capacity to produce and consume
things, insisting on freedom in some compartments of life and obedience in
others (Foucault "Problematics" 125). It is concerned with the ability to
make people manufacture goods by the most rational allocation of resources
available. Governmentality is destined for a place *beyond* sovereignty, in
the social field. It will be other-directed and instrumental; its target, the
whole population.

Yet the eighteenth century continues to wrestle with sovereignty,
through the early career of public law. And the model of the household as
an economic matrix also continues, despite its weakness in an internation-
alizing, postmercantilist world. A further transformation is needed. With
the externalization of the state, following a brief moment of territoriality
that looks exclusively inward, new industries and modes of production
emerge. Empire and economy require reconceptualization. For Foucault,
the arts of government have been freed from the strictures imposed by
sovereign and household motifs. Not only has "population" displaced
"prince" as a site for accumulating power, but "home" is displaced by
"economy" as the newly anthropomorphized dynamic of social intervention and achievement. This is the moment of the numeric figure. The populace becomes the province of statistics, bounded not by the direct exertion
of juridical influence or domestic authority, but by forms of knowledge
that grant "the people" a life that cannot be divined from the model of the
family. City and country substitute for home, with all the hierarchical dis-
location that implies. The epidemic and the road map displace the home
meal and the father's word ("Governmentality" 98–99).

Clearly, the emergence of modern capitalism is connected to the rise of the sovereign state, which was concerned with delivering a docile and healthy labor force to business; but not only to business, and not merely in a way that shows the lineage of that desire. Cholera, sanitation, and prostitution are figured as the business of government in the modern era through "the emergence of the health and physical well-being of the population in general as one of the essential objectives of political power." The entire "social body" is to be assayed and treated for its insufficiencies. Governing people means, most centrally and critically, obeying the "imperative of health: at once the duty of each and the objective of all" (Foucault "Politics" 277). This presents contradictions for the state-economy mix of contemporary cultural capitalism: enterprise is accumulable nationally, based on individual initiative, but morality remains tightly knotted inside mythic family arrangements that do not apply to most citizens. At least paradoxically, governments become, more and more, guardians of an economy that is meant to be self-actualizing and a civics that is supposed to derive from the nuclear family. But the statistical functions of the state, while in part beholden to political knowledge and phantasy, reveal societies that are just not right for the myths empowering ideological discourse. And the categories of knowledge informing and informed by the census—and related governmental programs—produce/treat/uncover a split society. In this space, between the empirical knowledges of governmentality and the mythic ideals of sovereignty, creativity, and economics, the cultural politics of a counterpublic sphere take place: the family is said to be "a model," when it is really "a segment." This space permits inquiry "into the forms of power and authority that the practices of the present help to sustain" (Foucault "Governmentality" 100; Shapiro *Reading the Postmodern* 14).

Foucault proposes a threefold concept of governmentality to explain life today. The first utilizes economics to mold the population into efficient and effective producers. The second is the array of governmental apparatuses designed to create conditions for this productivity, through bodily interventions and the promulgation of fealty and individuality. And the third is the translation of methods from education to penology that modifies justice into a technology of amelioration. Put another way, we might understand this as the indoctrination of the state by the social, the infesting of sovereignty with demographics (102–3). In *The Well-Tempered Self*, I point to the difficulties liberal-democratic and conservative political theories experience when they deal with the consumer-citizen couplet. As a number of recent studies have shown, governmentality provides a useful way of pondering this complex relationship of consumption and citizenship by centering the population as desiring, producing, and committed subjects that manifest contradictions (see George Yúdice's summary). I have sought to utilize these tools to understand how the population knows itself and its duties, redisposing genre, audience/nation, and modernity/postmodernity as categories of governmentality.

▶

## Genre

> Readers have often noted that genre invites . . . [an] analogy from daily experience: the way a social institution, such as an established church or a legislative body, functions. It is often possible to challenge such institutions, sometimes to over-throw them, but it is virtually impossible simply to exclude them from our lives.
>
> ::   Dubrow 3

The concept of genre derives from the Latin *genus*, from the word for giving birth. Originally, the term *genres* referred to kinds of people, often by class, race, or family. Genre has also signified forms of communication and their ownership. In economic discourse, a "genre monopoly problem" stands in the way of competition when certain regions are dominated by a single cultural producer or space, notably in the nonprofit sector; for example, the regional museum is often solitary and relatively impermeable. The significance of genre as a force determining textuality continues from Roman imitations of the Greeks on to late Hollywood's proclivity for re-makes and quotation, where mimesis spans correspondence and coherence theories of truth: realism is matched against the social world *and* prior cultural representations (Hodge 21; Durkheim and Mauss 8; Hunter "Providence" 213; Chartrand "International" 162–63; Dehon).

Generic classifications in literature and the natural sciences characterize nineteenth-century European attempts to embrace physiological and psychological categorization, a crucial part of the modern application of knowledge. Popular culture replaces the person as its basic cataloging unit by the notion of a text. Collocating texts that share characteristics or repeat stylistic moves does the work of forming a genre. Genres are about the interplay of repetition and difference and their organization and interpretation by producers, audiences, and critics. This can happen at the levels of cultural production, scheduling, regulation, and interpretation. There is enough in common between the components of certain texts to justify grouping them together, and enough that is different about them to mean we want to experience more than the exemplar. This represents a continuity in the history of literary and screen genres: they are always related to the

cultural attributes of a population at a certain moment, sometimes as reactions to those attributes, and sometimes as sources of them (Dubrow 7,
78–79; Hunter "Providence" 215). Just as the expansion of printing and
print literacy held implications for the emergence of the novel, so the
spread of the videocassette recorder and technological familiarity influence
the mixed genres of latter-day TV. Genres both train the population as
readers and agents and are themselves understood as representative of that
population, spatial markers of governance and resistance.

Knowing how to construct texts along generic lines is more than a
matter of knowing syntactic or programmatic rules. It is also a question of
knowing economic rules: having one's product quickly and easily recognized as a documentary, a museum, or a sport. But there is a great deal of
crossover. *Twin Peaks* can be understood as horror, comedy, soap opera,
special-event television, quality drama, or auteurist text, given its connections to David Lynch and his repeated recitations of fatherly bastardry.
*Northern Exposure* could also be cross-cataloged. It has elements of the
*Bildungsroman* quest for personal development and the "fish-out-of-water"
comedy, a subtext to do with center-periphery geopolitical relations, and
an engrossing series of problems posed in terms of ethnicity, gender, and
sexual practice. Not to mention the moose. Tzvetan Todorov argues it may
be "anachronistic" to classify generically because of the crisscrossing
among categories. Cultures may anachronize, domesticate, and proliferate
genres, but certain texts blur boundaries and encourage their audiences to
question how to decode what is presented. An example is the bizarre blend
of confession, hagiographic autobiography, cinema verité documentary,
action-adventure series, citizenship education, and Grand Guignol violence
characteristic of the infoedutainment of *Rescue 911*, *I Witness Video*, *DEA*,
and their equivalents from Sandinista-era Nicaraguan TV. Does this intertextual blurring mean the end of genre as a method of analysis? Or, perhaps more complicatedly, have texts emerged that disobey the iron codes
of genre, but still derive from them? Such texts do not imply that genres
no longer exist; on the contrary, they demonstrate the centrality of genre as
a sounding board and point of resistance against which originality can be
measured, and without which originality cannot function as a concept.
And even as such texts of innovation mount up, they undergo generic classification (Todorov 14–15).

When critics describe a film as "a genre flick," this is a put-down. It
derides the text under discussion for being formulaic, mechanical, and
without the connotative message beyond a denotative code that Christian
Metz speaks of; but these very characteristics suggest a dependability
and certainty—still with the possible frisson of surprise—that engages pro-

duction executives and viewers. The TV serial or series is "reliable." This reliability derives from the intensely categorical process characteristic of cultural production. Here, television is at the apogee of the culture industries, a scientifically managed institution for the mass production of entertainment. Risk and innovation are minimized (Caughie 127–29). This is a bureaucratically organized regime of pleasure; bureaucratic in that it is systematically planned and run, but pleasurable in that its products are permutations of the everyday and the spectacular, designed to capture audiences and deliver them to advertisers, in the case of commercial networks, or government, in the case of public stations. Genres combine the memorandum and the commodity; one ensures standardization, the other marketability.

Tony Bennett describes genres as "historically and culturally variable systems for the regulation of reading and writing practices." As Robert Hodge reminds us, a "system of genres is the product of an act of classification and classification is always a strategy of control." It is equally significant that such an act of classification connects text to performance, by what Ian Hunter calls an "occasion." This refers to "the practical circumstances governing the composition and reception of a piece" (the daguerrotrope). The distinctive point about electronic popular culture is its expansion of textual availability. Genres come to be defined in market terms as well as through the morality of administrators of conscience and taste, at the interstices of "a new practice of piety and a new communications technology." Consider the appearance of confessional narratives in early-nineteenth-century North American journalism. Originally a broadsheet phenomenon (the reverse physical association from our own tabloid moment), they gave voice to notorious criminals prior to execution, concluding with moralistic codas. At the same time, the spread of industry saw social scientific gazes fall onto working and nonworking people through the new human sciences of anthropology and its kind. This generated an interest in classifications of normalcy and deviance through observation, gaining expression via migration of the confessional form into popular-newspaper interviews. We can see traces here of four components of genre: rituals to determine boundary markers, shifting relations between universality and specificity, a hierarchical ranking of preference/worthiness, and institutionally delineated borders. These genre qualities are in turn defined by commercial, professional, and administrative logics (T. Bennett *Outside* 81; Hodge 21; Hunter "Providence" 215, 220; Bell and van Leeuwen 29, 32; DiMaggio "Classification" 441, 449).

Hunter's account of occasionality encourages us to note the close relationship between what is offered in a text and what is expected of its readership. There are certain amounts of autonomy in both these settings: the generic conventions animating a cultural product are not always known or enjoyed by audiences, and public opinion does not always coincide with its use as a cliché by producers. Both groups have different points of reference in a text and its proximity to reality. But the repetition and difference that characterize the relationship of a genre to an individual work occur somewhere between textual rules and spectatorial expectations, for this is "a received collective practice," subject to the pressures and conflictual relations of any social act (Greenblatt *Learning* 101).

The late avant-garde filmmaker Hollis Frampton offered an allegorical story about genre and its pre- and proscriptive, regulatory sensibilities and limits: "I am told that, in 1927, a Louisiana lawmaker (haunted by the ghost of Pythagoras, no doubt) introduced into the legislature of that state a bill that would have made the value of *pi* equal to precisely three" (quoted in Lunenfeld 7). Pi is useful as an infinitely long fraction, its mercurial indeterminacy helpful in calculating circumferences, arcs, and volumes. Attempts to legislate neatness against a surplus of meaning are improbable. Four centuries earlier, Albrecht Dürer's *Painter's Manual* proposed a rational cultural policy that would instruct young people in perspectival and geometric relationships (Greenblatt *Learning* 99, 101). Stephen Greenblatt's gloss of Dürer's plans for civic monuments glorifying historical events indicates how contingent legislated meaning can be:

> A victory over rebellious peasants calls for a commemorative column—after all, the fate of worldly rule, that is human civilization itself, depends upon this struggle—and yet the enemy is an object of contempt and derision. The princes and nobles for whom such monuments were built could derive no dignity from the triumph, any more than they could derive dignity from killing a mad dog. . . .
> . . . The peasants, of course, have no titles to seize, and can yield up no trophies to adorn the victor's monument. Indeed, in the economy of honor they are not simply a cipher but a deficit, since even a defeat at the hands of a prince threatens to confer upon them some of the prince's store of honor, while what remains of the victorious prince's store can be tarnished by the unworthy encounter (*Learning* 108–9)

This duality is also present in Herodotus. His fifth-century BC *Histories* begin with what read like today's options for treating the past: to recount "the astonishing achievements both of our own and of other peoples; and more particularly, to show how they came into conflict" (43). So it is with generic descriptions and their infinite regress toward a specificity that is never reached, but at least ensures family resemblance. Genres shift between the necessary and the negotiable, the given and the contingent in the composition of texts and their referentiality in the social world.

Recent developments in the social psychology of television watching organize genres and audiences as reciprocal movements within the self, with forms of TV programs understood in relation to interiority. There is, then, a dynamic relationship between rules as a static code and rules actually in play at the site of audience interpretation. Our "texts arise within ceremonials": the difference between the audiovisual tape of a TV program and its broadcast and reception (Preston and Clair; Freadman 70–71, 88, 91). Genres provide a vehicle for establishing community standards of aesthetic taste and pedagogic direction, akin to what Hodge sees as "classifications of people—readers and writers—and of what they write or read about and what they should think and mean" (21). Hence the tie-in to governmentality and the role of the popular as a primer in public morality. But this is no simple model of sender-message-receiver. There is a sense in which only the collusion of the audience with the producer can guarantee a genre is just that, so rooted is the concept in the apprehension and processing of repetitions and differences: the space between different moments of governance.

▶ ─────────────────────────────

## Audience/Nation

> *"There's a widespread feeling that just because a man has a large office he's an idiot."*—Edward S. Norton, president of the Pacific All Risk Insurance Company
> ::   *Double Indemnity*, Billy Wilder, 1944

Does an identifiable figure in an office of cultural production decide the meaning of meaning? Where does the transformation from text to reading to practical uptake actually occur? These are critical issues, flowing from Hunter's concept of the occasionality of texts. Eric Michaels poses the following related questions:

> Just what is the TV text—and where is it? Is it the performance that occurs in a TV studio in front of a camera, or the radio waves that circulate from the transmitter, or the picture that appears on any given home TV? The technology and economics of this medium generate many texts diverse in space and time, sequentially or simultaneously. Which is to be taken as the unit of analysis? (8)

He decides "to specify the media production processes so as to situate TV's 'readers' and 'writers' in their actual institutional relationships," to ascertain how audiences, producers, and technology negotiate meaning as part of the creation of texts, starting from the presumption that the media "engage unprecedented numbers and classes of people in coordinated, if not efficient, signifying activity" (9, 11).

Umberto Eco commences his analysis of television similarly, asking how signs move between senders and addressees and what meanings are produced by that movement. Eco is concerned with theorizing the communicative uniqueness of electronic audiovisual information. He stresses the promiscuous path of such messages as opposed to ancient forms, which were encoded for particular audiences by senders who could predict with reasonable confidence exactly where and how their signs would travel and land. Now, what he calls "aberrant decoding" is the rule. Signs move through and toward "an undifferentiated mass" that cannot be guaranteed to disinter the same meanings encrypted by TV producers. Eco shows that the televised code couples signs to semantic units, or meanings. This coupling is paradigmatic; it involves choice, and hence potential substitution. Such choices are made during production, but become invisible once that selection has produced what may then seem to be inevitable syntagmatic combinations. However, when added to varied audience reading protocols, TV's modus vivendi is clearly a polysemous combination of sound, image, seme, sign, and person, with the prospect of dissonances among them ("Towards" 104–6, 108).

The transformation of textual meaning from origin to interpretation takes place at the three primary sites for defining and refining popular culture: the industry, the state, and criticism. Each of these devotes a great deal of time to audiences as part of its reason to be (Hartley *Tele-ology* 105). In this sense, the audience is always fictional, a theoretical construct of various agencies that act upon their creation to exercise power. As John Hartley says:

> The energy with which audiences are pursued in academic and industry research bespeaks something much larger and more powerful than the quest for mere data. The TV audience is pervasive but perplexingly elusive: the quest for knowledge about it is the search for something *special*; literally, knowledge of the *species*. (*Politics* 84)

Laments for civic culture in the United States correlate a decline in membership in the Elks Club, the Red Cross, and Parent-Teacher Associations with heavy TV viewing. But unlike such institutions, the cultural audience is not a specifiable group within the social order so much as the principal site *of* that order. The audience participates in the most uniformly global (but national), collective (yet private), and individually time-consuming practice of making meaning in the history of the world. Just as people are parts of a collectivity (the citizenry of Switzerland) while they are also individuals (Frankie and Johnny), so the concept and occasion of being an audience provide a textual link between society and person. Whenever audiences act, they do so as a group (watching the detectives), but through individual processes (making sense of what a character does). So viewing television involves solitary interpretation as well as collective behavior (Roberts; Hartley *Politics* 85).

How is the audience understood? W. Russell Neuman suggests a six-way split. The "quantity argument" points to the enormous reach of the media, the sheer proliferation of messages. It stresses the insidious effects of saying the same thing over and over again. Quantification produces a Malthusian gloom: TV emits 3,500 images per minute per channel, radio stations broadcast a hundred words a minute, and newspapers publish 150,000 words each day. An abundance of signs and overlapping sign systems is thought to paralyze individual critical faculties, as North Americans go through daily exposure to 1,600 advertisements. Overloads of information produce convergent networks of values. The "targeting argument" addresses the control cultural producers exert over texts: magazines selling lists of their subscribers to specialist mail-order companies, for instance. The "modality argument" concentrates on new technology and its impact on our means of making sense, especially in a time of intense simulation of humanness by machines. The "scope argument" applies these other perspectives across the globe, underscoring the transnational reach of the media and its implications for world politics. The "addiction argument" was used by businesses associated with new visual technologies in the 1970s to announce their future success, predicated on a putative buildup of desire among future consumers for the arrival of video games, videotext, and related fashions. Finally, the "subtlety argument" discerns increasing professionalism in persuading people to believe and buy, working with targets and modalities in order to circumvent the loss of specificity in scope and quantity through the proliferation of TV signals and formats (81, 90–91, 83–85).

Americans spend about half their daily media time of seven hours with the television switched on. The average adult is watching during four and a half of those hours, mostly in prime time. Even teenage girls, the lightest of viewers, watch three and a half hours per day. Listening to the radio averages two hours, much of it in the car. Newspapers are read for between twenty and fifty minutes a day, magazines for up to half an hour, and books for twenty minutes. Most of the empirical information about people's use of the media comes from Britain and the United States. If we combine the material on TV, the composite picture looks like this. Average viewers watch more than twenty hours each week, although some are much more casual or chaotic in their patterns. People adopt and reject particular series in a wonderfully unpredictable, wayward mode. So habitués of a major nighttime soap opera, such as *Dallas*, are no more likely to be followers of *Dynasty* than is anyone else. A given popular prime-time series holds only half its viewers from week to week, and less successful texts lose and gain audiences even more spectacularly. This is so even with the option of delayed viewing by taping off-air, which is much less frequent than simply watching "live." Low-rating texts are not usually very well liked by those who *do* watch them, except for high-culture and information programs. Television occupies time, but not intellectual space. Everybody watches it, but individuals do so differently, many lackadaisically and cynically. TV is domestic, and therefore subject to a strong sense of the everyday and the controllable. It can be criticized and talked over, like some pet or vaguely dotty relative. Television is there to be used, laughed at, and given its due. British figures show that commercials in prime time escort 20 percent of viewers from the room and encourage another 10 percent to talk; 30 percent continue with the reading or discussion they were involved in during the principal text (Neuman 89; Barwise and Ehrenberg 5–7, 9; Ang 161).

What are we doing when we anxiously analyze audiences through the discourses of psychology, sociology, and economics? We are buying into Harold Garfinkel's notion of the "cultural dope," a mythic figure "who keeps society stable by acting in compliance with preestablished and legitimate alternatives of action that the common culture provides." The actual "common sense rationalities . . . of here and now situations" used by people are obscured by this overarching category (68), because when the audience is invoked as a category by the industry or its critics and regulators, it immediately becomes such a "dope": Ien Ang's "socially-constituted and institutionally-produced category" (3). Ratings and shares derive from the need of commercial television, the advertising industry, and public broadcasters to know whom they are addressing. In addition to the size of that viewing group, they want to find out how it relates to the population's sexes, ages, races, tastes, patterns of consumption, and politics. Such systems arose from measures of consumer activity that developed across the

United States over this century. (In the 1950s, the U.S. Audience Bureau of Circulation went so far as to devise tests for determining the number of articles perused in a magazine that led to photochemical experiments indicating how frequently a given page had been exposed to light [Lazarsfeld 43].) This is as much a desire to *control* through measurement as a desire to *sell*, with the audience a childlike object of experimentation (it would also work for tenure review).

TV executives invoke the audience to measure success, regulators to organize administration, psychologists to produce proofs, and lobbying groups to change programming. "The audience" is never available in pristine form, but is scarred by origins such as these that bring it into discourse (Ang 46; Fiske "Audiencing" 353; Hartley *Tele-ology* 105). Hence the link to panics about educational underattainment, violent behavior, political apathy, and social anomie supposedly engendered by television and routinely investigated by the state, psychologists, the left, conservatives, religious groups, neotemperance feminists, and others, as well as the panics over the lascivious female look detailed in chapter 3 and the overly inquisitive citizen in chapter 6, with their corollary of well-disciplined citizen-viewers sought in chapter 5. The audience as consumer, child, criminal, voter, and vegetable engages such groups. There can be no better reason than the existence of such concerns for seeing how audiences to popular culture are made to represent society.

The noncommercial tradition of TV, for instance, regards the audience as a public of thinkers beyond the home, carers beyond the self; as participants in a political and social system as well as an economy of purchasing. Public service broadcasters have complex, competing missions. When such services operate alongside commercial stations, they are expected both to win viewers and to train them in a way that complements the profit-driven sector. There is an infantilizing quality to this relationship of network and viewer. The masters of the system conceive themselves as both members of that audience and somehow beyond and above it, capable of transmitting improving, uplifting stories and values—in the vanguard of *forming* tastes as well as *meeting* them. Entertainment is secondary to providing programs the commercial market would not deliver. The model is one of enlightenment alongside pleasure, but in a different balance from the profiteering stations, which are principally dedicated to information-as-entertainment. Audiences are encouraged not just to watch and consume, but to act, to be better people (Ang 28–29). They are supposed to become cultural critics beyond the mall and inside the polis: citizens of a nation.

*Where* is the cultural nation? It is hardly an empirical audience arrayed in front of the set as before the flag at a citizenship ceremony. Binding people together through culture is a concept derived from social and political theory and public policy. Consider the following, from the 1920s:

> Broadcasting, properly handled, will make a material contribution towards greater understanding and amity between Nations, the cementing of home life and the happiness of the individual. (Marconi, 1924)

> It was soon evident that the Central Powers had laid careful plans, not only for a stupendous campaign on land and sea, but also for a war in the aether of space . . . to broadcast military and naval communiqués, having as their object the creation, in neutral countries, of an impression favourable to themselves, and if possible a feeling of disquiet amongst the wireless sections of the Allied armies. (Burrows 24, 1924)

These two statements appear in the same volume. One is authored by Guglielmo Marconi, the person generally credited with the first wireless transmissions. The other comes from A. R. Burrows, an early British broadcaster who was given "responsibility" by his government for ensuring that wireless news from the recently created Soviet Union was "handled with discretion." Their remarks establish the grand paradox of electronic media: broadcast texts transcend boundaries in their magical voyage through the infinite, but are subject to regulation by those who control the landscape they traverse. When insurrections or invasions occur in countries, outsiders look to who has control of the national media; once, the capital city was their focus. Owning the airwaves is identical to controlling the country, to defining its members and their needs. Because the mobilization of feeling into administration and vice versa can take place only within a rule-governed system—especially one that overtly enunciates a sense of the public interest as its reason to be—we are forced toward the large, but not limitless, boundary of the nation as our primary delimiter of the audience. The nation is the unit of appeal and organization for commercial networks, for public broadcasters designed to instill unity in the populace, and for viewers seeking to influence the allocation of space and content. Although the idea of public interest can be applied to smaller units than the nation— for example, readers of a specialist magazine—the conception of the public driving this logic is intertwined with national unity and service. The recent televisual internationalization of this process—whereby British, French, American, Asian, and Australian news services function as commercial entities outside their patrimonial spaces—complicates the issue without removing the category of the nation; it continues to be their geopolitical organizer as a textual entity and a business target.

Nations are recent and popular, increasingly so. Although not as easy to identify as states, which can be marked out in legal terms, they are multiplying. We live in an international age, which by its very formulation decrees we are also in a national one. The nation is a oneness of imagination that binds citizens to states, transcending the everyday apparatus of repression. It is a means of identification with persons and places beyond the horizon, but not so distant as to be foreign. It may be founded on genetics and/as history, or it may exist despite either or both of these, on the basis of policy, perhaps a postcolonial hangover of boundaries drawn to suit metropolitan bureaucrats and industrialists. It may be complicated by all of the above, and it can be a matter of settled agreement or collective anxiety. Given these differences, how can we render so slippery a term of belonging analytically useful? Why should "everyone" want to form nations, just as the more mindless or utopic among us continue to insist on their obsolescence in a new era of global capital? And how do we deal with a "dirty" object for the left, one associated with the worst chauvinisms? As an apparently unified form that needs decomposing each time it is applied to particular circumstances. Billy Bragg has pointed recently to the need for his English national pride to sit alongside his internationalism and his socialism. This might appear regressive at first sight, given that country's sorry history of imperialism. Bragg offers three arguments against such a position. First, it gives the right a monopoly on ownership and control of patriotism. Second, a multicultural agenda should appreciate both host and donor cultures. And finally, there is a trend toward nationalism across the United Kingdom that is politically progressive everywhere other than England, because of the left's squeamishness about the topic. As Tom Nairn paradoxically remarks, "Small is not only beautiful but has teeth too (speaking both technically and politically)." This is the difference between the apparently *outmoded* "medieval particularism" of small nationalism that Lenin derided and the really rather *modish* "nonlogical, untidy, refractory, disintegrative, particularistic truth of nation-states"; 1989 made medieval particularism the future (157–58). Our contemporary moment equally references intra- and transnationalism, with diasporic subjects and First Peoples gathering political momentum.

The state articulates the nation as a spirit-in-dwelling that gives it legitimacy, but that it also reserves the right to name and monitor, for nations are always coterminous with systems of government. This is a paradox. Even as the nation is manufactured, it is said to be an already existing, authentic essence of statehood and peoplehood. The nation is a one, true culture. Benedict Anderson argues we can study nations as "cultural artefacts" that draw on "a deep, horizontal comradeship" (13, 16). This collective identity was historically achieved through the spread of the printed word using local forms of European language after the sixteenth century. It came to represent political sovereignty instead of the religious one communicated through Christian Latin's previous monopoly on the book. Printing opened up the prospect of simultaneity, of knowing that people like oneself could be reading identical texts at another place but at the same moment. Two new forms of writing translated the old sense of time into a modern order that came to characterize European life in the eighteenth century: novels and newspapers. Anderson thinks they made it possible to imagine a nation through the invention of *meanwhile*, a term to describe action taking place elsewhere, but also now; part of our world as connected individuals looking at a text, but not available to us as connected individuals at a single site (24–25, 28–31). Documentary film, the newsreel, Internet discussion groups, and TV current affairs are their twentieth-century equivalents. Hence the panics over electronic culture that characterize the discourses of cultural imperialism and protectionism detailed in chapter 4. There was a related iconographic change. The era of sacred internationalism had produced images that elided time and space by denying the passage of history. They represented the foundational Christian myth as a spectacle that was always contemporary and local. Medieval European paintings of the crucifixion depicted medieval European people gazing at Jesus. For audiences such as these, time was coming to a rapturously cataclysmic end. Sacred power would be witnessed firsthand, as at a Second Coming. For us, this is anachronistic. Our sense of the simultaneous is of events occurring at the same moment in different places. But this chronotropic logic was not available then. Past, present, and future were essentially one. Now, we think we can distinguish among them, and do so to delineate a shared national cultural history (Anderson 24–25, 28–31).

As Philip Schlesinger sees it, national culture "offers respectability and brand identification" for state actions, either taken or called for (*Media* 138). The expressive interiority attached to national sentiment legitimizes public education's displacement of oral language through writing that spans distance and difference, in the very way popular culture binds people who have never met and do not expect to do so. Identity becomes transferable through literacy and a formal method of educating people, once responsibility for this task shifts from church to state. Can anyone seriously countenance a history of the United States without due treatment of Noah Webster's eighteenth-century spelling book? Webster was the first to produce primers that distanced themselves from what he called the "folly" of Europe, with its declining morals and outmoded political systems. At the same time, it would be silly to endow these developments with the happy face of functionalist sociology, for this very period is equally one of intense differentiation. Industrial culture divides even as it rationalizes, creating diffuse collective identities as well as officially endorsed ones (Gellner 757; E. Barker 4; Kohn 301–2; Schlesinger *Media* 160). Inside certain democratic forms, this is a relatively cozy arrangement, but it can be something else under different circumstances. The departure of state socialism from Europe has left a space of explanation, a theory-of-everything manqué, along with traces of "demons from bygone epochs," as Adam Michnik calls them. These are not about reclaiming collective memory or defending national identity; they are forms of ideological Darwinism (758–59). What are the contours to this oddly contradictory European heritage?

After the First World War, as national self-determination was proving to be panacea, placebo, and disorder all at once, Ernest Barker outlined three material bases to the nation: race, as a source of human identification; environment, as both physical border and internal geography; and population, as a set of statistical forms. Now, whereas the first and second terms were conceived as natural divisions (although never encountered as such, given the political venality and scientific illogic of racism and the inevitable struggles over resources), the idea of the population as an object of care, to be quantified and qualified, modeled and bettered, derived from social theory. Barker almost celebrates the fact this last category, already muddied, is the only one really applicable to the architectonics of nations (2–3, 12). We can see a logic similar to Foucault's in "Governmentality." As May Joseph says, "There has never been a pure space within the nation-state" (3).

The rapid exchange of information held out by audiovisual technology in the twentieth century mirrors an extraordinary expansion in the rate and extent of human, intellectual, and financial migration. Just as music, radio, TV, video, the Web, and cinema may link nations and blur their differences through international trade in text and ownership, they also constitute inter- and intranational difference. Such horizontal, technical, and vertical generic developments have always brought debate along with them, because the nation has routinely been for the taking as a group of readers. Such concerns are amplified and projected in the light of the screen; its mimetic hold drives administrators of the public psyche to apoplectic fits that outdo the impact of written and spoken genres, and even the contemporary demonization accorded to rap. The audience/nation becomes simultaneously dangerous and vulnerable: worryingly powerful as individual and social actors, apt to undo the fabric of their communities, and peculiarly fragile as symbols of the very reading and civic collectivities they constitute.

> *Generally speaking, a cultural industry is held to exist when*
> *cultural goods and services are produced, reproduced, stored*
> *or distributed on industrial and commercial lines, that is to*
> *say on a large scale and in accordance with a strategy based*
> *on economic considerations rather than any concerns for*
> *cultural development.*
> ::   UNESCO, quoted in Schiller *Culture* 30

Andrew Lang wrote a nineteenth-century best-seller called *Angling Sketches*
and also edited the *Blue* and *Red Fairy* books. His *Letters to Dead Authors*
(referred to in the dedication as "exercises in the art of dipping") appeared
in 1892. Lang praises William Thackeray for resisting the trend of the day:
"Fiction in your hands was not simply a profession, like another, but a
constant reflection of the whole surface of life" (3). This calls up the complexity of the modern: the arts are industries, but industries of life and its
expressive quintessence. The quotation that commences this section comes
from the international body—the United Nations Educational, Scientific,
and Cultural Organization—that has been most clearly identified with a
critique of culture as industry, because the latter is thought to obliterate
cultural differences and, nowadays, to produce a global American hegemony of knowledge and custom. The expression of these positions as
politicized policies and programs encouraged the United States to leave
UNESCO in the mid-1980s (bizarrely enough, given that the United States
wanted the organization to embody debates over communication in its
original charter, and also insisted on the dismissal of American citizens
from UNESCO in the 1950s for failing to reply to a precisely political—in
this case, a congressional—investigation of loyalty [Sewell 142–43, 156]).
But as the Lang quotation suggests, it would be wrong to associate criticisms of popular culture with "developing" countries alone. Consider the
following statement, made by a U.S. television producer in the mid-1960s:

> Success in American commercial television in 1966 is measured not by the
> content and artistry of the program or by how much it has meant to an indi-
> vidual viewer, but either by its ability to attract a maximum number of sets-in-
> use, or even by the ingenuity with which it utilizes a studio's permanent sets
> and contract players. (Schaefer 24)

The nomenclature of the culture industries brings to mind a nonorganic,
distanced, remotely conceived but locally delivered, sense of culture. The
culture industries may be understood as "those institutions in our society

which employ the characteristic modes of production and organization of industrial corporations to produce and disseminate symbols in the form of cultural goods and services, generally, although not exclusively, as commodities" (Garnham "Concepts" 25).

The idea that culture industries "impress . . . the same stamp on everything" derives from the work of Theodor Adorno and Max Horkheimer. Their theory of production-line culture says that as demand is dispersed and supply centered, management operates through administrative logic. These arrangements are defended by their proponents because they are said to reflect the already established and revealed preferences of consumers, a reaction to their tastes and desires. But for Adorno and Horkheimer, such an account denies a cycle of power. They see consumers as manipulated through the mobilization of cultural technology by those at the economic apex of production. Whenever it is claimed technology has an innate logic, this is an instance of "domination" masquerading as choice in a "society alienated from itself." Coercion is mistaken for free will. Culture becomes one more industrial process subordinated to the dominant economic forces within society calling for standardization. The element that *might* stand against this leveling sameness is "individual consciousness." But that consciousness, according to Adorno and Horkheimer, has itself been customized to the requirements of the economy.

Away from critical theory, Dwight Macdonald insists on the use of the term *mass culture* rather than *popular culture* because of its standardization and reach, which he equates with chewing gum. Once parasitic of high-cultural innovation, by the 1950s it can also draw on its own dubious archive as a source of dross, integrating the populace into a condition of "political domination" guaranteed by a predigested ordering of audience response that is democratic in its constituency but antidemocratic in its effects (167–69, 171). For in place of the "rigorous training" that enables an appreciation of high culture, the popular is regarded as a "domain of simple, bodily pleasure" (Rowe 3). As Ross Gibson says, this discourse elevates "true art" by contrasting its virtues of courage, innovation, and energy. The popular is found to be "lazy and craven in its 'contentment' to deal with prefabricated signs and materials" (201). We might connect that laziness to the concerns about industrial incompetence and ethical turpitude identified earlier as new social anxieties that accompanied the truth-telling convictions of the daguerrotrope.

Whereas much of this Enlightenment disappointment was shared by conservatives in their negativity toward the notion of "the mass," for some 1960s theorists, such as Edward Shils, mass society represented the apex of modernity. Far from being supremely alienating, it signified an expanded civil society, the first moment of history when central political organs and agendas were receptive to and part of the broader community. The population was now part of the social, rather than excluded from the means and ends of political calculation. Centralized authority is lessened, individual rights promoted, and interpersonal, large-scale human interaction necessitated by industrialization and aided by communication systems, while advertising breaks down barriers between high and low culture (Shils 505–6, 511). But once this permissiveness goes still further, how can such calculations, made at the core of society, extend to encompass all, and what if consensus and civility are different things for different categories of person, as the rise of social movements such as feminism, environmentalism, and antiracism might suggest? Is this not a splintered society? And what part does the popular play in this new world? Is it the opposite of the modern project, as per Adorno and Horkheimer, or its acme, as per Shils? What if the modern has, in any case, passed into history?

> The past—since it may not be destroyed, for its destruction results in silence—must be revisited ironically, in a way which is not innocent. For me the postmodern attitude is that of a man who loves a woman who is intelligent and well-read: he knows that she knows he cannot tell her, "I love you desperately," because he knows that she knows (and she knows that he knows) that that is a line out of Barbara Cartland. Yet there is a solution. He can say, "As Barbara Cartland would say, I love you desperately." (Eco "Stefano" 2–3)

If modernity is about applying rationality to social problems, utilizing reason and developmentalist notions of progress in search of truth and joy, postmodernity is concerned with the occasioned value of reason, the sense that it always serves a particular purpose and set of agents as opposed to having a transcendental hold on truth and value. The popular and the postmodern are often equated with an instantaneous, vacuous culture that has overtaken the careful argumentation and two-way communicative protocols associated with its predecessor. Roger Silverstone refers to this as a time of "cultural inversion." The principal figure of speech is the oxymoronic juxtaposition of real and unreal, to the point where the place from which the two might be *dis*tinguished is itself *ex*tinguished. Even a concentration on the form of historical narratives is lost in the oral, visual, and literary performances that fragment the experience of reception (104–5, 112). This has serious ramifications for the more conspiratorial among us, be they left critics or capitalist adventurers.

The postmodern is many things to many people. It is often taken to include an aesthetic style, in architecture or novels for example, that tropes or quotes other forms and styles in a mélange of cultural features; a historical template designating certain moves within the economy toward internationalism and a turn away by industrialized states from manufacturing in the direction of trade in services; a philosophical discourse that deconstructs existing forms of knowledge by using their own precepts to undermine them; a specific form of identity politics, beyond constitutional and class bases for defining political agents; the decline of the major forms of social reasoning of the past century (liberalism, Marxism, psychoanalysis, and Christianity); and cultural theories derived from and informing the above (J. Collins 327).

As objects that transmit information, television, radio, and film reference much of this. They are service industries, predicated on communication as a good; they are mixed-genre media, that rub together and blend a variety of narrative forms; they interpellate audiences as social subjects, by gender, age, and race; they are anti-ideological, in their broad appeal to a common sense that supposedly exists as part of the community, rather than as the property of discourse ethics; and they are always new, always speaking from the now. Through innovations such as music video, they incorporate modernist avant-garde techniques into the everyday. Multiple production responsibilities disrupt the status of the author as a single originating source of texts. And their demotic appeal—mixed with the idea of the niche audience—subverts doctrines of an elect readership capable of comprehension beyond the norm. Like the postmodern, the audiovisual media deny the primacy of personal, physical experience through their promiscuous journalism and eye-line tourism. From the morphed special effect to the hand-painted video clip, they are about simulation, the sense that setting up replicas is not merely a displacement of personal, material art and experience, but actually preferable to them. TV is better than the best view available to a single person at a sporting event. And the videocassette recorder offers viewers their own editorializing. The reality of everyday life includes TV, which is also the primary metacommentator on that everyday. As the television era itself becomes the object of historical investigation, cable channels emerge to recycle early material, while contemporary programs see characters refer to television itself. When the United States inaugurated national programming in 1951 with a live split-screen picture of the Brooklyn Bridge and the Golden Gate on *See It Now*, Edward R. Murrow said, "We are impressed by a medium through which a man sitting in his living room has been able for the first time to look at two oceans at once" (quoted in Meisler). This is the ultimate daguerrotrope.

Realism is quickly displaced on the screen by intertextual referentiality: rather than the social world acting as a check of verisimilitude, other signs do so, quite overtly. The reader becomes a casual assembler of meanings, a *bricoleur*. But at the same time, the world around undergoes commodification as payment exacted by the culture industries in return for semiotic travel. The commercial media's self-justification through doctrines of consumer sovereignty, and Adorno's counterclaim that "the customer is not king" of the culture industry, "not its subject but its object" (275), are both alive in the newer cultural technologies: pay-per-view, cable, home video, VCR time-shifting, remote controls, interactive modes, virtual reality, electronic mail systems, satellite dishes, and home computers.

Perhaps the advent of prototypically postmodern genres, notably infotainment, is not a symptom of mass indeterminacy and triviality but a new point in the history of negotiating differences and similarities between notions of truth and forms of communication. What is endowed with the status of infotainment by producers becomes a complex morality play about social structure for some audiences. The current moment in popular culture is one of textual change, akin to Hunter's account of the initial criticisms leveled at *The Life and Strange Surprising Adventures of Robinson Crusoe* (Daniel Defoe, 1719). Much of the book's early negative reception derived from two competing senses of truth telling then in circulation. One of these was bound up with existing notions of epistolary letters, confession, and the calculating self, the other with the emergent concepts of the novel and "publication." In addition, the book anticipated the demographic fictions of a later time, with its consideration of population themes (Gans "Reopening" 31; Hunter "Providence" 219; A. Fogel 316). A moment of epistemological generic rupture produced a new textual form, guaranteeing its prototypes a difficult reception, precisely because new classificatory modes of writing (the novel) and subjectivity (the calculating self) were intermingling. Today, *America's Funniest Home Videos*, *The Real World*, *Sylvania Waters*, *Oprah Winfrey*, and *America's Most Wanted* are similarly problematic for critics because they blur genres to utilize the skills of the audience as these have developed over sixty years of documentary and forty of TV: skills in presenting the self to the camera, using the relevant media technology, acting as two-way agents with the state and the media, and redefining the subject matter of current affairs.

The negotiated, contradictory pattern of making and transmitting truth in these genres captures the intrication of rationality and the modern with irrationality and the postmodern. For Foucault, this conjuncture offers the prospect and the necessity of questioning reason: How *has* it been used and how *could* it be used, when one form of rationality, based on Darwinism, led to racist ideas, and another, based on bureaucracy, enabled Nazi labor camps? The spiraling points of the postmodern demonstrate the uncomfortable closeness of reason's danger as well as its value ("Ethics" 268–69).

# [ 1 ] *Sister Morpheme*
## *(Clark Kent—Superman's Boyfriend)*

*"College boy, huh? Got your degree?"—Harry Callahan*
*"Sociology."—Chico Gonzales*
*"Sociology? You'll go far—if you live."—Harry Callahan*
:: *Dirty Harry*, Don Siegel, 1971

It is 21 November 1993, Sunday night in New York. The evening is given over on numerous networks to the formation of public memory. Program after program is dedicated to jogging, creating, or supplementing a recollection of thirty years ago tomorrow. Just as the umpteenth screen version of *The Three Musketeers* (Stephen Herek, 1993) comes to the theaters— Douglas Fairbanks, Walter Abel, Don Ameche, Gene Kelly, and Michael York displaced by Chris O'Donnell—*Trente Ans Après* is happening, anachronistically, in public affairs television. CBS offers a reprise of *The Waltons*: twenty-five diegetic years after the Depression and fifteen after the nondiegetic cancellation of the program, John Boy comes home, companion-in-love in tow. It is 1963 ("While a nation mourned, the Waltons saw more clearly than ever what was most important . . . family"). ABC offers *J.F.K.: Reckless Youth*, a miniseries on Kennedy off the leash in the 1940s ("If you knew him when he was young you'd never believe he would become president: His battle with deadly illness / The wild parties / The story behind PT 109 / The women he loved before Jackie / Finally, thirty years later, the untold story"). On cable there is a 155-minute profile of Lee Harvey Oswald and five and a half hours are reprised from broadcasts of the assassination and its aftermath. E. G. Marshall narrates highlights of the late president's press conferences by turning his 1993 NTSC gaze in a State Department media room away from the camera and toward the angle from which Kennedy will suddenly appear in monochromatic, eye-line-matched archival footage from 1961 (did critics respond as they had to Oliver

Stone's 1991 *JFK*, alleging that archival footage merged with a reenactment amounted to trick photography?). "November 22, 1963: Where Were You?" finds Larry King with Clinton/Gore/Nixon/Belafonte/Carter/Cronkite/Streisand/Connery plus a special toll-free number allowing viewers to "share your memories" with "celebrity guests." And elsewhere, a repeat of a TV film about the good Kennedys versus the bad Hoover (no trademark); Warren Beatty in *The Parallax View* (Alan J. Pakula, 1974) uncovering murder in public life; a re-creation of the Dallas event; and finally, Cliff Robertson emerging from his triumphant role in *Wind* (Carroll Ballard, 1992) to conclude our night's viewing with *PT 109* (Leslie H. Martinson, 1963) (or maybe not; Brando follows as *Julius Caesar* [Joseph L. Mankiewicz, 1953] at 2 a.m.: I come to bury America, can I help but praise it?). Let's not bother with the schedule for the day of the anniversary itself, other than to note that Linda Ronstadt hosts a special commemorative episode of *Good Morning America*. Because the networks had day after day of commercial-free TV from the time of the assassination through the funeral, the occasion is often held up as the moment when television matured and became the principal forum of national expressiveness; but the week of the thirty-first anniversary, in 1994, was the moment Jesse Helms chose to say that Bill Clinton "better have a bodyguard" on any visit to North Carolina (Jameson *Postmodernism* 355; Helms quoted in Greenhouse). So this is also a metatextual space for popular public culture to rework its own history as reprogramming—*with* commercials, as the Helmsman steers the course.

That same 1993 Sunday saw obituary notices for Kenneth Burke, dead at ninety-six, announcing him rather idiosyncratically as a founding parent of New Criticism. (This followed close upon the passing away of E. P. Thompson earlier in the season, which produced a critique of Althusser, and the death of Christian Metz, which passed unremarked; twelve months later, Gilles Deleuze was dead and Guy Debord had suicided, again to a U.S. media vacuum.) Burke continues to be anthologized not merely for his criticism, but for his notion of "literature as equipment for living." He begins the essay in question with a consideration of proverbs, asking how they make their point and insisting that interpretations of such figures of speech must be provisional, or rather, "active" (77), mobile in accordance with the occasion of their telling and hearing. Burke extends his analysis to literature in general: just as proverbs offer advice on dealing with recurrent issues, so the less epigrammatic form of the novel is a strategic document in how to handle information. Critical classifications are determined by the situation at hand (a very Marxist/Rogerian/ethnomethodological formulation). We need an integration of the available methods for understanding texts as *"equipments for living"* (81). At the same time Burke's obituaries appeared, Routledge's successful cultural studies collection edited by Lawrence Grossberg, Cary Nelson, and Paula Treichler was being advertised with this front-page puff from the *Voice Literary Supplement*: "If you plan to continue living in America, read this book." Ethical criticism lives.

There *was* one other event that evening: the prime-time continuation, edgily up against *Murder, She Wrote* and Spielberg's *Seaquest*, of *Lois & Clark: The New Adventures of Superman*. The series is about desire and confusion, calling up the work of René Girard. For Girard, desire is essentially imitative: I desire people because of their desirability to *others*. In addition to the desired and the desiring, there is always a third term: the rival. The more you turn in on yourself and your relationships, the more you are actually interrogating your own standing in the world by contrast with another. So texts become a series of triangular narratives (145–49). *Lois & Clark* is the first comprehensively Girardian program. If you are Superman in the opening seasons, your rival is Clark—who is you. Whenever Lois is with Clark, she desires Superman and tells Clark so. When she is with Superman, she is speechless. When Clark is with Lois, he desires her and is speechless when she refers to Superman. When Superman is with Lois, he is just speechless. As the impostor Clark (invented by his "parents" after he arrived in Smallville), he wants to be desired as the real Clark. As the real Superman (invented only in the first episode of the series), he also wants to be desired as the real Clark. He loves Lois for the way she is with Clark, but wants her to feel around Clark the way she does next to Superman. Deceit, desire, and krypton/tonite. (Henry Louis Gates, the principal of African American male literary criticism, thought it wonderful. The first audience figures were all right among urban intellectuals, poor in the viewing heartland outside the cities. *Lois & Clark* drew viewers from the right demographic for key reasons and survived for a second, third, and fourth season. Despite rating well behind *Murder, She Wrote*, it was "worth" about U.S. $16,000 more for each thirty-second commercial [Riggs 312]. In concert with increased displays of her cleavage in opening credits in the later seasons, color images of Teri Hatcher [Lois Lane] were made available to America Online subscribers in October 1994. Within eight weeks, they had been downloaded twelve thousand times, a record for a person, but still far behind the desire for *Star Trek* replicants. Hatcher, hoping "it's not one guy with a computer and 4,000 pictures of me," saw the figures as a positive remark on her character's capacity to be "intelligent and feisty and sensual all at the same time" [quoted in Kim].) Discussion on alt.tv.lois-n-clark focused on her body through the 1995–96 season.

## Have You Just Been Reading "Cultural Studies"?

Cultural studies continues to be magnetic. The period between 1993 and 1997 saw the appearance of numerous anthologies: an omnibus internationalist survey; a reader on black British cultural studies; national mixtures of solid gold and future memories from Australia, Germany, France, Spain, and Italy; and a Canadian-Australian book (During; Baker et al.; Frow and Morris *Australian*; G. Turner *Nation*; Burns; Forbes and Kelly; Graham and Labanyi; Forgacs and Lumley; Blundell et al.). A volume of the *Southeast Asian Journal of Social Science* appeared ("Cultural Studies in the Asia Pacific"), along with a special issue of *boundary 2* dedicated to the region ("Asia/Pacific as Space of Cultural Production"), while *South Atlantic Quarterly* offered "Ireland and Irish Cultural Studies," and globalization and cultural studies is also on the map (Cvetkovich and Kellner). Textbooks have been available for some time (Brantlinger; Punter; G. Turner *British*; Alomes and den Hartog; Dirks, Eley, and Ortner; Gray and McGuigan *Studying*; Jenks; Storey; Thwaites et al.). The gigantic *Cultural Studies* collection already mentioned (Grossberg et al.) came out in 1992, and family-resemblance volumes exist in lesbian/gay/queer, legal, multicultural/postcolonial, regional, Jewish, and "other" studies, and there is a call within biomedicine to adopt a cultural studies research agenda (Abelove et al.; J. Leonard; Redhead; Dent; Williams and Chrisman; Herr; Boyarin and Boyarin; Beemyn and Eliason; Good). The journal *Cultural Studies* has been relaunched in the United States, its origins in Australia wiped from the slate of history, and the *Review of Education* redesignated as the *Review of Education/Pedagogy/Cultural Studies*, while the *International Journal of Cultural Studies* has been announced (see G. Turner "Dilemmas" 8–10; Craik "Cashing" 25; Shannon and Giroux). Honolulu hosted a major conference in 1993, with one block dedicated to cultural studies journals from New Zealand, Australia, India, the Philippines, and the United States ("From Cultural"). On the right, readers of *Partisan Review* and the *New Criterion* have been alerted to the danger (Wolfe; Kimball). Finally, a sure sign of arrival via (a) authorship fetish—Routledge's *Stuart Hall: Critical Dialogues in Cultural Studies* (Chen and Morley), a *Festschrift* for someone who doesn't write books; and (b) Ivy League uptake—Brown University's Malcolm S. Forbes Center for Media and Cultural Studies, a monument to a proudly capitalist adventurer.

Revisionist critiques are well in place, including claims that Dr. Johnson, Pierre Bourdieu, or the Kamiriithu Community Education and Cultural Centre in Limuru, Kenya, invented the discipline (I. Davies 115; Le Hir 77;

H. Wright 355), the *Reading into Cultural Studies* volume of exegeses (Barker and Breezer), Jim McGuigan's assault on cultural populism, an Anglophilic account from Fred Inglis, Antony Easthope accounting for cultural studies as literature's child (*Literary*), reclamation by social history (Chaney), question and answer from political economy (Ferguson and Golding), and the inaugural number of the journal *Parallax* announcing the field to be "at a stalemate because of its overinvestment in radical pluralism, liberal humanism and the Academy" (also see Nelson and Goankar; T. Bennett "Useful"; Cunningham *Framing*; David Harris; Trigger). Attempts are made to return the area's constituency and methods to "literature, art, and history" (Jordan and Weedon xi). Across the humanities, courses proliferate, research award categories adapt, journals rebirth themselves, and Chaucerians lay claim to funds to assist powerful "cultural studies" readings of the *Prologue*. The genre of heroic introductory essays to new anthologies is beginning to take on the appearance of the Shavian preface: the metatext delivers more than the essays that follow. New research contributions are being collected, such as Sarah Franklin, Celia Lury, and Jackie Stacey's and Terry Lovell's feminist readers, and James Curran, David Morley, and Valerie Walkerdine on communication, along with special issues of *Critical Studies in Mass Communication* and *Critical Matrix*, each titled "Cultural Studies"; *Critical Studies* ("Cultural Studies: Crossing Boundaries"); the *Journal of Communication* ("The Future of the Field— Between Fragmentation and Cohesion"); the *Canadian Review of Comparative Literature/Revue Canadienne de Littérature Comparée* ("Cultural Studies/Les études culturelles"); *University of Toronto Quarterly* ("Cultural Studies in Canada" and "Cultural Studies: Disciplinarity and Divergence"); *Callaloo* ("Rethinking Black [Cultural] Studies"); and so on. The *Quarterly Journal of Speech* asks whether "neo-Marxism as a metadiscourse" is "alien to rhetorical sensibilities" in evaluating the impact of the *arriviste*, while *Victorian Studies* is anachronistically moved to run a review symposium on work about the 1980s and 1990s (Rosteck 397; "Review"). Routledge publishes an on-line *Cultural Studies Times* and American Express, inter alia, sponsors Infoseek's index of cultural studies Web sites, numbering 114,775 as of October 1996.

Segments of the humanities (literature, film, communication, social theory, cultural anthropology, and social history), themselves splintered by feminism, queer theory, and the postcolonial, are confronted by those trends within and alongside cultural studies. When I was appointed from an Australian program in communication studies to the Cinema Studies Department at NYU, I was asked to introduce a graduate seminar in "screen cultural studies." As I began developing the course, it became fairly clear that whereas various aspects of literary and television studies were reforming themselves under the sign of cultural studies in ways that were recognizably similar to Australian and British cultural studies, the area of film was somewhat absent. Absent not in the sense that the words *cultural studies* failed to appear alongside the analysis of the cinema, but absent in the same sense that English departments in Australia at the long-established universities have recently reformed themselves to catch up with the work done at Griffith, Murdoch, and Curtin Universities ten years earlier. Both American film "cultural studies" and Australian literary "cultural studies" seemed to be plying the faithful textual analyst's trade—sit in a comfortable chair, analyze a text, divine its intertexts in the social world, pronounce on the political valency of both the text and those intertexts, sit in another comfortable chair, and produce a piece of writing about it—whereas the cultural studies I was familiar with had looked very seriously at the subcultural aspects of everyday life as well as different means of knowing them, such as ethnography, ethnomethodology, social theory, and collective research work. In other words, finding new ways to deal with new objects, rather than using secondhand techniques and people to protect academic space. And this had tended to involve a concentration on TV, music, clothing, sport, cultural policy, and young people, rather than *Citizen Kane* (Orson Welles, 1941), *Clarissa Harlowe* (Samuel Richardson, 1747–48), mise-en-scène, narratology, value, and ethical substance.

Cultural studies is "loosely coherent," a "group of tendencies" rather than "a fixed agenda." So what is it? For the editors of a recent introduction to the field, the "what" *question* is a legitimate one, but no conclusive *response* would be legitimate. Instead, the reaction must comprise "evasions" and further "questions that are much more pertinent than the desire to achieve comfort" by describing/prescribing definite coordinates to the area, which would "do violence to the values of openness." A similar logic rewrites history to nominate Stuart Hall's early work on deviance as a vanguard of lesbian and gay studies, and Bourdieu on sport as the last word on cultural studies in the area. No wonder even proponents call cultural studies "ill-defined and problematic." Rather like therapy, it seems one is either in denial of cultural studies or in recovery with it. But, to repeat, what *is* "it"? Even if this question is singular and powermongering in its drive toward a fixity of signification, surely attempts to elude it are similarly complicit with a network of power relations. The former exercises authority by requiring the highly circumscribed and heavily policed definitions usually associated with social science, the latter by engaging the mystification of contingent meaning favored in humanities-based textual commentary. Is one of these so clearly preferable to the other? And doesn't a refusal to set limits indicate a certain arrogant imperializing (Brantlinger ix; Gray and McGuigan "Introduction" vii; Stuart Hall "Deviance"; Bourdieu "How"; Kaplan "Introduction" 398–99 n. 3; Grossberg "Introduction" 5)? (The proofreaders of the journal *Southern Review*, for instance, make "cultural studies" and "popular cultures" interchangeable. The title of an article by Alec McHoul and Tom O'Regan in a 1992 issue appears on the journal's contents page as "Towards a Paralogics of Textual Technologies: Batman, Glasnost and Relativism in Popular Cultures." The last two words become "Cultural Studies" in the heading to the paper.)

One way to know what constitutes cultural studies at present is to investigate these prefatory or synoptic discourses. Such accounts allow the reader to say, "Yes, that's me; I'm doing cultural studies," or alternatively, "No, thank you anyway; it was a nice offer." Occasionally these heraldic announcements are little more than anecdotal addresses ("On my way here I was served braised chicken on Japan Air Lines. Rearranging the food, I was drawn again to Barthes and the meeting of cultures as stylistic brico-lage"). But even when they take this highly impressionistic tone, such texts generate other discourses, offering manifestos for redistribution by deans, newspapers, magazines, funding agencies, journal and book editors, students, cultural workers, and parents. In this chapter I examine the genre of the summary text and lay out new agenda items for the field that will be demonstrated throughout this book via a combination of the humanities and the social sciences.

▶

## The Heroic Summary

Manthia Diawara, author of *African Cinema* and later director of a film about the documentarist Jean Rouch, sat on a stage with Rouch at the 1993 Margaret Mead Film Festival in the American Museum of Natural History, a key date on the annual calendar of ethnographic, postethno-graphic, and First Peoples' media. Rouch had insisted that participants in a panel discussion about his work sit together on the stage floor rather than in the chairs provided. Denuded of the technology of form, they were to greet him as he did his "African friends." Diawara, eventually given just five minutes to deliver his talk, said he had both prepared a paper *and* prepared himself to sit, stand, and deliver in the conventional manner. He made the move, good-humoredly, of underscoring that he was quite keen on the modern, thank you very much.

Diawara has also provided a multicultural trace of cultural studies. He connects the old Centre for Contemporary Cultural Studies at the University of Birmingham, London-based black cultural workers, and people of color in black and feminist studies areas in U.S. colleges. This trajectory involves certain key transformations of perspective. The initial animating force to cultural studies came from a desire to understand British culture in terms of class dominance and resistance. Its methods derived from cultural-ist and structuralist protocols of reading and research. The common point has continued to be a search for an agent of history to move radicalism forward in class terms. But the agency is now in doubt, with Britishness/Englishness up for debate in a way that criticizes "ethnic absolutism" and seeks signs of a new aesthetic molded from black diasporas. These revisions to canonical cultural studies involve a denunciation of left as well as right for mythifying a lost white working class (by critic Paul Gilroy), and a critique of moralistically antirepresentational avant-gardism in cinematic technique (by filmmaker Isaac Julien) (Diawara "Black" 262–63).

Diawara thinks these dual heritages explain something about U.S. cultural studies today. Race is quite central to a North American debate about black modernism, sexual relations, hybridity, and essentialism, bridging cultural practice, criticism, and teaching. The other side to cultural studies has closer affinities to Birmingham, without the London influence. The focus here is on popular cultural artifacts, the meaning of the everyday, and the general production of sexual and ethnic difference, but in some isola-tion from black studies, often on the grounds of a critique of essentialism. This latter note may be tied to the very literary basis to the new discipline, the detritus of its successful displacement of deconstruction as a critical site for text-based radicalism in the humanities that means a continued obses-sion with discovering essentialist reasoning in the Other to mark out one's own terrain. History, identity, and development—in short, the modern— look rather different if viewed with a knowledge of African American and global cultural discourses as well as grammatologically inflected literary ones. But Diawara does not favor keeping these strands apart. Rather, he calls for a synthesis of ethnographic urban method (Birmingham) and race sensitivity (London) inside the cultural, political, and economic specifics of the United States and diasporic contributions to a black public sphere, hap-piness, and creativity; in short, a black modernity unafraid of ghettoization and uninterested in dedifferentiating integration, which focuses instead on defining and achieving the good life (Diawara "Black" 265–66).

This historicity eludes pessimistic predictions of a settled existence for cultural studies inside "the elephantine structure of the US academy" (Straw 87) thanks to its connection to groups such as black gay and lesbian filmmakers who merge community, theory, *and* popular appeal, as Kobena Mercer emphasizes (238–40). This is why Handel Kashope Wright suggests the work of Ngugi wa Thiong'o, Ngugi wa Mirii, and others at the Kamiriithu Centre was so significant for cultural studies: it linked cultural critique to production and was institutionally located within the community. Only Eurocentrism and repression by the Kenyan state have prevented this becoming a standard component of cultural studies history (355–56, 361). He also elucidates why Brian Barry thinks the principal task for cultural studies in Britain today is finding a nonsectarian civic culture that broadens tolerance and narrows uniformity: the communal norms of a white working class are not so much nostalgically yearned for as supplemented and redefined by diasporic voices and subjects. Living together requires permitting difference to remain and flourish. The difficulty, of course, lies in where we draw the line between matters central to tolerance that must transcend specific cultural locations and become part of a shared civics and those that are culture-bound and intolerant of difference.

Limit cases occur at liminal sites: subcultures and import-export intellectual relations. Notions of subculture have been crucial to cultural studies as part of a concern with culture as domination rather than culture as empowerment. Subcultures are understood as simultaneously opposed to, derived from, and informative of dominant, official, governmental, commercial, bureaucratically organized forms of life. According to this logic, the socially disadvantaged use culture to oppose their repression. Historical and contemporary studies conducted through the 1960s and 1970s on slavery, crowds, pirates, bandits, and the working class emphasize day-to-day modes of noncompliance with authority: dragging your feet, stealing pencils, sabotaging faculty members' payslips, and so on—in short, making do with available forms of expressiveness. The Birmingham Centre concentrated its subcultural research at this time on teddy boys, mods, bikers, skinheads, punks, and Rastas. The Centre's magical agents of history were often truants or dropouts, and unlike obedient working-class youth, some were violent. The two themes were deviance and appropriation. The deviance thesis examined structural underpinnings to the creation of a style, whereas the appropriation thesis was a semiotic decoding of these styles that assumes subcultures are subversive *bricoleurs*. This research and its political agenda were opposed to the achievement-oriented, materialistic, educationally driven values and looks of the British middle class. Consumption became the epicenter of subcultures. Paradoxically reversing their status as consumers, young people were theorized as producers of new fashions, inscribing on the body their difference and powerlessness. This also provided a sphere of social comment. The decline of the British economy and state were said to be exemplified in the punk use of rubbish as adornment: bag liners, lavatory appliances, and torn clothing (Leong). This work, focusing on how relations of consumption and the redisposal of commodities manifest relations of production, has turned into an articulation of everyday and marginalized life with the means of communication.

Just as black British critics questioned lamentations for a racially homogeneous Anglo working-class world that underpinned early cultural studies, similar questions of national origins and transfers can be seen in importation rituals to the United States and other countries since the mid-1980s. Thomas Streeter reminds us of the danger in celebrating transgression, because mainstream U.S. politics interprets such appropriation within a model of consumer sovereignty (317). Similar issues have arisen from other quarters where cultural studies has been adopted. In his review article on the *Cultural Studies* collection, Fredric Jameson notes "the noisiest detractors of grand theory are the Australians," in keeping with "the idiosyncratic and anarchist roots of Australian radicalism." This hitherto "harmless anti-intellectualism" also has a "sinister variant." He derides Tony Bennett's "Althusserian hectoring" for proposing "reformist structures" that ignore the specificity of Australia's 1983–96 period of social democratic governance in extrapolating from that decade to propound cultural policy studies (discussed in chapter 2). Jameson takes this as emblematic of the incapacity of the volume's Australian contributors (Bennett, Meaghan Morris, Graeme Turner, and Ian Hunter) to distinguish between national circumstances. At the same time, he quite likes Australians when, as Canadians have long done, they themselves attack what he calls "American parochialism" and insist on spatiality as a defining quality of cultural studies: a focus on the material coordinates of critique that acknowledges specificity but does not take this as its end point, seeking difference in place of centering their deliberations on the national, regional, or A. N. Other self. Cultural studies has gained force as it has become clear that the local sovereign state is no longer the primary axis of knowledge in the humanities. Whereas Western social science always knew to find its relevance across the map, litterateurs were slow to make such a move. The new internationalism is Janus-faced. Rey Chow explains that business students' interest in "culture" offers teachers of non-European language and literature institutional kudos. This leads to conservative pressure at the point of demand, but it delivers research time and facilities. At the same time, we must understand the appeal of cultural studies to university bureaucrats who reduce staff numbers in the humanities and social sciences by imposing an interdisciplinarity that is really about attrition and retrenchment. Here, cultural studies is perversely transformed into labor market structural adjustment. Francis Mulhern points to the incongruity of a "project of radical innovation and reconstruction" flourishing when austerity characterizes political and university life. The supply of professionals into many humanities and social science fields remains relatively inelastic; until signals from the market reach students or faculty impose stricter limits on intakes in order to make for an equilibrium, there is liable to be a long period of unemployment. For Robert Ray, the oversupply is already with us. Hence the effectivity—for the moment—of cultural studies as a kind of humanities conglomerate, engaging in unfriendly takeovers of job positions throughout the area in a task of consolidation that may even ultimately diminish difference. (Graduate students across several disciplines have reason to fear obsolescence as much as they have reason to welcome a breaking of disciplinary bonds.) And university presses have moved on to operating on a full cost-recovery basis. "Routledge theory" is no longer cross-subsidized by the Arden Shakespeare, and it seems to be getting harder for first-time authors to obtain contracts across the board: tenure review, which has grown dependent on book production over the thirty years that government subvention has underwritten college publishing, will need rethinking. Cultural studies is a response to the new ethos of scarcity (Jameson "On" 28–30, 46–47; Chow 130–31, 137; Mulhern 32; Altman 25–27, 30; Ray 59; Rosaldo "Whose" 525).

Conflicts over space are evident in methodological as well as geopolitical and industrial terms; hence the uptake of ethnographic tropes and their critique inside cultural studies, and the often vexed reaction from ethnographers (Rosaldo "Whose" 526). The anthropologist David Trigger has registered intense irritation at this combination of borrowing and attacking. In place of attempts to account for cultures by interpreting texts, he calls for "empirical evidence drawn from careful study of social action, *i.e.* from what members of Australian society actually do and say in the course of their everyday lives." One of Trigger's particular concerns is Bob Hodge and Vijay Mishra's treatment of anthropologically reported Aboriginal meanings (Trigger 607, 611–12). In turn, Hodge and Mishra bring him to the bar for ignoring the epistemological and professional crisis within anthropology that is itself *represented* by cultural studies. Trigger distances anthropologists from literary critics (whose tendencies he identifies with cultural studies). Hodge and Mishra, however, consider cultural studies "a critical tendency" inside the humanities and social sciences as a whole, *including* the discipline of anthropology, which itself depends on textual analysis to interpret inscriptive practices in the form of notes, tapes, drawings, and photographs (614). And indeed anthropology has housed cultural studies in some places, such as New Zealand (G. White 17–18). Questions of method and politics can coalesce, as when the major disciplinary journal *Current Anthropology* runs a debate on "objectivity and militancy" between what participant Laura Nader calls "white-coat and barefoot anthropology" (426).

This notion of cultural studies as a tendency across disciplines rather than a discipline in itself is evident in practitioners' simultaneously expressed desires to refuse definition, insist on differentiation, and have conventional departmental credentials as well as pyrotechnic capacities for reasoning and research. We might in turn connect such ambivalence to centering the everyday inside the academic, which points uncomfortably to a logocentric interdependence of the student and the object of study (Rosaldo "Whose" 525; Frow and Morris "Introduction" xxi). That can leave the area somewhat vulnerable to mainstream critics such as Kenneth Minogue, who warns readers of the *Times Literary Supplement* against this "politico-intellectual junkyard of the Western world" (27). At the same time, the *"weak programme"* side to cultural studies has some positive aspects, rather like the family-resemblance model of genres I have outlined in the introduction. The continuities come from shared concerns and methods: the reproduction of culture through power, structural determinations on subjects versus their agency, and discourses that operate through semiosis and historical materialism (Morrow 3, 6).

Some sociologists, confronted by departmental closures, amalgamations, or a transmogrification into social policy, bury their heads in methodological anguish when confronted by cultural studies, or claim the turf and terminology as their own to depoliticize it. What do you get when you cross Talcott Parsons with Émile Durkheim and Harold Garfinkel? "A New Proposal for Cultural Studies." This position says Marxism has been overtaken by a revised functionalism that uses interpretative cultural anthropology and "subjective perceptions" to link meaning with social structure. Symbols and ideals rather than power relations are the appropriate focus. To underline the point, Cambridge University Press's new "Cultural Social Studies" series is an avowedly Durkheimian project. It echoes both the "Editor's Note" that inaugurated *Prospects: An Annual Journal of American Cultural Studies* in 1975, an attempt to "elucidate the essential nature of the American character," and claims that cultural studies is just symbolic interactionism (Alexander and Smith; Sherwood et al.; Salzman; Becker and McCall). Of course, sociology always poses questions of method: How exactly does one "do" cultural studies? The answer comes in such books as *The Unobtrusive Researcher* (Kellehear) and *Researching Culture* (Alasuutari). In the first reply, civil society is retheorized through values analysis; in the second, social research methods are used to analyze the everyday.

John Frow and Meaghan Morris contrast the view of elite power brokers, who see culture as a route to economic efficiency, with cultural studies, which questions power and subjectivity rather than seeking to extract surplus value of labor or educate into obedience. Frow and Morris want to audit the denial, italicization, assimilation, and invention that occur each time nation, community, or society is brought into discourse, preferring to move away from essentialist definitions of national identity in the direction of a plural account of person and polity ("Introduction" viii-ix, xv). Tom O'Regan deploys a similar logic in contending that cultural studies can be understood in the same space as the analysis of policy, but in terms of capillary action rather than the descent of meaning from an apex of power (192–93). This propensity to identify resistance from below, while also constructing (and acting from the presumptions of) a power profit-and-loss sheet, leads John Fiske to try to "Gramscianize Foucault while Foucauldianizing Gramsci" (*Power* 255). For communications scholar James Curran, a "new revisionism" in the study of media culture sees the radical and liberal-pluralist traditions in communication research passing each other. Just when Marxism is prepared to allow textual autonomy, pluralism begins to acknowledge the accumulation of power. Perhaps cultural studies refers to a shift in knowledge, akin to the foundational moments of the human sciences that marked out nineteenth-century Europe and twentieth-century North America: the location of academic respectability moves from the cloisters to the town, a grand reversal of legitimacy in keeping with the awkwardly simultaneous emergence of the citizen and the consumer as representatives of the civic and the selfish in the nexus of community and market, with cultural studies' "squeamishness about orthodoxy" a sign of such changes (T. Miller *Well-Tempered* 154–58, 165–66; Hartley "(Hair)Brush" 7).

▶

## A New Agenda

Among utopic and dystopic announcements of the decline of grand theory and the old world order, the question of international cultural relations is increasingly pressing. In particular, disparities in the means of communication between the United States and most other countries (the extraordinary imbalances in textual trade), allied to a lack of methods and materials for learning how readers actually make sense of this trade, leaves cultural studies in a dilemma. This is where economic and interpretative turns really should meet, in ways that most theorization simply has not tried. Textual reductionism separates economic determinations from the text, which is sufficiently rupturous to elude the grip of capitalist ideology. But it offers no account of the occasion of reading. Conversely, economic reductionism separates cultural determinations as relatively autonomous from the text; no rupture of ideology here, because the truth of the text resides in the relationship of its producer and receiver to the means of communication. The balance of radical inquiry has shifted between these over the past two decades, with practices of consumption and personal meaning of increasing importance. Today, even political geography has substituted subjectivity for productivism (Sayer). But this does not have to be an either/or choice if we use cultural materialism as a guide.

The expression *cultural materialism* is usually associated with Raymond Williams's attempt to understand culture. He is critical of purely idealist conceptions that assume culture moves toward perfection as determined by universal values of the human condition, rather than being grounded in particular conditions of possibility. And he also questions documentary conceptions of culture that seek to record the artistic work of people in order to preserve specific insights and highlight them through aesthetic critique. His third path is less hierarchized. The product of reportage, it records a way of life and system of values of particular communities at particular times, while noting the benefits and gains in representativeness made by such changes. Cultural materialism works with Marx's insight that people physically manufacture their own conditions of existence, but without necessarily a conscious, consistent, or even enabling agency. Social activity, not nature, genius, or individualism, forges a way of life and changes it over time. This insight directs us away from a view of historical and contemporary culture that privileges a noble reach for aesthetic civilization or salvation, the experiences of rulers, or the impact of religion delivered from on high (*Long* 57 and *Marxism* 19).

Art and society—Williams came to call them "project" and "formation," respectively—are intimately intertwined, with no conceptual or chronological primacy accorded to either. The relations of culture, their twists, turns, and often violent and volatile patterns of change, are part of the material life of society. That allows a certain autonomy to intellectual work from the prevailing mode of economic production, but not from its own economies of person, place, and power (*Politics* 151–52, 164–66). There can be no notion here of an organic community that produces a culture of artworks, or a culture of artworks that symbolizes an organic community, for both have internal, nonreflective politics. Williams's cultural materialism refers to the specifics of material culture (buildings, films, cars, fashion, sculpture, and so on) within the dynamics of a historically changing social order. Language is a signifying practice that neither precedes nor follows the world, but is part of it and itself material. And most hierarchies of taste are established by co-opting and reordering the popular culture produced *by* ordinary people and repackaging it as mass culture delivered *to* them.

Along the way, this multifactorial approach to cultural studies got a little lost; hence the departure of the social sciences from the space of the emergent discipline. But we can see such work today; for instance, Jane Gaines's study of image ownership and control began as an examination of commodity tie-ins to films. This research design was clearly located within Marxist understandings of commodity fetishism: how screen texts endow associated merchandise with some of their aura. An interview-based methodology of encounters with former publicists inevitably led to a consideration of legal questions: Who owns the image? Who owns the right to replicate it? Who owns a star image, with all its confused lineage in diegetic and extradiegetic meaning—when does Bela Lugosi cease to be Dracula and vice versa, for instance? This set of difficulties turned Gaines in the direction of licensing character. In this sphere of knowledge, canonical texts circulate in altogether different ways from the aesthetico-symbolic currency of conventional cinema studies. *Dark Passage* (Delmer Daves, 1947) matters because of its status in the history of copyright. *Gaslight* (George Cukor, 1944) figures in case law as the object of a parody on radio. *The Maltese Falcon* (John Huston, 1941) is central to disputes over serial rights. No account of the diegesis or ideology of the new version of *The Three Musketeers*, for example, can explain the French government's *droit d'auteur* banning the film there because the producers refuse to name Alexandre Dumas as one of its authors. Such a revelatory sense of the radical restructuring of texts in their circulation leads Gaines to situate her work inside cultural, rather than film, studies because it offers a way to combine theory and method across sites (xiii-xvi).

This propels me in a couple of directions, first toward Herbert Schiller, a founding figure of international cultural political economy (ICPE). His books from the 1960s are being rereleased in updated versions; their scholarly commitment to liberatory cultural definition continues to inspire. Schiller's recent work endeavors to account for readership protocols and the globalization mythology of the new world order. He is dubious about the former *and* the latter. Schiller explains the present moment of ICPE as the triumph of "transnational economic interests" over the mechanisms of accountability that derive from sovereign states and their international organizations. The world communications system is dominated by commercial rationality. There *may* be significant sense-making practices at all points on the continuum of a text, from origins in a U.S. production house to destinations in audiences elsewhere, but the flow is unidirectional, and increasingly provides the dominant source of information in recipient cultures. The model of the consumer society is being taken up by more and more countries under pressure from global economic organizations such as the World Bank and the International Monetary Fund. The institutions and cultural contents that animate this model are determinedly American in their ownership, operation, and signification. And indigenous cultures are often modeled on Hollywood genres. In terms of what actually *constitutes* the United States, Schiller says "the corporate perspective" is dominant, because potentially opposing positions of farming, labor, and civil rights have been subsumed by the sanitizing culture industries. Adversarialism is displaced by a flattened-out mediocrity that privileges confessional comings-into-consciousness to the exclusion of structural inequality ("Transnational" 47, 49–52): the *Bildungsroman* rather than epic theater. This is close to the critique of cultural studies in *Monthly Review* for a distance from its supposed constituency and a neglect of the workings of contemporary capitalism (McChesney 2).

Another direction is toward Annamarie Jagose, who is prominent in the newer field of queer theory. She questions accounts of lesbianism that suggest it can exceed sex and gender discourses by fixing lesbianism inside a compulsory utopics. Jagose favors a feminist cultural analysis that will produce "increasingly precise articulations of unassimilated difference." At the same time, she is aware that this "new magical sign" of pluralism may elude critique by pluralizing all noun forms. This should not provide an alibi for some return to foundational humanism; the work of feminism must always be to *produce* "woman," not *claim* "woman" as its already achieved impulse that can be known outside contradiction, beyond "cultural legislation." Her intent is to evade the conventional feminist binary of voluntarist libertarian desire and structuralist determination through the bonds of language (265, 272–73, 276, 278, 281).

Can we synthesize the perspectives of Schiller and Jagose, placing both positions inside cultural studies and taking them as methodological and political cues? Perhaps we can borrow the interpretative strengths of textual analysis and the distributional strengths of cultural economics, a "middle-range" methodology that has been essayed in the study of Australian TV (Cunningham and Miller). To this end, Alec McHoul and Tom O'Regan have introduced the notion of "textual technologies" to cultural studies as a means of productively bracketing politics and reading. They criticize the idea that "local instances" of people refusing the dominant interpretations preferred by global producers can be made to "guarantee any general statement about textual meaning." McHoul and O'Regan are concerned that the search for resistive readers who can delegate their wildness to researchers inflates transgression. Aberrant decoding becomes a professorial passport to the popular and a means of making the output of the culture industries isomorphic with a demotic, anticapitalist, antipatriarchal, antiracist politics. Criticisms of such methodological leaps tend to be answered by a translation a few degrees away from notions of reading and toward the space of morality: opposing the search for resistance becomes itself opposed to resistance. Instead, McHoul and O'Regan propose a shift away from this system of delegation and its all-encompassing politics, commending a "discursive analysis of particular actor networks, technologies of textual exchange, circuits of communicational and textual effectivity, traditions of exegesis, commentary and critical practice." In other words, the specific *uptake* of a text by a community should be our referent, but not because this is guaranteed to reveal something essential to the properties of that object or its likely uptake anywhere else or at any other time. We can only ever discern a "general outline" of "interests" that can be applied to specific cases "upon a piecemeal and local inspection" that may in turn influence the wider model. Politics and texts are both about the means of communication as they function along a continuum of time and space (5–6, 8–9). That still leaves the question, Cui bono?

Morris glosses the concerns of cultural studies as "racial, ethnic, sexual, gender, class, generational and national differences (roughly in that order), as these are produced and contested in history," along with "a critique of cultural universals." At the same time as generative/categorical devices from the social sciences are being deployed as grids of investigation, their status as machines obliterating difference is brought into question, the result a productive intellectual polyphony that draws out contradictions and dissonances as per governmentality. If we link this to Frow and Morris's litany of interdisciplinarity, we can specify a desirable cultural studies as a mixture of economics, aesthetics, formalism, politics, gender, ethnography, history, physical objects, textual analysis, policy, and the inscriptive self, undertaken as a way of seeing who controls the means of communication and culture and with a constant vigilance over their own raison d'être and modus operandi. This could be connected to Grossberg's map of cultural studies along axes of cultural method and social theory. He sets up a grid comparing five forms of method (literary humanism, dialectical sociology, culturalism, structuralist conjunctures, and postmodern conjunctures) with eight formations of theory (epistemology, determination, agency, social formation, cultural formation, power, specificity of struggle, and the site of the modern) to offer a historicized system for conducting cultural analysis. Such an approach frees us from the semantic reduction of "culture" criticized by Williams, opening up a sense of its material effects in the sphere of "social management." For instance, with holiday travel emerging as the largest global industry, the concept of "heritage," that most ambiguated of aesthetic and anthropological cultural tropes, becomes central to marketing and finance (Morris *Ecstasy* 11; Frow and Morris "Introduction" xvi–xviii; Grossberg "Formations" 35; T. Bennett "Useful" 69–70; Boniface and Fowler xi, 1).

The drive toward new methods is occasioned by material factors. Within twenty years, digitization, compression, and monopoly capitalism will potentially see TV signals from around the world available to any personal computer for the price of a local telephone call. Initially, profits are expected to come from game-playing compu-nerds (the "nasty little boys" market, as it is known), home shoppers, and betting people. Then the techneophyte will become a key moneymaking center. Multimedia applications of established figures and sequences from film libraries will be sampled for redeployment, much as the wave of violent crime TV in the late 1950s worked its way through archival footage from Depression-era gangster films. Cost structures are low for such genres, and cable companies in the United States are accustomed to making profits from just 1 percent of the available audience. Meanwhile, the newest programming innovation sees a limited number of high-budget films exclusively screened on pay-per-view television prior to theatrical release in search of instant recapitalization rather than servicing debts over the many years it takes screen texts to come into profit (the distributor could gross U.S. $50 million in an evening). The annual revenue of the North American gambling industry is U.S. $30 billion, six times the size of cinema ticket sales, but much of it from film-related activities. The new Luxor pyramid in Nevada has a theme-park casino designed by the special effects team from *Blade Runner* (Ridley Scott, 1982). It allows guests to boat on an indoor Nile from hotel registration to the elevator, and features past, present, and future virtual-reality theaters. MGM has the largest hotel in the world there, a casino organized around a huge Hollywood theme park. The usual moralisms about godliness and the dangers of organized crime have not been forthcoming, because the gradual spread of lottery systems across the country has seen church and state become dependent on finances from the area. And Native Americans have been major beneficiaries of the gambling industry, with casinos set up on sixty-five reservations between 1988 and 1993 producing a combined yearly turnover of U.S. $900 million.

These innovations, so easy to list in the characteristic pomo manner of presenting signifiers without analyzing them, have complex politics attached to their design, administration, regulation, availability, and reception. The new era suggests a chaotic plenitude of meaning, which we conventionally associate with the impossibility of sustaining grand narration. But two very grand narratives have emerged triumphant from the end of the century of Marxist revolution in the late 1980s. I am referring, of course, to the individual and the nation. One discipline within the human sciences has improved itself over the past two decades to the point where its account of *all* human activity is routinely employed by governments, businesses, organized labor, and charities: the discourse of economics and the rational calculator. Neoclassical economics takes certain givens about the person's instinctive drive toward self-improvement, combines these with assumptions about preference and method, and comes up with prescriptions for international trade, crime and punishment, marriage and divorce, homosexuality, the building and management of parking lots, drug use, minority discrimination—in short, life itself. This discourse claims to locate itself in each human body. By contrast, the discourse of national fealty positions itself between such bodies, lodging them together in the binding of invented tradition and memory, as we saw in the introduction. It travels under a greater plurality of academic signs than does economics. These include the idea of free public communication, citizenship, and prosocial collective values (Becker; Carey "Mass"; Murdock "Cultural"; Evans; Cunningham *Framing*).

As Schiller demonstrates, we may now be at a point when the nation is being used to impose a doctrine of free exchange and economic growth based on a model of the person that, after Jagose, seems utopic and untenable, but that has definite effects at the level of international policies of culture and communication. At the same time, we should beware reducing nationalism to the conventional Western political tradition of a unitary subject, thereby disavowing the force of culture. Partha Chatterjee has shown that postcolonial sovereign states are at risk of being constructed as "perpetual consumers of modernity" in such formulations. A more cadenced understanding of anticolonial nationalism in Africa and Asia would acknowledge this as a play of difference with the West's modular formulas that arose prior to specifically political claims being made of imperial powers. It worked in areas the West had not unpacked and displaced—the realm of the spiritual—prior to engaging in areas where the colonizer triumphed—the material/infrastructural. Embodied as a set of practices, this sentiment carved out a safe zone for ethical nationalism away from the constitutional and economic spheres of settler dominance (5–6). Perhaps it, too, provides a model for theorizing shifting relations of power between subjects, for the movement between these two sites of strategic thought (person and nation) is achieved again and again by very reactionary forces in public discourse, because areas of alternative identity formation such as cultural studies engage all too rarely in these sites and systems for handling information. It is crucial that cultural studies depart from its fixation on an opposition between the popular and the official as a binary axis, to look instead at the mutual imbrication of pluralized marginal and central cultural forms inside the discourse of the nation (Ross "Ballots" 28).

▶

## Outro

In the 1990s, David Cassidy became a Broadway star and a prime-time fixture on *Partridge Family* reruns and 1970s retro music programs. This followed two decades in which he stood for all that cultural oppositionality defined itself against (he was out of fashion with music and TV corporations). Cassidy has his own explanation of this transformation. It reads rather like an executive summary of Jameson's *Postmodernism, or, The Cultural Logic of Late Capitalism* or Stuart Hall's reiterations of the contingency of his personality ("Minimal"): "I've worked very hard at satirizing myself, the former self, my incarnation from television. In the 90's, it was almost like the curse had been lifted and almost overnight, I went from being yesterday's news to like a cutting-edge sort of kitsch hip" (quoted in Pener). Why should Keith Partridge be the only person to have such pragmatic access to contemporary cultural theory?

Whether people are "in denial" or "in recovery" over doing cultural studies, they, "the people," are many and varied. The issue of power and the person as expressed in the technologies of culture is raised each time the question "Have you just been reading or writing or reading cultural studies?" is put. The capacity to manufacture and control meanings that circulate within a community is not available to all, so cultural studies must analyze the ways in which the means of self-definition and promulgation are—and are not—up for redisposition (Allen 31).

In the final approach toward prescribing a revised cultural studies, I almost forgot my starting point. Twenty-three November 1993, Tuesday night in New York, brought an end to the *J.F.K.: Reckless Youth* miniseries ("Power. Women. Intrigue. Nothing you saw on Sunday will prepare you for tonight"). Do we call this capitalist desire, sexism, popular memory, prime-time history, white man's fantasy, grotesque intrusiveness, consumer responsiveness, or public service? Is it an exemplar of Richard Dyer's "born-again hedonists" at play (*Only* ix)? Or should we rewrite it? "*Cultural Studies*: power/subjectivity/the modern." Such a shift signifies the travel of commodity and person, sign and interpreter, through time, space, and knowledge, necessitating Grossberg's "radical contextualism" at work:

both a "theory of contexts" *and* a "practice of making contexts" ("Introduction" 5). This means shuffling between "cultural texts and social events or discourses," teasing out the often indirect relations between the two even as they intersect and come to be knowable as an ensemble (how do we understand *Batman* [Tim Burton, 1989] without looking at corporate entertainment logics, or *Do the Right Thing* [Spike Lee, 1989] in isolation from youth subculture?) (Ross "Ballots" 28).

Arthur Danto has persuasively argued that the signal achievement of pop art was to draw attention to art history as a series of erasures rather than obedience to the native beauty of a series of texts. By its very presence in galleries and museums, pop art showed that the difference between commercial dross and aesthetic address lay in the power to tell history and control institutional space and emphasized the democratic potential of everyday life, the liberating meaning it offers artistic representations (3–7). As the editors of *New German Critique* put it recently, "cultural" has displaced textual critique and social history as "a master-trope in the humanities," blending and blurring close reading with an impulse from the margins (Czaplicka et al. 3). Far from disavowing the means of production in favor of the production of meaning, as Nicholas Garnham charges ("Political"), the best cultural studies seeks to work through the imbrication of power and subjectivity at all points on the cultural continuum. We can see this in George E. Marcus and Fred R. Myers's collection *The Traffic in Culture*, which refigures art history and theory and anthropology from a cultural studies perspective without losing the strong analytic methods of either field.

The popular takes place in the everyday, which is also where we move between the obvious, repetitive sides of life—utterly formulaic and mechanical—and bizarre tastes, quirks, and drives. The everyday is invisible but ever present. It is full of contradictions, and it can be transcended, as when the drudgery of the workday is transformed through popular cultural forms and flings. But even the ordinary enactment of the everyday is, as Harvey Sacks puts it, a "business." This business "takes work, as any other business does," for being like others requires watching, training, and self-monitoring. To someone suddenly thrust into prison life, this might mean learning to examine the corner of a ceiling as a nightly activity, rather than engaging in a former pastime such as examining the diegesis of a TV drama. In Agnes Heller's words, if "individuals are to reproduce society, they must reproduce themselves as individuals." And beyond the physical means of reproduction, this involves the manipulation of material conditions of existence and coexistence. There is no need for such a "commitment to the local and the specific" to override "the broader social context of unequal power relations." Rather, cultural studies should focus on the articulation of human difference in a search for "how systems of domination are lived" and transmogrified (Sacks *Lectures* 216–17; Heller 3–4; Grossberg "Cultural" 72–75). Graham Murdock puts it well:

> Critical political economy is at its strongest in explaining who gets to speak to whom and what forms these symbolic encounters take in the major spaces of public culture. But cultural studies, at its best, has much of value to say about . . . how discourse and imagery are organized in complex and shifting patterns of meaning and how these meanings are reproduced, negotiated, and struggled over in the flow and flux of everyday life. ("Across" 94)

I close this chapter with an attempt to show how and why these methods might be combined.

> *Traditionally, people who take up textual studies of a given medium — literature or cinema for instance — are drawn to it because they think it's important or they like it. Television studies, perversely, was peopled by those who thought television trivial or despised it: a ratbag collection of tired ex-professionals seeking serenity in early retirement and vanity publishing; psychologists relentlessly pursuing the victim in order to justify their own brutal methods and personal nightmares; Marxist sociologists schooled in false-consciousness berating the media in the afternoons and watching telly at night (and never noticing the connection); renegade literary critics desperately looking for a way to grab the attention of card-playing hulks who earned more than they did but who were forced to attend liberal studies before they qualified as mechanics and mining engineers.*
> :: Hartley *Tele-ology* 158

> *These are the same people that sentenced what's his name . . . Salman Rushdie to death. So we didn't want to mess with them. . . . [laughter] We had the utmost respect for Islam and we'd have been killed if we'd done otherwise. And rightly so.*
> :: Spike Lee, speaking at a black cinema conference, New York University, 25 March 1994

John Hartley talks about academic condemnation of television in a clever alembic of the contradictory moralisms that constitute the way popular culture is frequently understood. Spike Lee refers to shooting in Mecca for *Malcolm X* (1992), a witty account that makes a serious point about self-interest, respect for cultural difference, and fear. Each statement models a postmodern movement across the spirals of governmentality.

What follows in this book clambers up and down many spirals in search of the architectonics of today's most critical technologies of truth that define the person, the polity, and relations of power through the deployment of daguerrotropes. These are *telling* technologies; they tell stories about who and how "we" are, in ways that make a difference to what they define and explain. This is a process of description and manufacture. The technologies produce truths about and for the very people who provide their receptive targets *and* their diegetic subjects. Audiences to technologies of truth are both a source of legitimacy in economic terms and a space of proof in scientific ones. Truth, then, abounds as an expression of power and the person. "It" takes place at the intersection of practices of interpretation embarked upon by readers, the "lexical signs" of texts, and their ongoing mutual citation by both sources. And so truth is much too important to be left to *fals*ification, when the flow is already toward its *multi*plication. The model of the sciences as handservant to the arts is as unsatisfactory as a relationship in which the first services the social empirically and the second emotionally, with the humanities intellectually subordinate to the truth claims of science yet somehow ethically superior. I want to illustrate these conflations by examining screen violence and its frottage with the real thing. Here we can see intermeshed concerns that will recur throughout the rest of this book: genre, audience, and the modern as tools of governmentality, individually beholden at certain points to aesthetic, psy-complex, and neoclassical models, but repeatedly exceeding the ties that bind texts to such discourses through the very fact of their intercourse. Wittgenstein queried the side effects of "our craving for generality." Scientific proofs such as correlations between TV viewing and violence exhibit many of these trends, reducing phenomena to finite numbers of rules and analogic, symbolic reasoning, rather than confronting and surpassing "'the contemptuous attitude toward the particular case.'" The effects of this unworthy contempt include a drive toward intellectual neatness that impels classification through the subsumption of difference. We might prefer a modest assembly of similarity through the more observational, less disciplinary notion of "family likeness," a concept that allows the bearer of a name to be other than the zero signified of that name and distinguishes between an order of knowledge and its actual deployment by persons. And there is some empirical support for such a position (Gerhart 177; Wittgenstein *Blue* 17–18; M. Hayward). This loose model of genre, allied to a pragmatics of meaning-in-use, informs what follows.

The intersection of violence and popular culture is a crucial site for the exhibition of contradictory and complementary aspects of the aesthetic, psychological, and economic registers. The "fallen woman" genre of early

1930s Hollywood, for example, can be understood at just such a meeting ground: as a feminist expression of autonomy, represented through the desire to be sexually active; as a threat to masculinity, such that the woman had to be punished for self-actualization; as a market niche for producers; and as a source of panic for private and public regulators. Denunciation and decline accompanied raciness and pleasure, as they have since at least John Cleland's *Fanny Hill; or, Memoirs of a Woman of Pleasure* (1748). The treatment of women in this part of Hollywood history has its running partner in the heterosexual pornography of today, which finds one feminism denouncing the genre as misogynistic and another celebrating the small space it offers in what is otherwise a tightly policed denial of women's lives as desiring figures with the right to sexual acting out. Here, straight porn is *both* a site for the enunciation of male power *and* the precise naming of it, added to the prospect of female agency and drive—"pleasure activism," as Annie Sprinkle and others call it. In one discourse, a rapist models his crimes on pornography, but in the other, a dominatrix might do so, in pleasurable mockery of conventional male power. The contemporary discourse on the dangers of untrammeled access to home video and cable texts is inextricably linked to moralizing limitations aimed at women in general, with working-class leisure and middle-class pleasure adding a contradictory texture to the assault on the home as the latest site of teenage liberties (Church Gibson and Gibson; Murdock "Figuring" 57).

What are we offered on this topic by the psy-complexes? Millions of (name your currency, but set it in vague parity to U.S.) dollars have been assigned to university departments of would-be science in search of a satisfactory explanation of media effects. Three models dominate. Social cognitive theory postulates that the screen offers a how-to guide for viewers in terms of both means and motivations for violence. Distribution and cue analysis argues for a more interactive relationship between environmental and televisual influences, such that TV has a reciprocal impact on social conduct. Arousal theory posits an enabling connection, whereby individuals' tendencies toward violence are heightened by their seeing it on the screen. Put together, these paradigms suggest that a number of factors determine the effects of media violence: its efficacy, its referentiality to actual existence and morality, and the susceptibility of viewers to textual influences in terms of their individual histories (Comstock 291).

The previous paragraph is summarized from the 1989 Oxford University Press *International Encyclopedia of Communications*, where we might anticipate finding an entry that balances competing accounts against one another. We get instead an essay by George Comstock that announces itself as a historical survey and then transmogrifies into a psy-polemic. Beginning with some acknowledgment of debates in the area, the entry rapidly becomes a set-to between science and commerce, as Comstock martials evidence from laboratories and surveys to demonstrate his point, noting the especial value of research undertaken on behalf of the U.S. surgeon general in the 1969–72 period. He neglects to mention his role as a chair of the surgeon general's Advisory Committee. This is in keeping with the location of scientific truth away from political contingency and toward timelessness. In contrast to Comstock's rather passive conceptualizations, uses and gratifications theory poses audiences as engaged in a form of emotional Benthamism that seeks out pleasure and its other in an ongoing dialectic of complex choices. Conversely, critical studies either concentrate on the capacity of the media to fix agendas that determine the field of activity for governments and citizenry and define what is newsworthy and legitimate or illegitimate violence or add up supposedly common, constitutive features to produce a content analysis of the number of violent acts occurring over time and space (Cunningham *Framing* 139, 138, 141, 144).

Literally thousands of studies later, debate continues over the link between audiovisual representations of violence and their replication in the real. The correlation between smoking and heart disease/lung cancer has not been matched. No one can decide whether screen violence produces, is produced by, or is unrelated to offscreen violence, against or by any class of person. There are many reasons for this. The overarching one, in my view, is that the question is always posed from the space of a problem about the popular. The transcendent, independent variable/nonvariable is, in short, the genre of popular culture, rather than images or personality types. For one researcher, repeated replaying of violent scenes from "video nasties" produces an antisocial desire in the audience to maim and destroy people. For another, it produces the properly Brechtian capacity to maim and destroy the Hollywood continuity system (Andrews 47). The first hermeneutic frame disabuses us of the possibility of a dramatic form innocent of social reference and impact; the second stresses that seamless special effects and editing can be made transparent and demystified by freeze-frame and rewind functions.

Recent interdisciplinary research turns away from those who commit crimes, toward those who suffer from them, in keeping with the logics of victims' rights. It seeks the meaning of TV violence for women in particular. The jumping-off point is gendered experience in a specific social formation, and the significance of screen violence for that form of life. So, for instance, British studies indicate that South Asian women read *The Accused* (Jonathan Kaplan, 1988) as documenting a quite foreign society, with loose controls on misogynistic assault, while Afro-Caribbeans complain of racist associations of people of color with violence in television drama. Class is a lesser source of difference. The most meaningful predictor of position on screen violence is prior exposure to personal violence, which produces strong responses and concerns about media effects (Schlesinger et al. 3–4, 164–65). We can see the benefits here of combining research methods to look at textual cues, narrative recollection, and emotions among audiences, acknowledging such factors as age, class, gender, and ethnicity. This type of research attempts to explain why in Australia, for example, working-class boys may be ready to accept violence on the television show *Tour of Duty* as entertaining in the context of their chances of exposure to real violence, the futility of their social position, and lack of access to elaborated codes for the purposes of renarrating screen stories (Tulloch and Tulloch).

The 1993 murder in Liverpool of a two-year-old by preteens, which I discuss briefly in chapter 5, is a gruesome and tragic exemplification of the violence debate. Video was said to have caused the crime (one of the killers grew up in a four hundred-videotape household, including sixty-four violent and/or pornographic tapes); video was said to be illustrative of the boys' callousness (they looked at cartoons after the death); and video was the source of their conviction (it captured them in the shopping mall, and they were interrogated before it in custody). A polysemous popular medium is simultaneously held responsible for the desire to murder, the absence of contrition, and the proof of guilt. In his discussion of *Schindler's List*, Geoffrey Hartman criticizes this bizarre double-deixis of video truth, whereby testimony satisfies generic conventions *as well as* being a supposedly unadorned record (137–38). How much truth can it produce? More specifically, how many bizarre continuities can we discern with anxieties over other audiovisual innovations? There is a routine, circular, homeopathic aesthetics/pathology at play here that tropes earlier fin de siècle predictions that the telephone would stimulate both criminality and police control (de Sola Pool et al. 136–37). Form and content merge, with problems and their solutions mythified into the essential properties of a medium. We need to disinter communication from such absurdities.

These modes of producing truth form the struggle-laden sphere of postmodern life. Greenblatt refers to a space of "the radical irony of personal dissent" opposed to "the harsh celebration of official order." Such a space can be found at the crossroads of genre (the aesthetic that is also the industrial), audience (the inscribed public that is also a vibrant and/or lackadaisical readership), and modernity (an idealized state never attained, certainly in its apparent successor), under the sign of a necessarily conflictual—because micropolitical—governmentality. As Foucault says in his epigrammatic way, "Truth is a thing of this world." It is produced in "multiple forms of restraint" and induces "regular effects of power." The apparent absence of such truth is a shocking moment. It occasions the pursuit of the popular, a search for an alembic of public health within the trace of sociopathy. Rather than counting expenditures or behaviors as a way forward to perfect knowledge, or allocating aesthetic value, my own pursuit of the citizen in this volume seeks to comprehend "population imageries" as they appear in popular culture (Greenblatt *Learning* 109; Foucault "Truth" 131; A. Fogel 315).

# [ 2 ] *Leavis to Beaver:*
*Culture with Power, Culture as Policy*

*Here are three recipes for doing cultural studies. First recipe. Begin a career as a scholar of English Literature. Become dissatisfied. Seek to study wider range of contemporary and "relevant" texts, and extend notion of "text" to cover media, performance, ritual.*

*Second recipe. Begin a career as an academic social scientist. Become dissatisfied. Reject misguided scientism, and pursue more phenomenological study of relations between public meanings and private experience.*

*Third recipe. Identify your major grievance. Describe resulting work as "Cultural Studies."*

:: Collini 3

Stefan Collini's conceit about cultural studies is both accurate and unfair. It is accurate in that it describes academic innovation and politics in general and the specific connection of cultural studies to the humanities, the social sciences, and identity politics. It is unfair in that it ignores the much murkier disciplinary histories of other areas, singling out the new field because its predilections are transparent and debatable rather than hidden and non-negotiable; it is unfair also because Collini fails to address recent developments. Noel King, by contrast, has pointed out that the tentacular extension of textuality has been brought into question by debates over policy formation and implementation in such areas as museums, gentrification, enterprise culture, and local and national heritage (King and MacCabe 164). But Collini's provocation is a useful jumping-off point for this chapter, because it neatly references some key themes: the division between the two arenas of knowledge that originated cultural studies and the complexity of connecting cultural studies to social change. More of that shortly.

As I stiffened the sinews and summoned up the blood to start writing this section of the book, I heard a reggaefied, question-answer, female-male version of "I Honestly Love You" playing on a Jamaican New York radio station, appropriating a song made famous by Olivia Newton-John. This record was once regarded as an exemplar of Australians' tendencies to take the blander elements of exported American musical culture and then sell them back (e.g., Air Supply, the Bee Gees, and Little R[ubb][iv]er Band). (As a colleague remarked, with pride in his coiffure, "They're Australian! I didn't know. I used to be told I looked like Barry Gibb.") The latest version represented a very complex maneuver in the histories of Newton-John in the United States. Remember, twenty years ago today, fifty famous people met at Tammy Wynette and George Jones's Nashville home to discuss the Country Music Association's choice of Olivia as Country Music Female Artist of 1974. Tammy and George's guests named Newton-John "cultural carpetbagger" of the year instead, and established the Academy of Country Entertainers to police the boundaries of their genre. As an afterthought, they redesignated the association's CMA acronym as "Country, My Ass" (Peterson "Production" 292–93, 292 n. 1, 293 n. 2).

We can see a host of complicated forms of cultural politics played out in this anecdotal frame. When first released in its Olivian purity, "I Honestly Love You"—syrupy country—was seen in Australia by correct-line music listeners as standing for the most regrettably formulaic, mimetic tendencies of a dominated, import culture. Conversely, export to North America alerted the administrative intellectuals of country music there to the dangers of a rival formation inside the new international division of cultural labor and the need to create a protective aura of marketing authenticity for their own work. In the 1990s, it embodies *creolité* and gender reversal—a nice example of the postmodern as historical, intertextual, international, and economic.

A little earlier in the day, I was tuned to a rock station when a presenter back-announced the title of Midnight Oil's "This Is the End of the Beginning of the Outbreak of Love." His fellow announcer (or maybe it was a tape) uttered a very guttural, "Uuuuhh. . . . Wot's that mean?" The response was "I don't know," and we moved to the next song—a nice example of the postmodern as banal, everyday, depthless, and localized. It is routine to categorize Midnight Oil as agreeably political. The band sings about indigenous people's rights, nuclear dangers, environmental hazards, and working-class life. But the uptake of their music in the moment I just described is less about vibrant cultural politics than is the uptake of Newton-John by the country music police. And that indicates why interpreting meaning purely from a text is inadequate. More relevant to my concerns here, it also shows how significant institutional politics should be to cultural studies, why some people are saying we should all become cultural policy wonks, moving from a critique of common culture—the F. R. Leavis of the chapter title—to an engagement with the "regulation" that permits Nickelodeon to program *Leave It to Beaver* to the exclusion of a comprehensive service.

This takes me back to another place and time: my parents and I went "home" (for me, not them) to Britain in 1965, three years after we had left. This involved a tour of Buckingham Palace under the aegis of a Beefeater. He pointed to the place where the Beatles had recently stood after receiving medals from Elizabeth Windsor for services to British balance of payments. I was the smallest person in the group (and probably the person who had spent the greatest proportion of his life in the United Kingdom). The kindly Beefeater asked me, a twinkle in his ye olde authentic eye, where the Beatles came from. I tensed for a moment, looked to my father for a (forthcoming) gaze of reassurance, and answered, "America." The kindly old gentleman laughed at me. So did everybody else. I was corrected; they came from Liverpool. I read a similar error three decades later in the *New York Times*'s major 1994 feature "Global Smarming: America's Pop Influence." It lists, among other things, key pop music exports from the United States. These include the above-mentioned Air Supply, actually an Australian export to North America that sounded—prior to their departure—quite American, as did and do the Beatles in their joint incarnation as singers, as opposed to lyricists and interview subjects. There is no multiaccented sign in this form of popular culture, until and unless its institutional setting is theorized alongside textual reading. We should not mock my seven-year-old "mind," or the fact checkers at the *Times*, but understand their errors as statements with specific histories that occasioned their utterance (1965 and trade awards, 1994 and trade negotiations).

I take up national patrimony in entertainment explicitly in chapter 4; for now, I want to look at the effects of governmentality on cultural studies. As I indicated in chapter 1, traveling among the levels of analysis required here is not easy: on the one hand, we need to traverse a space-time-genre-race-gender continuum in order to trace influence and meaning inside postmodernity and popular music; on the other, we should live with the essentially uninterpretable, commonsense *non*meaning of most encounters with popular music. There is an awkward tension in evidence here, between accepting the sense-making practices of musicians, owners, listeners, and dancers and deciding to embrace a hermeneutics of suspicion. This is in keeping with cultural studies' dual heritage of textual interpretation as its analytic mode and meaning-from-below as its demotic one. Wondering about that inheritance and the alternatives to it has produced what follows.

> *No longer serving power by representing it or embodying it,*
> *culture—as envisaged in the programmes of public museums*
> *and art galleries—emerges instead as an infinitely divisible*
> *and pliable resource to be harnessed, depending on the cir-*
> *cumstances, to a variety of social purposes: self-improvement,*
> *community development, improving the standards of indus-*
> *trial art and design. . . .*
>
> *. . . in place of those avant-garde critiques which, taking*
> *their cue from Adorno, place the art gallery on one side of a*
> *divide and life on the other, and which seek to liberate art*
> *from the former for the latter, there is opened up the life of art's*
> *bureaucratisation as a distinctively modern, "anti-auratic" form*
> *of art's use and deployment which, since no amount of cri-*
> *tique will conjure it away, needs to be assessed and engaged*
> *with on its own terms.*
>
> :: T. Bennett "Multiplication" 887–89

> *Cultural policy, the missing agenda.*
> :: McRobbie 335

Culture has always been about policy, in two ways. The first is artistic output, emerging from creative people and judged by aesthetic criteria. This
is an artistic definition that corresponds to the interests and practices of the
humanities. The second meaning, less specific, takes culture to be an all-
encompassing concept about how we live our lives, the sense of place and
person that makes us human. This is, apparently by contrast, an anthropological definition, from the social sciences. Conversely, *policy* refers to a
systematic regulatory guide to action, adopted by an organization to
achieve its goals. In short, it is bureaucratic rather than creative or organic.

But if we look at the meanings of *culture* and *policy* more closely, we
can see each is related to the other. Organizations train, distribute, finance,
describe, and reject actors and activities that go under the names of artist
or artwork, through the implementation of policies. Governments, trade
unions, colleges, social movements, community groups, and businesses aid,
fund, control, promote, teach, and evaluate creative persons; in fact, they
often decide and implement the very criteria that make possible the use of
the word *creative*. This may be done through law courts that permit erotica
on the grounds that they are works of art, schools that require students to
read plays that are "improving," film commissions that sponsor scripts on
the grounds that they reflect national concerns, or entrepreneurs who print

symphonic program notes justifying an unusual season as innovative. In turn, these criteria may themselves derive, respectively, from legal doctrine, citizenship or tourism aims, and the profit plans of impresarios.

The second understanding of *culture* may appear in academic anthropology or journalistic explanations of the zeitgeist. Again, this sense of the term is expressed in locations that use particular trainings and conventions to construct their categories. For instance, references to "Aboriginal culture" by anthropologists before land rights tribunals are in part determined by the rules of conduct adopted by the state in the light of a particular perception of political power and ethical rule. Similarly, references to "merchant-bank weekend culture" by feature writers are in part determined by the rules of conduct adopted by their editors/proprietors in the light of a particular perception of market segmentation. We hear about these lifestyle/ritual practices because of—and through—policy. None of this is especially new. If, for example, we go back to the uptake of English as the national language of England, the moment after 1400 when writing in Latin and French was disavowed, we can see the impact of a national language policy, animated by the desires of Henry IV and Henry V to reinforce their dubious legitimacy by encouraging national unity in the Parliament and citizenry. Similar policy histories account for the emergence of linguistic orthodoxies in India, Norway, Finland, Israel, and elsewhere. And from the first days of her empire, Queen Isabella's functionaries established Castilian as a language of conquest and management, while Basque separatists sought to repair this as one of their first priorities. Language policies have been critical aids to imperial rule and neocolonial "enterprise" over the past century, as critical linguistics, Afrocentric language planning, and examinations of triad antilanguages have shown. Complicated legal debates have taken place since the 1920s in international courts over attempts by former colonized peoples—such as the Flemish, Poles, and Irish—to assert their linguistic uniqueness (Fisher 1168, 1170, 1178; Phillipson 8; Urla 822; Mazama 3; Akinasso 139–41, 143; Bolton and Hutton; Berman).

So far so good. "Culture" and "policy" seem to belong together, or at least in close proximity. But consider the polemical beginning to a recent book about cultural policy, Stuart Cunningham's *Framing Culture*:

> The Prices Surveillance Authority's 1989 report on book publishing in Australia didn't make it to your local bookstore or to the review section of your weekend paper, yet it may have more impact than a dozen bestselling novels. "Sunday Afternoon with Peter Ross," the Australian Broadcasting Corporation's (ABC's) television arts magazine, didn't feature what happened in recent years in the latest round of international negotiations in the General Agreement on Tariffs and Trade (the GATT), yet cultural goods and services are

high on the list of tradeable commodities, and powerful nations view these markets as strategic sites for deregulation. Cultural commentators well versed in the intricacies of film style or art history may evince little interest in the commercial businesses, labour organisations, statutory authorities, or government departments without whose activities the world of culture as we know it would be unrecognisable. Happy consumers of culture are often in the Land of Nod when it comes to evaluating the infrastructure of cultural development in Australia. (1)

When we articulate culture and policy in the specific context of the state, more complex issues confront us. The state conjures up a number of attachments, depending on the nationality, historicity, subjectivity, and theoretical training of the person speaking, but these can include the notion that the state serves the interests of capital, patriarchy, or whiteness, or that it stifles individuality. The debate over cultural policy studies that I outline below is about certain sections of the humanities negating their histories as left intellectuals who used to articulate the theoretical correlates of public resistance in favor of a more measurable and measured influence inside the apparatuses of the state. The debate stands for much more than that, however, because it calls up the prospect of teaching the social sciences how to read and the humanities how to act, giving form to the agenda laid out in chapter 1.

▶

## Debating Positions

> *Many people trained in cultural studies would see their primary role as being critical of the dominant political, economic and social order. When cultural theorists do turn to questions of policy, our command metaphors of resistance and opposition predispose us to view the policy making process as inevitably compromised, incomplete and inadequate, peopled with those inexpert and ungrounded in theory and history or those wielding gross forms of political power for short-term ends. These people are then called to the bar of an abstrusely formulated critical idealism.*
> :: Cunningham *Framing* 9

> *"Personnel? That's for idiots."—Harry Callahan*
> :: *The Enforcer*, James Fargo, 1976

The notion that theory undergirds practice through a renewing critique taken up by bureaucracies has often seemed misplaced in the cultural field, where everyday academic critical practice eschews such relationships as either insufficiently aesthetic or too co-optive. Cunningham attacks this line for failing to acknowledge that public action on sexism in advertising and the status of women in the workplace have come about because of a shift from utopic critique to implemented policy. He calls for a "political vocation" that draws its energies and direction from "a social democratic view of citizenship and the trainings necessary to activate and motivate it." This "new command metaphor" will displace "revolutionary rhetoric" with a "reformist vocation." Its "wellsprings of engagement with policy" can avoid "a politics of the status quo—a sophomoric version of civics," because cultural studies' continued concern with power will always query Pollyannaish liberal pluralism (*Framing* 11).

A senior policy adviser to the Australian Film Commission, writing in response to Cunningham's work, finds "real hope that we might be something more than grubby little incrementalists" (Given 14). (But then the commission funded this work.) How supple is the new rhetoric? Cunningham maintains it can be extended to encompass cultural rights, access to information held by multinational corporations, the shape of international organizations like the European Union, the balance of power between developed and less developed countries, and how all these developments have an impact locally (*Framing* 11). As he contends in the opening to his book: "All global trends are local somewhere, and are therefore subject to specific actions by local agents, albeit in contingent ways. Outcomes are never totally predetermined by inexorable international movements; strategic thinking recognises this and acts accordingly" (*Framing* 13). Nevertheless, such a position is in sharp contrast to cultural studies as it was routinely presented in Britain, Australia, and the United States up to the late 1980s. Consider Lana Rakow's summary of feminist communication and cultural studies:

> How can we create a world that does not rank and tightly categorise people by race or gender, that provides materially for all its members, that treasures children and considers them not the property of parents but the responsibility of all, that is decided upon by all those living in it, not by powerful organisations or a small group of powerful men, that is based on values of cooperation and community rather than competition and individualism, where communication technologies are used not for private profit but for political and cultural participation by members of the society? (212)

This may appear not far distant from the utopic parts of the Cunningham peroration, but it draws on a much less sanguine account of capital and government and the culturally redistributive potential of social democracy. Cunningham wants a brace of skills in public policy as part of the everyday practice of cultural studies, which is decidedly heterodox. For example, readers opening the inaugural issue of the *Australian Journal of Cultural*

*Studies* in 1983 confront the following: "There is a single enterprise that can be labelled 'cultural studies'—[:] the conception of cultural forms as structures of meaning—[and] culture as a set of texts of different kinds— cultural studies is semiotics" (Hodge and Kress 1). This difference makes for a debate about cultural policy studies. If the semiotic approach is insurrectionist and textual, the policy approach is reformist and sociological. Where one is avowedly utopic, the other is equally incremental. That means not so much a neglect of textuality or high principle, but an embrace of institutionality and pragmatism.

Consider the foundational statement of the Institute for Cultural Policy Studies (ICPS) at Griffith University in Brisbane, set up by, among others, Tony Bennett. The institute's working definition of culture identifies agencies and practices that project a better, more developed world than the one previously in existence. So "*culture*, in the Institute's understanding, refers to the institutions, symbol systems, and forms of regulation and training responsible for forming, maintaining and/or changing the mental and behavioural attributes of populations" (T. Bennett "Culture" 6). This processual understanding of culture is concerned with moral uplift. The definition allows no form of policy life outside its own, and appears to have no anterior position, which renders it essentially mythic. It has an account of past and present textual criticism as a practice, but—as we shall see—no account of its own emergence in relationship to the wider domain of analyzing policy. Its autobiography continues to be articulated against aesthetic critique.

The ICPS's 1989 prescription for "cultural policy studies" says that the yet-unborn entity will examine "the factors influencing . . . policy objectives and operational procedures" of agencies that form and reform the "mental and behavioural attributes of populations." It also involves "assessing the outcomes of such policies and procedures with regard to their implications for different sections of the community" (T. Bennett "Culture" 6). The field is clearly being set up as evaluative: cultural policy studies will decide the legitimacy and utility of cultural policies and programs. It will not question the project of molding the populace, which is taken to be internal to culture and inalienable from it. There is a clear connection here to governmentality as a technology for managing the population. But unlike Foucault's ironized account, the institute's documents celebrate this development, using it to open up a space of influence for intellectuals: the cultural magistracy of consultancy.

This point becomes clearer in foundation director Bennett's *ressentiment* at other intellectual pastimes, principally "culture as an object for criticism" when such criticism is in search of "cultural artefacts" to transform into "a generalised form of social criticism . . . extending the sway of literary and aesthetic discourse into the sphere of everyday life construed as a rich domain of the unfathomable." There is a "correct" understanding of culture—the institute's definition—and a "correct" understanding of how to study it. This understanding is both piecemeal and mechanical. It is piecemeal in that it decries "positions deduced from general principles and applied across different histories, organisations, characteristic mechanisms, institutional arrangements, and so on." It is mechanical in that it perceives "the processes of government" as central to "shaping the attributes of populations, and particularly those of modern citizenries." This involves people being "superintended" ("Culture" 7, 6). Put another way, cultural studies is being told to pursue the popular under the sign of governmentality and the cultural citizen.

Bennett criticizes cultural studies as defined at Birmingham and since its "migration to the United States." The former approach is "misguided" on two counts: it persists in "attributing to the state and/or capitalism a monolithic unity" and "imagining the possibility of a populist politics" ("Culture" 7). Such critiques gain a special contour when we consider the curriculum vitae of their primary enunciator. Prior to his arrival in Australia, Bennett was a scion of English-language Marxist literary criticism and Gramscian cultural studies, with publications such as *Formalism and Marxism* and numerous essays on popular culture and social relations. His writings have been taken as celebrations of a class-based politics of resistance to aesthetics and the subcultural denial of behavioral codes. In Bennett's rapprochement with the state, it is possible to discern a movement from Lukács and Gramsci to a particular reading of Foucault. The shift is apparent both in his revocation of Western literary Marxism (*Outside Literature*) and in some of his tracts on cultural policy studies. It involves, inter alia, redemption through the neo-Wittgensteinian concept of rule rather than neoromantic elevations of resistance. "What we cannot speak about we must pass over in silence" is transformed from the closing paragraph of the *Tractatus* (74) into an ethic of empirical intervention. Bennett is arguing for the inevitability of rules, which have no necessary relationship to the mode of production within which they function. Hence the logic of evacuating spaces designed to be filled by some spontaneous irruption of political feeling that is declaratory and exhortatory in an emotionally expressive way, will not organize, and is basically libertarian. This libertarianism, an aestheticizing cultural critic's utopia, does not recognize the intramural rules of membership and critique that give it order, simultaneously failing to open itself up to using the rules by which the rest of the world is ordered ("Culture" 7).

I wish to welcome this shift and then criticize it for referencing but ultimately failing to breach the space between the humanities and the social sciences or attend to the extant field of policy studies. Although Bennett himself does outstanding work in the area of museums, the apocalyptic tone adopted by him and others needs recasting, as indicated by left and feminist dubiety-pieties expressed over this "original but somewhat perilous modification of theory and attitude in accordance with the ideology of governmental policy." Francis Mulhern, for instance, queries such a deployment of culture, distinguishing between politics as injunctions to the population and culture's dedication to difference (38–39). Not to mention the fact that the Policy Analysis Exercise Program at Harvard's Kennedy School of Government finds deconstruction and postmodern theory to be as necessary as other methods, problematizing the idea that such approaches lack application (Alomes and den Hartog 20; Grace; Morris "Gadfly"; Danziger).

In place of the "grand-standing of the cultural critic," Bennett offers "a third course for cultural studies." His brief programmatic statement opens up a field not necessarily catered to in the earlier definition of cultural policy studies. The "third course" entails "producing positive knowledges that can be effectively used within actually existing spheres of cultural policy formation as constituted in the relations between governmentally constituted spheres of cultural management and the agencies and constituencies operative within those spheres" ("Culture" 7–8). This "third course" has a place in the international intellectual/publishing stakes as well. Five founding members of the institute edit a series of Routledge books announced in 1993 under the title of "Culture: Policies and Politics," which calls for "a significant transformation in the political ambit and orientation of cultural studies." In place of a "prophetic and oppositional" stress on "resistance and empowerment," greater attention must be paid to "the policy instruments through which cultural activities and institutions are funded and regulated in the mundane politics of bureaucratic and corporate life." This means seeking out "a policy calculus" that can connect analysis to governmentality. The editors are aware that their "advocacy for pragmatism" may "be rejected as unprincipled" (Bennett et al. "Series").

Bennett's "third course" becomes apparent in this prospectus. We are *not* in an environment that criticizes cultural policy on behalf of those affected by it, or in terms of the meanings it circulates. We have entered another domain: consultancy. The value of cultural theory will be determined by the extent to which it can "be translated into programmes" amenable to implementation by government (T. Bennett "Culture" 8). This means work done directly on behalf of the state and other organizations that fall within the institute's understanding of cultural policy. But no indication is given of the ethical technology for distinguishing among cultural projects, between huge grants to ballet and small ones to street theater, no explanation of the precepts that govern the population, or of how the graduates in literature who run the institute deem themselves qualified to do so.

The unveiling of the *nouveau roman* called cultural policy studies took place at an especially providential and yet awkward moment in public politics, when Australian universities were being transformed by their principal source of finance: government. This transformation included the requirement for greater relevance in research and teaching as judged in terms of "the national interest," rewards for cooperation with private enterprise, and reduced time for professors to engage in the study of their choice. *Meanjin* dedicated an issue to the future of the humanities in this era. (The name *Meanjin* comes from the Murri Aboriginal word for a spike of land that juts into the Brisbane River.) *Meanjin* is a high-production-value quarterly, sold in bookshops and underwritten by private bequests and public subvention. For fifty years it has been prominent in the Australian literary-critical apparatus, publishing fiction, poetry, criticism, and history. Putting policy into its pages is both a provocation, for that enters the terrain of cultural criticism, and legitimation, because this is one of the principal places in which to be read on the matter of culture—but not, significantly, in political science. And *Meanjin* became a key site for debates over cultural policy studies, thanks to an article by Hunter.

Hunter criticizes claims by "the humanities academy" that it is "custodian of a recipe for human development that transcends all social purposes," and so must oppose attempts "to calculate the incalculable, to subordinate culture to bureaucracy." He locates such claims in the "persona of the critic," because they set "culture against utility, the liberal against the vocational, disinterested judgement against bureaucratic calculation." The humanities are construed as "central to the harmonious development of all the human powers," but in a noninstrumental, overarching, and unspecifiable sense that alchemically produces a "many-sided personality" ("Accounting" 438, 440–41).

Hunter, by contrast, favors a motivating force not of the well-rounded human, but the citizen, who must be furnished with "a specific set of ethical, legal and political competences," very much on a normative basis. These capacities will not develop spontaneously from "the study of literature and history"; such presumptions are nothing more than "a narcissistic expression of the aesthetic persona." Both aesthetic and cultural criticism defenses against the new relevance are said to depend for their analytic unity and intellectual history on nineteenth-century desires to counteract the anomic, alienating tendencies of industrial society that divided human subjects by labor: the vocationalism of the modern. But, argues Hunter, when the humanities displaced the classics in the curriculum—a central strut of modernity—they did so not in order to generate a unified, disinterested subject. Rather, they established the coordinates of "professional training for the liberal occupations." Governmental education in the late nineteenth century grafted "ethical and cultural abilities" onto the population, protecting it from "criminality, poverty and morbidity" by offering "a morally managed environment." Subjects such as literature and history were important because they established "ethical techniques and pedagogical relationships" ("Accounting" 441–44).

In short, it was from the Malthusian survey, not the Schillerian idea, that the humanities drew their reason to be. No one was being reconciled among their divided selves; rather, they were being warned about poor sewerage. This has contemporary corollaries: "The modern citizen is not just expected to be computer-literate; he or she must also develop and manage a self able to negotiate a range of statuses and duties associated with personal and professional relationships, parenthood, sexuality and the role of the democratic citizen" (Hunter "Accounting" 447). Training in the humanities occurs through the relationship of student to teacher, with norms and values transmitted not as ideology, but in the mechanics of knowing one another. This is Foucault's governmentalization of culture and ethics of self-formation alongside a Puritan admiration for rhetoric and civic models promulgated in the Jacksonian Republic. Hunter expresses a clear preference for procedurally oriented, disciplined bureaucrats over descendants of the originary pastoral model of aesthetic pedagogy, who mask their narcissism in a welter of expressive claims about identity. But what is the basis for this preference? If reproducing the persona of the critic is a given in the power relations of pedagogy, because bureaucratic authority has been handed down across generations of tutelary arrangements, then why should it be avoided, especially when precisely this brand of study has been popular with students and a matter of key engagement with a wide array of nonbureaucratic people and institutions (McWilliams 19–20, 28; Hunter "Humanities"; D. Bennett 205–6)?

This is a moment to juxtapose two favored authorizing perspectives, often cited by cultural policy studies. One is Bourdieu, the other governmentality, which derives, as I note in the introduction, from Barthes:

> To endeavor to think the state is to take the risk of taking over (or being taken over by) a thought of the state, i.e. of applying to the state categories of thought produced and guaranteed by the state and hence to misrecognize its most profound truth. (Bourdieu "Rethinking" 1)

I read a big headline in *France-Soir*: THE FALL IN PRICES: FIRST INDICATIONS. VEGETABLES: PRICE DROP BEGINS. . . . The signified or concept is what must be called by a barbarous but unavoidable neologism: *governmentality*, the Government presented by the national press as the Essence of efficacy. The signification of the myth follows clearly from this: fruit and vegetable prices are falling *because* the government has so decided. (Barthes 130)

Governmentality explains how second-order meaning can produce *post hoc ergo propter hoc* fallacies: headlines announce a drop in the price of vegetables, which the reader erroneously connects to the economy and then attributes to good management by the state. The problematically partial uptake of these authorizing perspectives is evident in Hunter's other writings.

He has progressed from work on the humanities to a critique of liberal, philosophical, and Marxist theories of education because they view contemporary schooling (presumably anytime, anywhere, although he does not engage with theorists or historians outside white settler colonies and Europe) as sacrificing "a noble ideal of human development to the grim reality of the social police" (*Rethinking* xii). In *Rethinking the School*, his major statement on the topic, Hunter opposes such positions with an account of nineteenth-century English and German schooling and religion based on policy documents and reminiscences from civil servants, clergy, and pedagogues, parceling together theories of education that rely on a public sphere, individualism, or collective self-government as assuming the subject has been split in language and divided in labor by cultural capitalism. Instead of remaining wedded to this wistful model of complete human development, Hunter favors a piecemeal approach (xii).

But he may, paradoxically, have restored us to Hegelianism. In place of a human essence unworthily divided through discourse and production, he gives government a *Geist* that propels it toward realistic social assays and interventions. The state can be trusted because any ideological component to its ministrations is inevitably compromised by the conditions of existence of the population. This transposition makes Hunter's work logocentrically interdependent with its damned other: he assumes the labor of government necessarily corresponds with existing social problems. Educational systems count, differentiate, and treat a variety of people in their actual social locations, a diffusion that is magically resolved by the state (Prussia is thought worthy and capable of emulation).

Hunter uses the concept *habitus* without taking great time over its definition and current circulation. In both education and the sociology of culture, the term is generally associated with Bourdieu, who gives it two meanings: "primary class upbringing" and "secondary habitus inculcated through schooling." These influences produce "prereflexive adherence" to a field of thought ("Peculiar" 9 n. 2). Bourdieu identifies secondary school-ing as a critical site for the transmission of state-defined and -described forms of knowledge, which are then loosened from their origin such that citizens "spontaneously apply" them "to all things of the social world—including the state itself." He is particularly concerned that the concept of the "bureaucratic thinker (*penseur fonctionnaire*) is pervaded by the offi-cial representation of the official," a peculiarly Hegelian seduction that ac-cepts accounts of the bureaucracy as a disinterested body of civil servants ("Rethinking" 1, 2). There is a clear resonance with the above quotation from Barthes.

Hunter also values Max Weber's explanation of how status propels people (in this instance, critical intellectuals) to exercise power. But again, Hunter's enabling category, citizenship, has been thought through by its en-abling theorist in ways that compromise its uptake as a piecemeal and/or universal sign. Weber discerns "three distinct significations" of citizenship. The first category is the divided "class citizen," understood in terms of an "economic interest" that binds people together through need as well as dividing them hierarchically. It is "peculiar to western civilization." The second category is "membership in the state," which signifies access to po-litical rights distributed on a universal basis, unlike the economic sphere. The final category is unitary class citizens, who share relationships to prop-erty and esteem that unite them against outsiders (233). Again, this lineage is not addressed in *Rethinking the School*.

This is not to deny the importance of Hunter's assault on the human-ism of much oppositional educational thought. His criticism of expressive totality and divided selves that can be magically reintegrated through charismatic discipleship is well made. But why should antiromantic models be privileged in his critique to the exclusion of how those characteristics are personalized? And why should curricular policies, which form the basis for much of Hunter's argument, be regarded as accurate representations of what is taught or received, especially as this relates to collective identities from beyond the school? When Hunter values the messiness of piecemeal work, this might ring truer if he engaged with the "muddling through" discourse of public policy. Its founder, Charles Lindblom, has recanted the position, recognizing that pluralistic fantasies about social groups sharing resources through interaction with governments fail to account for the business-based nature of most state actions. A fuller engagement with so-cial theory and research might displace assumptions, pervasive in *Rethink-ing the School*, to the effect that metacritical bureaucratic rhetoric has a necessary correspondence with *any* out of policies, programs, forms of cal-culating benefits and costs, and human agency. This would be in keeping with the critique from Barthes that attended Hunter's "good object," governmentality, at the very moment of its birth (on this point, see Craik "Mapping" 203–4).

Hunter's position is clearly at variance with what Alan O'Connor terms the "political currency" of cultural studies, that rather dubious chaplaincy of consciousness assumed by cultural critics in their search for the utopian progressive text (407). An example is Cathy Schwichtenberg's aim of uncovering "how cultural studies can be resistive" (204). The idea of teaching and research faculty in culture and communication connecting themselves to struggles over the provision of food, buildings, and harmony around the globe is coffee-shop self-promotion that denies what critics actually do. The sense of a rhetorically enlisted (but actually unengaged) extramural constituency of moral authority animating these positions is both absent and present in the sight of what Stephen Muecke calls "nostalgia for a lost unified front along which oppositional criticism could take place" (16): absent from material connections to that constituency, but present to speak on its behalf. To achieve this absent presence, the terms of trade of cultural analysis have extended beyond humanities high culture toward everything human, encompassing more and more practices and rendering them objects of study in a remorseless, tentacular hold that is forever lamenting its own conditions of existence; a former director of the Birmingham Centre refers to this "separation from popular forms" as an *idée fixe* of academic writings on the popular (R. Johnson 279). Much metareflection inside cultural studies is devoted to healing the aesthetic wound it forms.

For the ICPS, by contrast, representations are not so much reflections of material or psychic reality as forms derived from social institutions and practices. They articulate with bureaucratic rationality, which decides how texts are made to count and have particular valencies. Hence Hunter's adoption of "administrative intellectuals" over "prophets of culture" as pedagogic exemplars. He asks why "the administrative intellectual" is treated with a "mixture of condescension and veiled contempt reserved for those who have failed the great tasks of history through their lack of vision or their 'reformist' complicity with regressive forces." Such a denial supposedly fails to recognize that "cultural interests and attributes can only be formulated and shaped in the context of delimited norms and techniques. . . . the forms of their articulation and the degree of their integration must also be normative, contingent and organizational" ("Setting" 105, 113). But at the same time, the Institute is boxing with a very outmoded notion of oppositional culture. Figures such as Ruby Rich during her time at the New York State Council for the Arts, Deborah Zimmerman from Women Make Movies, and Ben Caldwell of the KAOS Network have long been acclaimed by cultural studies as people who run institutions and manage bureaucratic pressures while being dedicated to oppositional agendas that derive from social movements. Prominent left academics involved in cultural studies, such as Douglas Kellner, are nationally prominent figures for their grassroots media activism; not all cultural criticism is about education, not all humanities people use aesthetic exercises to re-create themselves in onlookers.

Perhaps the difference lies in the veritable embrace of the state evident in Bennett's renunciation of Gramsci as irrelevant to the Australian context. Instead of a fight to be waged over immeasurable consciousness, we are now presented with a revised view of the vanguard. There was a time when that vanguard comprised cultural critics, generalist intellectuals capable of acting as the heroic consciences of their time, eschewing utilitarianism to engage with broader moral questions. But the new model of intervention works inside the apparatus of the state, with a constituency that appears to have shifted. What is now thought to have been an imaginary world of the unvoiced oppressed is replaced by a supposedly symbolic world of the co-opted principled, but a world of the principled that derives from representative democracy. "The people" becomes sharper as an analytic device and a rallying cry, in that it is no longer located within cultural theory (categories derived from feminism, Marxism, and culture) but from political theory (categories derived from the social contract). The haute couture removal guaranteed by a purist Marxism is ditched, along with its culturalist sibling-in-disengagement.

▶

## Implications: Bourdieu Saved from Drowning?

> "Cultural Policy Studies" could be translated . . . into "Studies in the Relations of Government and Culture" . . . the "technologies" and minutiae of culture—culture as resources, culture as techniques, uses, tactics and strategies. . . . This is not culture as consciousness or ideology or text to be deciphered by decoding the rules, structures and conventions but culture as what Pierre Bourdieu calls practical orientation.
> :: C. Mercer 18

The signs of this rapprochement between critique and implementation are evident even in oppositional critics. Grossberg, who as we have seen is a major power broker in the translation of cultural studies into Americana, is no ally of the state. But this is because of the particular complexion of the U.S. government over the past two decades. Consider the following anecdote from his major statement on the field, *We Gotta Get Out of This Place*. Grossberg was at a conference to discuss the future of the Canadian National Museum of Civilization. Most of the papers trotted out the expected litany of bastardries, committed by the usual suspects: sexism, racism, Eurocentrism, and ethnocentrism were the crimes, with capitalism, imperialism, and architecture the criminals. Presenters called for the museum to be delivered to the people. Now, Grossberg concurred with their excavations, in the sense that traces of these systems of oppression were clearly present, but there also seemed to be an automaticity of condemnation at work. The machinery of critique was hauled into play without anyone's engaging the sense-making practices, pleasures, or otherwise of actual museum users. And museum educators were left with nothing to do—no ideas, no proposals. In this sense, Grossberg argues, "the politics of the museum seem to be given well before any real analysis" (89–90).

In addition to providing actionable options as part of cultural criticism, taking the risk and the opportunity to revise and reform in place of an oppositional negativity that carps but does not care to recommend, the institute's polemicists have another target: textual analysis. Given cultural studies' intellectual and administrative debt to the ideas and housing offered by literary and screen theory, this is a significant revocation. Embracing the cultural-capitalist state instead of denying it a role simultaneously turns away from the protocols of close reading that have characterized the hermeneutic imperative, markers distancing cultural theory from political economy and psychological approaches to the media.

This engagement with the state as a supplement to/rejection of cultural criticism is detailed in Bennett's contribution to the *Cultural Studies* collection. Coming from a semiparent of cultural studies, Bennett's account of "putting policy" into it is a denunciation of the past in favor of a self-revision. The latest academic persona is the superior one. But it *is* a principled and careful engagement with the state, utilizing systems of analysis connected to cultural studies, that Bennett favors. His gloss of the heterogeneous projects and methods grouped under the sign of this new discipline emphasizes one point of continuity: a concern with the connection of culture and power. But the break is, crucially, within the textual traditions of cultural studies. I shall return to the significance of this below.

I once acted, in a very junior way, in support of cultural policy studies as the first managing editor of the ICPS journal *Culture and Policy*. I remain bathetically pleased that the *Australian* newspaper suggested that Australian Prime Minister Paul Keating's 1994 cultural policy statement—which he referred to as "the day we drew a line under our postcolonial era"—would benefit from an engagement with *The Well-Tempered Self* (Craven; Keating quoted in Washington 281). Zoë Sofoulis even told me some years ago I was one of the "PPWBs" (postpolitical white boys) whom she has since disparaged in print (without naming them) for turning our/their "position envy" at feminists' political rectitude and theoretical power into a denunciation of political principle and radical politics (see T. Miller "Beyond" and "Film"; Miller et al.; Sofoulis 218, 213–14, 217). Although this critique does not engage with ideas, preferring instead to diagnose motivations, it does point to an important question of address. Why the anxiety on the part of cultural policy proponents to be recognized and emulated by cultural critics, people whose very professional lives they relentlessly attack? Rather than limit the answer to counterindicatively derived accounts of interiority, I argue below that we need to look at the real *non dit* here: the social sciences.

But first, lest it be felt this is a uniquely Australian or Grossbergian phenomenon, it is worth noting the interplay of cultural policy and the humanities elsewhere. There is not much of a critical apparatus surrounding the six decades of British propaganda sent across the world through cultural policy. But entrepreneurial policy developments in the ravaged postmanufacturing midlands and north of England have replaced identity politics with a commitment to new culture industries and the commercialization of heritage. This has encouraged a new (domestic) gaze from Angela McRobbie and others that also looks at government subsidies of art and literature. Cultural policy became a central strut of urban regeneration across Western Europe and the United States during the 1980s in response to deindustrialization—the boosterism of nineteenth-century North America revisited—and arts centers have proliferated throughout Southeast Asia since the mid-1990s (Mitchell; Frith "Knowing"; Jordan and Weedon 23–64; Bianchini and Parkinson; Whitt and Share; "Theme: Culture"; Groves "Arts"). The British-based journal *Screen*, long a major setting for Althusserian, psychoanalytic, feminist, and (latterly) postcolonial film readings, and resolutely committed to minute *explications de texte* across seconds of videotape, has undergone major revisions in the recent past, James Donald stressing the need for vocational screen studies. Cunningham's *Framing Culture* has been warmly received by Sylvia Harvey because "film studies, for so long the Cinderella warming her hands at the dying embers of textual studies" needs to be "animated by a new and useful scepticism" (170). (Of course, there are cultural studies exponents who argue that the British contingent has always been involved with questions of policy and broad politics, far from the security of the maddening text [Mellor 663–64].)

In Canada, the Research Group on Cultural Citizenship has produced a genealogy of Quebec cultural policy, and key debates over the appropriation of Native culture by whites have taken place under the auspices of the Canada Council. The Hong Kong Cultural Policy Study Group was founded the same year as the ICPS, and with much more of a public-sphere orientation to its work, as evidenced by its efforts to create open forums for discussion in search of a decentralized and democratic cultural bureaucracy. And there is now a *European Journal of Cultural Policy* (Allor and Gagnon; Rowell; Hong Kong 8, 17–18, 30, 232).

In the United States, communication scholar James Carey is vitriolic about the oppositional politics of some American humanities faculty. This politics denies legitimacy, efficacy, and relevance to liberal democracy and its infrastructure. For Carey, cultural studies should seek a common national patrimony of the American myth, in all the improbable grandeur of its folksiness, combined with an apprehension of economic dichotomizations of life into hardship and ease. An effective cultural studies must show how capitalist culture disadvantages people, of *all* races, genders, sexualities, and ages, not just the fashionably powerless at any given moment. This resonates with European media scholar Denis McQuail's agenda for communications policy. Similarly, Todd Gitlin, perhaps the left's most prominent media sociologist in the United States, warns, "Criticism must not dangle in social space." He is especially concerned about the way in which, on the one hand, phantasmatic agents of history in the Promethean discourses of the left (working people, women, and ethnic minorities) remain unengaged by self-appointed representatives in academia, while on the other, the public is forgotten by those who speak in the name of administrative intellectuals (Carey "Political" 56, 60–62; McQuail 45–46; Gitlin "Who" 184, 190, 192; also see McChesney 12). And when Annette Michelson accepted her honorary membership in the Society for Cinema Studies in 1994, she did so with an expression of regret that half the mission the founders of the field had set themselves remained unfulfilled. Film was now established as a legitimate site of university study, and it functioned as a model and methodological wellspring for other emergent interdisciplinary areas. The other dimension of the original project had been to extend these knowledges into public culture, but theoretical sophistication and linguistic prolixity had drawn a grand divide separating wider film culture from the university.

This divide between intellectual activity and cultural production is not so large on the right. The U.S. State Department's Division of Cultural Relations was established in 1938 to spread literature and teaching across Latin America as part of antifascist policy. By the time of Kennedy's presidency, North American international cultural policy was meshed very tightly with diplomatic, military, and economic strategies. The belated decision to join international copyright regimes had as much to do with a Cold War cultural policy of using books to win over nonaligned readers as it had to do with opening new markets. Since then, the emergence of public history as an academic discipline has been a significant force within North American government and on a consulting basis. In fact, the new field was brought into being as just such an applied field of knowledge (Phillipson 11–12; Mokia; H. Graham).

Public subsidy of culture has been of increasing significance since the 1960s. The right welcomed it as a means of ensuring the continued viability of high-cultural pursuits while shifting the burden from philanthropists, whereas the left saw it as a way to democratize art. Now, of course, disputes over moral rectitude in funding have become major sites of discussion in Congress and the media. Arts culture is transformed into a site of conflicting technologies: censorship, fashionable marketability, obscurity, and intellectual taste. The Clinton administration immediately translated proposals for a revival of New Deal politics into cultural domains: inner-city renewal through a "Culture Corps" of young people. Clearly, contemporary debates over political correctness are vitally concerned with policy: educational curricula, arts funding, museum management, and cultural pluralism. It is no surprise that the Republican Party's *nouvelle vague* of the mid-1990s promised to rid the country of federal assistance to culture, given that the enabling legislation instantiates a "multicultural artistic heritage." Critical multicultural textual analysis has been crucial to high school audiovisual pedagogy in the United States, as a site of antiracist discourse. Cultural studies is part of this policy-directed activity, despite Bennett's account of North American humanities radicals as narcissistically ludic; their successes led to great anxiety among aesthetic elites when the 1994 National Standards for Arts Education made no mention of textual appreciation (Rich 29–30, 45; Price; National Foundation; "On the Third").

This reference to social issues is inevitable for the humanities: U.S. universities remain premier civic institutions for large groups of demographically representative people coming together in purposive action. Peter Brooks is on the money when he stresses the fact that white freshman students at Berkeley in the 1990s are for the first time in a minority. Hence the need to address multicultural identity politics as an everyday reality of "young people living in daily contact." College humanities courses enroll students from groups that are in very open conflict in most quarters of society (10). This is no civilizing mission in the sense of training the working class how to sit still. It is about a space in which very different backgrounds commingle under the sign of an institution designed for and by a unitary group that must reform itself; the teachers learn cultural norms from the students as much as the other way around.

There *is* a very local flavor to the Australian debate. As a country founded on invasion and war, but without a revolutionary rebellion by the colonists, and still too distant and dry to be settled in large numbers, Australia has determinedly dwelled in the realm of state, business, and labor partnerships. A unique industrial relations machinery—routinely threatened but essentially unscathed after ninety years—enshrines tripartism in industrial negotiation. Three levels of government make both interference and representativeness ever present. You are never far from somebody telling you what to do in Australia, but nor are you very far from someone else to whom you can complain about it. There are corollaries in the subvention of culture. The country has a thirty-year-old policy of public funding for the feature-film industry, a sixty-five-year tradition of arms-length noncommercial broadcasting, and twenty years of peer-reviewed assistance for art. Only under such conditions—frequently funded by governments but managed by cultural workers rather than universalist bureaucrats—can the oppositionality of much recent textual theory so neatly animate a sense of affinity with the state. And only in a country with a powerful Labor Party (older than the sovereign state itself) can forms of cultural nationalism be so neatly imbricated with a change of theoretical gear from critique to enlistment. These preconditions facilitate Bennett's requirement that proponents of cultural studies "influence or service the conduct of identifiable agents" relevant to their concerns ("Putting" 23). At the same time, that requirement also meshes with Australia's sorrily utilitarian history, an odd mixture of tolerance and cutthroat competitiveness. As in other white settler colonies (Canada, the former Rhodesia and South Africa, and Aotearoa/New Zealand), there has been a strong motivation since the 1960s to find "an effective counterweight to the political and commercial power of Europe and the U.S." "The nation" has become increasingly significant as an ideal type—however flawed and risky—that could preserve and build culture through government (H. Collins; Bennett et al. "Introduction" 1–2).

That said, it is all very well for academics to deal with existing national traditions and participate in the political culture. But the requirement for intellectuals to perform such incremental work forgets, quite critically, how they came to be. This amnesia is crucial because of its impact on establishing the grounds of ethical conduct. These grounds are both intersubjective, referring to everyday proxemics, and metasubjective, detailing the very social system where our subjectivities exist and that is granted legitimacy by us. The problem for cultural policy studies has been its neglect of academic work already done as and about policy, because, in the true style of a professionalizing discipline, its real interest has been in establishing dispute procedures within its own domain.

▶

## Consulting Intellectuals/Where Have You Gone, Paul DiMaggio?

> *Let's remember that when we express concern at the "increased engagement of academics with bureaucracies as consultants" we are really concerned with the place of cultural academics as consultants. The rest have been doing it for years without the shadow of Dr Faust beckoning them to an ethical hell.*
> ::   C. Mercer 21

> *When I was a graduate student, I spent two years trying to discover a connection between typographic design, legibility, and reading speed. I failed at the task, having devised a number of unsuccessful tests, but my thesis was accepted anyway. My research had not generated any revelations about reading, but that is often the way with "pure" research. . . . Some years later, when I was responsible for overseeing a research project on the impact of the arts on the New England economy, I did not have the luxury of being allowed to fail. I was spending $50000 of public money to prove that the cultural sector contributed significantly to the economic vitality of the six New England states. Public agencies had staked their legislative appropriations at least partially on the results.*
> ::   Wolf 184

The quotation from Colin Mercer surprises in its denial of relevant intellectual history. Any examination of, say, language-spread policy and the part played in it by linguists would problematize such statements, let alone some contemplation of the work of economic advisers (Robert Triffin acting as plenipotentiary for the United States to the EEC and then as a European delegate to the IMF, just a few months apart, in the 1980s), political scientists (Project Camelot in the 1960s), biomedical researchers (relations with pharamaceutical companies), public relations consultants (a critical concern of professional associations), anthropologists (cultural-relativist defenses of male violence in court), and nuclear physicists (J. Robert Oppenheimer). The very existence of communication research raises questions of ideological distortion, given the discipline's formation under the sign of war and clandestine government activity and later corporate and foundation support. University consultancies date to nineteenth-century museums, observatories, and agricultural experimentation outposts, but the shop was really set up in the late 1950s. Considerable effort since then has gone into clarifying the significance of tailoring research priorities to contemporary political parties and corporations: pork-barrel science, as it is known. Ralph Nader's Center for Universities in the Public Interest was set up because of such concerns, which are even evident to former supporters of government/college/industry relationships who have experienced the obstacles they pose to disinterested research outcomes, such as Harvard's Derek Bok, and very traditional sociologists, notably Robert Nisbet. The policy sciences, originally conceived as a connection between democratic and executive action, have degenerated into "unrepresentative expertise" that lacks articulation with public life. John S. Dryzek's Foucauldian review of policy analysis suggests the animating subjectivity is either "clients or spectators," not active citizens, and Streeter points out that Australian advocacy of a policy focus may be less apt in the United States, where *policy* connotes a procorporate position that turns highly contestable positions into absolutes, with consultant professors simultaneously performing objectivity and applicability (*Language Problems and Language Planning*; Markoff and Montecinos 44; Ammon 6; Nisbet; Beauchamp; "Public"; Winkelman; Rieff; C. Simpson; Sholle 132; Rowe and Brown 98; Ruscio 209; Stahler and Tash; Bowie 5, 7; deLeon 886; Dryzek 117; Streeter 16 n. 14, 133, 136).

Consider the framework of public policy in France. Studies there emphasize three aspects of policy: cognitive, instrumental, and normative. Bruno Jobert, for example, has shown how semichaotic incrementalism is always leavened by a realpolitik that foregrounds probable outcomes. This realpolitik evidences a common intellectual understanding that can generally be reduced to a small number of variables and a particular account of the prevailing social formation and the institutions it should maintain. Consultants across the spectrum are prone to regulatory capture, their independence lost through close connections to those they are said to invigilate. Economists, so successful as consultants to government, have been shown over many studies to dedicate most of their time to finding "technical" alibis for preexisting decisions by the state, at the same time attaining high moral standing. They have become just the general sages of public wisdom—under the sign of governmentality—the ICPS so despises as a tendency within cultural criticism (Markoff and Montecinos 52, 56).

The "new" cultural policy studies seems to maintain a position of ignorance on the ethics of consultancy, something about which numerous public policy scholars have warned. Preexisting material clearly indicates bureaucratically driven academic research produces competitiveness, intellectual rivalry, and other concerns internal to the process, not to mention such external pressures as relations between researcher and paymaster and their joint connection to a field of academic endeavor. The record of successful uptake of public policy consultancy as an industry is more impressive than its record as an influence, other than when it is there simply to justify decisions: "The data show, in sum, that the data often don't matter." Studies of applied cultural policy work indicate the *process* of research consultancies—raising issues—is as important as their findings in terms of implementation (Amy; Nespor; Rogers; Streeter 159–60; Hoover 36–37).

It is vital to understand the differences among distilling, invoking, and reforming the public mind. The shift between policy analysis and policy service and advocacy is an important one. Public administration was the refuge of the worthy but dry academic, until public policy emerged as a site for carpetbagging academics in search of influence and consultancy clothing. A rich analysis of political discourse has come from both spheres. And the lessons of this literature should form the founding texts of cultural policy studies, rather than a lapsed left Leavisism. These lessons would provoke a skepticism about the fit between the rhetoric and practice of policy, because animating logics are often spurious or counterindicative. Most significantly, social research has cast serious doubt on the notion that policy works because of the utterance of actionable rather than expressive proposals. The literature demonstrates the error of aligning organizations and actors with their statements, their statements with their actions, or either with actual outcomes (Stark 514–15; Jobert 381; Colebatch and Degeling; Egeberg). But these lessons remain unavailable to a disciplinary diversion still seeking recognition from the empire of aesthetics—the cost of debating cultural policy studies inside the field of textual analysis.

Because the United States has such a strong tradition of academic study financed by governments and foundations, it offers an impressive review of how knowledge is used in sponsored research, how policy studies intersects with state and economy, especially think tanks (Hammack). Paul DiMaggio and Walter Powell have done important work on the structure of organizations that suggests a trend toward homologies between sponsoring and consulting bodies; when one institution depends on another for assistance, it tends to mimic its structures and reiterate its concerns ("Iron" and *New*). DiMaggio is interesting; he provides the trope for this section of the chapter, so he has to be. Over twenty years, his writings on cultural production and policy have been critical for developing social theory in the area. DiMaggio's strategic sense of the structures needed to make policy work in a field that is so unpredictable in terms of public taste is a reasoned call for randomness and serendipity that also works with the ethical restrictions presented by purse holders. He even wrote an article called "Cultural

Policy Studies: What They Are and Why We Need Them" years before the advent of the ICPS (DiMaggio "Can" 68–69 and "Cultural" 248; also see his "Classification," "Decentralization," *Nonprofit*, "Nonprofit," and "State"; DiMaggio and Useem; DiMaggio, Useem, and Brown; DiMaggio and Zukin). He is not alone. The urtext on the economics of cultural assistance was published two decades ago by Australian-based researchers, and it is more than twenty years since Herbert Gans's pathbreaking work on "taste cultures" provided a multilayered framework for intellectualizing the popular and its relationship to policy (Throsby and Withers; Gans *Popular* 121–59). In the 1970s, "cultural policy studies" was named and undertaken in part through the formation of the Association of Cultural Economics (which went international in 1994) and the Center for Urban Studies at the University of Akron. This was followed by regular conferences on economics, social theory, and the arts, and major studies of policy and program evaluation produced at Canada's Institute for New Interpretive Creative Activities, the Cultural Policy Unit of the Johns Hopkins Center for Metropolitan Planning and Research, the Cultural Information and Research Centres Liaison in Europe, and Columbia's Research Center for the Arts and Culture. Publications such as the *Journal of Arts Management, Law and Society* and the *Journal of Cultural Economics* have long provided a wealth of theoretical speculation and empirical reporting. This has led to queries about the relationship between a humanities and a sociological basis to the area: whether there should be, for instance, "a social science aesthetic," and how the new proxemics of administration, politics, and the arts should be ethically and technically managed, along with the need for both "historical analysis *in* policymaking" and "the history *of* policy" (Towse and Crain 1; Alderson 5; Hendon et al. x-xi; Chartrand "Subjectivity" 23–24; Peterson "Foreword" iii, v; H. Graham 21). But if you look to the "new" cultural policy studies for an engagement with this body of knowledge, you look in vain (with the exception of Jennifer Craik ["Mapping"]). These investigations were never referred to by the institute in its heraldic announcements—wrong target.

The protagonists share a conviction that accompanies renouncing an erstwhile self: there once stood I, on the Olympian heights of left cultural criticism, with a special hold on the radical entry to humanness that only the study of literature could provide. Now I have transcended this heroic role. Anybody who engages in the practices I have foresworn is abject and must be passed beyond. So kindly follow the *Quicunque Vult*. Paradoxically, the mantle of the prophetic and omniscient cultural critic is simply refashioned; instead of using a training in literary analysis as justification for "reading" shopping malls on behalf of "the people," the new task is to *de-*

*sign* them. Noel King alludes to the need for some restraint by the participants in his meditations on delaying the task of reading Cunningham's *Framing Culture* ("Its topic daunted me . . . mainly because, as Sam Cooke almost sang, 'don't know much about policy'" ["'Play'" 8]).

Until their resignation from a former career is complete, and followed by a serious engagement with a complex literature on policy and sponsored research, ICPS protagonists should be more modest, because they are repeating a move that is *very* traditional. As Colin MacCabe reminds us, Marxism was a momentary interlude for cultural studies that tied the emerging area to a romanticism about the working class and its collectivism and provided great moral verve. A left Leavisism that insists on the social ramifications of aesthetic culture and calls for a rapprochement between the humanities and social life has driven various phases of cultural studies and now its policy variant. Richard Hoggart, Raymond Williams, and E. P. Thompson all taught in adult education, and Hall was the original secondary-modern Leavisite with a conscience. Debates about groundbreaking Open University courses on popular culture in the 1970s and 1980s involve a struggle over origins, with some parties stressing the anti-institutionalism of the project and others its deep embeddedness in a project of governmental social uplift (Bennett "Out"). Should we be surprised to find Hunter, Cunningham, or Bennett seeking ethical agency in such classrooms, at the site of citizen formation? No; but we are entitled to see the relevant discourses in place.

▶ ——————————————————————————————————

**Reconsidering History**

> *Cultural Studies is spiralling out of control. Britain's answer to existential chic was last seen checking out of the Madonna Inn clutching a one-way ticket to Wayne's World. Okay, so the publishers love it, it's got conference kudos, it's even established a beach-head in Australia, supplanting surfing as the indigenous leisure industry. But that's just it. The study of popular culture has become too popular. It all smacks of a terrible mistake. Academics enjoy being serious. They've always preferred the snap and crackle to the pop. Now they find themselves sharing a seminar with Smashie and Nicie; coasting towards analytic entropy. Was the leap from Leavis to Beavis too fast?*
> :: ffytche

There *is* a role for cultural studies in debating policy. What Meaghan Morris (*Ecstasy* 75) calls "the public pedagogy of neocorporatism," that odd hybrid of neoclassical economic doctrine and consensual dirigiste statism characteristic of the Australian Labor Party through the 1980s, saw the media become critical sites for the articulation of a major intellectual shift in the ground of public discourse. The developing hold of economics in that decade, making its way from one more discipline to a semimedical model of enlightenment that stands ready to bring pricing systems to bear on any problem, anytime, anywhere, was an extraordinary act of discursive parthenogenesis. The Australian government's attempts to make the people "economically literate" were abetted by a news corps geared toward the handy slogans and tantalizingly seductive *reductios* of market logics. The media were making a double move. At one and the same moment, the fundamental humanism underpinning neoclassicism, with all its presumptions about the fully formed intellect awaiting perfect knowledge, was matched and overstretched by the anthropomorphization of the economy, which itself adopted human qualities of health and sickness, even as its technical needs started to outweigh the ability of consumers and producers to act "rationally."

This is surely the space where protocols of reading and problematizations of the relationship between culture and person should meet, with aesthetics and policy intersecting. That *has* occurred in Bennett's work on museums, but it has been absent from the pedagogy arguments about the humanities and government. Cultural policy studies is right to push for limitations to the political pretensions of cultural studies "proper," and to participate in the institutional networks of ethical formation. But in a country where multinational corporations and fictive capital have been the successes of a deregulation undertaken in the name of flexibility and the endless search for comparative advantage, that notion of the person must be geared against rationality as a catchphrase for the reforming right and its taste for dismantling social welfare, minority assistance, and the like (McKay et al. 10–12, 18–23). As Morris says, there is much to commend shifting away from intellectual practices that forever seek "a 'fraught space' of ethical grandiloquence, in which massive, world-historical problems are debated on such a level of generality that they cannot possibly be solved" (*Ecstasy* 119), but not at the cost of generating visions of preference. Anthony May cogently argues that the essentially Enlightenment-driven agenda of cultural policy studies, matching teaching with research in a model for the production of a knowledgeable, ethical, and tolerant citizenry, will not come about under contemporary government pressures to turn a training in the humanities into a directly vocational one (121).

I want to turn to Hoggart at this point. The oldest of the three men conventionally cataloged as the founding parents of cultural studies, and the first director of the Birmingham Centre, he is often listed alongside Williams and Hall, but is rarely made the subject of equivalent exegetical projections. It is worth remarking that in Hoggart's time, cultural studies had a significant engagement with the bureaucratic public sphere. He gave crucial testimony at the *Lady Chatterley* trial, and Penguin Books subsequently made an endowment-in-gratitude that helped establish the Centre. He also served on the United Kingdom's Pilkington Committee on Broadcasting, and the British Government's Television Research Commitee of 1963 gave much of its work to Birmingham in support of his team (MacCabe 29; Hoggart 182–96; Murdock "Visualizing" 177).

Hoggart also wrote a startling essay in the mid-1960s, titled "Higher Education and Cultural Change." In that essay, he theorizes the value and compromise involved in brokering relations between universities and public life. For Hoggart, "one of the virtues of the university . . . has been its impurity," the dirt that comes with application. This is not to celebrate—or even condone—opportunistic academics who "trim their intellectual sails to the wind." Rather, it acknowledges the shared social democratic, utilitarian, and social movement requirement that "the life of ideas be properly tested against the life of choice and decision" (95). But he poses some discomforting questions:

> What is one to make of a medieval historian or classicist who finds nothing odd—that is, nothing to be made sense of, at the least, if not opposed—in the sight of one of his new graduates going without second thoughts into, say, advertising; or of a sociologist or statistician who will undertake consultant work without much questioning the implications of the uses to which his work is put? (100)

For Hoggart, cultural studies is not simply an ethical training in "acquiring certain 'manners,'" any more than it is the acquisition of aestheticized tastes and their elaboration. Rather, culture is concerned with "the growth of the responsive and responsible imagination" (101). There are lessons here for our own time. Democratic governments in cultural-capitalist states have mandates that are general and contingent. So the broad political culture represented and fostered by democratic constitutionalism—especially the lives of social minorities—must animate cultural theory's account of governmentality. As Hoggart goes on to show in another essay, engineering metaphors in culture are preoccupied with machinery over decency, their discourse "more about 'adjustment to' than about the rightness of the 'what' to which people are supposed to be being adjusted." This describes the critical distinction between functional and substantive moralities (108–9). Let's indulge for two paragraphs in just such committed cultural study.

In 1965, BBC television commissioned Peter Watkins to make *The War Game*, a film that looked at the implications of the proliferation of nuclear weapons and predicted that by 1980 such weapons would be used in Western Europe. The BBC banned screenings of the film anywhere in the world in November 1965 and kept up that ban for almost twenty years. The German TV company Sudwestfunk hired Watkins to remake it in 1968, then sacked him ten days before work was to begin. The same thing happened with proposals for productions in Canada and Denmark over the next decade. These cancellations were sometimes justified in terms of scientific plausibility and sometimes in terms of aesthetics. When the BBC shut down *The War Game*, it sent a mass letter to the British public, advising that although TV was rightly regarded as a medium of experimentation, the innovations in this production had failed, which made it unwatchable. In short, the film was no good. It posed a cultural-political threat because it was close to documentary conventions for establishing truth; as per *Schindler's List*, this made it troublesome as fiction. *The War Game* was an overtly ideological intervention into television culture, and yet one that was brought down on aesthetic grounds to divert attention from the politics of its content. It describes an engaged, contested ground of screen culture in both its textuality and the material circumstances of its noncirculation. The film needs theorizing as a political-economic-governmental *and* textual category, utilizing both policy analysis and the oppositional underpinnings of cultural studies.

In 1993, the U.S. government imposed emergency restrictions on the importation of antiquities from Mali, principally artifacts from the Tellem Caves and clay sculptures from the inland Niger delta. The limitations were in accord with UNESCO's 1970 Convention on the Means of Prohibiting and Preventing the Illicit Import, Export and Transfer of Ownership of Cultural Property, but they were the first instance of any First World art importer applying the ban to exports from an African country. Alpha Oumar Konaré, president of Mali at the time, once presided over the International Council of Museums. He emphasized the importance to the republic of the struggle against illegal archaeology, appreciating the stand of the United States given the prestige on the international museum circuit that goes with such holdings. In this instance, the very materials of a people, their customary and artistic heritage, are placed within a market system of value connected to the seemingly benign operation of aesthetic relativism, the outcome a blow to the artifactual history of a nation. Mali's sovereignty is then mobilized as a protocol by an international organization to prevent such losses. Prevailing museum policies in the United States assist this safeguarding. The cultural politics of the situation revolves around four material pressures: the desires of wealthy foreigners to own these objects, the poverty of traditional owners, a push toward global appreciation of cultural production, and the notion of cultural maintenance. It is telling that the United States does not offer equivalent cultural protection to its own people, with the exception of Native Americans (McNaughton; Clément; Zolberg 11). Again, an appreciation of the problem necessitates some attempt to comprehend the shifting politics of the market, nationalism, textuality, and social meaning.

▶

## The Policy Ideal Type

> *I did not know much about what economists did. As I began to work with them I realized they were like lawyers when I was young. A lawyer was a professional who could do anything. Actually, well-trained economists were excellent in performing any task, and we had many tasks to do.*
>
> :: anonymous ex-Chilean military officer who became a minister after the coup of 1973 — quoted in Markoff and Montecinos 37

Pitting an abstracted empiricism of cultural policy studies against grand moralistic divides in cultural studies leaves one half lacking vision, the other lacking space, and both without a warrant. Each operates with constituencies enlisted for academic purposes ("relevance" for one and "resistance" for the other). But while a general social critique is too verbose and complex for the neat chunks of digestible material proffered by, for example, neoclassical economics, policy work is frequently incapacitated by the "lure of influence" (Gitlin "Who" 195). A rapprochement between the two, where policy studies is not valorized over critique or vice versa, is the polite return to a network of interlaced concerns that *has* always been part of left culture, as Paul Smith reminds Bennett, and *should* always have been part of cultural studies. But it was not, until the late 1980s in Australia *half* brought together, by proxy, the humanities and social sciences in the study of culture, as readers from literature discovered policy and liked what they saw.

But they were operating from an ideal type of policy. Ideal types derive from empirical observations, themselves interpreted from a particular theoretical position. Because such positions are devoutly held and totalizing in their accounts of human subjectivity, they are not capable of being countermanded by research. Ideal types are constantly ramified rather than falsified, undergoing so many successful extrapolations that they assume the status of *donnés* far beyond the conditions of their initial formulation. Let's take another, more extended and metacritical, look at economic ideal types.

Deregulatory policies and programs on television in cultural-capitalist states are routinely peppered with dogma derived from two ideal types: the consumer and the public interest. I have two questions of these approaches: (a) Do they prescribe particular types of human subject? (b) Do they prescribe an implied theory of textuality? These are impertinent queries, because the consumer is a priori sexless, stateless, colorless, ageless, classless, and irreligious, capable of perfect understanding and ratiocinative calculation along Benthamite lines. This ideal type is not amenable to discussion a posteriori; it seems to be hard to see a consumer from behind.

The public interest sometimes appears inside this first ideal type. At other times, it seems to exist in the space of the citizen. I want to explore this other space briefly by asking what would happen if the public were not a consumer, but a processual norm that recurs in the space of intersubjectivity. This move construes rationality as a model of public life not through dialogue between individual desires and the costs of attaining them, but a dialogue over mutual and different civic problems, between diverse subjects. This dialogic model of the public interest is overtly textual; it generates systems of signification and reading that are predicated on translatability and politesse. The implications for media policy differ from those that derive from the chief paradigm of the Federal Communications Commission and other screen agencies operating in the domain of neoclassical economics. For such bodies, creating arenas of competition in which persons can exhibit preferences is *the* means of establishing the public interest and its orbit.

A theory of the text already underpins much of the policy made and implemented by such organizations. The consumptive model sets up the rules by which it and all others are judged. Neoclassical dogma exemplifies *Eigengesetzlichkeit*, the quintessentially modern movement toward legislative and disciplinary intellectual processes within self-proclaimed autonomous spheres of knowledge and endeavor. The market model is absolutely rigorous in its exclusion of political factors, for example, as other than distortions. It does this in the name of an absolute, objective truth. Yet these rules are putatively demotic, subtended by what "the people" show they want. I have already demonstrated at a theoretical level why this is only one account of "the people." Now I want to indicate how, at an enunciative level, it generates a textual problem.

Public policy today is driven by the desire of the state to make markets, arenas where it excludes itself and encourages new entrants to industry to stimulate competition—a desire for diversity. In the case of the FCC, this is a diversity of broadcast television, for which viewers do not usually pay. It is subsidized by workers and consumers of advertised goods, whether or not they choose to constitute themselves as a TV audience. A theory of the text now enters the terrain. Content onscreen and its uptake by readers (as, say, shoppers or killers) matter in ways not amenable to an understanding founded on sexless, stateless, colorless, ageless, classless, and irreligious actants or spectators. The implicit assumption is of an intersubjective dialogue of projection and introjection between diegetic characters and viewers. This presumes there are desirable and undesirable components to such a process. All of the above emerge enunciatively even when marginalist economics is in the ascendant as a calculus of policy (crises over audiences and violence/education). It is no accident that the consulting TV professoriate in the United States has flip-flopped over the past two decades between effects studies and deregulatory projections—one to measure fear, the other competition (Streeter 138). Thinking back to the slicing of the population described in the introduction, we see that what is broken up by governmentality is only conditionally reunited in the sovereign consumer.

A discussion in *Dissent* between Richard Rorty ("Intellectuals" and "Richard") and Andrew Ross ("Intellectuals") plays out cultural policy studies issues by pitting two different university settings against each other: the American New Left (white welfarism and Dewey-eyed identity politics) against American social movements (culturalism and postcolonial identity politics). It is possible to see this as a much older split, between a social sciences focus on power and a humanities focus on meaning. Such a divide is disabling. Just as the first cultural studies knew this, so the debate over cultural policy studies in Australia gestures at this unwarranted space. For the necessary changes to happen, self-appointed representatives of "the people" in academic cultural studies need to "abandon the chance to talk of everything" in the name of "fantasmatic general subjects" of oppression and resistance, while self-appointed representatives of "the citizenry" in academic cultural studies must acknowledge that "bureaucracies form only some of the sites in which to struggle for social and political change" (Saunders 15, 13; Levy 552). And there should be a corresponding humility of intent and execution. When Bennett calls for "useful culture," he stresses the need to move beyond "cultural critique as an instrument for changing consciousness," in favor of "technical adjustments to its governmental deployment" (406). These are not opposites. Their *shared* task must be mutual respect, not dismissal. We saw descriptions of cultural studies in chapter 1 as a critical tendency within the humanities and social sciences. Cultural policy studies can be thought of as "an extension and retooling" of that tendency to engage the infrastructures of cultural power (Craik "Mapping" 201). Then the inexorable intertwining of culture with policy will be less arcane, less compromised, and less heroic.

The message of Part I of this book is in a sense rather disappointing and intramural: let's combine the social sciences and the humanities. That seems less exciting than the prospects for social change promised by resistive and consulting dons. But it suggests the need for intercourse between important intellectual traditions as a point of continuity with cultural studies' animating forces: subjectivity and power. Cultural policy studies can add to this dyadic sign the idea of governmentality, perhaps more as I outlined it in the introduction than as appropriated by certain apparatchiks. In Part II, I undertake interdisciplinary analyses that I hope will model a way forward for others to consider. In doing so, I will be instantiating what *can* be taken from, in particular, Bennett's reading of Foucault and his redesign of cultural history as successive processes of manufacturing and administering subjectivity. The principal benefit of this approach is that it conceives of subjects as given by a position in social structure and engages with the intersection of institutions and persons as sites and processes that constitute the rules of subjectivity and the exercise of power (Osborne 290–91).

In a generous moment of autocritique/*apologia pro vita sua*, Cunningham revisited *Framing Culture* to take account of its critics, acknowledging the need for a principled distance from the state on the part of marginalized groups. He had made policy advocacy and policy studies too close together and yet too far apart, in that they have both parallel and overlapping trajectories of critique and implementation. In short, he recognized the need for a thoroughgoing questioning of the state, while hanging on to criticisms of a purely expressive cultural politics. But this still fails to admit the falseness of such a dichotomy ("Cultural" 34; see the essays in Gunew and Rizvi).

When we think about oppositional theory, Umberto Eco, Noam Chomsky, and Jean-François Lyotard recur as signs. Some of their most famous work was born of cultural consultancy and state funding: Eco's TV semiotics for Italian state broadcasting ("Towards"), Chomsky's transformational generative grammar for the Joint Services Electronics Programs of the U.S. military, and Lyotard's report on the postmodern for the government of Quebec (*La Condition*). This is more than an investigation of how "taste" becomes "technique," or the "promotion of the good, the true and the beautiful," as the editors of a 1980s volume on comparative cultural policy would have it (Cummings and Katz 5; Ridley 11). This is cultural politics itself. The intellectual "enters a conversation with power," perhaps to broaden and destabilize what counts as tasteful, beautiful, and true under the sign of contemporary social movements—in short, the art of cultural governmentality (Alderson 2).

The 1990s move by U.S. arts intellectuals to counter Republican assaults by establishing think tanks to lobby politicians, community groups, and voters is based on dual strategies: public policy formation and social movement politics. This dual literacy—how to talk to the state and whom to listen to in the community—is a way forward. It is not easy. There was great fanfare when David Ellwood left his post as a prominent academic expert on welfare to become assistant secretary of the Department of Health and Human Services in the Clinton administration. After initial difficulties, a news conference was held to announce that Secretary Ellwood had decided to "go out and talk to some real people." He did so, perhaps in recognition that Harvard had given him a unique understanding of welfare needs (Carr; Wyszomirski 71; conference quoted in deLeon 895–96).

Thinking back to the geopolitically naive seven-year-old from 1965 who failed to locate the Beatles calls to mind the Liverpool they emerged from and helped to carry forward internationally. The city's music, clothing, football, and voice became part of the fabric of youth culture across the world. As Angus Calder notes, the city governors of the time were "innocent of 'cultural' objectives." And its rich 1980s television drama was produced under a radical-left administration that concentrated on public housing rather than aesthetics (454). Now, the city's reformist local government uses culture to attract capital investment in heritage tourism, but there is no clear correlation with cultural innovation. Instead, policy is a mop for deindustrialized waste, with gentrification assisted by government. Is this an appropriate application for cultural studies?

Whenever we operate as intellectuals in a university context, we do so with a very special role given implicitly—and otherwise—by public trust: tenure is grantable to academics precisely so they can make judgments away from the conflicts of interest that arise from having an involved paymaster. If the prelates of cultural policy studies had really renounced their training, they would have been devoting their time to the rich literature in business and professional ethics that has arisen over the past dozen years. But that was never their intellectual concern. And this neglect of the disciplines that engage with the arts of state also signifies the exclusion of political economy and textual analysis from the lists. We might as well know the nature of the dirt that is going to give us *les mains salles*. The "celebration of trespass," as Murdock calls it, must include breaching the divide between accounts of culture. In a diasporic world where debates over First Peoples, migrants, invaders, and commercial empires have an impact on all sovereign states, any attempt to uncouple the pragmatic from the ethical is dubious (Davis; Murdock "Across" 90–91; Washington).

PART

## II   *Applications*

# [ 3 ]  *A Short History of the Penis:*
*ET's Rendezvous at HQ*

*Enter the era of the body: the male body. We guys are flaunting*
*it. A new aesthetic is well and truly in: tattoos adorn beefy*
*arms; silicone pectoral implants are not unknown; the chest*
*hair that once so perfectly complemented that heavy gold*
*jewellery is being shaved off to complement "cut" muscles*
*and Paul Mercurio is obviously to blame for the recent prolif-*
*eration of white Chesty Bond singlets. . . .*
*    . . . Women are taking notice. . . .*
*    . . . A woman can pore over "Willy of the Month" with her*
*friends without fear of such comments as "That's degrading to*
*men" or "Why do you need to look at stuff like that?"*
*::   Worssam 3–4*

It is a step down from the summative heights of Part I to the low tone of
this chapter. But lowering the tone makes it more complex, as any shift
from metadiscourse to specific sites *must* do. Part II is about how technologies of truth create meanings and police conduct across popular culture.
Throughout, my purpose is to demonstrate the intrication of genre, audience, and the modern under the sign of governmentality in contemporary
somatic, national, and international cultural politics played out at legal,
economic, media, and policy sites. With those elevated terms reprised from
previous chapters, let us move to murkier territory.

    We live in an age of penis augmentation, by surgery and fantasy. It is
difficult to decline the penis; even Latinists seem confused about how to
pluralize it. Because this age is simultaneously concerned with the penis as
an artifact of meaning, medicine, law, and money, all these discourses must
be assembled to understand its diverse techniques, institutions, modes of
comportment, and methods of transmission and diffusion (Foucault "La
Volonté" 10). This can be a conflictual ensemble, for the male body is sadly

dissociated under modernity: torn by the divide between industrial labor and organic community in sociology and Marxism, terrified by women's castrating tendencies in psychoanalysis, and caught in the tight jaws of discourse and the wound of language that separates meaning from truth in aesthetics. Augustine's *Confessions* nicely capture the position of the male body between women and other men, alongside the governance of belief:

> As I grew to manhood I was inflamed with desire for a surfeit of hell's pleasures. Foolhardy as I was, I ran wild with lust that was manifold and rank. In your eyes my beauty vanished and I was foul to the core, yet I was pleased with my own condition and anxious to be pleasing in the eyes of men. (43)

I am seeking to open up man and his penis to approaches that are rarely deployed in cultural studies. They are not beholden to the unsaid, the repressed, or the hermeneutic, but are productive of truths. So, I utilize interpretation when that is a key paradigm in the relevant public domain, but not as a reading protocol from beyond. To illustrate this method as a working system, we might consider the account of phallic power that compels psychoanalysis. This is a factor in what follows to the extent that and on the occasions when Freudianism and its kind are evoked as systems of thought, but not as extratextual truths to be used as metatruth. Spotting symbolic genitals is a common public exercise, perhaps the most enduring of Freud's legacies. Within this discourse, the absence of the penis from much art is found to suppress homosexual desire, rerouting it in the direction of "social obligation." We can "effortlessly and unembarrassedly identify the *phallus* in dream objects, domestic objects, and civil objects" (Easthope *What* 15; Scarry 282). As Chris Straayer has said, "Fetishism is no longer the pathological condition of a few but rather our collective semiotics" (*Deviant* 266). Because all these entities deny their basis in sex—on this reading—that is where their real nature can be known. Objects that foreground their sex, such as the penis, become literally unknowable, because they fail to secret themselves.

What of the flesh attached to the penis? Men are on the agenda, or rather a series of agendas—research, critique, investigation, seduction, consumption, revulsion, and repulsion—across administrative, journalistic, domestic, academic, and occupational terrain. Instead of being the implicit center of the social and antisocial sciences (through the putative universality of "man"), men are now considered in their particular and peculiar formations. Feminist and queer theory critiques of masculinity have clearly been pivotal in this shift. They have problematized practices and concepts and provided the stimulus to a certain amount of self-reflexive (and frequently defensive) examination of men by pressing for consideration of "the man question" and drawing connections between men's bodies and sexual violence (K. Ferguson). And sport is critical in this. To quote Margaret Morse:

> The discourse on sport is like no other in our culture insofar as its object is the male body; its currency is statistical comparison of performances, of exchange rates and ownership, of strategies for deployment of bodies and of the particular weaknesses, quirks and gradual submission to injury, illness and aging of those bodies. (57)

This chapter brings sport and the penis together: one as an arena of intense self-control, the other as an arena of profound risk. The male body is standard currency in sporting discourse: on display, at work, measured, and evaluated—in short, objectified for the purposes of pleasure—as nowhere else in contemporary life. After years of automatic denunciation for oppressing women, sublimating homoeroticism, heroizing violence, and developing and sustaining nationalistic chauvinism, men's sport must be seen as a useful place for doing work because it mixes the primordially natural with postmodern nostalgia.

Attempts to professionalize sport for sponsorship purposes, a loosening of working-class masculinist domination, the appearance of women as broadcasters and journalists in the area, feminist sports scholarship, the "pink dollar" market among gay and lesbian consumers, increasing desires on the part of cable TV to broaden coverage as traditional sports are purchased by the networks, and political inquiries into biases against women's sport in the media all problematize the old shibboleths about male domination of sport. Sport allows men to watch and dissect other men's bodies. It is a legitimate space for gazing at the male form without homosexuality being alleged or feared. Admiring individuated body parts ("Look at those triceps") gives a scientistic pleasure and alibi. To see a man weight lifting is to experience at close proximity physiognomic signs of pleasure akin to facial correlatives of the male orgasm in a way otherwise denied to men defining themselves as straight. As one lifter has said, a good pump is "better than coming." This is "the paradoxical play of masculinity," whereby "a satisfying sports competition is much the same as a satisfying homosexual, that is paradoxical, fuck." It amounts to an erotic meeting of coeval power displaced from the site of the overtly carnal (lifter quoted in Shilling 144; Pronger 181). Sport plays up physicality and plays down sexuality, but the act of looking *can* cause problems. Paul Foss suggests that "shower-room banter, that slightly nervous parading of one's personal capital before the other boys at school or after sport, never entirely leaves us when we finally grow up to learn that this is a forbidden subject" (8). Jon Stratton connects sexuality to sporting vigor, with desire simulated through work and spiritual uplift: Corporal Hitler meets Cardinal Newman and Lord Reith on Eton fields. But a less politically and personally dubious reading practice is available as well: for the gay male in 1950s Britain starved of images, boxing, wrestling, and bodybuilding magazines became a significant pleasure (P. Lewis 23). Some important questions need to be addressed here: What does the successful body look like? Does such examination of the male body represent a historic shift?

Joseph Maguire offers a four-way typology of the sporting body as an area of discipline, mirroring, domination, and communication. The disciplined body is an object of allo- and autoregimentation, remade and remodeled through dietetics and training in search of policeable nuances of performance. The mirroring body functions as a machine of desire, encouraging mimetic conduct directly, as the desired other, or synecdochically, through the purchase of commodities associated with it. The dominating body exercises power through physical force, both on the field and off it, frequently in a gendered way. Finally, the communicative body is aestheticized as an expressive totality, balletic and beautiful. As Maguire points out, his typology is neither exclusive nor hermetically distinct. Its categories bleed into one another, and are conflictual as well as functional. They are also the outcome of history, publicity, and privateness: human, commercial, and governmental practices that implicitly negotiate boundaries and show traces of changing volatilities in the display of body parts ("Bodies").

▶ ───────────────────────────────

## The Bodily Commodity

> Desperate Living [1977] was the least successful of my films at the box office. I can't imagine why—a movie about a lesbian sex-change who realizes she made a mistake seems just what the doctor ordered for the mall cineplexes of Mid-America.
> :: John Waters Trash x

> While his important appendage was dingling and dangling as he moved, I kept a straight face, trying to ignore the entertaining idiocy of the act. . . . I couldn't help thinking how far from impressive were the dimensions of the apparatus which he displayed with such evident pride and satisfaction.
> :: Australian Governor-General Bill Hayden, referring to Prime Minister Bob Hawke

In the 1930s, advertisements for men's underwear were discrete: "Be comfortable and acquire poise . . . by wearing Jockey. Jockey's patented Y-front construction gives mild, restful support, eliminates squirming, assures convenient no-gap opening. Fits the male figure everywhere, no bulk, no bind, no buttons to rip off" (quoted in Martin 57). But from May 1967, Sélimaille ("Ceinture noire") promoted itself through sharply focused close-up nude photographs of Frank Protopapa, and English teenage boys of the early 1970s were encouraged to buy underpants by being told that "Mother wouldn't like it"; these items would "awaken the beast in you." This was the era of Andy Warhol's cover for *Sticky Fingers* by the Rolling Stones (1971). It showed formfitting jeans from belt to upper thigh, with the penis in hyper-outline, and a zipper to emphasize the central point at issue (Haug 168 n. 61, 84, 86). The penis is now an ordinary part of merchandising: mainstream shops offer Marks and Fleetwood's "Penis Pasta," complete with guidance on use — "Warning! Increases in Size When Cooked" — and "Mighty Man Magnets" from Blue Q, a selection of cigar, banana, obelisk, and rocket that is "Perfect for the Well-Hung Fridge."

An increasingly competitive men's underwear market uses bulging, muscular personalities in advertisements as a means of product differentiation. The early 1980s saw pole-vaulter Tom Hintnaus dwarfing Times Square in nothing more than underpants. And from the moment in December 1992 when Marky Mark grabbed his Calvins lycra boxer-covered crotch and pouted for the camera (which sent Australian sales of the new line 70 percent beyond expectations) the previous underpant decorum that airbrushed sightly bulges from history was over. For Daniel Harris, the mark of Marky is "a pivotal moment in the history of fashion" (131). New sex methods saw Jockey's Australian receipts double between 1990 and 1993, part of what marketing services manager Allan Mackey described as "a general feeling of equality in society. . . . If women are portrayed like that then why not men?" In Australia, 70 percent of men's underwear is bought by women. Janet Godon, general manager of Davenport, argues that "women like looking at a good-looking bod as much as men do." Davenport became notorious for a 1993 billboard poster of a seventeen-year-old schoolboy with boxer shorts around his ankles and the following lettering across his midsection: "EVERY DAY EVERY MAN SHOULD DROP HIS PANTS, LOOK DOWN AND SMILE" (R. Ryan). Teal Triggs says the master signifier of fashion-magazine masculinity is "no longer the garment but the male nude," an emergent discourse associated with such photographers as Bruce Weber and Herb Ritts (25). The overtly gay address of the Sheraton sheet advertisements from the 1980s and the International Male catalog from Southern California have made postcoital languor and the precoital erection familiar market niches. Mesh "V" Bodywear, for example, is underwear modeled on the condom, a form of gentle armature that combines lightweight packaging with intense visibility. Hyundai enlivened 1993 with its commercial in which women suggest that a man with a large car "must be overcompensating for a . . . shortcoming." And by late 1995, Calvin Klein underwear advertisements featured a model who, as the decorous *New York Times* put it, was "apparently sexually aroused" (Savan 228; Elliott).

The commodified penis has a link to male sports, which are moving away from violence and toward sexually inclusive audience strategies; boxers give way to pinups. The lengthy process of ocular invigilation that Norbert Elias has demonstrated, a progressive displacement of speech by sight as the critical hermeneutic method in early-modern Europe, has moved onto men in the sexualized way it colonized women much earlier. As Sam Fussell says, "Muscles are the latest props of the dandy" (577). Male centerfolds are common fare in teen magazines and British tabloid newspapers. It is now possible for 1993 Miss Wintersun at Surfer's Paradise, the first step toward election for the Miss Australia competition, to be Damian Taylor, much to the consternation of the Endeavour Forum (previously known as Women Who Want to Be Women). The local Chamber of Commerce, which promotes Miss Wintersun, endorses his candidacy. The fairly recent phenomenon of male striptease shows performed for female audiences references not only changes in the direction of power and money, but also a public site where "women have come to see exposed male genitalia; they have come to treat male bodies as objects only" (Dyer *Only* 104; Harari "New"; Barham 62). The burden of these events is clear: the penis emerges with commodification of the postmodern male subject under the bright key lights of narcissistic day.

At the same time, this passage out of darkness is not without difficulty. For example, sportsmen kissing on the field of play in congratulation and ecstasy have become objects of administrative, legal, and promotional gazes, as well as approvingly hedonistic ones. The English Football League has considered banning the embrace, latterly with the alibi of the supposed risk of HIV infection. And in sentencing a man for indecent exposure in 1989, an Australian magistrate blamed the national cricket team's "homosexual-type behaviour" and "unmanly practices" for loose public morals. Two weeks prior to that decision, a prominent Australian sportswriter, formerly of the *National Inquirer* but also laying claims to New Journalism, devoted his bylined column to this fantasy: if he botches a play, his team suffers; if he is successful, he is kissed by another man and shames his family on national television. In June 1993, Adidas (Canada) Ltd. announced it would no longer advertise in the Canadian edition of *Sports Illustrated* after the company was presented with an advertisement prepared by Young & Rubicam that showed a male soccer team naked save for the distinctive three-striped footwear. The slogan read: "Your team won't be taken seriously if it's not wearing Adidas." Trophies, soccer balls, and hands obscured genitals from view. The issue received coverage on *Hard Copy*, *Entertainment Tonight*, *Good Morning America*, and *Geraldo*. Then the Canadian National Soccer League suspended the club from competition, supposedly for unrelated reasons. Feminist critics pointed to a double standard that saw "the font of manhood" protected from view in a magazine notorious for its annual (female) "swimsuit" issue (Peters 1, 3; M. Simpson 88; Wells; Christie "Ad" B1 and "Uninhibited"; Ormsby). By the following year, men were included in *Sports Illustrated*'s "swimsuit" issue for the first time.

The male pinup draws out insecurity, instability, and contradictions in masculinity. Which kind of gaze is expected to consume it? Contrary to conventional masculine icons, the pinup pacifies the body. The feminized associations of soap opera seem to run counter to the presentational logics of sport, but the media circulations of soaps and sports are quite similar, not least as genres that have traditionally polarized TV audiences by gender (the Sports Network in Canada claims, "We deliver the male" in its self-promotion to advertisers). Even this aspect is undergoing powerful changes. The increased appeal by sportscasters to single women and gays, because they have high discretionary income, means that a formerly exclusive address to straight men has been deflected toward other communities: consider NBC's humanizing narrativization of the 1996 Atlanta Olympics, which focused on emotional life histories rather than results. And the Australian Rugby League authorities undertook a management audit of the game in the early 1980s, when the code faced bankruptcy. Along with a rationalization of clubs and more professional administration, the new post of marketing manager, initially held by Graeme Foster, was created. He aimed to "get away from the game's 'thugby' league image and promote the players as fit, skilled athletes." TV ratings went up 10 percent in 1989 (including a 21 percent increase among women) after the airing of a preseason promotional commercial with Tina Turner, described by the game's officials as "a ballsy campaign that appealed to women and young men, broadened the game's appeal and reached into the white-collar audience without alienating league's traditional blue-collar supporter base." By 1993, 30 percent of Australian women were regularly watching televised league games. Of course, women have long formed a preponderance of the television audience for professional wrestling, and half the twenty-four million people in Britain watching a 1990 World Cup soccer game between England and Germany were women, leading to speculation that TV production houses and female viewers were both engaged by the "bum not the ball," as the *Observer* put it (Medhurst 4–5; Foster quoted in Shoebridge

"League's"; Pearce and Campbell 18; Packard 77; *Observer* quoted in O'Connor and Boyle 116). When bum *meets* ball, as we shall see, the female gaze becomes very troubling.

▶

## ET

> Take a cappuccino-drinking copywriter from Paddington, a man who has never watched a game of Rugby League in his life, and turn him into a fly on the dressing-room wall during the 1990 Kangaroo tour of England. This is what he'll see: HUNKS.
> :: James Kerr 95

This section is centrally concerned with understanding the debates and discourses surrounding the April 1991 issue of the glossy monthly magazine *HQ*, which addresses its readers as people who "know Umberto Eco isn't a sounding device" and has recently been doubly transformed from the former *Good Housekeeping* and—briefly—*GH* into a magazine of knowing style. The issue in question was the least successful to that point. It sold 22,000 of a 30,000 print run, but *HQ* claims an actual readership of 154,000 (Hickie "Rugby" and "ET"). The April 1991 number contained, inter alia, interviews with Hanan al-Shaykh, Sonia Braga, John Cale, Paul Bowles, John Updike, and Quincy Jones; advertisements for Chanel No. 5, New Caledonia, and the Northern Territory desert; a contest for the best film script about the assassination of John F. Kennedy; fiction by Tim Winton; and (according to the Supreme Court of New South Wales two years later) a shower-room photograph of Andrew Ettingshausen's penis. The front cover advertised the magazine's contents as including "some naked Kangaroos," referencing the nickname of the Australian Rugby League team. The article in question promised to answer the following questions: "How big is Big Mal?" (team captain Malcolm Meninga) and "What does ET look like under the showers?" responding with, "Big Mal is indeed big, the biggest and ET is built like a Greek god."

From the moment of his appearance as a professional footballer in the mid-1980s, Andrew Ettingshausen has been glamorous. His looks have brought modeling contracts and television appearances, his speed of foot repute as a sporting star; a former coach said, "He's so quick he can flick off the light switch and be in bed before it's dark." These qualities, allied to his surname, have led to the genially oxymoronic sobriquet of ET, a great paradox when beauty provides so much of his recognition factor. It is claimed

Photo courtesy ACP Publishing Pty. Limited. From *HQ Magazine*, April 1991.

that he is "the face" of the sport, his "boyish good looks" attracting thousands of female spectators to the game. Readers of *Cleo* magazine (a competitor on the Australian market with *Cosmopolitan*) have voted him the "Sexiest Man Alive" (Harari "Crotch"). And he is part of an intensely visible sport: a few months after his penis was captured, Ettingshausen could be seen in an interstate game that set an Australian TV ratings record.

In February 1993, a jury of two women and two men awarded Ettingshausen A$350,000 tax-free in damages against Australian Consolidated Press (ACP), the owner of *HQ*, on the basis that he had been defamed by the photograph's publication, which implied that he had consented to his "genitals [being] exposed for reproduction" to a wide readership. By contrast, a person who lost his penis through an industrial accident might expect upward of A$45,000, or A$80,000 for a leg. Another comparison might be drawn with Darrell Bampton, a player who received A$11,000 in a settlement out of court in 1978 when his penis was broadcast nationally (and gratuitously) from the dressing room. The award to Ettingshausen drew criticism on these points from the New South Wales Law Society. Michael Lavarch, formerly chair of a parliamentary inquiry into the status of women and later federal attorney general, remarked that there was at least a paradox at play when alarms over this image were compared with daily media representations of women. Anne Deveson, chair of a federal government working party on the portrayal of women in the media, spoke of double standards, while hoping that men would now understand women's feelings about pornography. There have been various related developments in the United States. In 1980, Ann-Margret unsuccessfully sued *High Society* for reproducing a seminude image from one of her films: the text was considered newsworthy and hence protected by the First Amendment. But when a model brought a suit against the magazine the same year for an unauthorized nude shot, she won, because the photo was not deemed newsworthy. Five years later, a couple protested that a guide to nude beaches included a picture of them, but again this was protected as information of public concern rather than a commercial representation. When Tonya Harding's ex-husband Jeff Gillooly circulated a videotape on tabloid TV of her getting undressed on their wedding night, however, New Jersey politicians unveiled plans to punish people who sell or display nude photographs without their subjects' consent, on the ground that this resembles an assault ("Publisher"; Hickie "Nudity"; Harari "Crotch"; Coombe; Gray).

Ettingshausen initially claimed that the publication imputed he was an "indecent and lewd person" who had "willingly pandered to the prurient interests of . . . readers" by posing for the picture, later revising this to say it was suggested he had allowed his genitals to be reproduced for a wide readership (quoted in Hunt 3–4). For its part, ACP did not accept the penis was exposed and argued the photograph would not cause Ettingshausen any harm. It further claimed he had consented to the picture (despite the fact the magazine had published an apology to the contrary in August 1991). The defendant's counsel, Ian Callinan, said Ettingshausen's work as a model was predicated on sexualizing himself for women, which the player conceded. This meant "no sense of modesty could reasonably be offended" by the photograph. In an expansively metaphorizing mode, Callinan described the shot as "something much less than . . . [a] storm in a teacup . . . a great deal of fuss over nothing much at all . . . [a] tracery of deep shadow and greyness and darkness." Ettingshausen's reputation had "never stood higher" and his modeling career was flourishing. ACP appealed the finding and the amount, while agreeing to pay court costs of A$180,000 and A$20,000 of the damages. A court of appeal found the amount awarded "excessive." The payout was reduced in a second case to A$100,000 ($20,000 more than Ettingshausen had requested three years earlier). Australia's Free Speech Committee applauded the reduced amount (Harari "Crotch"; O'Neill; Hickie "ET"; Falvey; Fife-Yeomans; Pullan).

ET's counsel was Tom Hughes, a former politician famous for his period as attorney general in 1970. (On one occasion, annoyed by anti-Vietnam War demonstrators in his garden, Hughes had pursued them with a cricket bat.) In the ET hearing, his antipathy toward Kerry Packer, the richest man in Australia and owner of ACP, who had just discarded Hughes in favor of another law firm, was a strong subtext. During the case, Hughes cross-examined Brett M. Cochrane, who took the photograph: "His penis was in the photograph, wasn't it?" Cochrane looked at the magazine and replied, "There's no denying that." He said he could make the penis out "on close inspection." Cochrane added he had not asked the players for permission to take pictures, although he was there as an official tour photographer with a general authorization to film from the Australian Rugby League, and had never been asked by anyone to stop work. (Cochrane later told a reporter, by way of background, that many members of the team regarded women as "just objects to root.") In questioning Shona Martyn, editor of the magazine, Hughes asked whether she would be offended by a suggestion that she had consented to her genitals' being photographed and published for mass circulation. Martyn responded she would not, providing the outcome was "a tasteful shot" in a magazine such as *HQ*; she thought the picture "flattering" to Ettingshausen. She would agree to having her genitals reproduced, but had received no offers. Martyn dissented from Hughes's view that a reasonable reader would now consider it inappropriate for Ettingshausen to continue in his job as a school development officer for the rugby league (Sandra Hall 8, 12; Hughes and Cochrane quoted in Hickie "Photographer"; Martin quoted in McAsey).

Shown a massive enlargement of the image, Martyn conceded she was "careless" to allow a picture in the magazine with a "shaded area" that might be taken for a penis. She had "been struggling to look at it" and could just make out "some shadow." Martyn denied there was a "white shape with what looked like pubic hairs"—Hughes's description—but would come at an interpretation of the image as "an off-white shape" that "could be a penis." The following exchange then took place:

HUGHES: Is it a penis or is it not?

MARTYN: Well, I assume that if it's in that part of the body, maybe it could be and maybe it might not be.

HUGHES: What else could it be?

MARTYN: I guess it could be a shadow . . .

HUGHES: Is it a duck?

MARTYN: I don't think it would be a duck. (quoted in Hickie "Editor")

The line about the duck references Martyn's Aotearoan/New Zealand accent. Its flat *i* turns "six" into "sex." "Fish and chips" becomes "fush and chups," and "dick" swells into "duck" ("Judge Attacks"; "Judge Slams"). ET and his counsel were less playful: "Is that your penis in the lower half of the photograph?" "Definitely" (quoted in Harari "Crotch").

The presiding judge in the New South Wales Supreme Court believed the damages payment reasonable, and criticized subsequent media coverage. Justice Hunt emphasized that the "award was made not simply because the plaintiff's penis was shown in the photograph," but because publication in *HQ* amounted to "an extraordinarily serious imputation about a well-known young sportsman with an unchallenged good reputation for observing standards of decency" in the eyes of "the ordinary reasonable reader." He added A $13,416.66 as interest, noting the defendant had conducted the case like "a death wish." Justice Hunt stressed that Ettingshausen "is entitled to a good cushion." For his part, photographer Cochrane went on to appear as Ashley Taylor's entry for the Archibald portraiture prize, captured showering with a camera dangling over most of his penis (Hunt quoted in Hickie "Judge Defends" and in O'Neill; Borham).

The critical case cited as a precedent in ET's duck was *Burton v. Crowell Pub. Co.* from 1936, in which the Second Circuit Court of Appeals for the Southern District of New York heard a previously dismissed action. The plaintiff, Crawford Burton, complained that an image published by the defendant made him look "physically deformed and mentally perverted," as well as "guilty of indecent exposure." The court found the defendant had a case of libel and slander to answer, even though the "trivial ridicule" that might descend on Burton was "patently an optical illusion" and part of an advertisement in which he had consented to appear.

The image in question? Crowell Publishing had printed a photograph of the plaintiff in an advertisement for Camel cigarettes. Burton, a renowned amateur steeplechase jockey, was quoted as endorsing Camels for their calming, restorative effect after "a crowded business day." This annotation accompanied two photographs. The first, which did not excite legal action, depicted him in riding attire after the race, holding cigarette, whip, and cap; "Get a lift with a Camel" was the caption. Problems arose with the other picture. It represented Burton after the little death, the race finish, when it is time for all good jockeys and horses to draw deep breaths. Burton is shown carrying his saddle en route to the weigh-in, with one hand under the cantle and the other beneath the pommel. The seat is about a foot below his waist, and the line formed by a loose girth appears to connect him to it. Herein lies the problem: it looks like a dick. Or, in the terminology of Circuit Judge Learned Hand, "The photograph becomes grotesque, monstrous, and obscene; and the legends, which without undue violence can be made to match, reinforce the ribald interpretation. That is the libel." Burton had posed for the photographs—unlike ET, except in the most generic sense— but he had not been shown the outcome. His penis had been unrealistically constituted—the power of cropping. Knowing Judge Hand was a strong supporter of free speech adds to this sense of a problem with proportion and person rather than penis *qua* penis (*Burton v. Crowell* 154; Heins 172).

These cases haul us toward definitional issues. Surely the penis is one of those well-hung signs, weighed down beyond the capacity of the postmodern to float it? But if there is no penis where one should logically be in the ET shot, is ET a man? What *is* in that space? As Peggy Phelan has shown, the "visible real" of photographs is quickly enlisted by "representational notions of the real" that come from the human sciences and government. This enlistment serves to establish the effect of transparent truth beyond the recorded image, grafting onto the photo-effect the discourses of these sciences in order to render theory empirical. Mimesis goes guarantor for the subject who utilizes it (3, 6–7). This contradictory penile semantics suggests we should consider some organic history.

▶───────────────────────────────────

### Religion and Race

> *Abraham said unto his eldest servant of the house, that ruled over all that he had, Put, I pray thee, thy hand under my thigh. . . .*
>     *And the servant put his hand under the thigh of Abraham his master.*
> ::   Genesis 24:2, 9

> *An erection on Rodin's* Thinker *is a shocking thought. One cannot decently "have a hard on" everywhere.*
> ::   Fanon 165

Augustine explains Adam and Eve's postapple physical shame as a problem of control: what had been easily operated organs prior to the Fall became liable to "a novel disturbance in their disobedient flesh" homologous to their own disobedience of God, leaving the rest of us with original sin. The *pudenda*, or "parts of shame," are named as such because people now find lust can "arouse those members independently of decision," the "movements of their body" manifesting "indecent novelty." Like Ettingshausen's embarrassment, negative feelings derive from the capacity of objects to get out of whack. The "genital organs have become as it were the private property of lust." What were once "like the fingers" in obeying the will of their owner elude his control, a punishment for Adam's own attempt to evade God's will. Man exemplifies the Fall in the mutability of his penis. So Renaissance paintings of Jesus routinely depict him pointing to or touching his genitals as a sign of his human side: a begotten rather than created Son (Augustine *Concerning* 522–23, 578, 581; Foucault in Foucault and Sennett 14; Porter 206).

Circumcision dates back six thousand years to Egyptian notions of suitability for leadership judged through personal cleanliness. Its most direct significance in our own time derives from directives in the Jewish Bible/Old Testament, the Koran, and medical theories about untimely ejaculation, hygiene, cancer, and masturbation. Circumcision allows divine entry into the human form. *The first book of Moses, or Genesis*, finds God appearing to Abram to form a covenant. Renamed Abraham, the mortal man will become "a father of many nations." In return, all male children born or coming to live in those nations must lose their foreskin flesh. An uncircumcised man's "soul shall be cut off from his people." This is problematized in the Epistle of Paul the Apostle to the Galatians, which identifies Jesus' legacy as freedom from the "yoke of bondage" masquerading as membership of the chosen people: "I Paul say unto you, that if ye be circumcised, Christ shall profit you nothing." Faith through love offers salvation; purity of life begins to inflect the genitals, rather than purity of ritual (Wallerstein 7; Scarry 204, 235; Genesis 17:4, 14; Galations 5:2).

Gender relations among Western Desert Pintupi people in Australia are symbolized in male circumcision processes. The penis is an index of age and position, again through a reciprocal covenant. The circumciser provides the young man with his daughter as a wife in exchange for the pain he has inflicted. Ritual knowledge and the gift of women are paid for with the foreskin, just as initiation is indexed in the penile sheath as signs that the initiate is a relatively autonomous subject. The penis is a public object, but it is not weakened by this condition. Rather, as per the Merina of Madagascar, highly formalized circumcision is transferable with shifts in the loci of male power across the history of a people, precisely because the changes are not so much propositional as ritualistic. Despite a loss of modishness for Christians, the practice abounds. Neonatal circumcision has routinely been the most common surgery performed in the United States since the beginning of the twentieth century; people here just can't leave the thing alone. In Britain, it was taken up in the early 1900s in an attempt to replicate Jewish child-care practices, which were thought to diminish infant mortality. Now there is a reaction: in 1996, twenty men sent a letter to the *British Medical Journal*, signing themselves "Norm UK" and announcing a support group for the circumcised in protest of popular logics of the 1960s, which held that sexual pleasure would increase from the operation. On the other side of the ledger, penile modification workshops for "Modern Primitives" are prominent in the United States today, as thick descriptions of genital burning, branding, cutting, and piercing in San Francisco and Oregon's Living in Leather Convention have shown (F. Myers 174, 236, 239; Bloch 190–95; Gollaher 5; Hyam 77; B. Cohen; J. Myers).

This notion of primitivism raises questions of race. *National Geographic*, long a key onanistic aid to straight North American men in search of female breasts, has not felt able to represent the penis, even when publishing photographs of men from cultures where no sheath or clothing is worn. Airbrushing techniques remove male genitals of color, in keeping with white anxieties about the size of the black penis that go back four hundred years in written records; in the seventeenth century, black men were referred to as "large Propagators." After the American Civil War, the discourse escalated, in keeping with the direction of postslavery racism. Frantz Fanon's account of white projections onto black male genitals is central here. Fanon (when he is not pronouncing clitoral orgasms immature) argues that "everything takes place on the genital level" in white imaginings of "the Negro," which endow him with "tremendous sexual powers," supposedly enhanced by constant mating in the jungle. Such absurdities illustrate white men's "sexual inferiority," which elevates the phallus to omniscience and hates African Americans for being the ultimate "penis symbol." As per Augustine's notion of genitals out of control, Fanon points to the equation of black maleness with penile excess and the risks of uncontrolled lust (Lutz and Collins 172–78; Hyam 204–5; Fanon 157, 159, 165).

This hierarchized difference—"the Mandingo complex"—continues to trouble academic invigilators of the public psyche, who correlate race with size of testes, incidence of twins, "copulatory frequency," and female breast cancer. J. Philippe Rushton and Anthony F. Bogaert share with us via the *Journal of Research in Personality* their attempts to connect human reproduction, "sexual restraint," and "size of penis" with race and criminal activity. They place "blacks" at one end of a continuum and "Orientals" at the other, with "whites" the golden mean. The article claims black men "had larger penises, at a different angle of erection, and maintained intromission for longer" than other races, in keeping with their sociobiological destiny: high birthrates, multiple partners, many orgasms, "low self-monitoring" socially, excessive criminality, and early death. Rushton and Bogaert rely on Kinsey's research and, most wonderfully, the anonymous "French Army Surgeon" who spent much of the 1890s measuring body parts of Third World peoples in all conceivable places and conditions of tumescence. These findings are described as "the ethnographic record" (Foss 10; Diamond; Rushton and Bogaert 529–30, 536, 539; also see "Invited Reviews" and Boone 94 for critiques). Even before that, sexual organs had been critical to the imperial project of delineating white from black by positioning the latter in "a twilight zone between nature and culture." Saartjie Baartman, categorized as "the Hottentot Venus," was "shown" in London and Paris museums in the early 1800s because of her buttock shape, and an autopsy was publicized to point out the "animal-like" form of her genitals (T. Bennett *Birth* 77–78).

The continuity of concern between contemporary research and panic over black sexuality is perhaps most relevant here. The size, shape, and swell of men's genitals are sites for projecting a seemingly inevitable horror onto African Americans. (At the same time, we can find elsewhere a similar mythification of the white penis. Gasowe of Makiroka Village in Papua New Guinea recalls his first encounter with white men in the 1930s. He assumed their habit of wearing considerable amounts of clothing was designed to cover up "a huge penis . . . so long it was wrapped round and round their waists" [quoted in Connolly and Anderson 44].) But the power differential is very marked, as David Marriott notes in his discussion of U.S. racism: "The taking of photographs at mass lynchings, the taking of body parts from the mutilated victim as *memento mori*—the most highly prized being the black penis—seem to have been central to the compulsively ritualized ways of looking at the black man's body at the moment of its annihilation" (9). Commissioned photographs at lynchings were staged for the daguerreotype process, which necessitated a camera mounted on a tripod and a set arrangement of the body. Once the box camera came on the scene, greater variety and individuality were available for poses. Such violations continue. In the 1960s, Ku Klux Klan members castrated a black Alabama man with razor blades, doused his wound in kerosene and turpentine, and passed around his testicles in a cup. Patricia Turner's latter-day study of rumor in African American culture identifies contemporary beliefs that work through such tensions: the Klan is thought to own a national fast-food franchise, a malt liquor company, and a soft-drink firm that sterilize black men through additives. Whites and blacks across the twentieth century have run a "Topsy/Eva" legend in which a black/white preadolescent boy is castrated by white/black men in a public toilet (Marriott 18–19; P. Turner 73, 2–3, 227, 149–50).

▶

## Pornography

> We felt like joining hands in a prayer of thanks for the two or three actors willing to do a scene involving real sexual intercourse. . . .
>
> The problem was the man. Nearly all the men flinched at the idea. They all said, "I'm afraid I won't get an erection when the time comes."
>
> "You have a big one, don't you?" I asked audaciously over and over.
>
> "I'm confident that it'll be big at the crucial moment, but I think that normally it may be a little smaller than most people's." Eight out of ten men gave that response.
>
> Two out of ten said theirs was average. I considered them to be the confident ones.
>
> I am one of those lacking in confidence, but I was delighted to find out that there are so many of us.
>
> :: Oshima 262

For Baudelaire, photography is porn's natural ally through its indexical link of image and object, tied in the popular imagination to a sexual charge. The camera is a tool of seduction. To pornography police in our own time, it is said to have a "coercive immediacy." The late-nineteenth-century spread of the photograph coincided, of course, with imperialism, and Britain saw hundreds of thousands of Orientalist male porn shots seized by the state. The Kinsey Institute for Research in Sex, Gender, and Reproduction, which houses more than seventy-five thousand dirty pictures, benefited for many years from the careful nurturance of relationships with metropolitan law enforcement agencies. Its archive includes a wide array of physical culture shots seized in the 1940s and 1950s, most of which are homoerotic and/or sadomasochistic (Gever 175; Falk 201; Solomon-Godeau 235; Hunter et al. 89; T. Smith; Crump).

Gay pornographic texts dedicate a great deal of time and space to penis dimensions, sometimes for commercial reasons, but not entirely. The periodical *Straight to Hell* (also known as the *Manhattan Review of Unnatural Acts*) began in the 1970s with a remit to combine sexual and political arousal. Its "underground folk-raunch" was a Godsend to Tom Waugh as "a trembling grad student in New York City . . . wondering whether marching in Gay Pride could blow my comprehensives" ("Gay" 30). Its photographs and autobiographical essays show the penis to be desirable *and* abject, as messy and troubling as it is reliable and attractive. This is no utopia. Hierarchical evaluation is at work, with appreciation of the penis a taste culture of its own (*Meat*). For Dyer, there is an unremitting ontological anchor here, the key to his pleasure in watching much gay pornographic film: these people really did this, that penis really experienced those pleasures. Self-reflexivity is a routine aspect to gay porn, through filmmaking, auditioning, live performance, movie-house sex, and intertextuality ("Idol" 49–54).

Gay and straight porn alike search for the best angles and coverage of the penis at its climax through overlighting, extreme close-ups, multiperspectival montage of the same action, and "spatial lability." But there are major differences. Until the appearance of feature-length, fully narrativized straight porn in the late 1960s, the "beaver shot" and the close-up on women's faces at the *crise* were dominant motifs, with the penis implied (Dennis 123). Contemporary porn video aesthetics call for the "meat shot," a close-up of genitalia interacting, and the "money" or "cum" shot that closes down a section of the narrative and proves men are having fun. This quest will not conclude until either a cum-cam can go anywhere or porn involving women is able to "imagine the difference," as Lisa Katzman puts it (33). Whereas safe sex is a nostrum of gay porn, much straight sex on-camera is euphemized as "prochoice" (Indiana 34). And there are many violent and degrading films. Tania Modleski takes as exemplary *The Devil and Miss Jones, Part 3*, in which a black woman is raped, dying at the point of male climax. The violent notation that sees her at one point penetrated both vaginally and anally by two nearly touching penises is intensely disturbing. For Modleski, the phallus and penis overlap in this text. The link lies for her in male social dominance, which she sees as a point of continuity between hypermasculinity and the feyness of figures like Boy George and Pee-wee Herman (160–61, 90–111).

Gertrude Koch has drawn attention to the need, however, for consideration of the commercial and industrial circumstances of porn. She explains the dramatic efflorescence of the genre in Victorian Britain as a consequence of economic modernity: scientific management and its correlation of new modes of communication and textual apprehension produced new sites and forms of looking, as porn's association with the brothel was broken (31). The editing rhythms of Candida Royalle's genital coverage in her recent Femme Distribution films substitute middle-class, heterosexual feminist lyricism for conventional male-produced straight porn in ways that give some women the sense of actually seeing their own lives onscreen, while women stars in straight porn reportedly make twice the amount paid to men (Katzman 31; Faludi 65–66).

It used to be a given of liberal-humanist feminism to deride porn, not least for the money shot's gendered point of view. But that position is under critique. In keeping with its stature as the principal cultural genital, the reality effect of the spurting celluloid penis turns its uncontrollability into a confession. Exposure may mean women will decide "the penis isn't a patch on the phallus," that the public exhibition of masculine force in other body parts is an acknowledgment that the wrong object has been selected to signify power; and when the penis appears apart from its personal function as a private part of the body, its symbolic connections to public power are brought into question (Patton 105; Dyer *Only* 116; Hearn 88; L. Williams 25). For many who feel metaphorically excluded from mainstream sexual aesthetics, the work of porn in making the penis visible can certainly make a positive difference. Richard Fung argues that the general absence of male Asian sexuality from film has given him a "lifelong vocation of looking for my penis, trying to fill in the visual void" (149).

The male form just isn't up to standing for the phallus in this latter-day epoch of calibrated differences. Jean-Luc Godard's "metapornography" makes allure formulaic by returning to it again and again as a supposed excitement that finds the penis less and less satisfying, as Jane Fonda tells Yves Montand in *Tout va bien* (Godard and Jean-Pierre Gorin, 1972) (Stam 178). The mockery of dicks in recent films, chronicled by Peter Lehman, looks like a women's countertextual initiative. Cruel comparisons are made in *The Witches of Eastwick* (George Miller, 1987), *McCabe and Mrs. Miller* (Robert Altman, 1971), and a series of other Hollywood movies from the past two decades (if often with the wry affection that one can read in Judy MacInnes's "Small Penis Poems"). It's one of the nice conceits in *Tank Girl* (Rachel Talalay, 1995), and a key to gender relations in John Singleton's *Poetic Justice* (1993), when Ayisha tells Chicago, "Your dick's the motherfuckin' problem," explaining that his previous liaison ended because "You can't hang." In *The Last Seduction* (John Dahl, 1993), Linda Fiorentino's character, *noir*-like unto cliché, references both resistive and hegemonic attitudes to women and the penis. When one (white) man advertises himself to her in a bar as "hung like a horse," she insists on seeing and touching his goods and services then and there. But her method of dealing with a black investigator who is trailing her involves requiring him to take out his penis, when he has expressed no sexual interest in her and is feeling put-upon by her questions and intimations ("Is it true what they say?"). He does what she wants in return for a quiet ride. Then she causes the car to crash, simultaneously incriminating him for sexual harrassment and killing him.

The episode alluded to earlier in a quotation from John Waters about his film *Desperate Living* is worth describing. Mole McHenry, very butch, loves Muffy St. Jacques, very femme. Muffy expresses the desire for sex with a penis, so Mole makes the ultimate sacrificial addition to her life by going to the Johns Hopkins Sexual Reassignment Clinic, armed with lottery winnings. Pulling a knife, she persuades the clinic's receptionist to put her ahead of others in line. Mole continues with this reverse bedside manner ("Come on, quack. I want the sex change and I want it fast! . . . Cut the sermons and give me my wang! I want a wang and I want it NOW!"). Reversing the example of the psychiatrist in *I Led Two Lives* or *Glen or Glenda?/I Changed My Sex* (Edward D. Wood, Jr., 1953) (who refers to the "removal of the man and the formation of the woman"), the surgeon proceeds. The deed done, Mole goes home and reveals her new self. Muffy gags. Far from being pleasantly surprised, she calls the penis an "ugly deformed worm." Muffy orders Mole to cut it off, vomiting with disgust in response to the promise that it "never goes soft." Crying, "So much for science, Muffy!" Mole reaches for a pair of scissors and slashes the cock. Muffy picks it up from the floor and tosses it outside, where a dog eats it. Waters's cheerful irreverence touches on Bruce Beresford's mockery of white Australian men in *The Adventures of Barry McKenzie* (1972). After numerous references to urination, such as "siphon the python," and "shake hands with the unemployed/the wife's best friend," we discover Barry is a virgin. This bravado is compensation. The film's troping of the penis concludes with a scene in which a fire on a BBC-TV set is extinguished by a group of men—including the Hitchcockian director—pissing on the flames.

Juxtaposing the good, the ugly, and the hard references the ambiguity of the organ's aesthetic career. Consider the cutting and shot/reverse-shot relations in *Viva Zapata!* (Elia Kazan, 1952). Jean Peters, a remarkable composite character who stands in for the historical Zapata's twenty-six wives, pulls a knife from her hair, touches her finger with it, and looks knowingly at Marlon Brando. The dialogue is telling. She says she would go with him wherever, without the need for force. But this is followed by "sooner or later you would fall asleep." We cut to Brando: "And then?" This is the feisty woman onscreen; not a metaphoric castrator, but ever ready to resist masculine power, which will, indeed, need to rest somewhere, sometime, letting its vigilant tumescence descend for a moment. (Can it be an accident that, regardless of his splendid name, John Wayne Bobbitt's television performances are perfect reenactments of Brando's "diction," and that *John Wayne Bobbitt Uncut* [Ron Jeremy, 1994] was released at the same time as Brando's autobiography? It can.)

The presence/absence dance of metaphysics that the penis engages is also a tool of marketing. Consider *Color of Night* (Richard Rush, 1994). After initial indications of a subdued audience response, Disney publicists played up Bruce Willis's nudity, which was then cut to gain a broad exhibition rating, but left in place for the video release (Brodie 7). We are confronted by audience response here, with iconography overdetermined in the definition of porn by what takes place in the body of the spectator. The key issues become *whose* body is that, and *where* is it? Since the nineteenth century, the reality effect of genitals on film has been connected with specific audiences and their practices, for it is the peculiar talent and shame of pornography to be perfectly targeted. To critics of the genre, it has "one simple, unequivocal intention: to excite its consumer" (Dyer "Coming" 27; Clover "Introduction" 3). By joining the conservative's anxiety about unruly audiences to the aesthete's concern for proper self-management in engagement with a text, porn loses the capacity to live as a stable set of signs. It is consigned forever to being cataloged by who watches and how they do so.

The penis has always been central to documentary, in keeping with a genre absorbed by audience conduct, not just audience receipts. The male nude was crucial from the earliest days of photography in lending the new image a mimetic capacity, while many of the six thousand films about tribal Australian Aboriginal people have implicitly presumed upon nudity as a means of differentiating tradition from modernity and paganism from God. This has put them beyond the civic concern of censorship. Conversely, documentaries and docudramas explicitly concerned with sex have routinely troubled governments and critics since the beginning of the screen, whether they take the form of training films or attempts to legitimate titillating narratives through an informational alibi. In the first category, we might consider the sex education of *The Gift of Life* (1920) and *Fit to Fight* (1919), which warned of the venereal disease threat to men and the defense of the nation posed by prostitutes. Such films were produced by the American Social Hygiene Association to advance public understanding of sexuality, but frequently drew some concern from those less liberal (Hatt 135; Bertrand 104). Their blend of broad-appeal narrative fiction with a public health remit leads Annette Kuhn to name the genre "the VD propaganda film" (50). Sex-segregated audiences of the day could watch a double bill of a documentary investigation of the impact of sexually transmitted diseases on the body, followed by some rather dubious fictionalized social-problem film (Stevens 84).

In the second category, combining both these forms, we could place Richard Franklin's 1976 sexploitation film *Fantasm* (some way distant from his polite 1995 release *Hotel Sorrento*) and Julia St. Vincent's *Exhausted* (1981). Such texts adopt the conceit of educating their audience, playing with new censorship classifications that permit a franker treatment of sex. In the United States of the 1960s, this genre takes the form of visual "reports" on the Danish pornography industry that are themselves essentially diegetic frames legitimating the rerepresentation of erotica. But again, the modal shifter that operates between training and entertainment is complicated. It is currently referenced by the acknowledgment that safe-sex videos may be most effective if they are explicit and enjoyable, in keeping with their public viewing destiny in gay bars and other sites dedicated to pleasure rather than didacticism. And supposedly academic publications quickly move into the realm of audience titillation in their marketing. So, the Milanese Incat System's 1990 CD-ROM of erotic photography, drawn from five universities and seventy-one archives, includes the title "Germany: Pale Asses und Whips 1839–1930" (L. Williams 24; "Seedy").

Like the complicated legal determinations on *Titicut Follies* (Frederick Wiseman, 1967), which for many years allowed limited release based on the professional qualifications of the audience, this specification of recipient design is a strong point of continuity with much older imperatives in the policing of pornography. *Miller v. California*, a 1973 U.S. Supreme Court case, established three tests of obscenity that are almost a palimpsest of how eighteenth-century Revolutionary France policed such matters. They indicate the implausibility of a purely textual, content-driven definition. The categories refer to audiences (Would a reasonable person find this prurient?), regions (Do the depictions resonate with sexual definitions under particular state laws?), and interpretations (Does this lack intellectual value?) (Hunter et al.; Darnton 41, 44–45; Adler 324). Once more, there is no stability to this series of qualifications. The first and third rely on divining average and specialist opinions, the second on matters of time and space. Wiseman's *Zoo* (1993) contains a sequence dedicated to the castration of a wolf that makes the point within its own diegesis. Reaction shots of one person visibly disturbed by this event, as opposed to more professionally inured onlookers and participants, underscore that specific reading protocols are the ultimate determination on the penis as sign. These imperatives are neither formalist nor ideological, but occasioned by the nature of a textual encounter: how the reader is trained to respond to signs.

> *I am in favour of leaving the penis alone.*
> :: Dr. Benjamin Spock, Olympic gold medalist, quoted in
>    Wallerstein 24

> *The penis consists of three corporal bodies: the two corpora*
> *cavernosa dorsally and corpus spongiosum ventrally.*
> :: Batra and Lue 251

> *The sexual organs are so tough that almost no amount of*
> *ordinary use, prolonged even for sixty years, is of itself*
> *capable of injuring them.*
> :: Hyam 7

In the late nineteenth century, the observation that feebleminded men frequented their genitals led to an etiological link between their condition and their hands. Medicine fixated on the penis as an index of mental illness, offering wire cages and spiked rings to ward off masturbation and electrical alarms to wake up recipients of Morpheus's tug. From that point on, the textualized penis has conventionally been circumcised in U.S. medical and paramedical publications. Today, most attention is given to the "mechanism of penile erection and its hemodynamics," not to mention the six phases of swelling. A fully fleshed-out debate surges over measurement of the penis at rest and otherwise, with advocates for penile plethysmography, rigidity monitoring, nocturnal penile tumescence, axial buckling pressure measures, the postage stamp loop, the Potentest, the Rigiscan, penile blood pressure indices, radioactive xenon washout and infusion cavernosography, the penile strain gauge, penile volume response versus penile circumference response, pulse Doppler ultrasound studies of penile blood flow (related to NBC's Doppler 4000 weather radar), and the Miami Sexual Dysfunction Protocol. The test conditions usually require sleep or exposure to sex on film, along with some allowance for PERM, or postejaculatory refractory mechanisms (Gollaher 8, 20–21, 25; Porter and Hall 144–45; Batra and Lue 252–55; Buvat et al. 272–73, 284, 290; McConaghy; McAnulty and Adams; Ackerman et al.; Moss et al. 11).

The definition of a penis has also been something of a research tease: Do you prefer cellular structure, engorgement, or function? Phallometry has a hard and long road to hoe. Although Fanon suggests the average penis length of white and black men is 12 cm, the exact physical nature of the penis changes with medical fashion, as science and circumcision continue their uncertain dance. *The Complete Dictionary of Sexology* offers an average at rest of 3 to 4 inches top to bottom and 1 inch across, extending to 5–7 in length and 1.5 in diameter *in extremis*. At the other end of the spectrum falls the "micropenis," which is 2.5 standard deviation units smaller than the norm for the age group of the "affected individual." Whereas the adult male can be "stretched" to an average of 6.6 inches, micros cannot make it past 4.68. Alternatively, the penis may be "permanently bent upward," a case of "phallanastrophe." In advice literature, the essential quality of the penis is its mobility. Size, shape, and inclination vary across time, space, and function, even with the one owner. Walter R. Stokes's *Modern Pattern for Marriage* (1948) defines the penis as an "erectile male organ, adapted to penetration of the vagina," with changes in size central to its being. In keeping with their liberalizing project, books of this genre emphasize that "rarely does [penis] size have much significance for the matrimonial union." But twenty-five years after the first such support, *The Joy of Sex* finds men still preoccupied with dimensions. They "need reassurance and a different attitude" (Garber 102; Fanon 170; Keuls 68; Francoeur 475, 397, 481; Stokes 9, 36; Groves et al. 109; Comfort 45).

Physical reassurance is close at hand. Bernarr MacFadden, a guiding light in the turn-of-the-century physical culture movement, gave us the "peniscope" to pump up the penis. Equivalent techniques today require shaving the scrotum and the base of the penis, which both attracts attention and facilitates drawing the dick through a vacuum tube or attaching two- to four-pound bell-shaped weights—the "rock on a cock" exercise. Piercing cosmetics include the "Prince Albert," which Queen Victoria's consort never traveled without, the ampallang from Southeast Asia, the Dydoe, the Apadravya, the Persian Gulf region's Hafada, the European Frenum, and the South Pacific Guiche. Prostheses, splints, and enhancers are also available. This preoccupation is on the increase. As the *Archives of Sexual Behavior* recently put it, there is an "expanding body of literature concerning developments in diagnosis and treatment of erectile dysfunction (ED)." Impotents Anonymous and the Impotence Institute of America are waiting to assist sufferers, while university tests like the Leiden Impotence Questionnaire are at hand to establish that feminists are the best partners for men suffering from ED. Recent surveys of the professional psy-literature reveal that the sign "impotence" has displaced "frigidity" in the period since 1970. Impotence cures now appear in TV commercials and full-page *New Yorker* advertisements, insisting on a physiological basis to the problem. Since the mid-1980s, self-administered injections of prostaglandin to relax penile tissue and heighten blood flow have been on the market, and in 1996 the U.S. government for the first time approved one such treatment,

Advertisement courtesy Pharmacia & Upjohn.

Caverject (Francoeur 474–75; Kimmel 21; J. Myers 279, 300–301; Fussell
581; Speckens et al. 159, 161; Tiefer 579; "Injected").

There are also fertility issues. Contemporary numbers, shapes, and
motilities of sperm are wanting compared with the free-flow norm of the
1950s male, and 1996 will go down as the year the *British Medical Journal*
published material on the great disappearing sperm count and the *New
Yorker* went on a global hunt for correlations among urban stress, toxic
chemicals, and increased estrogen. Commenting on these findings, the Lon-

don *Daily Telegraph* identified the "Victorian era" as a golden age when "most men . . . had enough sperm to sire a great many children." The only hope was that the burgeoning science of andrology would see gynecologists and pediatricians supplanted by real experts on the new crisis of masculinity (L. Wright; *Telegraph* quoted in Nolan 20).

These three discursive formations—the pornographic, the legal, and the medical—come together, albeit in reverse order, in the summer 1993 case of John Wayne Bobbitt and Lorena Bobbitt. Following what appears to have been coercive sex, she cuts off her husband's penis as he sleeps and drives to the home of her boss. Lorena later told *20/20* she had difficulty negotiating tight right-hand turns en route: "I try to turn, but then I saw that I have it in my hand." She throws the penis out of the car. When John wakes to his half of the discovery, he goes to a hospital, where he is cared for by a Dr. Sharpe. The police hear about the episode from both parties and take off in search of the organ. Once found, it is packed in a zipper-type plastic bag, brought to the operating theater, and reattached.

James Sehn, a surgeon involved in the operation to sew John's penis back on, reports countless demands from women to see his before-and-after photographs. And as William Safire's tracery of the penis in print journalism demonstrates, "July 13, 1993, will be remembered as the day the word *penis* appeared in 30-point type in The New York Times." The police described their search for the well-flung penis as "looking for an extremity"; Lorena Bobbitt called it "the body part." This extremely isolated emasculatory incident produced a zeitgeist search by journalists for a new, dangerous feminism supposedly connected to Valerie Solanas's Society for Cutting Up Men *Manifesto*, a ridiculous quest given the limited concern expressed by some women for the alleged rape of Ms. Bobbitt, mixed with horror at her retributive method (West and Zimmerman 135–36; West and Fenstermaker 9, 20–21; Masters 170; Margolick; Deem 513; Udovitch).

Two law cases saw the parties acquitted. Ms. Bobbitt's lawyers argued that her life was worth more than his penis. Mr. Bobbitt sought financial assistance from the sale of T-shirts emblazoned with "A Cut Heard around the World," "Love Hurts," and "Severed Part," and Howard Stern held a New Year's Eve telethon on his behalf. JWB informed viewers of *Jenny Jones* (21 December 1993) that Lorena "tried to destroy me in the worst way possible." (The program showed a video of their wedding, holding on a frame of her cutting the cake.) Elsewhere, Lorena's supporters mimicked the motion of scissors with their hands for news cameras. Camille Paglia pronounced the act to be "kind of like the Boston Tea Part." The Jurassic Penis company offered a "Penis Protection Plan," complete with full cloning service. Details were faxed across Manhattan to offices of all kinds in

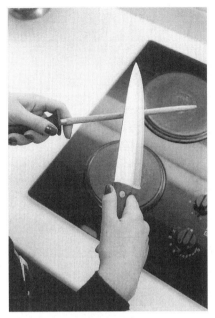

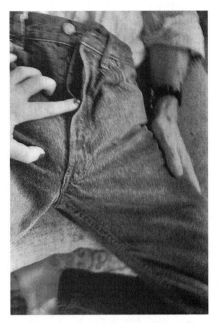

Photo courtesy Kristine Larsen.
Copyright 1993 Kristine Larsen.

Photo courtesy Kristine Larsen.
Copyright 1993 Kristine Larsen.

early 1994. *Martha Stuart's Better than You at Entertaining*—a parody of
the publications of Martha Stewart, albeit published by HarperPerennial—
included circumcision menus: how to keep knives and palates equally sharp.
It was impossible to deny the story or cordon it off from humor. The re-
sultant porn film was a jokey reenactment of domestic and hospital experiences from that historic summer's night. *John Wayne Bobbitt Uncut* introduced the genre of "hardcore docudrama." It won several awards at the
1995 Adult Video News Awards, including highest number of rentals. The
protagonist's acceptance speech referred to "my battle wound." Anxiety
over his new size was as great as the prospect of renewed multiple functions. John Wayne ended the year with a heavily publicized operation by a
urologist to extend the length of his penis by three inches and the width by
one (Paglia quoted in Masters 170; Connor and Downey 24–29; Gleiberman; Faludi 82–83). Daniel Dervin looked to psychoanalysis for help in
understanding these events. But Freudianism's hermeneutic commitment to
"wishes rather than deeds . . . the absences within presences" left it with
*nothing* to offer on the penis as a material, or rather dematerialized, entity
(253). Similarly, we need to query assumptions that the penis is crucial for
"masculine identity," given ethnographic research on men who have had a
testicle removed because of cancer and appear to deal very effectively with
all the anxieties projected by theorists (Gordon).

Jurassic Penis ad. Anonymous.

The Bobbitt crisis provides the ethnomethodological equivalent of a
sex change, "a 'naturally occurring' breach experiment," when someone
"who faces the problem of becoming competent in sexual conduct" is confronted by contradictions that bring to light what is otherwise unexamined
everyday conduct. The ethnomethodological notion of accountability was
developed to explain occasions when practices refer to themselves *as* practices. This is often done inadvertently, when actions draw attention to their
generic preconditions and features but pass these off as natural. The public

penis is always already accountable in this sense. It stands out, crying for recognition as a problem, as something to be attended to (McHoul 111).

## Penisthetics

> *Sex in erection is the image of man revolted against God. The arrogance of sex is the punishment and consequence of the arrogance of man. His uncontrolled sex is exactly the same as what he himself has been toward God—a rebel.*
> :: Foucault in Foucault and Sennett 14

> *"He looks so silly in his tennis clothes"—Anne*
> :: *Strangers on a Train*, Alfred Hitchcock, 1951

As we have seen, Freudianism is not alone in its inability to specify the object. Postmodern fiction joins the throng. The Dog Woman in Jeanette Winterson's *Sexing the Cherry* encounters a man who shows her "a thing much like a pea-pod." "Touch it and it will grow," he says. The result reminds her of a cucumber. He invites her to put it in her mouth "as you would a delicious thing to eat." She follows instructions, "swallowing it up entirely and biting it off with a snap" (40–41). Here the problem lies not in definition but in mixed metaphors. Criminology has its own difficulties in this area. Maureen in Elmore Leonard's *City Primeval* has spent eight years in the Detroit police department's sex crimes unit, dealing with how to spot an "infantile penis" in a suspects' parade. One hundred fifty-seven sets of pants were dropped, but no common agreement ever emerged on what amounted to penile infantalism (255–56). Boyish multimillionaire Robbie Daniels from Leonard's *Split Images* is wary of category mistakes about "big schlongs" (238), and Don DeLillo's football argot from *End Zone* comprises the following:

> "You're a nipple-prick, thirty-five. You're an eensie-weensie. You got your dong from a cereal box."
> "He's barely got a dong," Jim Deering said.
> "Nipple-prick. Nipple-prick."
> "Eensie, eensie, eensie." (136)

Deborah Cameron's experiments with U.S. college students on synonyms for the penis show that even knowing what it is doesn't rein in the desire to renominate. A group of female students had 75 names for it, the males 110 (271). It's all a bit of a laugh, in an anxious way. To quote Foss, "The *law of six inches* functions like some impossible threshold in the imagination, a 'minimum wage' subject to either regret or endless inflation" (8). On the Internet discussion group alt.tasteless.penis, pmedic@cybernetics.net tells us that, as of 8 August 1995, "most guys I have met who said they were 8 inches were most likely reading the ruler backwards or using the centi-meter side."

An element of parody is clearly present here, but this is also a move-ment away from discovering conscious and unconscious fears about propor-tions and onto strict calculations of difference. Britain's Obscene Publica-tions Squad defines as erect—and hence actionable—a textual penis at an angle to its owner of more than thirty degrees (M. Simpson 147). John Davidson's *Cleo* article "Does Penis Size Really Matter? One Guy Gets Honest" comes with a measuring apparatus to determine whether a man's penis is "SMALL" (1–10 cm), "AVERAGE" (11–20 cm), "IMPRESSIVE" (21–25 cm), or "OUCH" (26 cm and counting) (69). In January 1996, the maga-zine's TV campaign comparing penis sizes was criticized by the Australian Advertising Standards Council. These developments replicate lines of force traditionally drawn over women's bodies specifying "correct" mea-surements of breast, waist, and hip and "healthy" sexual response. Recent analyses of the North American labor market suggest that wage discrimi-nation based on beauty is as prevalent among men as it is among women (Hamermesh and Biddle). Men are the target of a disciplinary gaze, long experienced by others, that is excruciatingly precise in its calculations and comparisons.

The penis also invokes aesthetic anxiety. Pasi Falk dates the European investiture of penile cultural objects with evil iconic power to sixteenth-century attempts by Roman Catholics to counteract Protestantism by play-ing up the beatific nature of "good objects" and the turpitudinous nature of "bad" ones. The erotic in art is not mass-produced at this time, so there is no opposition between sex and purity. Manners, not texts, are the site of obscenity until the end of the seventeenth century. In the eighteenth cen-tury, Kant bifurcates the sublime and the beautiful through the exclusion of a third, less worthy term—the sensual—to describe bodily experiences that lack an apparatus of commentary (Falk 190–93).

From the eighteenth century, sex in Europe becomes "a symbiotic mechanism in the semantics of love," to borrow Niklas Luhmann's phrase. Fucking is domesticated and made isomorphic with intimacy, which pro-duces a new shyness and an ethic of communicative indirectness. Sex is theorized by Christians as simultaneously disgusting, tender, excessive, and necessary, and theorized by governments as simultaneously biological, psychological, given, and alterable (111–13). The late nineteenth century brings an end to veneration of *reliqua* from Jesus' foreskin, as sex-related bodily parts are redefined and privatized. At once sacred and demeaning, representing the genitals in search of pleasure raises the prospect of transcendence. The self may be objectified and surpassed by spectacular auto-secularization. This worries public and religious government. After the Great War, the notion of a second Fall enters the debate about pornography, as violence and maleness are intertwined in public discourse as problems: what was once noble is demeaned, and sacrifice is reconfigured as a moral failing on a continuum with antisocial sexual practices and texts. Consider Carolyn Dean's discussion of fin de siècle French discourses of virility. The meaning of tumescence alters over time, from a womanly incapacity for self-control to the manly representation of moral order. This oscillation of the penis between power and weakness is ongoing—public virtue is never in a stable relationship to virility. Rather, it is determined by a *dispositif* of textual criticism, able to endorse materials as uplifting or deride them as obscene (Wallerstein 10; Peckham 288, 298; C. Dean "Great" 61–62 and "Pornography" 74, 80, 84).

Although I suggested earlier that the penis is a weighty sign, its dimensions and effects are hard to tie up and hard to tie down. Male genitals embody holy beauty in certain aesthetic discourses dating from the nineteenth century. But problems arise when they are represented for the purposes of sexual excitation, because this necessitates a disproportionate, wandering penis that goes out of whack and sets the rest of its body askew. In short, such a penis becomes ugly. But more than this, the visible, material practice of libido, a sign of Adam's disobedience, renders isomorphic the relationship of the owner-operator to his penis and to the divine. So, in his redemptive use of aesthetics as a philosophical broker between the kinesis of desire and the ascesis of faith, Joyce's Stephen Dedalus employs a notion of appreciation based on a definite, knowable form to art and its rhythmic structure, a spirituality that transcends the limitations of somatic response or pleasure (Falk 196; Joyce 212–13). Govern yourself and you may govern others. Hence anxiety over the First Penis during Bill Clinton's presidency.

This duality continues. The *David* by Michelangelo, something of an oddity for its own time, has been both valorized as high art and derided as obscene well into the twentieth century, prints of it causing trouble for vice squads in the United States and Australia. Hollywood censors vetoed the original poster for *Six Degrees of Separation* (Fred Schepisi, 1993) because it showed a naked Adam from a detail on the ceiling of the Sistine Chapel. In 1985, a swimming-pool mural at a London nursing home was whitewashed by administrators to hide full frontal male nudity, leading Senior Registered Nurse Sian Hillier to ask whether this meant "young and innocent nurses" would be given blindfolds when "handling the unmentionable object" (Svetkey 31; Hillier quoted in Easthope *What* 16). You can touch, but you must not look.

When women appropriate the penis, definitions become problematic. The dildo is so commonly associated with lesbians they almost own the object, whereas "chicks with dicks" hermaphrodites masturbate their flaccid penises and display their breast implants to audiences keen to be penetrated by women, defying categories by stretching them. The Australian state-supported film *Sacred Sex* (Cynthia Connop, 1992) caused a great ruckus, notably the moment when Les Nichols, Annie Sprinkle's "lesbian-separatist-turned-macho transsexual" partner, inserts a plastic rod into his skin to manifest an erect penis. Sprinkle has also exhibited Les on Coney Island, highlighting the commodified and phallic nature of much commercial sex while problematizing gender binaries (Straayer *Deviant* 254–55, 242–44, and "Seduction" 162–63).

▶

## ET, Again

> The plaintiff, a well known Rugby League footballer, was shown in a photograph published in the defendant's magazine with two other members of the Australian Kangaroo team, naked under the showers. The photograph is capable of being interpreted as showing the plaintiff's genitals. Upon a separate trial as to the capacity of the matter complained of to convey certain imputations, it was also held that an imputation in the following terms:
>
> > "The plaintiff is a person whose genitals have been exposed to the readers of the defendant's magazine 'HQ', a publication with a widespread readership."
>
> was capable of defaming the plaintiff.
>
> ::   *Ettingshausen v. Australian Consolidated Press Ltd*

In evidence before the court, Ettingshausen acknowledged he had promoted himself as a sex symbol in calendar stills, posters, a TV commercial for jeans where he appeared without a shirt on, pulling up the zipper of his denims, and a posed photograph in pajamas—all said to have been designed to interest straight women. These appearances were, he thought, tasteful, but the *HQ* photo was "a very offensive shot and a pornographic shot." The difference between his promotional strategy and the offending image lay in a combination of his feelings about his penis and the genre of publishing in which it was reproduced. He found the picture affronting and pornographic "because it shows my genitals which I believe to be a very personal part of my body which I do not want to be shown to anybody" (quoted in Hickie "Nudity"). The body could not be known at ease, in an unposed, unanalyzed, unprofessional condition for "anybody" to see. As Foss notes in his reading of Robert Mapplethorpe's "Man in Polyester Suit" photograph, being shot "on the slack" is risky, signifying as it does a lack of strength in this most "downcast and reticent" of nude registers (8).

When Edouard Manet's *Olympia* and *Déjeuner sur l'herbe* were first exhibited, it was as much their air of languorous ease and unconcern as the depiction of nudity that enraged critics. The body at rest does not accumulate strength and productivity. The soaping ET, engaged in jovial self-repair and maintenance, is blissfully unaware of his duty of control. This issue connects to Kenneth Clark's distinction between nakedness and nudity. The naked form implies being "deprived of our clothes," a "huddled and defenseless body." The nude, by contrast, looks "balanced, prosperous, and confident." Where the photographed naked form encourages an invigilating gaze, reconnoitering imperfections in the specific human subject in focus, its nude sibling invites contemplation of the space between art and life, as the photographer seeks to reproduce the painterly nude. It is acceptable to engage an "erotic feeling" in the spectator under such circumstances, provided this is integrated with a philosophical worldview (Heins 106; K. Clark 3, 6–9).

The "anybody" in question who might have looked at ET's likeness was a particular kind of reader. Ettingshausen had been dogged since the magazine appeared by taunts from colleagues when posing for team pictures ("Hang your cock out, ET" and "Make sure you don't get ET's cock in the photograph" were representative statements) and received repeated requests from women to autograph the picture. These feelings extended to and were informed by the global standing of the penis, but that status again depended on questions of reproduction and reception. When asked if the simple sight of male genitals was offensive, Ettingshausen replied, "Not in an encyclopedia but in a book such as this, yes." But one of his teammates, Ian Roberts, has since come out, posing naked for a gay arts magazine and writing a fitness column for *OutRage*. Roberts now has a sponsorship deal with a major telecommunications firm that is targeting gay customers. And in 1995, the U.S. Supreme Court actually ruled that people in sports changing rooms have a diminished right to privacy because of the expectation of being observed undressed—a liminal space in the eyes of the law (Ettingshausen quoted in Hickie "Nudity," O'Neill, and Harari "Crotch"; O'Shea; Flannery 8).

There is the sense here that the penis can be a legitimate object of disembodied study, where it is a fetishized sign standing for a generic object without any specific human identification. Conversely, when it appears outside the domain of learning, as an item of personalized popular information about a concrete individual, the reader alters from a disinterested inquirer after knowledge into a gossipy subject of camp. This interpretation is enhanced through testimony given in the case by Wayne Pearce, a former international player: "I wouldn't want my pecker in the paper." Pearce is a nondrinking, nonsmoking, ever-smiling advertisement for beatitudinous living. He advised the court he had been unable to buy the magazine soon after it appeared because sales had been so rapid, but had seen the photograph when a female work colleague was handing it around. His reaction was profound: "I was just repulsed by it. I didn't want to read the article at all . . . and I still haven't read it." Again, the problem was not the sight of men's genitals in the shower, but their reproduction. Ettingshausen's wife, Monique, also gave evidence in support, noting that he didn't "do nude photos," had been anxious since the publication of this one, and was experiencing difficulty concentrating on the job. Robert Abbott, the Australian Rugby League's general manager, described Ettingshausen as "the epitome of what was good and healthy," somebody who "always portrayed an excellent standard of living and decency." At issue, then, is women observing men being ethically indolent (M. Ettingshausen quoted in Hickie "Rugby"; Abbott quoted in Thorp).

The pursuit of the popular by the law is necessitated by unruly citizens who may fail to comport themselves properly. Prurience seems to have been central to Ettingshausen's discomfort, as per Dedalus. This concern is about the ability of a formation of readers to balance their bodily responses to a text with aesthetic interpretation at a higher plane. Hence movements in the government of pornography toward specifying the occasion of reading and the practices and identities of readers, away from the suggestion that texts can be inherently obscene: pornographic status is daguerrotropic. Circulation develops as a test of pornography with the spread of print culture and its ability to cross boundaries of high and low aesthetics. This centers readers as citizens. Their unruly readers' activities must be evaluated and reordered in pursuit of obedience. Shona Martyn's defense in court stressed that the readership of *HQ* was "educated, intelligent women . . . interested in the world." Obscenity is determined by its readers, whose position in a social world of unevenly distributed cultural competence determines the risk and harm a text can produce. Controversy in China over Jia Pingwa's bestselling sex-and-scandal novel *The Abandoned Capital* in 1993–94 arose in part over the notion that a high-culture writer was producing *ditan wenxue*, "literature for the sidewalk stalls." The book was finally banned

# ET judge supports defamation payout

FAMILY man . . . rugby league superstar Andrew Ettingshausen with wife Monique and daughter Tiarne. He was this week awarded $350,000 compensation for a nude photo. Text and photo courtesy *The Courier-Mail*, Brisbane, Australia, February 13, 1993.

because it could harm the partially formed subjectivities of adolescents (Hunter et al. 211, 146, 138–39; Martyn quoted in Hickie "Rugby"; Jianying 238–40, 264). Fitness to govern the body is a crucial test here, for readers and writers; can they be relied upon to rule themselves?

Wayne Pearce's own team, Balmain, was taken to court for refusing dressing-room access to Jacqueline Magnay, a reporter with the *Sydney Morning Herald*. No postmatch interviews by women with players or officials were permitted in that area (not a policy held by other clubs in the competition), because Balmain men require particular privacy. This issue of equal access to the changing shed has legal precedent dating from the 1977 World Series, after women baseball reporters were banned from the locker rooms. Despite victories in case after case, many obstacles are still erected to women's free passage in such places, including sexist remarks and intimidating behavior by players and officials. Their "invasion" has produced specific anxieties about women and the penis. Lisa Olson of the *Boston Herald* was subjected to intense abuse by members of the New England Patriots after a 1990 football game. One man thrust his penis out and invited her to "take a bite." Challenged over their conduct, the players countered that she was "a looker," a woman who gazed at their genitals. This epithet is frequently spoken by men as they brush their wedding-tackles against women reporters (Sider; Fuller; Disch and Kane 278–80, 289).

Again and again, the lines of force dividing civility from its other are tested and redefined under these circumstances. The characteristically uneasy interdependence of journalism and professional sport is nowhere better traced than here. Every reporter needs to notice and every player needs to be the object of such notice. But no one is clear about what should be noticed, how far the inspectorial gaze should go, or whose it should be, given that women make up about a fifth of the readers of general sports magazines (Guttmann 130–31). Heartaches begin in the male changing sheds because the postmatch male letdown is a cathartic, liminal event, a space for body contact to be transcended. Perhaps it is the fear of a female gaze at shadows—or women's gaze at men gazing into that darkness—that so exercises men's minds. The shower scene from *HQ* is far from the tautness of ET in his pinup mode.

ET's gray areas are literal as well as metaphorical. ACP argued that the source of Ettingshausen's shame amounted to "a very, very indistinct collection of shadows . . . no more than in the groin area." Tom Hughes countered by telling the jurors this was "an insult to your intelligence." The penis was definitely in the text: "There is some suggestion that it's a shadow. I bet it's the only shadow you've ever seen that is lighter than the surrounding area." And legal precedent exists for a preoccupation with pubic hair as a Peircian index of a darker, tubular presence. When D. H. Lawrence's pictures caused great anxiety in Britain, police tests of obscenity included a search for hair (ACP quoted in Hickie "ET"; Hughes quoted in O'Neill; Hunter et al. 79, 141).

ACP claimed that even if the jury thought there was "the suggestion of a penis," Ettingshausen's use of his body as a sex object to advance his career as a model problematized any suggestion of defamation and the award of damages. (Perhaps. ET certainly modeled something for Tommy Raudonikis, an ex-player who offered after the hearing to "drop my ol' fella out anytime anywhere for that kind of money.") We are returned to the question of men's bodies under surveillance and the etymology that connects pornography with prostitution. The appeals court that set aside ET's payout remarked, "Common experience demonstrates that male nudity is now much more frequently seen." But by whom? Waters refers to the importance of the occasion of viewing and the nature of the audience in his discussion of the legal tribulations of *Pink Flamingos* (1972). Its blow-job sequence looks very different to late-night cult fans from the way it looks to midmorning jurors who have nothing in common with one another and have turned up unwillingly, expecting to try a burglary or whatever. When Waters showed the film to a prison class of convicted murderers he was teaching, the moment when Divine eats feces ushered African Americans out of the room, but no white people; audiences have culturally and historically variant interpretative codes (court quoted in Falvey; Waters "Out" 12–13).

▶ ────────────────────────────────────

## Conclusion: Reattaching Man and Penis

> *The Kennedy family . . . from what I've read, that they're very smart, but when they get horny their penises take over.*
> :: potential juror in Kennedy Smith rape trial during nationally televised voir dire, 1991

> Peggy Lee syndrome *The feelings of disappointment often reported by teenage girls in their first sexual intercourse (qv) when it is not as thrilling as expected. The term was derived by sexologist David Weis from Peggy Lee's popular song "Is That All There Is?"*
> :: Francoeur 472

R. W. Connell, perhaps the foremost academic writer on masculinity, has a *longue durée* approach to men that combines Marxist theories of imperialism with individual stories to map the psychic politics of men, articulating the spread of North Atlantic commercial republics into the lives and social systems of the rest of the world with anthropological *Annalesisme*. The result tends to make Western European and North American white male sexuality isomorphic with power: male body equals global organizational design and desire orchestrated to oppress women, albeit countered by the liberal promises of modernity. Those promises displaced highly formalized, ritualistic performances of femininity and masculinity that had endured and progressed within different formations around the world, permitting a rationalization of imperialism and neocolonialism (185–99). As a piece of very totalizing social theory that also cares about empirics, Connell's account is exemplary. But can it allow for a time when a man is not *being* a man, when his activities might be understood in utterly different ways, rather than being reduced to logics of sexual urge and agent? What of the microphysics of practice, which eludes overarching explanations and is as discontinuous, conflictual, and mundane as it is interconnected, functional, and dominant?

As Wil Coleman has indicated, two principal discourses interrogate masculinity. The first presents a dramaturgical view: men act their gender in public performances through practices that together amount to a role. By contrast, the second discourse treats its object as a hidden truth to be understood through symptomatic readings. In each case, various practices cataloged as "masculine" could be ascribed to other performances: teaching, voting, policing, or cooking. Masculinity is an occasioned activity, not a system (193, 195). It appears at such moments as the law case concerning Andrew Ettingshausen's body or in acts of sexual violence, when it is an analytic or aggressive category. But these occasions do not necessarily explain each other, or processes going on elsewhere. They may be local and specific to those sites, not necessarily an overall movement of masculinity.

When men are judged as such, and present themselves in anticipation of such processes, masculinity "takes place." Rather than looking behind masculine representations of the body as a phallic stand-in, we can follow ethnomethodology's lead and view gender as an occasioned, multiperspectival matter. Like film (and, more important, watching film), it emerges from social situations. In McHoul's hands, ethnomethodology demonstrates that the apparently normal is in fact a contingently achieved series of actions. Their contingency becomes inspectable when a penis is detached or willfully represented. New York performance artist Diane Torr's "Drag King" workshop for women keen to adopt male forms of bodily comportment as a means of controlling space urges participants to come with a "fake penis (the most convincing is a piece of tubular bandage, stuffed with cotton wool and sewn at either end—don't make it too large!!)." Masculinity is present; men are not.

The man simply "is" most of the time; masculinity emerges when it is called up (Coleman instances an occasion when a man is asked to carry a bag conventionally coded as feminine and becomes aware of sexual difference). Such moments are not secretions of what is otherwise denied: there are often no things to deny and nothing beneath the surface. If there are, they may not be part of a broader, coherent problematic, because too many other possible contexts must be accounted for (bell ringing, color, age, newsprint readership, gardening appliance purchase, or criminal activity) to encompass the diverse practices of all men all the time under this handily tidy sobriquet. Its very tidiness leads down one of two paths: either men constantly monitor their performance of masculinity, ensuring a seamless weave with no grammatical mistakes and specific semantic and syntactical shifts that underscore their gender, or they are constituted unconsciously and collectively by a mass ideology that can be uncovered only through the heroics of theorists. Rather than these remorseless antinomies, we would do better to aim the study of gender in the direction of explicit, knowable—and hence realistically contestable—occasions of maleness (Coleman 197–98).

In January 1997, ten male street sweepers from Tabasco took off their clothes in front of the Mexican Congress in protest over working conditions. Their grievances had begun in 1995 after they were fired for disobeying instructions to clean the houses of certain public officials. Here was an abject moment: powerless working people mobilizing their "shame" to shame authorities. Only one daily paper had the *cojones* to print photos of their dicks (Kobré). Such occasions can be understood through a variety of theoretical approaches and analytic techniques, bringing together the spheres of medicine, law, text, society, and economy. Treating, policing, aestheticizing, behaving, and spending are interlocked as never before in a lattice of technologies of truth. When Callinan questioned ET's complaint because the player-model-junior development officer had posed in sexually suggestive ways for women's magazines, he interpreted the male body as a unified subject that "deliberately, overtly exploited himself as a sex symbol." When Hughes responded, he found a significant distinction between "unoffensive, non-pornographic photographs that emphasise a person's sexual attributes" and "this wretched photograph" (quoted in Clifton). The threat of tumescence disfiguring the proportions of male beauty opens up the prospect of an organ out of control. This is its limitation for governance, and its possibility for cultural politics. As when Abe Sada cuts off her lover's penis "because of love" and wears it "next to her body" during *In the Realm of the Senses* (Oshima 285), something far more interesting and multifaceted than a repression narrative is engaged: the law, the image, and gendered power are brought forward.

Let us consider Maguire's typology of the sporting body again, redesignating its categories. The disciplined penis is trained to be obedient, to transcend but also operate alongside biology to be under control in a satisfactorily self-policed body as per Dedalus's ascesis and today's penile prostheses. Hence the concerns evident when, as in the case of ET, the owner of the penis is at ease and not in control or, as per Oshima or Bobbitt, loses it. The mirroring penis is a desirable icon, used directly in pornographic cinema to represent and produce excitement, and synecdochically through its commodification into advertising. The dominating penis is a physical sign and technique exerting force over others, especially women, in rape scenes. And the communicative penis stands for a combination of the aesthetic and the sublime in complex relations of size, race, and sexual activity.

The contexts for all of these organs are quite different, as are their recipient designs. Commercial and historical shifts in the protocols of producing and viewing heed Félix Guattari's call to "destroy notions which are far too inclusive, like woman, homosexual. . . . When they're reduced to black-white, male-female categories, it's because there's an ulterior motive, a binary-reductionist operation to subjugate them" (86–87). This is not to suggest transcendence through the discovery of an authentic self; as I seek to demonstrate in *The Well-Tempered Self*, that search is an unending one, given the power of ethical incompleteness. Rather, it is to call for an engagement with the sometimes murky, sometimes clear, often unworthy, and frequently insignificant historicism of man and his penis, their thick and thin past, in a practical encounter with occasions of masculinity. The socioeconomic shifts impelling the long, slow move that makes the male body the object of routine public ocular dissection also increase the options for toying with its symbolism in a very conscious, highly unimaginary series of material encounters. Sixty years after Crawford Burton's steeplechase got out of hand, Camel's notorious "Smooth Character" campaign features anthropomorphized, phallicized camels who play in the "Hard Pack" blues band, part of the company's attempt to win back male smokers from Marlboro (Savan 103–6). Dicks sell.

# [ 4 ] *How Do You Turn Indooroopilly into Africa? Mission: Impossible, Second World Television, and the New International Division of Cultural Labor*

*Iranian director Reza Badiyi vividly remembers the impact Mission had back home. "It was the number-one show in Iran," he says. "On the nights that my shows ran, people shut down and went home to see it. They called me Mister Mission: Impossible. I became so famous that the government sent me first-class tickets for my family and the baby-sitter and the dog to go to Iran. The National Guard came to the airport, and there were maybe five hundred there at one in the morning. When the jet arrived they played the Mission: Impossible music out of tune. It was fantastic. The people regarded it as much more than just a television show."*
:: P. White 428

*ABC, the network that has traditionally been in the avant-garde of video derrieregardism, has jumped on the bandwagon with a remake of no less an icon of "classic" prime-time mediocrity than Mission: Impossible.*
:: Marc 47

*Assholes Drive Imports.*
:: graffito in *Roger & Me*, Michael Moore, 1989

The anecdote that began chapter 2, about Olivia Newton-John imitating "authentic" U.S. country music, threatening its indigenous practitioners into establishing a national cultural police force, and then being roped in herself by reggae-rap, has resonances in the international division of cultural labor and the remaking of *Mission: Impossible (M:I)* by U.S. money, on Australian—initially Queensland—shores, with European, North American, Caribbean, and African "locations," fifteen years after its first life on American network TV. The state of Queensland was ultimately malleable in the hands of the U.S. Paramount company and Australia's Village Road-show Corporation (subsequently a joint owner of the Warner Bros. Movie World theme park and studios on the Gold Coast). Australia bought back the farm and called it a skyscraper.

"Buying back the farm" calls up anxieties about foreign ownership, balance of payments, and cultural imperialism, a rhetoric about natural resources/surplus value extracted and human resources polluted by "for-eigners": the seizure of irreplaceable physical goods matched by an equally reprehensible dumping of cultural ones. The United States provides the highest proportion of overseas investment in Australia (A$46 billion in 1992), with a balance-of-payments surplus of two to one—its second largest in bilateral trade. All this in an era (typical across the past seven decades) when the United States has dominated Australian cinema and video: 1992 saw 60 percent of all film releases coming from North America, and 85 percent of video rentals. As a program manager for the Seven network put it: "Sydney is regarded as the 51st state" (Bell and Bell vii-ix; Molloy and Burgan 3, 5; manager quoted in Phillips 86).

Signs of an apparent reversal to this trend in the late 1980s were most welcome, with Australian investment in the United States reaching two-thirds reciprocity. Christopher Skase and Frank Lowy, entrepreneurs who had just entered Australian TV ownership, were looking to buy into Holly-wood, and Skase's company had produced *Lonesome Dove*. Yahoo Serious and Paul Hogan were authorized as non-foreign-language filmmakers in the United States and Rupert Murdoch was on a media rampage. For a moment, it seemed as if the deaths of Phar Lap (a 1930s Australian race horse whose demise was supposedly contrived by American interests) and Les D'Arcy (a boxer who died on a World War I U.S. surgeon's table) were revenged and more. Pauline Kael might even have to rethink her prepared-ness to watch Australian films only "while I'm fixing vegetables" (quoted in Hamilton and Mathews 28). Foreign ownership dilemmas were to be overturned and the flow of cultural codes reversed (or at least partially rerouted). But this *recto-verso* triumph led a short life. Skase went bank-rupt and left for Spain, Lowy returned to real estate and shopping malls, Serious dropped from international view, and Hogan could not repeat his successes. In the 1995 "Down Under" episode of *The Simpsons*, a U.S. State Department representative briefs the family on bilateral relations: "As I'm sure you remember, in the late 1980s the U.S. experienced a short-lived infatuation with Australian culture [this is accompanied by a cartoon slide of Crocodile Dundee]. For some bizarre reason, the Aussies thought this would be a permanent thing. Of course it wasn't [slide of a boarded-up film theater with 'Yahoo Serious Festival' on the decrepit building]." By the

1990s, the one lasting intervention was that the internationally demonized Murdoch became an American citizen, a citizen who pursued the popular for himself. But the moment when Australia seemed to be reversing the balance of textual trade may have implications for the future. In 1994, Murdoch announced that Fox would build a film and television studio in Sydney—at low cost thanks to tax incentives and other state aid—and Kerry Packer (owner of Australia's Channel Nine TV network and *HQ* magazine, encountered in chapter 3) bought the Regency Enterprises production company (Groves "Pix" 46 and "Aussie" 45; C. Ryan). Examining the micropolitics of one program may help us understand the implications for cultural citizenship of contemporary global television.

In 1988, Paramount faced a Hollywood scriptwriters strike that led to a chronic shortfall in new programs at the same time Village Roadshow, which planned to build a studio near the Gold Coast, lost its joint venture partner, Dino de Laurentiis. Paramount responded by moving offshore, Village Roadshow by refinancing its investment. The 150-day strike by the Writers Guild of America over creative and residual rights payments cast attention toward Australia, where the A$5,000 cost of a TV script compared favorably with the U.S. figure of A$21,000. Paramount brought back *M:I*, a reprise it had contemplated intermittently over almost a decade, as 1989 became Hollywood's "summer of the sequels." Big budgets were available only for established formulas, an attempt to minimize exposure, while on TV, returns to *Columbo* and *Leave It to Beaver* promised a ready familiarity among the audience and minimal development costs. Four old *M:I* scripts were recycled and new ones written after the industrial action concluded. The idea originated at NBC, which called it the "American Revival"; as ABC said of the plan to remake *Mission* stories, "Why tamper with success?"; *M:I* offered "a built-in baby boomer audience" and the opportunity to avoid California unions (B. Lewis; "Moviemakers"; Corliss 68–69; Sharkey 40; "Hi"; McGillick; Hay; P. White 433; "ABC"; "New"; Chadwick). In Australia, dreams of a new Hollywood south of Brisbane were announced. *Mission: Impossible*, which Australians once saw in black and white, with tasks assigned via audiotapes that would shortly self-destruct, was now shot locally and in color, with videodiscs readable only after confirmation of Jim Phelps's thumb print.

But although southeast Queensland became a temporary production home for the series, it was never *Mission*'s significatory home. The physical location was subsumed or negated by edited-in footage of other cities, American accents and place names, and the very cultural register of memory and rhetoric surrounding the series. The Queensland Film Development Office advertised the state to prospective producers like this: "The produc-

Television still. In the revival, Phelps received his orders on self-destructing optical laser disks.

tion company of a recent American primetime television series found a diverse range of 'international locations,' from London to the Greek Islands in Queensland." The first ten episodes were set in nine different countries. As the executive in charge of production, Mike Lake, put it: "We have managed to successfully carry off the illusion, and make each episode LOOK as though the team are actually in the city they are supposed to be in." Seventeen kilometers from the Gold Coast lay London, Zurich, the Bahamas, Turkey, France, the Germanies, Australia itself, Greece, the United States, Africa, Czechoslovakia, and the Himalayas. Matte shots and Australia's multiple climates and settings made a mise en scène more exotic than any back lot. But the strategy failed. After two seasons of fairly poor ratings, usually third in its time slot and sometimes behind its competition on the nascent Fox network, the series was canceled in 1990 (Lake quoted in P. Clark 56; Benson; P. White 436). The Gold Coast studios continue to be used for Hollywood productions, including *The Island of Doctor Moreau* (John Frankenheimer, 1996) and *Mighty Morphin Power Rangers* (Bryan Spicer, 1995).

Television still. *Mission Impossible* returned in 1988 with (left to right) Terry Markwell, Tony Hamilton, Peter Graves, Phil Morris, and Thaao Penghlis.

Two sets of questions drive this chapter. In an era of internationalism and media deregulation, what constitutes local television drama? What, for instance, should Queensland look like in a California/New York TV series to qualify as Australian content in the eyes of policy makers and viewers? For this is not the Queensland epically described by Charles Chauvel in *Sons of Matthew* (1949), comically problematized by Jackie McKimmie in *Australian Daze* (1985), or caricatured in *Goodbye Paradise* (Carl Schultz, 1983), where Ray Barrett, as the Gold Coast's local soak/Phillip Marlowe manqué Michael Stacey, is heard to advise: "I have to warn you that this is Queensland, not California, and I can tell any lies I like." The State of Sunshine has an utterly changeable morphology and appearance. It can *be* California. (Consider the "Hollywood on the Gold Coast" slogan advertising the Warner Bros. theme park: "Enter the Grand Archway and you are there! . . . a place where fantasy is real"; at least the Australian-shot *Young Einstein* [Yahoo Serious, 1989] and *The Sundowners* [Fred Zinnemann, 1960] are featured, as "Blockbuster Attraction" and "Shopping Adventure," respectively.) Should we regard *Mission: Impossible* as metropolitan expropriation or local customization/ironized appropriation by a culture used to importing meanings? How does cultural identity sit with issues of genre, audience, and the postmodern? Second, what are the long-term implications of these developments for cultural imperialism and what I am terming the new international division of cultural labor (NICL)? Is there a trend toward offshore investment by the American screen industries, with major implications for disinvestment at home? Or was this a momentary aberration occasioned by the need to overcome striking workers, with no lesson other than a threat held in reserve, given the propensity of U.S. investors in the fairly undercapitalized screen sector to insist on much quicker returns from ongoing foreign production than in more predictable domains, such as car manufacture?

Put another way, in this chapter I look at the government of TV text, audience, and production as economic and cultural-nationalist questions. If we think back to the origins of governmentality, we find that ecclesiastical conflicts of the Reformation and its successor produced a void of everyday authority, with no clear guide to belonging and behaving. The state emerged to fill this lack. Today, the international cultural economy, particularly its audiovisual segment, is a space of new conduct that lacks norms of reception and management. Global television opens up the nation again to redefinition. The case described here is especially pertinent as a test for other places. Because it has a long-standing mixed system of five national television networks (one like the BBC, three like the U.S. networks, and one multicultural station), Australia is a model for the deregulating environments of Europe in its blend of public service and commercial broadcasting, within a regulatory infrastructure that acknowledges the need for local dramatic and news texts. It is Second World television, importing more than it exports, but actively producing as well, a country with sufficient capital formation and technological reach to put its stamp on audiovisual culture.

▶

## Cultural Imperialism

> *Theorists of cultural imperialism assume that hegemony is prepackaged in Los Angeles, shipped out to the global village, and unwrapped in innocent minds. We wanted to see for ourselves; and thanks to grants from the trustees of the Annenberg Schools and the Hoso Bunka Foundation, we were able to do so.*
> :: Liebes and Katz v

> *Think of the Mexican entertainment market, with its young population and fast-growing middle class, as a teenager out looking for a good time after being cooped up at home for too*

*long. For economically emerging peoples all over the globe,
Hollywood speaks a universal language.*
::    Gubernick and Millman 95

*When Saddam Hussein chose Frank Sinatra's globally
recognized "My Way" as the theme song for his 54th birthday
party, it wasn't as a result of American imperialist pressure.*
::    Eisner 10

In the 1950s, modernity was set up as an actionable condition, to be striven for through the implementation of policies and programs by government and capital in what were variously named "developing countries," "the Third World," and other teleological marks, a complex discourse of industrial, economic, social, communications, and political development. Its founders and husbanders were First World political scientists and economists, mostly associated with American foundations, universities, research institutes, and corporations, or with international organizations. Among the foundational premises were generating nationalism and state sovereignty as habits of thought to protect the "modern individual" from the temptations of Marxism-Leninism. Development necessitated displacing "the particularistic norms" of tradition by a "more universalistic" modernity to create "achievement-oriented" societies (Pye 19). The successful importation of Western media would be critical to this replicant figure, along with elite sectors of society trained as exemplars for a wider populace mired in backward, folkloric forms of thought that lacked trust in national organizations.

The export of modernity ignored the way the life of the modern had been defined in colonial and international experience, by distinguishing the metropole from the periphery, importing ideas, fashions, and people back to the core, and controlling representations of "civilization." The model was also inflected with assumptions from evolutionary thought, not only in its narcissism, but in its search for hidden unanimities to bind humanity in singular directions and forms of development. This enabled owners of the discourse to observe themselves at an earlier stage of maturation, by investigating life in the Southern Hemisphere and policing and coordinating what they found there, in keeping with a drive toward uniformity and optimality of human definition, organization, and achievement (Axtmann 64–65).

The post-World War II proliferation of multinational corporations (MNCs) united First World businesses and governments in a search for cheap labor, new markets, and pliant regimes on the margin of a globe designed to spin as a Northern Hemisphere top. MNCs emerged as significant players in the internationalized production of goods in the 1950s and

1960s, when governmental and academic logics of modernization were on export to the Third World. Today, multinationals tend to invest in industries with high levels of research and development, skill, advertising, and intangibles. Along with the expropriation of surplus value back to the core, there has been a significant diversion of funds away from investment at home. Relocating production has resulted in a domestic crisis in employment and balance of payments. Critics from within fear the process because it costs American jobs despite boosting American profits; critics from without fear mental and economic colonization, mediating their liking for the antichauvinism of globalization with the recognition that certain sovereign states are as strong as—or stronger than—ever (Reeves 24–25, 30; Gilpin 184–89; Markusen 172; Strange "States" 6).

Apart from its unreconstructed narcissism, this discourse disavowed the existing international division of labor and the effect of imperial and commercial powers' annexing states and their labor forces. Implausibly solipsistic, it was criticized from the inside by a locally sensitive acknowledgment of conflicts over wealth, influence, and status, and challenged from the outside by theories of dependent development, underdevelopment, unequal exchange, world-systems history, center-periphery relations, and cultural or media imperialism. Widespread reaction against the all-encompassing racist and self-seeking—or at best patronizing—discourses of modernization has foregrounded the international capitalist media as critical to the formation of public taste in commodities, mass culture, and forms of economic and political organization in the Third World, links by which ruling classes and states in the metropole run the global economy. Examples include the export of U.S. screen products and infrastructure as well as American dominance of international communications technology. The transfer of taste has seemed more profound and widespread than any transfer of the means of communication and distribution. The rhetoric of development through commercialism has overtaken the promotion of a local economy. The stronger the claim to the modern in, particularly, advertising, the weaker the allocation of resources to actual modernization. Emergent ruling classes in the dependent nation benefit by trading off local power against their own dependence on foreign capital and ideology (Molloy and Burgan 68; Fröbel et al.; Reeves 30–35).

In response to these trends, dependency theory became ascendant on the international left throughout the 1970s. It spread from Latin American sources across the globe, finding agreeable surrounds in international cultural organizations and Group of Seventy-Seven alliances. *Dependencia* resonated beyond the Third World to explain dedominionized white settler societies, notably Canada and Australia. But the position has declined politically and intellectually since then. Once adopted by UNESCO, it became vulnerable to that agency's complex frottage: a pluralism that insisted on the relativistic equivalence of all cultures was forever rubbing up against the equation of national identity with cultural forms (Schlesinger *Media* 145). The U.S.-U.K. withdrawal from the organization in the 1980s drew resources away from research and innovation designed to help create a new world order of culture and communication, while the discourse was attacked from the left for its inadequate theorization of capitalism, the postcolonial condition, internal and international class relations, the role of the state, and the mediating power of indigenous culture.

Cultural imperialism was said to lack research on specific issues and to fall short as a theoretical paradigm. Tamar Liebes and Elihu Katz's study of the reception of *Dallas* in Israel, Japan, and the United States "found only very few innocent minds" across these cultural groups. They queried the nature of electronic narrative: Is it understood universally, or is there so much renegotiation that it loses its originary referents? Liebes and Katz disavow cultural imperialism, requiring three absolutes to be established beyond reasonable doubt for *le défi américain* to exist: the text contains information designed to assist the United States overseas, is decoded as encrypted, and works its way into the receiving culture (v, 3–4).

In his history of the state, Michael Mann notes that cultural sovereignty has always been imperiled by capitalism, other than in the brief period between 1880 and 1945, when industries were constructed along national lines. Early capitalism predated the existence of the state, and questions of culture were usually organized by other points of affinity, such as religion or race. Cultural diffusion has always been international, but the velocity and profundity of its processes are ever on the increase. Mann asks, "[Do] Clint Eastwood, Sylvester Stallone, and the 'Dallas' and 'Beverly Hills 90210' casts remain American when speaking Portuguese or German slang?" (119, 132).

Finally, conspiracy motifs about export ignore U.S. elite fear of the popular and its capacity to produce "a progressive atrophy of the creative instinct of the average American" that disables national character through artificial emotion and instant gratification (Commager 420). And the extraordinary puritanism of some cultural protection disavows the liberatory aspects of much U.S. culture, especially as it had been experienced inside, for example, the stifling English class structure. (Reexport back to the United States of music the British had learned from African Americans—and taken credit for—may have helped to free rock from its Elvis-movie-Pat Boone-family deracination. Recall Muddy Waters's remark about Mick Jagger: "He took my music. But he gave me my name.") Most analyses of transplanted culture either concentrate on Hollywood in one market, in isolation from other regions, or take a very totalizing view that is insufficiently alive to specificities. The issue of customization is critical here, as evidenced in the capacity to fuse imported strands of popular culture with indigenous ones (*vide* Nigerian *juju* and Afro-beat), rediscovering and remodeling a heritage via intersections with imported musical genres (Waters quoted in Chambers 69; Reeves 36, 62).

The great talent of international cultural commodities is adaptability. But because culture is about discrimination as well as exchange, it is simultaneously the key to international textual trade *and* one of its limiting factors. Ethics, affect, custom, and other forms of knowledge enable and restrict commodification. General Motors, which own Australia's General Motors Holden, translates its "hot dogs, baseball, apple pie, and Chevrolet" jingle into "meat pies, football, kangaroos, and Holden cars" for the Australian market. This can be read as the paradigmatic nature of the national in an era of global companies, or as a requirement to reference the local in a form obliged to do *something* with cultural-economic meeting grounds. We need to avoid any sense that the transmission of U.S. material is straight out of a U.S. textbook on sender-message-receiver communications theory. Accommodation always already involves transformation by local cultures, and an increasing awareness of the fundamentally heterogeneous and conflictual nature of North American culture itself. As the *Economist*'s 1994 TV survey remarked, perhaps cultural politics is always so localized in its first and last instances that the "electronic bonds" of exported TV are "threadbare" (Jacka "Introduction" 5, 2; Frow "Cultural" 18–20; Schøu 143–45; Heilemann Survey 4).

Armand Mattelart and Michèle Mattelart, formerly prelates of cultural gloom, are now saying cultural imperialism was an enabling alliance of intellectual engagement rather than a sustainable theory. It mobilized people to think through the implications of international textuality at the nexus of "new" nations, their former colonizers, and the United States. It is no surprise that this concentration on unequal exchange initially emphasized directions in flow rather than signs and their reception. But the accusation of cultural imperialism brought local culture to bear against neoclassical economics' heroization of the sovereign consumer. More than that, it exemplified the export of theory itself from the Third World to the First. Revisions to the thesis do not mean that international television trade is a happily settled matter (Mattelart and Mattelart 175–77; McAnany).

Many positive accounts of cultural exchange have dubious political projects. Promises are made of "new economic citizenship," an updated version of ghastly 1970s employee participation. Instead of the old factory-based division of labor, each employee is to match productivity and cost with a specific competitor in another country. Global political economy is devolved to the shop floor, allegedly empowering the labor force in the process. This physiocratic globalization has a running partner known by that rather touching euphemism, the "multidomestic" corporation. Marketing pharmacists prescribe sensitivity to cultural difference as a category of business training. Consider a major IBM study comparing fifty countries. It put Australia close to the United States, and hence attractive in terms of modular approaches to management. On power differentials across society, the two countries ranked forty-first and thirty-eighth, respectively; on individualism, second and first; and sixteenth and fifteenth on masculinity. Nice to know these places are pluralist, free, and quasi-male. Rather than interrogating those categories as if they were helpful or unhelpful, accurate or inaccurate, we can take them as signifying emblems of direction, tools in investment and organizational planning: technologies of truth. These are formative knowledges, neither falsifiable nor ridiculous, but productive of the power to invest, manage, and govern. Similar logics apply to the "anticosmopolitans" and "home plus" business or tourist travelers seeking an argot and a site for work or leisure that can be utilized with minimal but optimal adjustments to their own cultural lives—a guidebook answering the "whether there is a Taco Bell in Mexico City" quandary (Miller and O'Leary 17; Chartrand 153; Hofstede 148; Hannerz 241).

▶ ————————————————————————————————

## Queensland and Difference

> Americans may know that Jaguar cars are now American. But do they know that Burger King or Winchells Donuts are British? Spaniards may know Seat cars are German and Pryca supermarkets French, but not that Texas Homecare stores are British and not American, that half their clothes are Dutch, and that Massimo Duti fashion clothes are not Italian but Spanish, more precisely Catalan.
> :: Mann 132

> Our locations could place you anywhere on earth, or off it. We have crystal clear oceans, palm fringed beaches, mountains, deserts, waterfalls and tropical rainforests, cities both old and new. Everything from Mars to Marrakech. Yet, you still have

*access to expert crews, world class facilities and the largest
studio complex in the southern hemisphere. It's heaven.*

*Making movies in Queensland can save you up to 40% on
production costs, which when combined with our attractive
package, makes the bottom line look simply divine.*

::    Pacific Film and Television Commission

I arrived in Brisbane in January 1988, at the same time as the Hollywood
strike, billeted with a prominent film scholar I had just met. We sat in front
of his ample television set that first night. A local politician was being interviewed on the news about plans for a "Cairns International Film Festival." The idea was that tourists would book to come to North Queensland
assuming "Cairns" was "Cannes." I looked across at my new colleague,
the hermeneut within me ablaze. What would local knowledge make of
this? His face was cast in a half-smile, comparing his response to the familiar with my encounter with the different.

Long before feminist and postcolonial psychoanalysis privileged "difference," people proudly said, "Queensland is different." And when *M:I*
actually came onscreen there, the state seemed to be under siege in ways
that *made* it "different." Out west, seven men were charged with 142 sexual
offenses; up north, a seventeen-year-old was sent to jail in the first witch-
craft case in sixty years; in Brisbane, a former commissioner of police was
arraigned, twenty others were up on ninety-three counts of alleged corrup-
tion, and (in an unrelated move) the lord mayor announced a five-year plan
to eradicate the cane toad (imported from Hawaii in the 1930s in the mistaken belief that it would control native pests). She declared herself chief
toad-buster and undertook to lead the city in a series of toad-eradication
nights (Massey). Why so?

Thea Astley finds that isolation from the political and economic
decision-making center of Australia's southeast has generated a mythical
alterity separating Queensland from the rest of the country. She stresses in-
formal architecture and attire, a slow personal atmosphere engendered by
climate, a sense of separateness exemplified in the U.S.-Australian military
decision to sacrifice points north of "the Brisbane line" during the Second
World War, and the derisory status of "being a cultural joke to Southerners"
(252–53, 261). Moving away from the atmospheric, Denis Murphy problematizes the rhetoric of Queensland's "difference." He stresses similarities
among Australian states: common religious, cultural, and legal backgrounds,
very similar language and accent, and the absence of interstate wars or culturally separate groups delineable by federalism. It is really the direction

and depth of economic development that divides regions: Queensland has a high rural population and an undeveloped manufacturing sector (D. Murphy 78–79, 82–83; McQueen 42). In keeping with an economic base that does not add great value to its resources, this is an import culture. (In the 1890s, for example, it had the lowest percentage of Australian-born citizens and a stage and music milieu dominated by overseas influences [R. Lawson 579, 581].) Former Premier Johannes Bjelke-Petersen may have said, "We are not Australians, we are Queenslanders," but Gillian Whitlock provides a more adequate context for such logic: "The Queensland state of mind is imported, derivative and, like many other things, comes to us from the south" (85–86).

This sense of separateness, disadvantage, and inferiority has specific resonances in the screen industries. A 1988 survey of Queensland film and television workers blamed scarce job opportunities on size and parochialism, leading to a drain of talent to other states. Films made there have been directed almost exclusively by nonlocals. Hence the harnessing of substructural developments noted above into a Hollywood discourse, a means of defining and valorizing Queensland against the place that really matters, the epicenter of entertainment innovation, sidestepping the national in the process. For Brisbane's *Sunday Mail*, the Roadshow studios were "Hollywood on Our Doorstep." The *Australian* newspaper's special feature on the Gold Coast made the point that "major film studios traditionally bring three main ingredients to an area—employment, money, and celebrity," a double move that put local people in touch with fame and then proceeded to define the locals as famous. This resonates with a broader national aesthetic atmosphere identified in Susan Dermody and Elizabeth Jacka's account of Australians as feeling "second best with their own markets and culture, forced to second guess what their authentic indigenous culture should be." For Sylvia Lawson, the country remains "a colony of Hollywood." Joint media ventures have attracted particular obloquy from cultural nationalist critics. They are held responsible for a "mid-Pacific genre in which the flavour of the film is about as distinctive as a McDonald's plastic takeaway" (La Planche; Pavasaris *Queensland* 2; Molloy "Screensland"; Veitch; Dermody and Jacka *Screening Vol. 2* 20; S. Lawson 6; McMahon and Quin 7).

Australian governments adopt contradictory postures on foreign investment. They want foreign exchange, job creation, and access to international markets. But ambivalences are caused by the intersection of such opportunities with nationalism, xenophobia, and the interests of an indigenous bourgeoisie. (Less chauvinism attaches to U.S. and European investment than to Japanese.) When de Laurentiis was choosing between Sydney and the Gold Coast as locations for a studio in 1987, one factor was the success of the then Queensland Film Corporation in patching together an A$7.5 million loan at low interest and then attracting A$55 million via a local share issue. His company collapsed after the stock market crash that year, and the space seemed destined to fail. It was touted as a new Disneyland site and a multifunction polis, but neither plan succeeded. But Village Roadshow-Warner Bros. announced a studio expansion in 1989. The state was ready to assist with an A$5 million secured loan, a construction subsidy that became part of the studios' promotional material. Well might the Queensland Tourist and Travel Corporation refer to the state as a "last frontier," replete with "smiling locals." For Stanley O'Toole, managing director of what later became the studios, Queensland was set to be "LA without the smog" (Pavasaris *Queensland* 16 and "Warner"; D. Stratton 9; Condon; Warner Village Roadshow Studios; Corporation quoted in Whitlock 85; O'Toole quoted in Amad and Hawker 9).

The Warner Village Roadshow Studios have been advertised overseas in terms of soundstages, production offices, dressing rooms, workshops, "reasonable" trade unions, costs, and external locations. The studio, theme park, and water slide traverse two hundred acres, with a further two hundred available as a back lot. There were more and more television joint ventures and coproductions in Australia from the late 1980s as a result of a specific conjuncture: funds available from tax write-offs for screen investment diminished at the same time overseas satellite and cable television services lost advertising revenue (La Planche; Amad and Hawker 4; Pavasaris "Warner").

The Village Roadshow group is jointly owned by Warner Bros. and Australian and British TV stations. This leads to intense cynicism among both filmmakers and critics. Opportunities for overseas producers are present because of local skill and governmental initiative, but the textual result amounts to foreign content. With the election of a corporatist government in Queensland in 1989, these trends intensified. The Pacific Film and Television Commission was formed to promote the state to international and Australian filmmakers, through a revolving fund of A$10 million for low-interest loans secured against guarantees and presales, rebates on payroll tax, and subsidized crewing costs. The commission claimed that local industry was revitalized by these initiatives, but the value of Australian currency against the American dollar in the early 1990s was equally critical; de Laurentiis's original interest in Australia had emerged at a time when foreign exchange rates rendered local facilities attractive (Jacka and Cunningham 21; D. Stratton 10; Bailey 92; Molloy "Film"; Dermody and Jacka *Screening Vol. 2* 15).

So we have here a willingness to undergo transformation from the outside, to collude in—and even subsidize—the destabilization of one's own allegedly innate and special difference. The only question asked of this comes from cultural nationalism. Partly because it is logocentrically dependent on the object it opposes, such a critique is never quite effective. But another, less conceptual, reason for this ineffectiveness is that Australian culture businesses have successfully appropriated the unifier of "nation" and interpellated consumers as citizens. For all the public policy/culturalist debate about the value of local drama on television, for instance, the sport- and U.S.-sitcom-dominated Channel Nine has been the most popular network in the history of the industry. Nine has said it would not produce any Australian drama without being forced to by successive regulatory authorities, notably the former Australian Broadcasting Tribunal (ABT). Brisbane's QTQ9 is particularly uninterested in the fictive local. A 1986–87 survey of six metropolitan commercial channels found that the station devoted less than 2 percent of airtime to Australian drama, and had halved the amount since 1983–84. That may have put a question mark against Nine in the eyes of the ABT, but it had seven of Brisbane's ten top-rated shows in 1988 (Boylen; A. Davies; Maloney 5, 27; Shoebridge "Networks"). The strategy was to move away from drama of all kinds and toward sports, as the following indicates:

In 1979–80, Australian drama and foreign drama accounted for 3.8 percent and 44.3 percent of programming, respectively; sports accounted for 8.8 percent.

In 1983–84, Australian and foreign drama made up 4.0 percent and 37.8 percent of programming; the figure for sports is not available.

In 1986–87, Australian and foreign drama made up 1.9 percent and 29.4 percent of programming; sports accounted for 14.7 percent (Australian Broadcasting Tribunal *Amounts*).

This also tells us some things about the local audience. Rugby league games between Queensland and New South Wales (featuring Andrew Ettingshausen) are QTQ9's equal highest-rated programs of all time, at 51. By contrast, the ABC drama *Police State*, based on the enormously newsworthy Queensland Royal Commission that had just brought down a government, lost its time slot in Brisbane against *Mission: Impossible* and the Australian nighttime soap *The Flying Doctors*, but won in Sydney and Melbourne, where its meanings might not have been expected to circulate so powerfully (Lynch). O, Queensland.

> *This tape will self-destruct in five seconds.*
> :: Bob Johnson, the taped announcer of *Mission: Impossible*, and
>    a Portland man; Portland, Oregon

> *Cultural Studies is dogged by a mission impossible, that of*
> *developing universal laws of significance around the most*
> *seemingly insignificant and banal phenomena.*
> :: ffytche

> *Mission: Impossible was created before its time. The rightful*
> *time for this series is now. Sponsored by the ludicrous Reagan*
> *administration. Because now they can quite cheerfully submit*
> *the absurd Rightist dialogue of "Your mission, Jim, should you*
> *decide to accept it, is to steal Nicaragua at night when they're*
> *not looking and hide it in Yellowstone National Park so that*
> *we, the U.S. government-by-any-other-name, can service it to*
> *our requirements. Of course, should you or any of your IMF*
> *guerillas be caught pulling off this slick trick, Ronnie will auto-*
> *matically disavow, ignore and permanently be out to lunch."*
> :: Vahimagi

A survey of two thousand viewers found that *M:I* was most popular with teenage boys from affluent backgrounds. Enough people watched it for QTQ9 to offer an almost immediate repeat of the 1989 series. Now, outside Sydney and Melbourne, Australian metropolitan stations have pitifully small amounts of local programming. In this context, the series had a special resonance, at least initially, for Brisbane journalists: "Naturally, a major interest in *Mission Impossible* for people in this part of the world is how many local locations they can spot"; "Where once you made love in the afternoon for hours, now you hold hands and watch *Mission: Impossible*." *TV Scene* magazine irreverently but affectionately referred to protagonist Jim Phelps and his Impossible Mission Force (IMF) as "Jimmy and the Boys," the intertext being an Australian new wave music group of the early 1980s. When production for the second season moved to "Australian Film Studios, Dallas, Australia" in Victoria, the line was, "We've lost it. Alas, no longer will south-east Queensland be on international display" (Kingston; Wicks; Appleton 27; P. Dean 20; Sills; Ronnie Gibson; "Made" 17 September; "Mission" 16 July).

The first series of *M:I* saw more than 150 episodes between 1966 and 1973, when Watergate presided over the decline of all U.S. spy series in a

Television still. Grant uses an ultra-violet visor to help him open a laser-protected safe in "The System."

TV world less taken with covert action. But it lasted much longer than the many spy series on network television through the 1960s. So the remake came from somewhere, from a past plus a place, an ideological locale and a geographic entity: an adventure series that brought together various influences under the sign of covert—but democratically "sanctioned"—enforcement. Overseas sales (sixty-nine countries by its third season) were said to give "many in the Third World . . . a wildly exaggerated impression of the Central Intelligence Agency's capacities." The program always steered clear of live issues such as the war in Vietnam. By the time it began, TV producers were under intense pressure to include black characters in positive roles, as civil rights groups challenged network license applications in the South and pointed to the ratings importance of the black audience. This meant "salt and pepper" combinations in *M:I* as well as *Ironside*, *Star Trek*, *I Spy*, and *Mod Squad*: the affirmative action quota of three white men to one black man and one white woman, a quota present again in the "new" *Mission*. *M:I* was held up by *TV Guide* in the 1960s as a paragon of virtue in its presentation of race. Barney Collier was hailed as one of television's "New Negro figures." This didn't avoid criticism for the token African American's being cast as a "backdoor" technical expert, one-dimensional and emotionless—the modern-day janitor. Collier seemed to have no connection to the ghetto turmoil of the time. He was ingratiating, willing, beautiful, competent, and obedient (Terrace 101; Halliwell 201; Marc 47; MacDonald *Tele-*

*vision* 196; Baughman 102, 111; R. Lewis 36; Mankiewicz and Swerdlow 96; Barnouw 119; de Roche and de Roche 70, 72; MacDonald *Blacks* 241; Hill and Hill 9; Goethals 135; Berger 44; Bogle 292).

The first *Mission* was critically validated for its bizarre plots. It was unusual for American TV drama to favor complex, overlapping, story lines at the expense of characterization. Following each program's twists became a talisman for the cognoscenti. The inversion of heroism, whereby treachery, theft, mendacity, kidnapping, and destruction were qualities of *good* characters, made the series seem intellectually and politically subversive. Once new people had been introduced in a segment, they immediately underwent bewildering transformations that problematized previous information about their psyches, politics, and conduct. Creator Bruce Geller's fantasy was that actants be figures that perform humanness, infinitely plastic and ready to be redisposed in a moment. The series had perhaps twice as many shots and cuts per episode as the norm for its time, to cover movements across the three sites of each text: the IMF planning group, the IMF infiltrators, and the enemy. Only when the series was in decline did the producers endeavor to personalize it, reining in this montage excess (P. White 1, 11, 35; Gardella). By comparison with network television of the time, such modular, depthless quality was positively Godardian in its prolixity and jaded *jouissance*. But it also offered the transferability required of flexible cultural production, obliterating local referents in favor of American supersigns:

> You can go back to "Robin Hood" and "Zorro" for the concept of the hero operating around the law for a good cause. People love that. Look at Oliver North. He thought his hands were tied, but he thought he needed to do what he did. He was his own IMF. Many people admire him for that. (Phil Morris, star of the new *Mission: Impossible,* quoted in Chadwick)

At the same time, its U.S. success said something to Arthur Asa Berger about national identity. He read it as "a classic reflection of the American mind." The lack of deep characterization tropes the absence of history, manifest destiny informs the IMF's self-appointed police role, and new identities adopted each week model the crisply efficient modern organization (36–37, 40–41, 43).

In keeping with this nonhumanism, technology was critical. Because its enemies were so powerful, the IMF required intricacy and secrecy (for which read "covertness"), and the technicist thrill of team gadgets depoliticized the execution of their tasks. But at the very time the famous words were being intoned in each disembodied, taped assignment ("Should you . . . be caught or killed, the Secretary will disavow any knowledge of your actions"), the real-life U.S. assistant secretary of defense, Arthur Sylvester, was supporting covert operations. Series writers were instructed to "avoid names of actual countries as well as mythical Balkan kingdoms by being vague. This is not a concern at early stages of writing: use real names if it's easier" (Dunn 346; instructions quoted in Barnouw 198 n. 19).

Geller's idea for *M:I* was to deploy "the everyman-superman" in "homage to team work and good old Yankee ingenuity." The earliest leader was Dan Briggs. He would choose a team for each task, usually composed of the black technical expert—planned for a white man before the advent of tokenism—a strong man, a female model, and a gentle man of disguise. Briggs was "a PhD in analytical psychology and highly paid as a behavioral analyst." In the first year, he stressed, "assassination is out as a matter of policy." Despite these stereotypical qualities, Geller instilled a knowing self-reflexivity into the series. He became renowned for the remark that "nothing is new except in how it's done," and liked to borrow characters from Hollywood, such as Victor Laszlo from *Casablanca* (Michael Curtiz, 1942) and Tom Dunson from *Red River* (Howard Hawks, 1948). That casual postmodern casuistry had legal consequences when a suit was filed against *Mission* by makers of the short-lived 1959 series *21 Beacon Street*, who claimed that a number of plots and settings from their series had been reused. The case was settled out of court. In addition to this troping unoriginality, there was an engaging postmodern quality in the texts themselves. When Phelps looked through a dossier of potential agents for each task, those rejected were represented mostly by photographs of people working on the series and their spouses, from Geller himself to hairstylists, producers, and writers. This segment modeled the high-technology, action-adventure, continuity drama as a screen genre: disguise, timing, technical deception, and pace (Meyers 122–26; P. White 9, 2, 235, 8–9, 14; Bergery 43).

The diverse critical summaries of *M:I* provide a hint about the need for caution in dismissing it as unidimensional:

> "An elite unit of last resort drawn from a secret army of diversely-skilled men and women who could be called to danger at the drop of a conjuror's hat . . . exists to sustain the democratic functions of non-NATO governments, counter the spread of communism and resurgence of fascism, free friendly scientists and undercover operatives from captivity, thwart the plans of enemy agents, expose traitors, retrieve stolen secrets and prevent wars" (Alsop 17).

> "The Impossible Mission Force is a multi-national organization which operates, independently of governments, against the forces of evil" (*Cinema Papers* no. 71).

> "Some sort of U.S. espionage group, presumably for the CIA," offering assistance to Third World countries, moving to a focus on domestic organized

crime in the light of a public critique of high levels of U.S. foreign aid; then a spy series (Mankiewicz and Swerdlow 96; Meyers 126, 137).

"Special unit of spies and saboteurs . . . trained to attempt the impossible" (Halliwell 201).

Classified by viewers as a science fiction story of a government agency (Rovin).

"Anticommunist," in keeping with the escalation of the Vietnam War (Monaghan 14; Kellner *Television* 50).

CIA-like (MacDonald *Blacks* 122; Brown 310).

"Watergate-type interference" by "freelance agents" (Wicking and Vahimagi 22).

"The 51-minute episodes are as perfectly symmetrical as ever: Jim receives the assignment and comes up with a Rube Goldberg plan to get the job done; one detail of the plan goes wrong during the execution, but the team improvises a solution that manages to work, though just barely; the enemy of democracy and freedom is neutralized by humiliation, death, or both; the credits roll" (Marc 48).

"Probably the most patterned of all television series" (Beatie 46).

"A kind of continuing celebration of careful planning and cool unflappable professionalism" (Rafferty 85).

This list makes it clear that precise definition of what the IM Force stands or works for is beyond us. The American executive government? The citizenry? The police force? Liberalism? Anticommunism? Anticriminality? Does it reflect the end of ideology, a place to search for the transcendentally good and worthy? Early seasons straightforwardly addressed the U.S. government's funding of entrepreneurial saboteurs, a means-ends rationality that went against conventional public wisdom about the state at that time. Complex populist oscillations between interference in others' affairs and withdrawal into the self saw later *M:I* episodes from its first life move away from "bailing out Third World countries" in favor of dealing with "problems at home." As Peter Graves put it in publicity prior to the 1970–71 season, "We'll be cutting out so many stories about South American dictators and Iron Curtain plotters." Twenty-five years later, Brian De Palma's film of the series has removed any credibility apart from personal integrity. East and West are united in greed and deceit. Governments are obsessed with surveillance and their servants with personal gain (P. White 22; Meyers 126; Graves quoted in Lowry; Arroyo 20).

David Buxton describes *Mission* as an exemplar of the 1960s British/American "pop series'—*Danger Man*, *The Avengers*, *The Prisoner*, and *The Man from U.N.C.L.E.* These paeans to the fun of the commodity, the modernity of design, fashion, and knowingness, leavened the performance of quite serious service/duty to the nation with a formula of "programmed action from an assemblage of characters who are ideologically rather than psychologically determined." But as the earlier litany of generic typologies describing *M:I* might indicate, this was also an ideological minimalism, open to a range of interpretations anchored only in the need to preserve everyday Americanness, in the most general sense of the term. The opening tape's threat of official disavowal in the event of failure highlighted entrepreneurial initiative and gave an alibi for minimizing references to politics. Episodes were devoted to a scientifically managed, technicist public-private sphere beyond the rule of law, with the IMF representing an efficient allocation of resources because of its depersonalized division of labor and consultantlike distance from the official civilities of diplomacy (Buxton 115–17; Katsh 168). By contrast, Bruce A. Beatie's Proppian/Jungian framework relates audience fascination with *Mission: Impossible* to "a dim, unconscious perception . . . a faint shadow of the spiritual quest that Magdalenian man imprinted in our blood" that gains expression in the characterization of fictional heroes (60); maybe.

The generic ambiguity surrounding *Mission* is on vivid display in tropes derived from the show. The title drew numerous spoofing quotations across the popular media: *Get Smart*, *Blue Thunder* (John Badham, 1983), *1969* (Ernest Thompson, 1989), *The Jeffersons*, *Revenge of the Nerds* (Jeff Kanew, 1984), *Airplane II: The Sequel* (Ken Finkleman, 1982), *Mad Mission 3*, an Oldsmobile commercial, and Bruce Springsteen's "I'm a Rocker." Australia's *Financial Review* appropriated it to refer to difficulties confronted by the Reserve Bank of Australia. An article in the Brisbane *Courier-Mail* aimed at schoolchildren on threats to the ozone layer was headed "Mission Impossible," in the same typeface as the program's titles; American ABC had offered a three-part environmental series in 1970 titled *Mission Possible: They Care for This Land*. The term was deployed by long-suffering New York Rangers ice hockey fans sporting a "MISSION ACCOMPLISHED" banner when their team won the Stanley Cup in 1994 and in BBC soccer commentary (29 October 1989), a *Weekend Australian* editorial on the New Zealand monetarist Roger Douglas, *New Yorker* coverage of U.S.-Vietnamese relations in the 1990s, an *Economist* story on the Colombia-U.S. drug trade, an article on space science, a French history of the Holocaust, and society jottings. A witness before Australia's Human Rights and Equal Opportunity Commission claimed police treatment of Aborigines in Sydney was "something out of the television series *Mission: Impossible*." It was also used to promote football on Channel Nine in 1989, ESPN2's 1996 NHL draft coverage, and Marilyn Lake's feminist revision of Australian historiography (P. White 14, 427; Rigby; Brown 193; "Mission"; Sheehan 78; Leech; Favez; J. Fraser 8–9; witness quoted in Reiss).

Lalo Schifrin's arresting theme music was equally significant. A flute played the descending melody while a thumping bass rose, all in a 5/4 rhythm that spelled sophistication and difference. The theme has reappeared on numerous anthologies and is quoted by Doc Box and B. Feresh's 1990 "A Mission Impossible" and the Jams/Timelords' "Whitney Joins the Jams" (1989). The tune was even used by Alan Copeland to the lyrics of "Norwegian Wood" (1968). The Lesbian Avengers hummed the melody as they marched on Bryant Park to unveil a statue of Alice B. Toklas next to the official memorial for Gertrude Stein, and Disney's *Homeward Bound: The Incredible Journey* (Duwayne Dunham, 1993) features the theme during the pets' search for their owners, setting the mood for adventure and serving as a mnemonic/wake-up call for adult viewers. This references the series' special status as a "knowing" text, watched with devotional regularity by college graduates who otherwise abjured TV in the 1960s, raising advertising prices to record levels for a show that was never close to the most popular programs in the ratings (Pareles; P. White 215; Lowry; Gelfand 129–30).

College anomie/jouissance continues: the visual trope that began each *M:I*, a hand striking a match to light a fuse, is a leitmotiv in David Lynch's *Wild at Heart* (1990), which repeats the *Mission: Impossible* sign in lovingly drawn-out close-ups, and Toyota's 1996 Independence Day dealers' sale. In *River's Edge* (Tim Hunter, 1987), the leader of a bizarre teen clique draws on the *Mission* logic of patriotic loyalty to justify concealing a murder. Producers of the original series were initially troubled by such troping, because it held them up to ridicule. The tape and "self-destruct" line were momentarily removed. But they simply had to return for the remake, and of course for the movie. Such tropes repeat and revive themselves, keeping the program in coining circulation and dramatizing the object described. When the revised series was flagging, ABC began a "radio trivia campaign" in thirty-five key U.S. markets to develop audience interest through just such postmodern circulation. Meanwhile, the BBC's major programming effort of the late 1980s to attract a youth audience, *Def 2*, ran old *Mission* episodes as retro fashion (Beck; J. Lewis 14–15; Rafferty 85; Frith "Youth" 77).

Australia's Channel Nine promoted the new series in a similarly postmodern way. Voice-overs referred to "Queensland's own *Mission: Impossible*," with teletext reading "SHOT ENTIRELY IN SOUTH EAST QUEENSLAND." Advertisements in the local papers made a virtue of Queensland's being transformed and internationalized; for instance, from the *Sunday Mail*'s television guide: "How do you turn Indooroopilly into Africa? Nothing's

Advertisements courtesy *The Sunday Mail*, Brisbane, Queensland, Australia; from *TV Scene*, May 28, 1989, p. 18; and September 3, 1989, p. 25.

impossible" (*Scene on TV*). *TV Scene* magazine boasted, "La Belle France is the country depicted in Thursday's *Mission Impossible*" ("Mission" 16 July) and "Tonight, Brisbane gets a Golden Gate. See, nothing's impossible" ("Mission" 3 September). Artifice becomes a virtue: "The Gold Coast is no Turkey! But tonight it's an impressive Istanbul. . . . The Gold Coast as you've never seen it" ("Mission" 17 September). Topographic falsehoods become self-reflexive/parodic promotional material. If this is Thursday, Queensland must be polysemous. Australian viewers could participate in the mock internationalism that was a feature of the series. Nameless but vaguely Eastern or Central European locales were identifiable by an ideolect called "Gellerese," which the initial producer and his researchers had developed as a "foreign" language that English speakers could identify as different but also understand: hence the first episode's sign on the door of a van in the small Latin American dictatorship of "Santa Costa" reading "EXTERMINADOR" and a stop sign reading "ALTO." Later neologisms included "'machina werke' (machine repair), 'zöna restrik' (restricted area), and the ever-popular 'gäz' (gas)" (P. White 16–17).

What of the episodes themselves? It seems almost unnecessary to analyze scenes and shots if this is a straightforward case of jobs and money, the simple operation of an international division of labor with no aspect of Queensland culture involved. The instructions to writers of the previous series encourage us to write the program off as Tayloristically formulaic:

> The tape message contains the problem. An enemy or criminal plot is in existence; the IMF must counter it. The situation must be of enough importance and difficulty that only the IMF could do it. The villains (as here and later portrayed) are so black, and so clever that the intricate means used to defeat them are necessary. Very commonly, but not inevitably, the mission is to retrieve a valuable item or man, and/or to discredit (eliminate) the villain or villains. (quoted in Barnouw 198 n. 19)

"Queensland's own *M:I*" was shot and screened at the same time the ABT was assessing commercial television with a view to tests for Australian content that would go beyond production factors (such as nationality of key workers) and count onscreen signs: theme, location, and accent. Leaving aside the ontological status of Australianness and ultimate revisions to program standards, it is worth noting that *Mission* was the limit case for unions, writers, the Australian Film Commission, other producers, the Tribunal, and public advocacy groups. They insisted that any new system must ensure *M:I* not count as Australian, even though it was technically local under the extant rules (Cunningham and Jacka 61). By the second season, it could be scheduled only as an import, Chris Berry lamenting this displacement by "macho Anglo-Celtic nationalism" (15).

I think it *is* worth devoting some time to asking what these disparate groups were watching that merged their divergent interests. *Mission* actor Thaao Penghlis, an Australian, uses a mid-Pacific accent, its tones somewhere between new Sydney money and method acting for the smallish screen. Recalling the difference between his time in Australian soap operas and life overseas, he told *TV Scene* about the difficulties of coming home: "People want you to be the same, but that's not possible" ("A Movie"); at least something is. (Even this bland voice troubled a writer for *Variety*, who found the "unexplained Australian accents" of two characters a "distraction" [Bier].) All the *Mission* actors sat in left-hand drive cars with non-Australian license plates. In a semiological tribute to Queensland's rocky democratic structures and their many corrupt inhabitants, Brisbane's Parliament House was transformed into a Prague hotel in one program. When allied to the populist tropes and self-reflexive promotional material, this mockery of mass culture resonated with the Brisbane audience.

The different episodes certainly contained elements of the script policy components listed earlier, but a lot more besides. "Reprisal," when telecast in Australia, contained advertisements for pizzas, other programs, rice, furniture, vases, a hotel, maxi-shields, toothpaste, soft drinks, nasal decongestant, alcohol, frozen food, canned soup, cars, sweetmeats, paint, and chips, interspersed with—and just as much part of the time slot as—the postmodern narrative of a misogynistic, homicidal IMF reject seeking revenge. In a moment of self-parody, the killer traps Phelps in a room that will "self-destruct in five seconds." This is a psychological study as per film noir serial killers, with the ex-IMF man descending into madness from his former sanity (bestowed through membership in the Force). Throughout a temporary loss of authority, Phelps remains calm, the unruffled gentleman running the show who in the last instance is an infallible father.

The same era is a source for the "Bayou" episode. High-camp Austra-

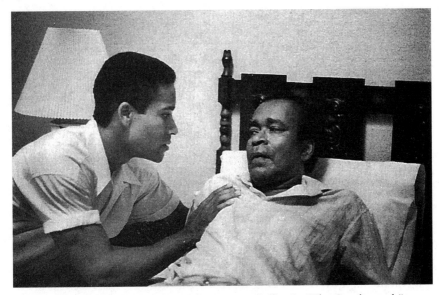

Television still. Greg Morris returned as Barney Collier in "The Condemned."

lian character actor Frank Thring presides over people hunts by dogs and armed men in a mangrove swamp, a subtropical distillation of Sidney Greenstreet and Lionel Barrymore. Thring is always already self-parodic because of his leer and TV commercials for "demonic" fire lighters. Self-mockery becomes automimesis when Phelps receives instructions from a movie director following this coded interchange: Director—"You can't beat this city for a backdrop"; Phelps—"Yes, well I've been a movie fan since I was a kid." "The Condemned" is intertextually self-reflexive. It casts Greg Morris (from the first series) alongside his son Phil. Phil plays Greg's diegetic son and successor as African American technical expert, in this case, disguised as his father to rescue the "real" Phil ("Real-Life" 72).

But it would be hard to cavort over the new *Mission* as sustained excess. *Mission: Impossible* is no *Miami Vice* or *Moonlighting*, let alone *The Avengers*. *Variety* contrasted the "time telling us how the IMF agents felt" in the revived series with the "intricate schemes" of its former life, which transcended the reaction-shot path to joy. Consider the IMF smuggling dissidents out of Eastern Europe in "The Wall." Posing as a Texan impresario keen to hire a chess player and a magician, Phelps is accused by a KGB officer of making "capitalist offers." He replies good-naturedly, "Business is business the world over." And so it is, when the IMF team can grant U.S. citizenship as it pleases. And of course, liberal openness—and therefore critique—is justified in terms of improved social outcomes, exemplified in technology and self-deportment that are always superior to the opposition. The IMF (what irony to share an acronym with a key tool of First World economic power!) establishes a sphere of the other that is harsh and repressive compared with its own goodness and light, captured in close-up as the East German Colonel Barty's highly polished boot grinds a little girl's lost doll into the mud when he arrests her defecting family. The shooting script calls for Phelps to have a "broad American smile" in contrast to the "slow, unfriendly" East German. The cut from unpleasantness at the Berlin Wall to Jim playing golf generates a lifestyle and polity distinctiveness, illustrating the IMF's efforts to assist elements "behind the Wall" that favor political and economic openness. Phelps's patriarchal condescension is as much geopolitical as gendered in his remark to a ravaged Ilse Bruck in act 3: "You're a very brave girl, Ilse. But we're still in East Berlin and you'll have to call on all your reserves to help us get back to the West." This is in keeping with his public circulation as a "craggy-faced, white-haired, all-business hunk of a leading man" (Bier; Meyers 124). It is difficult not to see this as a recondite hangover—the kind we regret the most—for a passing era. But it is as much a reminder of the casually ideological nature of American action-adventure: opposing names and affiliations may change, but disavowal of alterity and debasing moralism seem infinitely sustainable.

▶

## The Economy, Clever

*At the final accounting, it is the industrial organisation of media entertainments—at all points on the circuit of planning, production, distribution, exhibition and circulation—that determines the text.*
:: Gomery "Media" 44

*The massive, assured English-language market in America— and increasingly elsewhere—enables Hollywood studios to raise the necessary financing for production and marketing that it is not possible for studios in a much smaller, say, French- or German-language, market. This has given the American entertainment industry the ability to pick up the stories, stars, songs and talent from across the world.*
*I would argue that because of this, the entertainment industry of this country is not so much Americanizing the world as planetizing entertainment.*
:: Eisner 9

If we are to evaluate the local impact of *M:I*, the terrain must encompass the development, circulation, and reception of text, and one of the key factors is employment. Of the 250 people at Coomera that Paramount employed during the shooting of the series, 37 percent were Queensland residents. Benefits down the line included A$21 million spent with local businesses (Veitch). The care with which these figures were accumulated, organized, and disseminated is indicative of concerns enumerated earlier. They meet the desire for a return on state investment through a multiplier effect that benefits the citizenry, suggesting foreign capital assists the local bourgeoisie and petite bourgeoisie and does more than pilfer from an advantageous labor market and government.

Some of the production aspects *are* positive, or at least less a one-way street than the import back-lot fiasco of the 1950s, when "certain American location films, particularly *Kangaroo* ([Lewis Milestone,] 1952) and *On the Beach* ([Stanley Kramer,] 1959) . . . dangled the carrot of characteristic Hollywood largesse in front of largely excluded local film actors and technicians" (Cunningham "Nascent" 94). (These locals were also required to deal with Ava Gardner's unhelpful—if correct—remark that Melbourne was the ideal place to make a film about the end of the world.) In confronting the internal corollary of this difficulty, Jackie McKimmie described the problem in a letter on behalf of the Australian Writers Guild to her state premier:

> Most of us continue to work in Queensland despite the difficulties, because we believe that if Australian art and culture is to thrive, it needs to reflect the diversity of the country and its people. Regionalism and decentralisation are now the operative words in many areas of the arts, but in the most accessible and popular form, film and television, we are faced with the prospect of increasing centralisation. Local life as we see it now almost exclusively emanates from Sydney and Melbourne, and overseas. (41)

The homogenizing urban nonspecificity of many Australian programs renders this an employment concern. That Queensland is peripheral textually is not necessarily any more apparent in "local" drama and comedy than that New South Wales is central. So perhaps we should merely note, rather than celebrate, the fact that whereas 120 people lost their jobs when de Laurentiis fell bankrupt, about 150 Australians worked on the production of *M:I* at different times, and 60 percent of the first thirteen episodes were written and produced by Australians. Of the five lead actors, two were locals, and the sixty-person crew contrasted with thirty to forty on most Australian series. Extras were paid A$75 for a four and a half-hour call, and speaking parts commanded A$1,400 per diem where an American accent was required. But, as noted above, there followed the forever Queensland tragedy when the series was transferred south. After one season, Paramount elected to head elsewhere, lobbied by Film Victoria and a joint sub-

Photos and text courtesy *The Sunday Mail*, Queensland, Brisbane, Australia, March 28, 1989, p. 7.

mission from production company McMahon-Lake, Australian Film Studios, and local trade unions, amid suggestions that the Gold Coast lacked variety in its locations and that Melbourne's insipid light and aged architecture made European settings more plausible (Monaghan 14; P. Clark 55; "Film"; Amad and Hawker 4; McLean). This desire for an Old World trompe l'oeil raises the issue of Australia's regional and national vulnerability as a site for overseas production. Skills, technology, and landscape are advantages, but the travel required remains a problem compared with Northern Hemisphere production. Editing is straightforward: text can be beamed to the United States by satellite or processed locally. But recent attempts to weaken acting unions' control over imported stars have only gone a certain distance to satisfy producers, who continue to deal with the requirement that U.S. pay rates be applied to locals whenever Americans are on the set (Molloy and Burgan 63).

Economic tensions were evident in *Mission*'s first life. Paramount was owned by Gulf & Western Industries, a conglomerate with interests in New Jersey Zinc, South Puerto Rico Sugar, and Consolidated Cigar. It had two high-rated 1970s series produced by Geller, *M:I* and *Mannix*. An episode of *Mission* cost U.S. $225,000, for which CBS paid U.S.$170,000. Geller was shooting upward of fifty thousand feet of film per screen hour, more than twice the average, and spent 30 percent longer than the norm doing so. Special effects and writing costs also spiraled far beyond studio policy, in part to capture the feature-film look that was a key factor in the program's success. After three seasons without profitability, each episode was placed under intense financial restrictions. Economies were sought by a multinational that treated TV as a potentially down-market way to profit, leading to intense disputes over creativity versus commerce (R. Lewis 31). In this sense, we can see *Mission* as a microcosm of the political divisions that inform its patrimony as a text and a forerunner of new technology screen-production issues that are so pressing today.

We might consider these matters in the Australian context by looking at two films, *Kangaroo* (cited earlier) and *The Return of Captain Invincible* (Philippe Mora, 1983). Like *Mission*, they provide limit cases of U.S. screen investment in Australia, one chronologically and the other conceptually. Twentieth Century Fox dispatched an entire off-camera production team for *Kangaroo*, in addition to most of the cast, because its Australian-based capital reserves had been frozen by government to prevent foreign exchange leaving the country. Filming took place in a settlement that local authorities officially named Zanuckville, after the head of Fox—an emblem of supine attitudes to foreign investment. A formulaic western, the film failed to draw audiences, but then the need to use money lying idle was probably the sole innovation associated with the text (Pike and Cooper 281). For its part, *Captain Invincible* represents another outcome of the state's producing conditions for foreign filmmaking. Here, taxation incentives designed to make the industry less dependent on cultural bureaucrats and more attentive to the private sector saw the Australian Treasury subsidizing U.S. producers to make a film set almost "nowhere." It concerns a former American superhero, played by Alan Arkin, who migrates to Australia and dipsomania following McCarthyite persecution, reviving his powers and sobriety to thwart the villainous Christopher Lee. Recut by U.S. producers in reaction to difficulty obtaining American distribution, the text was disavowed by Mora and denied certification by the Australian government as insufficiently local by comparison with the original script. A court challenge against this ruling was successful (D. Stratton 79), but the tax haven was politically and culturally compromised from that point. (Interestingly, the judge who initially heard the case remarked that "the origin of the story idea" was irrelevant to determining a film's eventual Australianness in terms of its look or atmosphere. There was "no property in an idea," but in its material appearance [quoted in Dermody and Jacka *Screening vol. 1* 148].)

The end of the Australian government's 10BA tax rebate film financing system saw the head of drama at Channel Ten, Valarie Hardy, argue that the Australian industry had ended: "Everything's international now." Greg Coote, president of Village Roadshow Pictures, announced: "What I want to do is make movies in Australia — or anywhere else but preferably in Australia — that are international movies." The decision to shift *M:I* to Queensland left the text fundamentally unmarked by its *locus* of manufacture. In 1988, it cost on average U.S.$1.2 million to produce an hour of TV series drama in the United States, which would then be sold to other countries at prices they could afford (perhaps U.S.$36,000 to Australia, U.S.$7,000 to the Netherlands, and U.S.$30,000 to Italy). Despite local cost-cutting in production, 1988–89 saw Australian networks paying an additional A$79,000 an hour for local drama compared with these dumped imports, although that figure was half the disparity of a decade earlier (Hardy quoted in Maloney 39; Coote quoted in Urban 102; Molloy and Burgan 114, 94, 59). This environment is some distance from a neoclassical model that emphasizes undistorted equilibria in supply and demand through easy entry for new competitors across industries and continents, with efficiency determined by consumer preference through price. In an era of predominantly free-to-air television, the audience was no such creature.

The Australian experience of *M:I* fits a dependency-related model in political economy terms. First the U.S.-made program is imported. Then it is made locally but *still* "imported." And the United States doesn't buy Australian television. The ultimate "madness" occurred in June 1989, when Warner Bros. issued a prospectus to gain Australian financial involvement in Hollywood films when the local industry was almost without backing. An emergent Australian bourgeoisie put funds into new ventures overseas, while U.S. houses considered remakes shot in Australia. (Meanwhile, investment advisers were warning clients that the average return on investment in Australian film and television was 12 percent, down 8 percent from earlier in the decade.) And even as Australia becomes a key player in audiovisual trade (the third largest exporter of rock music and the third player in TV drama exports to Europe, where it sells more television than any individual Continental country), it attracts a negative reputation with many outside critics for a banal recycling of American-style material. The revived *M:I* was made in Australia to update a prior success "by using new locales and high-tech equipment without changing any dialogue — preventing union

trouble." This was an inherently conjunctural decision, diegetically referenced in the IMF director's planning methods. Just like a film producer, his
sifting process to select operatives was a contingent coalescence of management, intellectual production, technology, and somatics to meet the needs
of a particular task: a classic division of labor, borrowed for MTV's promotion for *The Real World V* in 1996. As the *New York Times* put it,
"The series' clunking cold war futurism" was equally about "patient cooperation as an almost religious obligation" (Shoebridge "No One" 135;
Chadwick; Jacka and Cunningham 18; De Bens, Kelly, and Bakke 93;
Holden C13). The Queensland studio space is an example of a site dedicated to just such formulas.

▶ ━━━━━━━━━━━━━━━━━━━━━━━━━━━━━━━━━━━━━━

### The New International Division of Cultural Labor

> *One man draws out the wire, another straightens it, a third
> cuts it, a fourth points it, a fifth grinds it at the top for receiving
> the head; to make the head requires three distinct operations;
> to put it on is a peculiar business, to whiten the pins is another;
> it is even a trade by itself to put them into the paper.* . . .
>
>     *The division of labour . . . occasions, in every art, a propor-
> tionable increase of the productive powers of labour.*
> ::   Adam Smith 110

There have been four distinct phases of trading history, corresponding to
developments in surplus production and the division of labor. In the four-
teenth and fifteenth centuries, a mercantile system arose from calculations
of climate, geography, flora, and fauna. Exchanging goods turned into ex-
changes of labor. As food commodities made their way around the globe,
so did people, often as slaves. When machinery was developed, work split
into an industrial mode, as cities grew into manufacturing sites and populations urbanized. Wages displaced farming as the basis of subsistence
across the sixteenth, seventeenth, and eighteenth centuries. This is the moment of Adam Smith's famous example of pin making, quoted above.

    When developed countries moved onto the global stage, new forms of
labor were institutionalized in empire. Manufacturing went on at the center, with food and raw materials imported from the periphery in the eighteenth and nineteenth centuries. Differences of opinion emerged about the
significance of the balance of trade to a country's well-being. Mercantilists
thought it should be controlled, but free traders wanted market forces to
rule in accordance with factor endowments and an international division
of labor. Keynesian responses to the Great Depression made protectionism

a more legitimate position in economic theory, until stagflation eventually emerged from the transnational phase that commenced after World War II. By the mid-1980s, the volume of offshore production by multinationals exceeded the amount of trade between states for the first time. Today, *division of labor* refers simultaneously to sectoral differences in an economy, say, between fishing and restaurants, the occupations and skills of a labor force, and the organization of tasks within a firm. Life-cycle models of international products suggest they are first produced and consumed in the center, in a major industrial economy, then exported to peripheral economic points, and finally produced in the periphery once technology has become standardized and savings can be made on the labor front. The carefully ordered certitudes of standardized processes lessen risk for investors. Goods and services owned and vended by the periphery rarely make their way into the center as imports. In screen drama, factors of production such as labor market slackness, increases in profit, and developments in global transportation and communications technology have diminished the need for colocation of these factors. Fragmenting production depresses labor costs and deskills workers. Any decision by a multinational firm to invest in a particular national formation carries the seeds of insecurity, because such firms move on when tax incentives or other factors of production beckon (Lang and Hines 15; Strange "Limits" 293; Keynes 333–34; R. Cohen 129, 133–39; P. Evans 27–28; Allan 325–26; Browett and Leaver 38; Welch and Luostarinen).

The idea of a new international division of cultural labor derives from retheorizations of economic dependency theory following the inflationary chaos of the 1970s. New markets for labor and sales and the shift from the spatial sensitivities of electrics to the spatial insensitivities of electronics pushed businesses away from treating Third World countries as suppliers of raw materials, regarding them as shadow setters of the price of work that competed internally and with the First and Second Worlds for employment opportunities. This broke up the prior division of the world into a small number of industrialized nations and a majority of underdeveloped ones. In its place, production was split across continents. Folker Fröbel and his collaborators christened this the new international division of labor (NIDL). I am suggesting that just as manufacturing fled the First World, cultural industries may also relocate. This could happen at the level of textual production, as with *M:I*, or in such areas as marketing, information, and high-culture, limited-edition work. There are two difficulties with the NIDL and the NICL: they aggregate investment and trade data, assuming a correlation between the movement of capital and the division of labor that is not necessarily appropriate, especially given the role of the state; and privileging production and distribution in the cultural area may negate the importance of meaning in the circulation of texts. So the model is tentative. The key economic question is, Will deindustrialized states lose jobs to the periphery, while retaining superprofits for their own ruling elite? Already, work is being done in a variety of cultural industries to examine the impact of global labor markets in advertising, architecture, accountancy, and sport, trying to balance out the positives—less chauvinism, less monochromatic whiteness—from the negatives—American dominance and deracinated peripheral suppliers (for example, 25 percent of Silicon Valley technicians come from Asia, while that region is desperately short of transferred technology) (Fröbel et al. 2–8, 13–15, 45–48; Miège 41–43; R. Cohen 130, 132; Beaverstock; Maguire "Preliminary" 452, 458, 466; Strange "Limits" 296).

Obviously, the U.S. film industry has always imported cultural producers, such as the German expressionists. But this was one-way until a combination of postwar antitrust decisions, the advent of television, and the suburbanization of America compelled changes to the vertically integrated studio system in the decades after 1946. There was a decrease of a third in the number of Hollywood-made films and more than a doubling of imports. Production went overseas as location shooting became a means of differentiating stories and studios purchased facilities around the world to utilize cheap labor. Between 1950 and 1973, just 60 percent of Hollywood films in production began their lives in the United States, with de Laurentiis a 1970s pioneer of global presales, garnering funds from distributors around the world in advance of production in Los Angeles. This opened the door to the United States for other European producers. And American financial institutions are now long-practiced at purchasing foreign theaters and distribution companies to share risk and profit with local businesses. By the end of the 1980s, overseas firms were crucial suppliers of funds invested in Hollywood or loans against distribution rights in their countries of origin. Joint production arrangements are now well established between U.S. firms and French, British, Swedish, and Italian companies, with connections to theme parks, cable television, and home video. Hollywood production is undertaken by small editing, lighting, and rental studio companies that work with independent producers and sell their services across a variety of audiovisual industries. Films may be shot across the world, but decision making and postproduction are concentrated in the L.A. entertainment sector (although animation work is frequently undertaken in Southeast Asia and Europe by employees at lower rates than those demanded by U.S. workers). In television, the networks pursued a variety of expansionary strategies over the same period. The 1960s saw ABC gaining minority interests in Latin American stations and CBS establishing CBS Japan, Inc., to distribute programs. The trend is clearly toward a horizontal connection with other media, a global scale of economy and administration, and a breakup of the old public/private distinctions in ownership, administration, and programming philosophy (Christopherson and Storper; Wasser 424, 431; Buck 119, 123; Briller 75–78; Wasko 33; Miège 46; Marvasti).

In 1994, American cinema made more money overseas than at home, for the first time. This is far from a unilateral exercise of power. The American Film Institute is anxious about a loss of cultural heritage to internationalism, critics question what is happening when local U.S. drama is scripted with special attention to foreign audiences, and political economists of cinema argue that a newly transnational Hollywood no longer addresses its nominal audience. Perhaps cultural nationalist arguments are shifting—tremulously but marginally—into reverse. George Quester laments that British costume history crowds out the space for indigenous "quality" television, noting that there is more Australian high-end drama on U.S. TV than locally produced material (Wedell 325; Quester 57).

Although it is difficult to generalize, I think the *Mission* experience shows the direction of such developments. Like the scenery and convenience aspects of tourism, the international screen has some peculiarities that do not apply to manufacturing. It is risky on all but a huge scale: the vast majority of investments are complete failures, a pain that can be borne only by large competitors. Whereas new technology problematizes the colocation of shooting, editing, and financing, it also reduces the need for "authenticity." Against this, coproduction is clearly something like an NICL, with host governments working together or with the United States. But the trend remains for North America to attract talent developed by national cinemas to compete with it. Peter Weir's postproduction might take place in Australia to satisfy offscreen indices of localism and to obtain state financing, but does that make for a real disinvestment away from Hollywood? Yet it is a source of pride, prestige, and intangible/invisible economic benefits to Australians that as of October 1994, *Variety*'s list of the hundred most successful domestic films in U.S. screen history included two Australian productions and four Hollywood films directed by Australians (not to mention Academy Award successes), while Michael Apted speaks with optimism of a gradual "European-izing of Hollywood." Perhaps the real internationalization occurs at ancillary levels, as international audience targeting becomes increasingly specific: Sean Connery is cast as a Hollywood lead because European audiences love him, and each U.S. film is allotted a hundred generic descriptions for use in specific markets (Kevin Costner's *Dances with Wolves* sold to the 1990 French cinemagoer as a documentary-style dramatization of Native American life; *Malcolm X* was promoted there with posters of the Stars and Stripes aflame) ("Top"; Apted quoted in Dawtrey 75; Wasser 433; Danan 131–32, 137).

The Grundy Organisation produced Australian drama and game shows from the 1950s, but looked to the United States and Europe as key sites twenty years ago. The company began to sell texts across the world, operating with a strategy called "parochial internationalism," which meant leaving Australia rather than exporting in isolation from relevant industrial, taste, and regulatory frameworks. Following patterns established in the advertising industry, it bought production houses around the world, making programs in local languages based on formats imported from Australia that themselves drew on U.S. models. From a base in Bermuda, Grundy's produced about fifty hours of TV a week in seventy countries across Europe, Oceania, Asia, and North America, until it was sold to a non-Australian company in 1993. This is the NICL offshore, utilizing experience in the Australian commercial reproduction industry to manufacture American palimpsests in countries relatively new to profit-centered TV. The benefits to Australia, where a regulatory framework birthed this expertise by requiring the networks to support such productions, are unclear. Similarly, attempts by the French film industry in the 1980s to attract U.S. filmmakers may have the ultimate effect of U.S. studio takeovers, while diplomatic efforts to maintain local screen subsidization continue even as Hollywood producers and networks purchase satellite and broadcast space across Europe. There may be more utility in the benefits to local networks that sell this drama in other markets: Australia's Channel Seven estimates that exported soap operas contributed 17 percent of its 1993–94 profit (Cunningham and Jacka 81–87; Moran; S. Hayward 385; Stevenson 1; M. Harris 76).

The Village Roadshow group represents another NICL model. With all the rhetoric about the Queensland film industry, it is significant that *Paradise Beach*, a soap shot at Village's Coomera Warner Studios in 1993 for simultaneous release in Australia and the United States, utilized writers, directors, and crews imported from the south on the basis that it was "not feasible, logistically, to use Brisbane writers" (quoted in Dawson 76). The Gold Coast Studio sets up a third tier of Australian-based screen production in addition to notions of culturally valuable film culture and commercially driven film industrialism—a floating multinational space that some accuse of promoting "cultural imperialism." It makes money for investors and keeps already trained personnel in work, but textuality and industrial impact are other questions. Village Roadshow has an in-house, high-production-values TV subsidiary, Roadshow Coote and Carroll, that makes quality drama. But this is of minimal revenue importance alongside the theme park; exhibition and distribution operations in Australia, Singapore, Taiwan, and Aotearoa/New Zealand; interactive compact disc manufacture; and offshore production investment. Village claims it can produce screen texts at two-thirds of the Hollywood cost. Such rhetoric is forever in need of renewal, with similar promises coming from Portugal, Spain, South Africa, and Mexico and increasing flexibility among U.S. unions to conserve jobs. But for all that Coote claims to want to make movies, his company has never made a profit from its studio business. Announcements of a new stage in 1995 concealed the fact that a set was being rededicated to the more successful theme park. The glamour and cultural politics of screen production may simply attract state assistance that cross-subsidizes more important matters to a firm that is joining Warners, Channel Nine, and the Westfield shopping chain in national merchandising (Bailey 83, 91–93; Cunningham and Jacka 87–95; Groves "B.O." and "Roadshow"; Molloy and Burgan 54, 51, 47; Hoskins and McFadyen 215; C. Ryan; Grant-Taylor).

In an era when U.S. network television is desperately cutting costs, there are opportunities for outsiders, but only major players. Where action-adventure texts such as *Mission* once took up perhaps a fifth of North American prime time, in the 1990s they occupy about 1 percent of the schedule. Infotainment has grown from nothing in the past five years to earning U.S.$1 billion per annum. An hour of reality television costs U.S.$700,000, as opposed to U.S.$1.3–2 million for action and U.S.$1 million for studio-based drama. At the same time, the past decade has seen hard-top exhibition moving toward "event cinema," where a tiny number of films are responsible for the vast proportion of receipts. Over this period, ten of the five hundred features released from Hollywood in a given year have made up as much as 40 percent of box-office revenue. The trend seems to be toward smaller investments in a larger number of programs for television, and larger investments in a smaller number of films for exhibition. This is the future in the simultaneously splintered and concentrated media domain of North America, where a huge increase in the number of channels and systems of supply and payment is also producing unprecedented concentration of ownership. The *Mission* example represents a form of vertical investment, in that production processes were fragmented across the world. But the remainder of the Warner Village Roadshow story may be more significant for the future: horizontal direct interests in licensing and joint ventures that mirror domestic retailing systems. For the culturalist remit of Second World TV, the ability to make locally accented infotainment is one way of nations' using the NICL, in addition to turning toward the Southeast Asian action-adventure film and video market rather than Hollywood as an investment source (Schwab 14; Roddick 30; Markusen 170; Buck 130). And with the demise of financial-syndication rules in American broadcasting regulation, the networks control and own more and more of the texts they screen. The reaction from independents, who currently produce a sizable proportion of TV drama, may well be to move elsewhere, to make foreign countries their principal profit centers for programs later sold as video packages in the United States, or to utilize the networks as secondary sources of revenue.

▶ ────────────────────────────────────────────

## Conclusion

> Emmett mumbled. He glanced at the TV and scratched Moon Pie's neck. Moon Pie rolled over on his back and stuck all four feet straight up.
> "You could go to Lexington too," Sam said. "You could go to Flagstaff, Arizona, if you wanted to. Or Japan. What's keeping you here? Or you could stay here and do something besides watch TV."
> Emmett grunted. "The TV goes everywhere," he said. "It saves a lot of fuel. I don't have to go to St. Louis to see the Cards. I can watch right here, and see better too."
> :: Mason 190

> "Made in Australia" is almost like a seal of Good Housekeeping on a film. If a young man goes out on a date, it is safe to take a girl to an Australian film.
> :: Pauline Kael quoted in Hamilton and Mathews 25

> When you're working 9,000 miles away, it's easy to feel forgotten.
> :: Phil Morris quoted in Beck

To repeat, two aspects inform the fear of "dumped" U.S. television: the production impact on the indigenous television industry and textual limitations confronting spectators. Very little empirical research has been done on this subject in Australia. What there is suggests that Australian children consuming American themes and accents on television do not regard these as indicative of a specifically American experience. Rather, they perceive a universal TV world that reflects their own conditions, so Aboriginal children assume African American characters are black Australians like themselves. Of course, it is easy to be skeptical about how much weight should be attached to such findings. All over the world, viewers prefer locally produced texts to U.S. ones. As Elizabeth Riddell has noted in another context, a "weekly injection of Peyton Place is not going to turn a Richmond River dairy farmer into an Idaho potato grower" (27). And in the decade after 1982, Australian-produced texts went from 60 percent of the nation's top ten programs to 100 percent, under the combined stimulus of regulation and industry assistance. But recent research on Australian schoolchildren reading *Tour of Duty*, mentioned in chapter 1, displays a horrific isomorphism of the United States with progress: South Vietnamese villagers are fortunate to have Americans in their midst who bring guns and television, signs of a desirable, sophisticated future (Pingree and Hawkins 193–94; Hodge and Tripp 140–42; Appleton 9, 23; Chanticleer; R. Collins 217; Mattelart *Advertising* 84; Pendleton; Molloy and Burgan 57; Tulloch and Tulloch 228, 234). This suggests that certain aspects of the global American presence are circulating in very uncritical forms.

In his discussion of Australian landscape and film, Ross Gibson argues for a long tradition of trying to cope with and explain life in the most arid of continents that has recently given way to a less transformative and aestheticized discourse, where the country is more than a wasteland or a picture (64–65). A European society away from Europe confronts this separation economically by a turn toward the Pacific Rim and emotionally through an obsession with wilderness in the most urban culture in the world. To lie beyond the city is to be homeless, a sign of vagrancy or liberty. The connotation changes with one's color, but the signification depends on an outsider's alienation from the land, washing its hands in dry despair or waving them in romantic gestures. This combines the denial of native title that characterized Australian law until the 1990s with the more pictorial, Edenic side to doctrines of *terra nullius*. The refusal of adequate land rights to the original inhabitants of Australia assured newer arrivals an imaginary space of self-fashioning. An inability to cope intellectually with the harsh new world associated Aboriginal people with a form of land-spirit harmony, simultaneously depriving them of that heritage (as it was less material than soulful) *and* utilizing the spirit-place as a substitute ethical center for deracinated white capitalist development.

The latter move positions all Australians inside an ambivalent love for land that cannot be domesticated. Its wildness and nothingness combine as reasons to quarry—or marvel at—grandeur that must be both commodified and elevated to a new life world. It becomes urban Australia's narrative other, a culture graft of expressive feeling onto a ravaging invasion. In filmic terms, this produced the notorious period costume dramas of the decade from 1975, in which lace and ruralism stood for a shared past and the difference between black society's myths of organic creation and more secular narratives that rely for their coherence on a sense of being trans-planted. This era led Kael to compare seeing an Australian film to "reading an old-fashioned novel"; the energy from years without a national cine-matic image had been misdirected into the faulty realism of Victoriana. Both forms lacked the capacity to break through "academic barriers" to raw feeling (Lattas; Ross Gibson 67–68, 72; Kael quoted in Hamilton and Mathews 21, 23).

In 1958, three decades before the All-New *Mission: Impossible* Shot Entirely in Southeast Queensland, Prime Minister Robert Menzies an-nounced, "Australia is an independent nation and has a perfect right to express its views whatever the result. But the fact is that we are not truly independent except in legal terms" (quoted in Catley 143). Do we find suc-cor from the local in *M:I*? For example, that Jim Phelps's bookshelf contin-ued to include leather-bound editions of the *Queensland Industrial Gazette* even after production moved to Melbourne? Or should we return to the Mattelarts: "The denunciation of an evil 'other' is never exempt from a certain holier-than-thou attitude to be found at the heart of the notion of cultural identity"? This can lead to an "asphyxiating localism," particu-larly where such localism ultimately amounts to familiar narrative styles anyway. Phillip Adams (who ran an advertising company as well as having careers as a film-culture bureaucrat, newspaper columnist, film producer, and radio host) is right to style *M:I* "gross and grotesque." But what would be the correct way to style local screen industry lawyers, accountants, and producers—or him? Programs such as *Mission* do not "represent" Queens-land and Australia. They "represent" investment patterns. Sydney has the world's ninth-biggest stock exchange, second in the Southern Hemisphere. And when Dentsu, the Japanese firm that is one of the top two advertising companies in the world, selected Australia as its base for a holding com-pany designed to move into Southeast Asia's newly industrialized countries, this was a sign of the contingent nature of locale *and* the significance of Australia in the service industries as consumer, host, and base (Monaghan 14; Mattelart et al. 22; Mattelart *Advertising* 15).

*Mission: Impossible* and its kind send a message about the interna-tionalization of production, which may lead to increasingly diffuse and di-verse pressures exerted on the Americana of TV. The economics of global television are characterized by significant elasticity at the point of sale. The large, multiple markets in the United States recycle material across net-works and cable through first-run programming, stripped schedules, and nostalgia opportunities. Until the 1990s, the English-language community was by far the biggest in the arena of television trade. The opening up to capitalism of Eastern and Central Europe makes those language groups important, and new satellites spread Hindi, Mandarin, and Cantonese. But English is currently TV's lingua franca, and it has a limited repertoire of "natural" accents. Whereas many American and British regional voices have long circulated in the United States as norms, Australian tones remain "other," in need of diegetic explanation. This makes for a "linguistic discount" in trading terms (Lee and Wang 146; Wedell 322; Hoskins and Mirus). We might recall here attempts to deal with Errol Flynn's still high-antipodean voice in *Dodge City* (Michael Curtiz, 1939). Initially introduced as an Irishman who fought with the Rebels during the Civil War, his character is more fully explained: time with the English Army in India (itself a technical impossibility, since no such force existed, but this *is* Hollywood) and fighting in Cuba. The account concludes with Alan Hale informing us that such a genealogy makes Flynn "either the greatest traveler that *ever* lived or . . . the *biggest* liar." Half a century later, James Coburn advised viewers of NBC's documentary *100 Years of the Hollywood Western* that "Flynn was such a charismatic actor that audiences weren't bothered by his Australian accent."

So we are finding language really is a model for understanding the screen, twenty years after seemingly inconclusive debates over the use of semiotics to unpack audiovisual forms of communication. English is a tool of governance. For those countries that already use it as their approved language, this sets up tantalizing opportunities to counter imbalances in television trade, in addition to shoring up local bourgeoisies and training citizens into a national culture. This point has been nicely taken up with reference to *Crocodile Dundee* (Peter Faiman, 1986), the most popular imported film in U.S. history. It was distributed in the United States by Paramount, which cut five minutes from the Australian version. The result removed picturesque segments, altered the mixing to foreground dialogue, and concentrated on forming the heterosexual couple to increase the film's pace. When added to the Hollywood-style story line and shooting already there, this might disqualify the text as an Australian product (Crofts 129, 137, 141).

But Morris distances herself from Australian critics who attack the film for merely mimicking Hollywood genres. Instead, she subdivides unoriginality into three: as a negative critique occasioned by a faith in the new and the specific, as a positive and necessary outcome of making a national cinema work at an industrial level, and a postmodern *combinatoire* of aesthete and financier that makes unoriginality a virtue. Genre is parodied as it is taken up, pirated, and *puré* to assert a hybrid Australian cultural nationalism (Morris *Pirate's* 247–48). The implausibility of Mick Dundee as a transplanted Manhattanite alludes to the fantasy of buying back the farm and calling it a skyscraper. This is no assault on hegemony; it is a reminder of difference. So too with *Mission: Impossible*. And parodic renderings of the text by the very network that was transmitting it to Queenslanders, in a form that made knowing reference to the sleight-of-signifier that typified it as American, allow the viewer to negotiate imported culture through a local lens.

The sign is truly detached from its referent through the positive unoriginality of a mediated diaspora. *Crocodile Dundee* and *Crocodile Dundee II* (John Cornell, 1988) and the *Mad Max* trilogy (George Miller 1979, 1982, 1985) offered new ways of dealing with landscape, revisionist westerns that were fabulously successful. The environment remained an ineradicable center to these stories, formed in dialogue with Hollywood fables and the inapplicability of manifest destiny to a country lacking river systems. When Billy Hughes, a former prime minister, inaugurated the radio-telephone link between Washington and Australia in 1938, he did so with these words: "What we are, you were; and what you are, we hope to be." *Dundee* is finally "about succeeding through *getting Americans to like us*" by making the landscape malleable and risible, a comparativist turn that displaces the more obvious "template of a national identity." The celebration of the modern has become a parable of the postmodern. This helps us understand Graeme Turner's observation that Australian cultural policy is characterized by the efforts of "a small and economically weak nation . . . torn between adjusting what it does in order to compete internationally . . . or alternatively maintaining a close relation between its activities and a sense of national identity" (Hughes quoted in Phillips 69; G. Turner "Cultural" 70). Being aware of that binary, as a textual determinant, audience propensity, or policy principle, is in some sense to subvert it, to turn generic predictability and spectatorial permissiveness into postmodern freedom, but to do so with a skeptical eye on the internationalization of cultural labor, the economy, and the texts exchanged. After all, De Palma's trailer for the *Mission: Impossible* movie could not be differentiated from Macintosh's "Mission: Impossible. The Web Adventure" TV commercial until their respective punch lines: either "Expect the Impossible May 22 1996" or "Your mission, should you choose to accept it, begins at http://www.mission.apple.com."

*The Truth Is a Murky Path:*
*Technologies of Citizenship and*
*the Visual*

---

*The King case haltingly and inconsistently rebuilt some of the*
*coalition lines that had eroded, and ultimately led to an aston-*
*ishing coalition victory—a popularly supported reassertion of*
*civilian control over the police.*
::    Sonenstein 212


*While the gay movement still has no Martin Luther King Jr. or*
*Gandhi it does have local heroes like Harvey Milk of San*
*Francisco, the martyred city politician. . . . Milk is remembered*
*in "Harvey Milk," a docu-opera.*
::    B. Holland


Americans must know a lot about the world, cradling it in their own populism as per chapter 4. But this seems an awkward thing to be saying in contemporary cultural theory, when the United States is thought to contain
infinite numbers of nations (queer, Christian, Native American, silent majority, of Islam, and others). In some sense it seems to *be* the world, or at
least its prime representative of economic and political infrastructure and
demographic intermingling. This poses additional problems when we remember that writings about popular culture conventionally juxtapose two
apparently antagonistic locations of power. Other than in cultural policy
studies, corporate capital and the state are characterized as agencies that
seek to subjugate the culture of the people, who exist separately from both
institutions. As we saw in chapter 1, "the people" function as a demotic
warrant for academics and a rallying cry for social movements, while nationalism is decried as ideological by contrast with popular culture. In
cultural-capitalist states, official culture (taught by government or supplied
by business) is set against unofficial culture (differentiation by subcultures
or consumption by readers). What value do such oppositions hold when

the very identities of state, capital, people, and geography are unclear, even—or perhaps especially—inside such regimes of truth as an amateur video that becomes courtroom evidence, a hagiographic realist biopic that assists identity politics, or a TV documentary that doubles as study toward a college degree?

When Americans speak as such, it is always in dialogue with diasporic histories and presences. The dialogue references an internal and external struggle over sovereignty as a popular technology—critical issues for citizens of the last superpower. In this sense, the United States truly is the apogee of the modern. Communities are molded from beyond, from spaces and times not their own. Film and TV enable North Americans to know the worlds they make and unmake. The culture industries and the sovereign state become intimately connected, through truth onscreen, for as the history of governmentality shows, a globalizing economy forces sovereign states to look outside for self-definition, even as they prize brief moments of unified territory, sovereignty, and ethnicity.

This chapter focuses on complex reciprocal movements of visual truth making inside documentary, as very broadly defined. These shifts take place between exteriority and interiority: between appearance and emotion in the case of the individual subject, and between the international and the national in the case of the sovereign state. And documentary is a training ground in conduct for individual persons as private people and citizens of a country. In this sense, the genre falls into the category of both psychology and policy, a kind of audiovisual etiquette guide. In this chapter I seek to indicate what is gained and lost for a democratic politics by it. What, for instance, might Dan Rather be telling us when he announces that coverage of the O. J. Simpson cases was "a civics lesson" (quoted in Rosen 24)? If he is right, who is the "we" being addressed, do we want such lessons, and who is our teacher?

Documentaries marshal systems of representation to encourage a point of view about something. Commercials are their apogee, for advertising performs truths and, increasingly, pronounces on them constatively in the same breath. According to one company's tracking survey, there were more than four hundred uses of the word *true* in different broadcast advertisements across the United States during 1993, and well over five hundred the following year. The 1994 season of truth began with AT&T's U.S.$100 million "True Voice" campaign. It promoted a range of "True" savings available on long-range services, attested to not only by Whitney Houston's "true" singing voice, but also by the "true confessions" of numerous customers who had left the AT&T fold, only to return to authentic value. The ne plus ultra North American theme of redemption is satisfied by the *con-*

*verso* who sees the error of her ways and returns. Marketing seeks to establish a rapport between concepts and events. The former encapsulate a product's historical, scientific, social, and artistic meanings (the truthfulness of a telephone company's claims), and the latter put these ideas into material play, giving them coordinates of time and place to verify the claims in song, documentary testimony, and so on. Hence the anxiety expressed by the U.S. Marine Corps over the reality effect of the digitalized Harrier jet sequences in *True Lies* (James Cameron, 1994). This concern was not brought on by some absolute notion of accuracy. Rather, impressions of reality in the mind of the audience were expected to promote recruitment, as *Top Gun* (Tony Scott, 1986) had done for the Air Force (Fitzgerald; Deleuze and Guattari 15; Magid 65).

As William D. Routt maintains, documentaries "try to tell the truth, and fiction films . . . do not try to do that" (60). The systems for establishing truth are familiar: sources from the past quoted by interview or archival footage, maps and tables to chart developments over time and space, critics who speak with disinterested expertise, disembodied narrators who intone truth from above, nondiegetic music and slow motion to evoke moods, crossing the line in a camera movement or edit to prove action dictated the shape of the film rather than the continuity system, focusing on individual stories inside a collective issue to encourage identification, or reversing any of the above as a means of distancing oneself from such systems.

But any text that relates an event is narrated. It is told from somewhere, by someone. And it is inherently representational. The documentary transforms its object into a spectacle of sound and image that draws on signs from the fictive and social worlds. Just as advertisements engage the viewer in a socioeconomic match between stories and human action, the documentary more generally is a personal and public artifact. Fictional and factual protocols become tropes of production and reception, as filmmakers and viewers draw on intersecting textual norms to make and decipher meaning. No surprise, then, that Court TV's subway and street-sign advertising campaign during preliminary hearings on the deaths of Nicole Simpson and Ronald Goldman advertised the network as "GREAT DRAMA. NO SCRIPTS. COURT TV. Watching the real life drama of justice," emphasizing the entertainment value that can coincide with truth-value (this of a telecast in which the only difference in coverage between Court TV and the four major networks was a seven-second delay). The genre-driven network differentiated itself at the time by claiming to offer "an objective, calm look at the proceedings," because of its standing as "*the* brand name in legal news," unlike purveyors of "soundbites or speculation" (Aumont et al. 70–71, 77–79; Court TV advertisement in *New York Times* 5 July 1994 C16).

A further, intercultural issue strikes us here. As truth emerges at the intersection of systems of representation, so may chaos and diversity. Eco discusses the 1977 Venice Biennale screening of Michelangelo Antonioni's *Chung Kuo*, or *China* (1973). Antonioni had gone to China with the intention of contributing to international understanding, but was vilified as reactionary and imperialistic for the text he produced. The Chinese "denounced the film as an inconceivable act of hostility, an insult." The People's Republic of China protested to the festival, and the Italian government tried to prevent the occasion from going ahead. Eco watched it with a Hong Kong critic, who elaborated a Chinese perspective to him frame by frame. Antonioni's concentration on individuals was complicit with antipolitical obsessions about personal relationships. Subtle touches of human conduct designed to gesture at other, deeper matters appeared trivial in a screen culture founded on broad-brush symbolism and dialectical narrative. Worst of all, Antonioni had looked to the simple, rural idyll of China. In place of addressing its prowess as an industrially developed nation, his vision was that of the Westerner in search of Arcadian serenity. Such primitivism revealed poverty and failure to a Chinese eye that is itself industrial (*Travels* 282). Put another way, Antonioni's staring point was wrong. He looked in the wrong places and showed the wrong things, in the process manufacturing a screen argument with opposed political valencies in different cultures of film interpretation. This encourages us to seek textual evidence that acknowledges the contingency of reading protocols.

The most ordered of empirical events—legal proceedings and college TV lessons—are concerned with truth telling and hence narration. They organize information by genre, not by some naturally occurring property of the data. And they rely on the capacity of people to explain themselves and understand others within the norms of a particular, elaborated code. Decades of sociolinguistics tell us how specific such codes are in terms of their availability to dominant social groups (Bennett and Feldman 171–73). I explore this in detail here with particular reference to the brutal beating of Rodney King and subsequent court hearings, a biopic on Harvey Milk, and TV teaching about Peru.

▶

### Video Truth: Rodney King and the Reading of Character

*Can it really be argued that repeated showings of this videotape on television helped maintain the hegemony of America's power elite? Or did this highly symbolic event—the white power structure mercilessly beating down a helpless person*

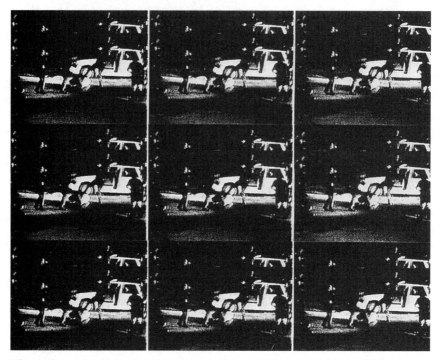

*The Rodney King Police Beating Disaster Series,* by Danny Tisdale, 1992/3, 24″ x 36.″ Reprinted with permission of Danny Tisdale.

*of color—actually undermine the special interests of the powerful? In effect, the Rodney King video became a one-minute commercial for racial discrimination.*
:: Lull 134

*This raw, crude footage in which a man is being beaten carries an indexical whammy.*
:: Nichols *Blurred* 18

*Regardless of what you think you saw, it was not what actually happened.*
:: Sergeant Stacey C. Koon 12

On 29 April 1992, video told the truth in a court of law in California. Simply put, this was a truth of emotion. Three L.A. police officers who beat up Rodney King were acquitted in *California v. Powell, Wind, Briseno, and Koon* (Powell was convicted on a charge of excessive force), one of the few cases in legal history popularly cataloged by the name of someone other than a defendant. The acquittal was obtained through the truth of bureaucratically calibrated emotion, interpreted from video footage shot by George Holliday and sold to a television station for U.S. $500. He had recorded the tape fourteen months earlier, on 3 March 1991, as these men assaulted Mr. King with extraordinary brutality (fifty-six baton blows, at least seven kicks to the body, and four shots from an electronic Taser stun gun) while seventeen other police officers watched on. Later, they taunted him with verbal abuse in the hospital as he lay before them with fractures and other serious injuries (Grabiner and Grabiner 90; Herbert 186 n. 1; Solomon 90; Jacobs 1239).

Houston A. Baker Jr. refers to the beating as "the image of the late twentieth-century." For prosecutor Terry White, the tape is the "most objective piece of evidence" imaginable. Laura Rabinowitz sees it as the moment when "Rodney King, one of the hundreds of black men roughed up by the LAPD," was "blasted . . . into history," visualizing the U.S.$20 million in damages paid by Los Angeles to more than three hundred victims of police brutality between 1986 and 1990 in a city with the highest proportion of killings by police in U.S. history. This was happening even as complaints against white officers by black citizens were markedly unsuccessful. In a federal trial a year later, Koon and Powell were convicted and Wind and Briseno acquitted on charges of violating Mr. King's constitutional protection against unreasonable arrest, an ironic use of legislation enacted during Reconstruction to protect black citizens from the states. The judge breached federal guidelines in minimizing their sentences, on the grounds that Mr. King's conduct contributed to the beating. Furthermore, his award to Mr. King of U.S.$3.8 million in a civil suit was less than the private funds raised for Powell. Meanwhile, the proportion of African American men aged between twenty and twenty-nine in prison had gone from one in four to one in three over the life of the trials (Baker *Black* 102; Rabinowitz 209; Jacobs 1240; Grabiner and Grabiner 91; Reed 177; Herbert 186 n. 1; Thaler 51; Noble; "Black" 3).

The video recorded what Alfred Hitchcock called "noncinema man, man who is not doing things primarily for the camera," exactly as Martin Luther King Jr. had predicted decades earlier: "We will no longer let you beat us in the dark corners," but "make you do it in the glaring light of television." Yet despite the denotative clarity of the original text, these policemen were initially found not guilty of the use of excessive violence by a nonblack jury (four were members of the National Rifle Association and eight had served in the military). Koon and his colleagues had obtained a jury from what they called "John Wayne territory, Green Beret country . . . overwhelmingly white": Simi Valley, geographically distant from the beating but historically and demographically close to it (the number of current and former police officers in Simi Valley exceeded the 1,800 employees of the district's biggest firm). Then Los Angeles became the site of a riot, with

58 people dead and 11,700 arrested. Jesse Jackson was sociological about it: "This is just a part of urban abandonment." John Singleton was incredulous: "We're sitting on a time bomb." But it was a television issue for Dan Quayle. His speech to a California club shortly after the riot tied it to the decay in family values he had witnessed two nights before on CBS, when Murphy Brown produced a child without a husband. Michael Bradley thought it was to do with sociobiology. He explained the beating and its aftermath in terms of the "Neanderthal ancestry" of Jews and other white people, which made them "needlessly brutal" (Hitchcock 215; M. King quoted in Swenson 81; Herbert 191 n. 9; Grabiner and Grabiner 92; Abelmann and Lie 2; Walkowitz 40; Bradley 218–19). This cross-referentiality tells us more than we already knew about Quayle or anti-Semitic Afroscience; it suggests something about the reading of character.

The prosecuting attorney didn't even call Rodney King to testify—silenced again, in Baker's view. Instead, the case relied on video evidence as its "star witness." But that overt, essentially horrendous footage was not read as evidence of overt, essentially horrendous deeds, brutal force captured in seemingly unmediated form. It was read for the externalization of emotion, as per highly produced melodramatic excess. When the *Los Angeles Times* first reported the beating, its coverage emphasized the irrational and unrepresentative nature of the officers' conduct. The defense attorneys had the same focus, but from another angle, stressing the reasonableness of what occurred. They focused on a shot-by-shot breakdown of the tape and a highly directive verbal commentary, concentrating on two aspects: the extent to which the police officers' bodies (a) could be interpreted through a feelings discourse and (b) manifested the principles of L.A. Police Department training. If the police displayed fear, their characters felt it. If their movements expressed this fear and translated it into actions they had been taught, no offense was committed. Careful trial preparation of the defendants by psychologist Elizabeth Loftis assisted in their humanization. Michael Stone, counsel for the defendant Laurence Powell, explained that the plan was for the jury to interpret and identify "not through the eye of the camera but through the eyes of the police officers," officers who were not, as he put it, "paid to roll around in the dirt with the likes of Rodney Glenn King" (Baker "Scene" 42–43; Jacobs 1246–47; Stone quoted in Koon 128 and Mashon 7).

Disaggregation of events is an accepted legal precedent (albeit with a notable dissenting opinion in a U.S. Supreme Court decision from Thurgood Marshall). In this case, violent images were disaggregated to reinvest them with a narrative twinning that simultaneously moved Mr. King from victim to violator *and* instantiated indexicality through standard policing procedures. The officers' anxieties could then be articulated with Mr. King's body by "use-of-force expert" Sergeant Charles Duke, through policies for dealing with a citizen whose "buttocks area has started to rise." The assault was separated into "ten distinct uses of force," with each one weighed against the LAPD manual on beatings and a hermeneutics of the King body: "application," "departmentally approved," and "power strikes" describe the officers' actions, while "cocked," "trigger position," and, finally, "compliance mode" account for Mr. King's body. The two vocabularies make the victim a nonsentient brute by contrast with the policemen's reasonable anxiety (Koon's memoir describes Mr. King as "different . . . big . . . a really monster guy"). At times, the idea of the victim as a savage is declined in favor of a rational-choice model, where his actions are calculated to break the law and endanger police. Astonishingly, the *New York Times* could offer the following headline as late as 1993: "Blows Saved Rodney King's Life, Officer Testifies." As Marita Sturken says, by "rupturing the persistence of vision," this rearticulation "rescripted Rodney King as the agent" of this interaction. Koon's account ultimately *blames* LAPD policy. The elimination in the 1980s of the "chokehold" as a use of force because of "minority leaders" and "the political establishment" made the beating inevitable. Had the chokehold been available, the event would not have occurred: the carotid artery in Mr. King's neck would simply have been held in an armlock, cutting the flow of oxygen and blood to the brain. In short, the actions of all those involved were governmentalized, assigned certain meanings, tensions, and valences in accord with forms of narrative and genre that emerged from the chronology re-created and the empirical relationships established for and by the jury (Stone quoted in Herbert 195; Rabinowitz 210–11; Crenshaw and Peller 58–59; Duke quoted in Goodwin 619; testimony quoted in Goodwin 617 and P. Williams 52–53; Sturken 39; Koon 20–21, 56, 23, 54; Herbert 189; *Times* quoted in Nichols *Blurred* 23; Garfinkel 107).

Harvey Sacks talks about Adam and Eve's guilt and the problem of unruly conspicuousness, encountered in chapter 3: the realization "that they are observables" links "being noticeable" to "being deviant." The idea that "the sinner can be seen" is a standard component of police practice, along with the requirement to account for being in a place and behaving in a certain way. Without such a justification, suspects are subjected to "incongruity procedures," which transform, for example, being a woman walking on the street into being a streetwalker. Such procedures are listed and explained in police training manuals, tying the means of establishing suspects to the means of verbalizing inferences in an ordered, bureaucratic manner. Picking up from Sacks's lead, others have noted how police justify their violence through a combination of rebuttals to implied critiques in questions from attorneys that build a narrative and accounts that emphasize constraints on their conduct: the police are always *weak* as a justification for the failure *or* success of their actions, and this is routinely related to paralinguistic, inferential interpretations of character. As Garfinkel found, juries draw on many sources in order to differentiate themselves from other compartments of existence: the official handbook, the underlying norms of the voir dire, the conduct of officers of the court, screen dramatizations, and civics classes (Sacks "Notes" 280–83, 285, 288; Atkinson and Drew 163–66; Brannigan and Lynch; Garfinkel 110).

Connotative devices used by the defense and others have themselves been retroped. Their doublespeak is shown up in *Demolition Man* (Marco Brambilla, 1993), in which the escaped criminal Simon Phoenix is confronted by police officers who are subject to microphysical instruction from a centralized computer source. It tells them what to do next, following machinelike steps up from verbal to physical reprimands and violence in response to his more spontaneous acts. Phoenix, cryogenically preserved from another age, is bemused by this anal scientism. The King intertext is called up, ironically, on Phoenix's face. His bafflement contrasts with the police officers' blankness, mirroring public horror at the alibi for the violence enacted on Mr. King. Elsewhere, the original tape of Rodney King's beating prefaces Spike Lee's *Malcolm X* (1992), and Branford Marsalis's saxophone in *No Justice, No Peace* (Portia Cobb, 1993) is rhythmically synchronized with the number of blows delivered to Mr. King's body. Ice Cube's 1991 *Death Certificate* release has a dialogue between a police officer and the singer. The policeman says, "We're gonna treat you like a king. . . . Rodney King! Martin Luther King! And all the other goddam kings from Africa!" The Afrocentric Not Channel Zero collective's tape *The Nation Erupts*, broadcast on Deep Dish TV, commences with the Holliday footage, then shows news and documentary accounts of racial riots, culminating in actual incidents from the 1992 rebellion. Throughout the text, the Rodney King beating recurs. The *Oprah Winfrey Show* dedicated a series of programs to racism in 1992, with the Holliday footage a regular. One episode cut from disturbing audience disputes between Korean and African Americans to the tape, along with Mr. King's pleas for tolerance, ultimately seguing into the saxophone that begins Marvin Gaye's "What's Going On." More prosaically, O. J. Simpson's legal team in 1994–95 included an investigator who had worked on LAPD racism during the Rodney King cases (Ice Cube quoted in Kellner *Media* 184–85; Ouellette 177–78; Hamamoto 235–37; Lynch and Bogen 241). The literal is rendered symbolic, as a video of record is connotatively transformed into a metonym for race relations.

Steven Brill, founding chair and chief executive officer of the Courtroom Television Network, defended himself against accusations of sensationalism with reference to the King hearings (this from a man who promoted the nascent service to Time Warner cable as "soap opera meets C-SPAN"). Brill argued that the audience had made up its mind on the basis of an eleven-second tape of the violence shown on network and local newscasts. When added to the testimony, the full seventy-one-second version made the case "ambiguous." (The defense asked his network to petition federal authorities for the right to broadcast the second case.) This echoed the position enunciated by many police advocates and conservative critics, who disparaged the excerpted version. Television news programs defended their decision to excise some material on aesthetic grounds: it was not of broadcast quality/clarity. On the other hand, Rush Limbaugh replayed part of the tape frame by frame on his television show to produce a new context, that of Mr. King advancing on the police. At New York's Museum of Television and Radio in 1995, Limbaugh mockingly impersonated Mr. King's plea for everybody to "get along," to applause from the audience. As Mwatabu S. Okantah said of the first trial, here was "America's black/whitemare raging / once again in the streets" (Sikes 34; Solomon 95; O'Heffernan 7; Alexander 92; Okantah 136).

The video record should have guaranteed what the prosecution ruefully referred to after the event as "the slam-dunk case of the century." But video also provided points of reference against training and interiority. Humanistic interpretations were not solely responsible for what happened; racism was clearly the key. But because law is often about interpreting doctrinal materials, systems of reading are also important in explaining miscarriages of justice. The King tape was subject to plural viewing practices, contexts, and occasions that turned members of a jury into habitués of white violence (prosecutor quoted in Anna Smith xxi; Dumm 186).

How was this achieved? Through close-reading protocols: repetition, reversal, freeze-framing, and slow motion. The defense's shot-by-shot still photographs, mounted on the whitest of backdrops, were akin to grisly postproduction storyboards. Textual analysis, of the kind TV viewers teach themselves and university professors teach their students every day, animated the rationale, if not the drive, of the jury's verdict. Consider the following from one juror, cited as saying Mr. King was responsible for the violence. She knew this thanks to her inspection of the videotape in slow motion: "he was in full control" and resisting arrest, she told local television. So, as with the defense's assertion that the officers were afraid, character interpretations based on what people look like they are feeling justify brutality. Now, I am not saying the psy-complexes are, or should be, irrelevant to the processes of law. Rather, I want to suggest that assigning emotions on the basis of physical acts, and in explanation of them, informs the architecture of this decision and much film and TV interpretation. This was clearly understood by the defense, and it is a problem. It is part of a developing tradition of reading character that extrapolates from the internal to the external of human figures and back again, often with scant regard for questions of a more social kind, such as institutional power. The prosecution in the second case understood this. It successfully negated issues of interiority by juxtaposing the scientistic administrative model of LAPD manuals against civil rights discourse (Herbert 196).

▶ ────────────────────────────────────────

### Facing the Truth

> *President Eisenhower used to say, "Look me in the eye when you say that," . . . says Robert Fogelnest, president of the National Association of Criminal Defense Lawyers. "If you're a loan officer in a bank, would you want to make a decision based on statements someone made to you over a television screen?"*
> :: C. Johnson B1

> *Videotestimonies make a double claim: they convey "I was there," but also "I am here"—here to tell you about it, to take that responsibility despite trauma and pain, despite the divide between present and past. The "I am here" is the present aware of the past but not seeking its grounding there.*
> :: Hartman 137

> *Zapruder's film footage . . . retains a privileged position . . . a central yet marginalized piece of film, scandalous and long sequestered for its content, prized as vérité, dissected for its narrative, a thinly veiled subject for the commercial movie industry (Brian De Palma's* Blow Out *after Antonioni's* Blow-Up*), and a structuring absence for the film avant-garde (Bruce Conner's* Report*).*
> :: Simon 35

The struggle for meaning in the King case was waged over referentiality among image, event, rule book, and interiority, as well as race. Physiognomic hermeneutics and police rules provided a master code that initially won the day.

It is important to trace the history of legal/industrial truth telling to see how "actuality" footage is understood. Film theorist Michael Renov suggests the defense attorneys in the first case "had perfected their tactics through a careful reading of contemporary film theory" by encouraging the jurors to identify with the accused (9). And the Society for Cinema Studies passed a resolution condemning this application of its own favored pastime. SCS was quickly attacked for a positivistic faith in empiricism: the prosecution should have trained the jurors in contextual semiotics that would add a history and currency of racism to the images. So Avital Ronell calls for an exposure to the tape that will avoid "immediate sense perception" in favor of "reading" (Gooding-Williams 167; Murphy and Jung 478–79, 481–83; Ronell 3). But there are times when it is strategically necessary to accept profilmic surface images and couple them to the rule of law, to the exclusion of depth readings. The visceral immediacy of this violence for spectators is itself informed by a fundamental ethic of care that is as powerful as the seemingly incommensurate racist terror that may accompany it.

Where does this will to physiognomy come from? Guillaume-Benjamin Duchenne, a key figure in the early life of neurology, published *The Mechanism of Human Facial Expression* in 1862. Duchenne's work merges medicine, photography, and aesthetics to correlate muscles and feelings. He records and interprets the body as a physical manifestation of a psychic state. A decade later, early Darwinian theory claimed that each emotion produced a universal facial correlation. Challenged since by cultural relativism, this position has been revived in recent years. Against it, we confront V. I. Pudovkin's "Types Instead of Actors" talk from 1929, in which he relates an "experiment" conducted by Lev Kuleshov that stresses the insignificance of profilmic events by comparison with their combination after the fact, illustrating that editing can produce new meanings barely prefigured on location or the set by altering the sequence of shots. The "experiment" intermingled smiling and frightened looks with a revolver, radically transforming facial subjectivity as the actor in shot is ascribed a range of interiorities from cowardice to bravery, depending on the choice of image bracketing the weapon. Although there is controversy about this experiment *qua* historical event, it has canonical status in screen studies and much film production. Hitchcock's essay on production for the 1965 *Encyclopaedia Britannica* calls the Kuleshov effect "pure cinema." He admires the capacity of editing to alter evaluation of the person so comprehensively, simply by reordering a sequence (Amirault 62–63; Baron-Cohen et al. 40–41; Pudovkin 167–68; N. Holland 79–82; Prince and Hensley; Hitchcock 215). Physiognomic interpretations heave themselves remorselessly onto reading character, even when close-ups are juxtaposed without any frame to fix actants in a single space. A cause-and-effect relationship between shots, as per the Kuleshov effect, is even instantiated in *Uhl v. Columbia Broadcasting System*, when the Supreme Court

> found that the juxtaposition of three film clips—one of geese in a field, one of plaintiff shooting horizontally, and one of plaintiff holding a dead goose—made it appear that plaintiff was unsportsmanlike in killing a goose on the ground. . . . Actual malice was found in the fact that the film editors had put the film together "to produce the effect of shock they were seeking." (Zimmerman 416 n. 282)

The beating of Mr. King was recorded in long shot, which is classically associated with establishing space and time rather than individuality. But it was subjected to the humanistic readings associated with the Kuleshov effect. In other words, the capacity of video and other evidence to establish the identities of those in the frame—which some might have regarded as sufficient grounds for conviction—was obliterated by an overlay that sought and found interiority among the violators.

Wittgenstein understands a picture as "a situation in logical space, the existence and non-existence of states of affairs" that position the picture "against reality like a measure." The picture touches reality through "correlations . . . with things." Truth and falsehood depend on this process of comparison and measurement (*Tractatus* 8–10). Abraham Zapruder's 8mm film of John F. Kennedy's assassination has probably been the subject of more controversy and close reading than any other film text, in just this way. Zapruder's footage shows how actuality material gains connotative complexity as it moves through time and space. Once the film was developed, copies went to the FBI, the CIA's National Photo Interpretation Center, Zapruder himself, and *Life* magazine. The first public exposure was in *Life* a week after the murder. The magazine published thirty-one frames, excluding the president's head wound and thereby eliminating chronology from the text. This aided the promulgation of a lone-killer, magic-bullet explanation, as it removed evidence of multiple sites of fire. Three years later, *Life* published an interview with John Connally—who had always maintained he and Kennedy were hit by separate shots—along with additional frames. Legal battles ensued over the Zapruder images when the magazine claimed copyright against a book publisher. The court found the film to be a "particular form or record" with "many elements of creativity," such as the decision to use moving pictures, color stock, a telephoto lens, and a specific physical setting. As the entire reel became publicly available, so the forms of interpreting it multiplied: optical enlargements of Kennedy's head exploding, computer measurements that confounded what could be seen with the human eye, arrested and enhanced film speed—all serving as evidence for incommensurate conspiracy and anticonspiracy explanations (Simon 35–54).

Recorded images have been equally complicated in less-known crimes. The very public abuse of black bodies has often led to riots, even without actuality footage: 1917 in East St. Louis, 1919 and 1967 in Chicago, and 1943 in Belle Isle. But the pace and quality of information flow increases immeasurably with TV images. Footage of a 1980 trial in which five Dade County officers were acquitted of killing black businessman Arthur McDuffie led to three days of riots in Miami. The same year, TV crews caught on film North Carolina Klansmen murdering five demonstrators. African Americans were excluded from juries in successive trials of the Klansmen over the next four years, and the killers were acquitted. In 1989, two Long Beach, California, police officers were taped pushing Donald Jackson though a plate glass window. Jackson, an African American and an off-duty policeman, was known to be critical of excessive force and claimed that KKK literature was being circulated in police stations. In the early 1990s, white Australian officers videotaped themselves at a party in "blackface" and hanging gear, mocking the many Aboriginal people who have died in custody. Public release of the text produced the predictable apologia of humor. Just before the King verdict, Soon Ja Du, a Korean American grocer in Los Angeles, was given a minimal sentence for killing Latasha Harlins, a young black woman, the act captured on videotape. The Soon Ja Du and Rodney King tapes meshed, producing a riot that pitted Asian and African American against one another. Further outcry followed the airing in 1996 of TV-crew footage of the end of a high-speed chase when police in California brutally beat people who had run from a truck thought to be carrying illegal immigrants (Jacobs 1252; Thaler 30; Fukurai et al. 6; Simmons 144; Abelmann and Lie 9, 148; P. Turner 207; "California").

There are direct parallels to the King case in Western Australia. Reaction to the initial acquittals there included the poisoning of baby food in supermarkets, allegedly in protest. And a few days later, Joseph Dethridge, a seventeen-year-old, was beaten senseless and his jaw broken by Sergeant Desmond Smith in the Fremantle police station. He had been taken there after he questioned the arrest of a friend for refusing to "move on" from the main street. A videotape of the charge room shows Dethridge being tossed against a wall, kicked, and taken out of screen space. A scream is then audible on the sound track. (When U.N. Security Council delegates were shown videotape of Israeli border guards killing Palestinians gathered at the Al-Aqsa mosque in Jerusalem, the screams for help and medical supplies made as big an impact as the visuals, as did Mr. Dethridge's cries. Conversely, the amateur videotape of Israeli police officers kicking Palestinians near a Jerusalem checkpoint in 1996 relied on image for its impact.) Back in-shot, his face covered in blood, Dethridge accuses Smith of assaulting him. After months of secrecy, the tape was shown in court and then on national TV, leading to a massive outcry about police brutality. Smith was fined A$5,000, which was paid by an anonymous benefactor; after further public protests, he was sacked from the force but was later reinstated on grounds of wrongful dismissal. Smith's defense referred to stress—an alibi—and service—a mitigation—that supposedly transcended his brutality (Hammond; Jayyusi 51 n. 25; Greenberg).

In less public forums, videotape encourages psychologists to make hermeneutic strides through slow-motion investigations of the human face, which produce so much knowledge that they can allegedly assist in the early identification of senile dementia. Citizens are subjected to proxemics, choreometrics, kinesics, and family therapy through tape and analysis. In the 1970s, ethnographic film and video theorists sought both democratizing and disciplinary aspects to their work. Video would enable "the people" to create their own truths, to become cultural producers. But it would also provide science with new truths, through its time-shifting capacity to lay bare processes hidden from the unaided human eye. Perhaps the most spectacular research moment was the Bronx State Hospital's Project in Human Communication, which placed video cameras in homes to analyze caring and sharing domestic moments (inter alia) (Hanson 219, 225; Asch et al. 179; MacDougall 407).

What of video trials? Miami has a long history of misdemeanor arraignments recorded in prison chapels. Public defenders criticize this practice because it hinders counsel, defendant, and family communicating with each other and the bench. The Australian High Court conducted its first telehearings in 1988. With justices in Canberra and counsel in Brisbane, the dramaturgy saw lawyers standing at a lectern fifteen feet from the video screen that showed members of the bench, in keeping with the rules when they are physically in the same room: distance discourages the physiognomy engendered by close-ups. While clearly animated by pompous legalisms, this rule pays tribute to the need to go beyond personal emotional meaning in due process. Of course, it connects to a very long tradition of cinema and television courtroom drama. That tradition itself makes an impact on jurors' expectations of the performance of attorneys. Lawyers borrow from screen drama to engage knowledge of the genre: spectatorship in one domain influences performance in another. So William Kunstler once asked a client to raise his shirt in court to reveal bullet wounds allegedly suffered as a result of police aggression, because such a maneuver had proven effective in *Philadelphia* (Jonathan Demme, 1993) when the protagonist displayed his lesions to the jury (Surette and Terry 245–48; T. Harris).

Critics believe TV coverage cheapens proceedings, encouraging participants to engage in excessive conduct that is driven by television genres rather than due legal process. Others think cameras in court open the law to public discussion and increase understanding of how it works. The U.S. Supreme Court favors open media access to judicial proceedings under the First Amendment as a means of cultivating citizens' confidence in and knowledge of the system. It overturned the 1965 conviction of Billie Sol Estes on the grounds that permitting TV to show the trial violated due process, but left the way open for this to change once television had become an ordinary part of everyday life rather than something new and strange. The popular—TV—could lend the unpopular—the law—some of its glow. Coverage has been problematic on occasions such as the 1984 New Bedford rape case, when the victim's name was broadcast by mistake. The first major international debate about trial television occurred with the 1989 Steinberg case of homicide/manslaughter/spouse and child abuse. The judge, Harold Rothwax, was publicly tutored by his wife to drop gestural and facial mannerisms that were producing unfavorable media comment. One juror questioned whether "her psychological, therapeutic suggestions" were appropriate guides for judicial performance. Witness Hedda Nussbaum, whose credibility relied on her continuing to look abused twelve months after she had last seen the accused, at first wore a colorful scarf to testify. This was seen as a major error, because it signified joy, and her subsequent appearances were carefully orchestrated, through videotape coaching, to guarantee authenticity (Chance; Gerbner "Cameras"; McLeod; Thaler 146–47; Surette 15; juror quoted in Thaler 172).

The status of video evidence was addressed in a 1987 case before the Supreme Court of Victoria. The plaintiff was suffering from lung cancer allegedly connected to the actions of the defendant. Terminally ill and in the hospital, the plaintiff gave evidence on tape for a jury to consider. The defense argued that close-ups would make the jurors sympathize with the plaintiff, outweighing the value of testimony that would otherwise have been unavailable. This position was not supported by the judge hearing the case, because he believed the pain and suffering experienced by the plaintiff were useful records. In other words, the tape was more accurate than a written transcript. Reenactments using the testimony of truthful and mendacious witnesses, read on tape by actors and interpreted by jurors, suggest that deception is routinely, and often wrongly, suspected when close-ups are available. The close-up *is* crucial to establishing the plausibility of testimony, but long shots help jurors remember details, because they contextualize and afford relief from intense interiorization. In addition to shot type and length, of course, jurors are also influenced by the class, race, gender, occupation, and body shape of witnesses and their own backgrounds: the rate of guilty verdicts in the United States delivered by people with Northern European backgrounds and high incomes is high compared with the rates of the rest of the population, and people across the board tend to acquit folks from their own racial backgrounds and convict "the other." The Constitution empowers juries to be partial in the sense of coming from the locale where the crime was committed and from a community that is demographically representative; hence the call for racially mixed juries, unlike the white male-dominated juror and black/immigrant-dominated defendant profiles we still have (Surette 224; Starke; Miller and Fontes 188–89, 205, 172; Kaminski and Miller 96, 100; Barber 64; Skolnick and Fyfe xiii; Dane and Wrightsman 104–5; Fukurai et al. 3–6).

Tapes of police interviewing suspects present another issue for the courts. Should such evidence be admissible if it has been edited? If confessions are not on tape but other material is, should it be admissible? What about taped *Miranda v. Arizona* warnings, especially as videotaped confessions have been promoted to police as ways of getting around *Miranda*? (For more than a decade, various jurisdictions have equipped patrol cars with video systems that automatically begin recording when blue lights flash or ignitions are turned.) There is already proof that confessional narratives on video encourage jurors to emphasize states of mind in their deliberations on criminal cases. This also has implications for video reenactments: the accused can provide a voice-over commenting on the validity or otherwise of the acting. Conversely, where there is a Grand Guignol aspect to actuality tape, this is frequently toned down by presenting the material to juries in black and white. The process also involves certain telegenic protocols. For instance, the police often position the camera over the interviewing officer's left shoulder. This concentration on the accused conceals what is going on elsewhere in the interview room. Many police are worried that shifting depth of field from wide angles to close-ups through use of a zoom will alienate jurors by emphasizing critical moments. Hence their negativity in the face of requests from the bench for such camera movements. University studies indicate that exclusive concentration on the suspect, as opposed to wide-angle coverage of everybody in the room, encourages viewers to believe there has been minimal coercion, even though audience sympathy is engaged with the subject in-shot. When point of view centers on the detective, the assumption of coercion is more prevalent. The legal system defends its attention to the confessor on the grounds that any coercion out of shot will be reflected in the body of the suspect. Courts of review are unclear about privacy rights from taped confessions versus the public's right to knowledge of the judicial process (Waye 234–39, 241; Sechrest et al. 257, 260–61; Surette and Terry 243; A. Grant 166–67; Lassiter and Irvine; Freedman 68–70).

At the same time, tapes showing entrapment, such as those in the John DeLorean and Marion Barry cases, raise questions about the conduct of officers and informers onscreen. The Recruit Cosmos bribery scandal, which rocked Japanese politics in the late 1980s, was sparked off by tape of a member of Parliament, Yanusoke Narazaki, shouting "Wow!" as he made his way through piles of 10,000 yen notes offered by Hiroshi Matsubara, a director of the real-estate development company. Much was made of the worry in the director's voice as he urged the politician to accept the bribe. The rejection of the money uncovered the whole scandal. The use of concealed cameras by the news media has led to public embarrassment and complicated lawsuits many times across the 1990s, but the practice goes back to 1928, when a photographer from the *Daily News* shot an electrocution in Sing Sing using a camera strapped to his ankle. TV programs used concealed cameras frequently in the 1950s. This became much easier in 1989, with the development of new lipstick-size technology. When added to TV's interest in cheap actuality genres, this has produced new programs and ethics. Lawyers for those exposed by hidden video move inside the psyches of their clients, going deeper than the technology to plumb feelings and privacy in opposition to ideas of the public interest. Again, we encounter interiorities overpowering acts that contradict the law (Ries; Lissit).

We might return here to the aetiological and evidentiary use of video in the 1993 murder in Liverpool of two-year-old James Bulger, mentioned in chapter 1. His abduction by preteens Robert Thompson and Jon Venables was captured by a shopping-mall security camera, its image distorted and fragmentary. Then the search was on to explain why they killed the little boy. Venables's father had just rented *Child's Play 3* (Jack Bender, 1991), and the film was closely analyzed for tropes in the Bulger case (train tracks, paint splattering, battery use, and child abduction; much was also made of a woman's report that her six-year-old son had "become possessed" after seeing it, the evidence being his attempt to kill the family pet). The two boys were psychologized with reference to the fact that they watched cartoons on video after the killing and were themselves recorded over twelve hours of interrogation, the tapes later played in court. These videos showed police encouraging Venables to narrativize the events in filmic terms. He did so through a fictional story that was then judged to be a historical account and hence a confession (Morrison; Alton 170). Keneally and Spielberg hovered in the ether.

In short, Edenic fantasies projected onto children had to have their failure explained, with popular cultural technology used to transform relations of truth and falsehood, itself both the culprit and the investigator of wrongdoing. Like the King defenses, courtroom melodrama of Hollywood's silent era frequently pitted the identificatory power of impassioned testimonies of innocence against external credibility. This is the simultaneously reliable and unreliable narrator that we encounter in *Sunset Boulevard* (Billy Wilder, 1950), a story told by a corpse, or *C'est arrivé près de chez vous* (*Man Bites Dog*) (Rémy Belvaux, André Bonzel, and Benoît Poelvoorde, 1992), in which a film crew documenting a serial killer's murders participates in his crimes. In each case, the viewer depends on flashbacks or recording methods that themselves depend on impossibility: we learn how a man died in *Sunset* by listening to him as he floats, lifeless, in a swimming pool, and *C'est arrivé* tells us about the filmmakers' complicity through the very techniques of truth telling that are impelling them on to gang rape and homicide. Perhaps the best instance of film narration as proof of its own duplicity is *Laura* (Otto Preminger, 1944). Waldo Lydecker's recurring voice-over and flashbacks about Laura's life and death are retrospectively revealed to be accurate because he played a part in a murder. Continuity rules of storytelling, performance, and promotion merge fictional with factual spaces of truth telling, as when CNN cut from Edward Kennedy's testimony in the 1991 William Kennedy Smith rape trial about his family's many tragedies to a commercial for Oliver Stone's *JFK* (Turim 53–54; Thaler 48–49).

Clearly, even relatively unmotivated, highly indexical footage, such as the Rodney King video, is open to high-handed interpretation in search of interiority. But there is always a public politics of governmentality to suggest other directions. Raphael Sonenstein locates the video and its aftermath in a history of L.A. coalition politics. The remarkable if inconsistent links among liberal big business, African Americans, and Jews that had propelled the city from the direst of conservative backwaters to a comparatively progressive place during Tom Bradley's decades as mayor seemed all but over by 1991. Economic issues had become central, along with questions about the mayor's financial probity. But racial and social policy matters returned to the limelight once the video was broadcast. Proposition F, a proposal to reform the LAPD and make it more accountable, was voted on in June 1992. The old coalition of downtown finance capital, liberal whites, and ethnic minorities swung behind the proposal, which passed by an overwhelming margin (220, 224–25). That kind of politics, in some ways much more hopeful than culturalist perspectives on the King incident have allowed (or discussed), is crucial to our next case.

## Harvey Milk

> *History and memory intertwine; meaning and action, past and present, hinge on one another distinctively. Documentary and fiction, social actor and social other, knowledge and doubt, concept and experience share boundaries.*
> :: Nichols *Blurred* 1

> *Dragnet was one of the great instruments to give the people of the United States a picture of the policeman as he really is. It was most authentic. We participated in the editing of the series and in their filming. If we had any objections on technical grounds our objections were met. This program showed the true portrait of the Policeman as a hard-working, selfless man, willing to go out and brave all sorts of hazards and work long hours to protect the community.*
> :: William H. Parker, LAPD police chief, 1962, quoted in Skolnick and Fyfe xi

> *Several occupational groups, including federal polygraphers, robbery investigators, judges, and psychiatrists, were not significantly more accurate at detecting deception than college students. . . . only secret service agents were more successful. . . . humans are poor lie detectors . . . only slightly more accurate than a flip of the coin.*
> :: Miller and Stiff 69

*The Times of Harvey Milk* (Robert Epstein, 1984) is a film about both representative and representational issues: the life of a gay politician murdered in office. It won a 1985 Academy Award for Best Feature Documentary, was named Best Documentary by the New York Film Critics Circle, and gained three Emmys the following year. The film had begun as a dialectical enterprise covering the 1970s debate over banning homosexual men and women from teaching positions in California. Director Epstein says Milk "emerged as someone worthy of being the centre of the film I was then researching" (quoted in M. Smith). That sense intensified with his assassination, shortly after the plebiscite on teaching. To solicit financing and provoke community discussion, the filmmaker sent pamphlets about the movie to fifteen thousand people, and a sampler reel circulated for years.

The text now stands for a "brief golden age of gay freedom, coalition politics on an unprecedented scale and the emergence of an identifiable gay community." For while the mainstream media honed in on its depiction of conflictual values, *Harvey Milk* also stood for an international alliance and outrage and a linkage of interests across minorities and classes. The producers strove to avoid having *Milk* classified as "a gay film." They wanted to stress that "the human experience of being gay . . . is inherently political" in the sense of gains made in the arena of civil rights and counteractions against those gains. The central character's status as a culture hero inside the mainstream political infrastructure was posthumously eponymized in San Francisco's Harvey Milk Gay and Lesbian Democratic Club and Manhattan's Harvey Milk School for Gay and Lesbian Youth: a nice instance of identity politics moving between counter-public-sphere sites of self-formation to produce change inside the public sphere "proper." For the right, Milk remains a troubling sign. John Agresto, for example, accuses the NEA of promoting "*conformist* art of the highest degree" because it favors an orthodox set of liberal values. His sine qua non for relieving himself of this view will come "when I hear that the NEA funded an artist who urinates on a portrait of Harvey Milk." The Houston Grand Opera's 1995 decision to stage an opera based on Milk led to "stormy board meetings, the loss of accustomed corporate sponsorship, and the wrath of fundamentalist Texans" (Russo 318; Waugh "Lesbian" 264, 268; Erens; Agresto 336–37; Schwarz).

The film comprises nine segments. The establishing shot is effectively the title, because a voice-over is already telling us that the text is headed toward the death of its protagonist. There is offscreen verbal reaction, an extreme close-up and freeze-frame of Milk, and a still of him smiling. The camera zooms in as a sound recording to be played in the event of his death is announced. As the tape runs, we cut to slow-motion footage of a gay pride march: Milk cuddling another man, marchers bobbing up and down in forward motion, Milk atop a float, and then the conclusion to the audiotape, where he tells us, "I have never considered myself a candidate" but rather "part of a movement." So the protagonist is not all there is to the text; this is about his *Times*. (The director did not interview Milk's boyfriend or those with a "personal interest in his life" because the filmmakers "weren't going after a biography of the man, but a portrait of the times" [quoted in M. Smith].) The other eight segments deal with people's first encounters with Milk, electoral reform and the Castro subculture, Milk's campaign and election, the early months of his term in office, the issue of gay rights in the light of repressive legislative proposals, his murder, the trial, and its aftermath. The text mixes cinema verité with history through news footage from the time, other archival material, and interviews shot for *Milk* itself over four years. The biggest issue for the director was explaining the murderer's motives, "to bring him into the film so that he's a character." The filmmakers edited out most retrospective discussion of Dan White, the killer, relying instead on old television interviews: his own words. They elected not to feature people with an institutional involvement in the murder—politicians and police—but rather "common folk" (Erens).

*Milk* is a very straightforward documentary. It is narrated by a voice-of-god that growls good-humoredly and trustworthily onto the sound track. Weird underlaying music begins as the camera moves to an extreme close-up on a still of White's face. The music is subliminal and haunting at times, evocative of an anthemic procession at others. A heterosexual working man who formerly disliked "fruits and kooks" is interviewed. His implication that the political culture murdered Milk and then acted poorly after the fact is both an overt counterweight to the successful psychologization of the murderer by his defense (resonances?) and an index of Milk's appeal. There is a sense of Harvey Milk as a Christ-like figure: he united the interests of minorities, predicted his own death, stood for principle, and was Jewish. (Bernard Holland criticized a later docu-opera about him, claiming a "small-time entrepreneur" could not sustain this heroic parallel.) The sense of San Francisco as *the* site for a messianic figure to appear is inordinately strong. We are told he contrived publicity and could be temperamental, even childish (the fate of men). There were clearly ways in which he connived politically, in keeping with the necessities of public office. But he kept the faith in speaking for people excluded from politics by their identity.

This text has many ingredients that could lead me to hate it: the disembodied tones of an elderly gentleman telling me what to think, TV news presented unproblematically as factual, interviews with participants that deny any role to the camera crew (other than when a woman fruitlessly asks them to stop filming), and relentlessly straight continuity editing. In short, everything about the form and content of *The Times of Harvey Milk* denies the contingency of truth and cries out to be read for character through liberal humanism and expressive totality. Others may get it wrong, but this film and its sympathetic watchers will not. Elliott Stein said of a screening at the New York Film Festival:

> The end product is well-crafted, entertaining and functional. It will reach the hearts and minds of mainstream liberal heterosexuals; homosexuals will get out their handkerchiefs of varied hues and, understandably, shed tears for California's first openly gay elected official—the first gay martyr. . . .

> . . . somewhat antiseptic[, i]t has been packaged to make festivals, not
> waves. The raunchiness of Milk's life, the raw sexuality that was an intrinsic
> part of gay liberation in San Francisco in the Seventies have been kept at
> bay, domesticated. The attractive talking heads that yak brightly at length—
> gay, straight, working-class, middle-class—all have this in common: none
> was really an intimate of Harvey Milk. Not one of his many lovers was
> interviewed. (71)

Harvey, in short, did all right for himself. This promiscuity, a new ethic of
relating, was integral to the counterideology of 1970s gay politics. That
politics took as its rallying cry the unlikely slogan "Think we're lowdown
and disgusting? Damn right we are." For Leo Bersani, gay men define
themselves by turning homophobia into a force of desire that jumbles drives
and identifications in a cathectic excitement that seeks self-questioning in
place of mannered tolerance. Such a logic informs D. A. Miller's search for
"a gay writing position" rather than the special pleading of identity miser-
ablism that can "bore or terrorize with a 'positive image'" (Bersani 208; D.
Miller 41).

*Milk* is not concerned with this form of identity adventurism. It is
relatively quiet and demure—hot and disturbed when the liberal cultural-
capitalist state acts out of order with its own discourse, but essentially
polite and controlled. It wants to do away with stereotypes. Hence the
silences over the protagonist's appetite for sex and the fact that pornographic home happy-snappies were a staple for his camera store. In keeping with this tame-gay discourse, there is no mention of prevalent conspiracy theories that the killer did not act alone. We can dimly hear marchers
shouting, "Dan White, Dan White, hit man for the New Right," but no
reference is made to police officers' wearing "Free Dan White" T-shirts
under their uniforms during the trial, in keeping with their loathing of
Mayor George Moscone (shot along with Milk) for having appointed a
liberal chief of police. Nor are we told of the systematic exclusion of gays
from the jury (Waugh "Lesbian" 257; Stein 71; M. Smith).

And yet this is the most moving documentary I have seen. I love the
avuncular voice-over, because it mixes ironized delivery with identification
(matched by the concern of an elderly, straight, white, organic intellectual
of the working class). I love the TV news, because there is very dramatic
shooting on the run and we see a reporter interviewed after the event talking about her pretense of impartiality. I love the interviews because the subjects are spectacularly articulate and varied: yuppie consultant, dyke-bikie,
Chinese lawyer, union ancient, gay activist, and faggy schoolteacher. I love
the notion of Harvey as a saint, because of his nose, his muscles, and his

voice. I forgive that he ran his own business and the sanctimoniousness of it all, because I remember how excited I and so many others twelve thousand miles away were when Milk was elected, devastated when he and Moscone were murdered, and outraged when Dan White was found guilty of voluntary manslaughter rather than first-degree murder. (This was similar to our feelings when Rodney King's assailants were originally found not guilty.) When it is claimed White ate too much junk food (the "Hostess Twinkies defense" that blames popular culture for heightening emotional distress) and was acting instinctively as a former police officer by reloading his gun after killing one man prior to murdering another, it's just like the notion of Mr. King's violators behaving in accordance with the rule book given their interpretation of his body and the jurors' reciprocal reading of their interiorities. And the Twinkies defense continues to be used (Haberman).

There is another reason this text is so important: it merges the representative with the representational. Constitutionality and sexuality converge, showing the prospects and limits to such a meeting. In place of absolutist oppositionality, a rapprochement was arrived at between minority and majority politics and infrastructure. Harvey Milk was political on behalf of all the disenfranchised. He worked with the system. There followed an incident when that rapprochement was shown to be underachieved, as forces of evil betrayed decency. Now our understanding of this in retrospect—and the same applies to Mr. King—could be achieved only through documentary, and through a notion of government inside the state and also against it. The court of appeal *against* the state *remains* the state, in its complex amalgam of citizenry and population, who in turn serve as its legitimacy, in the form of an electorate, and its target, in the form of a body of bodies. So what makes the film political? Bob Ellis describes *Milk* like this: "as vivacious and lacerating a mural of the lunacy that is American politics and law as that greatest of radical documentaries Harlem [sic] County. . . . It confronts the poofter basher in all of us . . . moves all of us to tears of rage." Again, we see the shift from the external to the internal so characteristic of screen truth. No wonder the incident produced the short-fiction subject *A Letter to Harvey Milk* (Yariv Kohn, 1991), Stewart Wallace and Michael Korie's *Harvey Milk* 1995 opera, Emily Mann's play *Execution of Justice* in 1986 (she went on to direct Anna Deveare Smith's *Twilight: Los Angeles, 1992*, about the riots), Bill T. Jones's 1991 *Another History of Collage* choreography, and the Dead Kennedys' "Lily White Dan Sings I Fought the Law (and I Won)." Not to mention Dianne Feinstein's TV commercials from her 1990 California campaign for governor, which used footage of her tearfully announcing the Milk-Moscone murders to the press, to show that she could hold people together in a civil crisis. This is the same Feinstein who as a Democratic senator distinguished herself during hearings on the *Enola Gay* Smithsonian controversy in 1995 by bemoaning reforms to the study of history since she had majored in the subject at Stanford: "I have seen history change" from "essentially a recitation of fact, leaving the reader to draw their own analysis" to "a writer's interpretation. . . . I wonder about the wisdom of presenting any interpretation" (Clendinen; Feinstein quoted in Thelen 1035). It is to the question of historical truth that we now turn.

▶

## The Americas

> Chile and Peru are narrow coastal territories, and they have no culture of their own. . . . it did possess an indigenous culture when it was first discovered by the Europeans. . . . We do have information concerning America and its culture, especially as it had developed in Mexico and Peru, but only to the effect that it was a purely national culture which had to perish as soon as the spirit approached it.
> :: Hegel 157, 163

The intersection of truth, Latin America, and U.S. television forms the remainder of this chapter. General news coverage of the region in the United States is rare by contrast with reports of disaster and revolution, and there is normally no ongoing media presence or background to stories. *The Americas* television series, which screened in prime time in January–March 1993, was designed to rectify this problem. A coproduction of WGBH Boston for PBS and Britain's Central Television Enterprises for Channel 4, it was funded by Annenberg and other foundations (including Carnegie and Rockefeller). The series and its ancillary written materials were authorized by academics from Tufts, Columbia, and Florida International Universities. To participate in the passage of the broadcast text into social and pedagogic space by enrolling in a course for credit, viewers merely required access to the inevitable touch-tone phone: "To find out more about any of these features, call our friendly customer service staff at 1-800-LEARNER" (Day 306; Corporation).

Promotional material for *The Americas* includes *Biographical Notes* that contain, inter alia, information about the achievements of Yezid Campos and Marc de Beaufort, who jointly produced the ninth episode of the series, "Fire in the Mind," an investigation of recent military struggles in El Salvador and Peru. Their short biohistories speak of a recent film "for British television" called *The People of the Shining Path*: "the first report from the inside on Peru's revolutionary organization, the Sendero Luminoso" in the data on Campos, and a film made "with inside access" in the case of de Beaufort (WGBH *Biographical* 2).

There are three reasons for attaching significance to these facts. First, they are indications of the filmmakers' quality and experience that legitimate the series. Second, the form of words describing *The People of the Shining Path* is a complex generic classification of texts that are, indeed, made "from the inside." The third reason is that, effectively, *The People of the Shining Path* was produced as half of "Fire in the Mind." It was recut for American broadcast without the producers' endorsement, but screened in the original version back in the United Kingdom as part of the *Dispatches* series. This to-ing and fro-ing took place because Campos and de Beaufort's work was said to portray a one-sided view of the Peruvian revolutionaries, what the North American screen establishment calls "point-of-view" documentary. (Much, perhaps, as *Cathy Come Home* failed to consider the needs of landholders in 1960s Britain and the first *Four Corners* reports on Aboriginal living conditions did not consult adequately with government officials in 1960s Australia.) This fantasy about value-free film has very interesting constitutional ramifications. The U.S. Information Agency has litigated, unsuccessfully, to deny customs benefits to documentary filmmakers whose work it deems propagandist, not educational, because of "point-of-view" nonsense. The courts have derided any such neat separation of positionality from learning, but censorship is frequently internalized by filmmakers anyway ("Panel" 351).

The academic advisers to *The Americas* decided a positive presentation of Sendero Luminoso (the Shining Path) was unacceptable. It is now left to the Berkeley-based Committee to Support the Revolution in Peru to distribute *The People of the Shining Path* in the United States. (The more available sign is the Che Guevara lookalike who rules a netherworld of 2013 on Sendero Luminoso principles in *John Carpenter's Escape from L.A.* [1996].) But remarkably, the very partiality of the suppressed documentary, the quality that required its alteration, resurfaces in publicity material for *The Americas*. Perhaps this should not surprise us in a series that claims to offer "An Insider Perspective on Contemporary Latin American and Caribbean Society," even as it distances itself from de Beaufort's film (WGBH *Series* 1; Winn Introductory).

This controversy, publicly paraded in the *Boston Globe*, sheds light on the ethical zoning procedures of screen citizenship. A major educational-TV initiative lies before us: all fifty U.S. states offer such programs of study, with more than half a million students enrolled in "telecourses" each year. This is not a textual-analytic debate over ideology but a problem in a textual career, an occasion of critique. Nor is it Robinson Crusoe: WGBH's career also includes notorious interventions into *Korea: The Unknown War*, jointly funded with Thames Television in 1988, again involving multiple publishing spin-offs and opportunities for asinine mystification. Here, Bostonians were concerned with the cosmetic horror of "thick British accents," as well as "anti-Western bias," according to WGBH producer Austin Hoyt. So they hired Richard Stilwell, a retired U.S. general who had been in charge of covert operations during the Korean War, to make what he called "accuracy checks." Stillwell found the original text "not appropriate for an American audience." And Ali A. Mazrui's 1986 BBC-PBS series *The Africans: A Triple Heritage* ran into problems in the "New Gods" episode, where he referred to Marx as "the last of the great Jewish Prophets." This phrase was safely broadcast to audiences in Israel, Jordan, Australia, Finland, and Nigeria, but not the United States, where PBS thought it might offend viewers. That did not prevent the press from attacking the network and Mazrui for creating a program that included this message in other versions, accusing him of being anti-Western. The National Conservative Foundation urged readers of *Broadcasting*, a trade magazine, to watch *The Africans* and then "threaten to withdraw financial support for public broadcasting" (Orr xix; Cumings 231–67; Stilwell quoted in Jacobsen 47 and Cumings 231; Mazrui 90; Matabane and Gandy 6, 14 n. 1).

■ ──────────────────────────────────────────

## The Nation Abroad

> *At what precise moment did Peru fuck itself up?*
> :: Stavans 18

> *Peru, Peru, Peru—Macy's Bridges the Americas.*
> :: store advertisement in 1930s New York quoted in Hamburger 290

A specter is haunting educational TV—the specter of citizenship. It has been difficult to bring into discourse. We ask questions—Is this propaganda? Is it balanced? Who is its author? Is it true?—presuming there is an ontological space of metacritique alongside experiential knowledge and intentionality. Such activity is beyond me, for I am a viewer. That position inclines me a few degrees, toward more modest space. This space poses certain questions of statements made, but it does not do so in terms of a *non dit*, the secreted unconscious of deceit and mystification that can be related to a subject position or absolute distinctions between truth and falsehood. Rather, this space says, "You cannot tell me the statements I have heard deny their true meaning if you also wish to use them as evidence of that denial, for that indicates these statements say something you claim they do not say." (See the formulations of Foucault *Archaeology* 109–10).

This will *not* be a symptomatic reading, but a reassemblage of the materiality of the event called "Fire in the Mind." I do this as an outsider, an engaged but unenrolled viewer, in the knowledge that the Shining Path has been locked in a struggle with sovereign and not-so-sovereign authorities for more than a decade. More than twenty-five thousand lives have been lost, with violence on all sides and accusations of "narcoterrorism" problematizing the group's left-revolutionary claims (Poole and Rénique; Tarazona-Sevillano; Winn *Americas* 537). I shall refrain from comparing these films with the *real* Americas. But I "know" a great deal about *The Americas*, thanks to a *Series Backgrounder*:

> The 10 programs focus on themes that often draw together several countries. The film on racial identity, for example, moves smoothly from Bolivia to the Dominican Republic to Haiti, illuminating the unique ethnic and racial problems of each country through human stories, a filmmaking style that succeeds through the deceptively simple means of looking and listening.
>
> Behind those images, however, something quite complicated is going on. Entire armies of scholars, researchers, producers and production staff are, in effect, on the march. "I sometimes feel like a general," says [the executive producer]. (WGBH *Series* 2)

This process is meant to produce an innovative amalgam of diegetic individuation, whereby experiential narratives personalize public history and extradiegetic academicism serves as a pedagogic warrant. Promotional descriptions make this quite apparent: "The series presents personal stories that highlight the issues behind the limited images and incomplete information that capture public attention in newspapers and popular magazines" (WGBH *Fact* 1). Popular culture distorts, but it can be pursued and utilized homeostatically to educate (as per video and the Bulger murder). But to say what?

Cultural technologies such as the TV series analyzed here create, and sometimes inhabit, the masks of an other. Countries of the region are defined as different but similar. "The Americas" emphasizes certainty (the definite article) and difference (the plural form). And just after the programs' identificatory humanism quoted earlier, self-promotional material adds an assurance from academic director Peter Winn that the "complex arguments and historical background," which "books are better at presenting," will promote reason rather than tourism. But wait; if books can argue and provide history, and film is good for what he terms "images and sounds," then the original account of the Shining Path was not worth recutting. Its material always already lacked complexity, depending on "images and sounds" immune to subtle agonistics. But the material *was* reedited into an acceptable form. Winn himself said of the sanitized version that it was a "better film . . . significantly improved throughout." Was the film's content improved through a telegenics of truth that satisfied the Star Chamber of Historiography? The answer to this question resides in the contingent protocols of the academy. For instance, Ken Burns's 1994 *Baseball* series, another PBS venture into pedagogy for fun and profit, is advertised in *American Quarterly*, the key American studies journal, as "Directly Correlated to the New Standards in U.S. History" ("Teach"; WGBH *Backgrounder* 2; Winn quoted in P. Bennett B30). And no doubt it is. But are those standards shared by Dianne Feinstein, Peter Winn, and *dependistas*?

These questions relate to publicity for the *Americas* series that authenticated it through the carefully rewritten promotion of two producers who made "insider" texts for the United Kingdom: traces of value that *are* only traces, because *what* they produced is deemed unsuitable. A cosmic ambivalence is at play here in the chalking of territory. Uneasy marks of extraterritoriality characterize the United States as a military, economic, diplomatic, and intellectual seeker of a self riven by the fault lines of an immigrant but export culture and the lost project of its own invention: civics. The formula for the surface, diegetic truth making of the series, "personal stories," simply doesn't work with the original Peruvian footage. Even when Shining Path members are in-shot—imprisoned, masked, or caught on home video—they speak ideological language unsuited to the series and contemporary world politics. Time is out of joint, if not coca. In short, these folk appear antediluvian to the Whiggish narrative that overcame the series during the ten years it took to produce, as the politics of the continent shifted welcomely from the horrors of the 1980s. With that shift, North American policy—part *of*, as much as a reaction *to*, these transformations—recast itself, adopting a new posture toward those it had once abjured in El Salvador. But such revisionism was not applied to the Shining Path.

> *Lloyd DeGrane's recent book of photographs is called* Tuned
> In: Television in American Life. *It retails for U.S. $11.95 from
> the University of Illinois Press. The front cover depicts three
> television viewers watching a large-screen set. To the left of
> the frame a woman is in an armchair. A man is sitting directly
> opposite her. The central position in the photograph and in
> front of the TV is taken by a llama, attached to the man's left
> hand by a leash.*

By now my intent will be clear. This section of the chapter does not center
Peru or El Salvador. Nor is my referent the Byzantine—but structurally
predictable—rent-seeking wars of university intellectuals versus media intellectuals. My concern is the stalked creature whose imaginary presence
animates those conflicts: the much sought, oft-analyzed, but never-subdued
creature encountered in the introduction, the television audience. Specific
to this case, I am concerned with tracking how various telegenic protocols
inscribe viewing positions for that audience together with the extratelevisual
pedagogic objects created for *The Americas*, producing ethical zones of historical citizenship. But where should I, the armchair analyst lacking a green
card that is reportedly pink, begin? Is there a text in this chapter?

"Fire in the Mind" is decidedly not "a" text. Peter Winn and his team
of advisers could not control its production or circulation in the United
Kingdom. Marc de Beaufort and his team of technicians could not control
its postproduction or circulation in the United States in the face of what he
called "a particular generation of academics." The text itself is set up to
be interpreted through study guides, the seminar of the mind, and teaching
manuals. As *The Americas* series' executive producer, Judith Vecchione,
said, it "seems a shame to do all that work and broadcast the results only
once. . . . I really like the idea that we're doing programming both for
prime time general audiences *and* for student audiences" (de Beaufort
quoted in P. Bennett B30; Vecchione quoted in Maurer 3). This is a *series
of events*, in need of explanation as such.

I shall not go into a detailed empirical contrast of the Channel 4 and
WGBH versions. Suffice it to say that such an account might refer to the
excision in the United States of narration that describes the Path as "a
highly organized political party" with "rapidly growing support," in favor
of its nomination as "one of the deadliest revolutionary groups in the
world." And it would probably note *military* atrocities displaced by *party*

atrocities, plus the removal of scenes showing Shining Path peasants peacefully herding llamas. The American version locates resistance to the ruling regime and the Shining Path in organic community opposition, whereas the British version centers the Path as the organ of dissonance. I shall concentrate on the call to citizenship that occurs at the elision between the two halves of the American version to establish an equilibrium-disequilibrium struggle across two unrelated histories: El Salvador and Peru did not need to be seen together, but they were *brought* together, through a "Monroe" strategy of narration.

Consider the interpellative address that begins the film: "The Americas"—an atmospheric, apolitical, geographic syntagm—accompanies an image track of the sublime through a mountainous establishing shot. Then "a rich, vibrant region" is matched by the shot of a twirling dancer (in itself perhaps amenable to a politicized reading, but here reduced to the "rich cuisine" end of multiculturalism). This is soon supplanted by "close to our borders," accompanied by a close-up on a Shining Path woman in uniform—that most disturbing of *Mädchen*—marching and charging under the sign of the red flag. You will be astonished to learn that "their choices will change our lives." And guess what? "All of them are as much Americans as we are."

The Monroe strategy works either because we know the terrain or can reshape it to *look* familiar. I refer here to the words spoken by Raul Julia, the offscreen narrator, for it is his voice, the script, and perhaps the authenticity offered by Julia's public *persona* as a Puerto Rican and the feature-film lead of both *Romero* (John Duigan, 1989) and *Kiss of the Spider Woman* (Hector Babenco, 1985) that merge these essentially unconnected stories. We begin with the tragedy of El Salvador. Blame is equally apportioned: the violence is set in play and reinforced by a combination of the state, rebels, and U.S. foreign policy. The horrors we enter into, particularly shocking in the death that was felt around the world, the death of Archbishop Romero (an occurrence that, even at this distance and in this film, makes my eyes water), are very retroactive, bundled together as a history lesson for future policy makers, participants in the viewing public sphere. They are about former errors. Specifically, it is acknowledged that previous disasters made revolutionary violence inescapable. Or, put another way, as U.S. policy on El Salvador recognizes its complicity in this past horror, that insurrectionary violence is made understandable. The new, improved U.S. foreign policy means there is no need for such activity anymore. Equilibrium is restored to country, film, and viewer: El Salvador is a democracy, the screen sequence is over, and the citizen-spectator has an exemplary instance of former foibles to read against current wisdoms.

Halfway through "Fire in the Mind," there is a cut between armchair prognostications about the settlement in El Salvador and a political march through the hills of Peru. One site is individuated, named, and subordinated to the intellectual space of argument. The other is visceral, demotic, and namelessly threatening. Unlike in Hollywood, where we might expect a dream sequence to articulate this shift in diegetic space, there are no concessions to continuity outside Julia's narration: "In the 1990s, the unfolding drama of Peru might be a grim indication of more radical ways of revolution." There is an absolute logic splicing Peru into El Salvador in this chillingly arrogant manner. Regardless of authorial intentionality, matching the two situations sets up a particular ethical practice available only to Monrovians (and you know whom I mean when I use that term). We are shifted from the site of former revolutionary violence. At its zenith, this violence was considered illegitimate by the United States. The film takes it to be reasonable now that it has ended (partly *because* the United States ceased to regard it as illegitimate). The crossover takes us to contemporary violence, which—surprise, surprise—is rendered simultaneously illegitimate by both the U.S. government and the narration of the program. The edit achieved by Julia's voice track connects a *historic* violence that was *right*—rather like the American and French Revolutions—with a *current* violence that is *wrong*.

In the 1990s, most of Latin America became democratic, much to the satisfaction of the United States. With major trading blocs emergent across the globe, often working against North American investment interests, the prospect of economic growth in the region was equally pleasurable, leading George Bush to propose a free-trade zone through his "Initiative of the Americas." When Peruvian president Alberto Fujimori suspended the Constitution and dissolved Congress and the Supreme Court in his April 1992 *autogolpe*, the economic portfolios in Washington lobbied for inaction. Bush suspended financial aid, but when the rest of the continent remained comparatively silent, pressure on Fujimori from the United States diminished. The maintenance of good relations between Washington and other capitals in the region was reasserted as a priority. The Clinton administration was only marginally more prepared to criticize the regime (Vargas Llosa 126–30, 141 n. 4; Madalengoitia). Meanwhile, Fujimori was offering powerful experiential narratives of his encounters with the oppressed and the efforts he makes on their behalf:

> On weekends, I generally try to go out to the slum areas of Lima and the poverty-stricken areas elsewhere in the country—precisely those areas where Shining Path is supposed to be present—to see with my own eyes what they are living through.

> My car has been stuck in the mud many times in such places, where I've
> seen that water costs an unaffordable one dollar per container. Having seen
> that, I immediately put the armed forces to work to build the necessary infra-
> structure so that water will cost half as much. (11)

Perhaps the water has scarcity value because vast amounts are needed to
make the mud to bog down his limousines.

Such issues are superficially far from students of *The Americas*; you
don't need to know about the economy of Peru, the beliefs of its peoples, or
the activities of the state to pass *The Americas*. The book guiding students
in their work begins with a two-step operation that articulates the Monroe
strategy by its paragraphic slippage. The first thing to know is that the next
century will find Latin American and Caribbean people as the biggest minority group in the United States, the second thing that "our relationship
with this vital region" is of great importance. The "our" is suddenly historical and yet contemporary: "we" are about to be internally differentiated,
so now is the time for "us" to learn about the process, but also to influence
it by adopting a knowledgeable position on U.S. foreign policy (one of the
course's principal educational goals) (Orr xi, xii, 134).

There is a crucial choice in the "Test Bank" of questions for viewers
enrolled in college courses associated with the series. In that splendid false
syntagm, the multiple-choice section, questions 17 and 20 are concerned
with Sendero Luminoso. The account of the party's leadership offers the
following possibilities: (a) opposed to violence against the peasantry, (b) in-
spired by other regional revolutionaries, (c) opposed to drug trafficking,
and (d) favoring violent overthrow of the state. There is one right answer.
The other question has *two* correct answers, which tell us that the movement adheres to Maoist principles "despite the discrediting of international
Communism" and "has used terrorist tactics against the civilian population." The essay question on the topic asks students to find ways of disso-
ciating the Peruvian crisis from other revolutionary conflicts in the history
of the region (Orr 125–27). An ethical zone is upon us. It is not a zone of
active, engaged citizenship, I fear, but a homology between liberal-humanist
textual strategies and governmental policies. Ongoing academic debate
about the Shining Path indicates its complexity (L. Taylor). The address
and narration of *The Americas* are massively conditional even as they seem
to rest on an unsignifying native turf of personal and collective memories
and rights and absolutist professional history.

Perhaps, however, the artificiality of that turf, its contingent dependency on a policy consensus, is ironically made available to redress by the
little cut between otherwise disparate countries and struggles, through

Julia's voice of authority, for surely that cut alerts us to silliness. Contrasting the British and American versions of truth in Peru stresses that, as the materials could so easily be rearranged to make a different point for the sensitive eyes and ears of North American viewers, they could have been added to in another way: left as they were diegetically, but accompanied by additional discussion and debate, if necessary heated—an encounter between differing positions on the film, a "live" advisory. Alternatively, might a way be found to add information and critique that makes academic study and prime-time television performatively dialogic, rather than disassembling the work of documentarists? There are two immediate options for doing this: conflictual voices inside the primary text, a multiperspectival narration, and associational editing; or a hypertext variant on the studio-discussion model, with software enabling viewers to "choose their line" (e.g., "Would you like to hear a pro/anti-government position on these topics?" I endeavor to show something of this approach to citizenship in chapter 6). At least something could be done to alert viewers that the multiple-choice and essay questions make sense *only* if this readership shares the concerns of U.S. foreign policy at the moment the questions were written. Such thoughts come as a consequence of that little opening, the space between El Salvador and Peru that Julia's butterfly vocal suture could not close. And if this gesture toward reconsidering that hinge of truth has been suggestive, then I shall feel satisfied.

# [ 6 ] *Historical Citizenship and the Fremantle Prison Follies: Frederick Wiseman Comes to Western Australia*

*The concept of the museum in the modern age, and it is a distinctive concept, is that it is public property. This is a founding event in the history of the modern museum from the French Revolution on, the assertion of the principle that the people through the government exert collective ownership of cultural property. I think that is a tremendously important and founding principle of democracy and of modernity.*
::   Bennett in Puplick and Bennett 74

*The defendant did not comply with conditions imposed on the privilege of making the film, that, through his wide ranging photography, he abused the privilege by showing identifiable inmates naked or in other embarrassing situations, and that each individual portrayed was only important to the film as an inmate suffering from some form of mental disease and undergoing a particular type of custody or treatment, it was held that in the circumstances the final decree should prohibit showing of the film to the general public in order to protect the inmates' right of privacy . . . but that, since the film gave a striking and instructive picture of the life and problems at the institution, the final decree, in the public interest, should permit showing of the film to specialized audiences of persons with a serious interest in rehabilitation and with potential capacity to be helpful.*
::   judgment in *Commonwealth and Others v. Frederick Wiseman and Others* 252

The two genres discussed in this chapter are critical sites for the production of truth. The museum stands as an Enlightenment object dedicated to the curation of other objects. It embodies the selection and control of an artifactual national past and lessons in how people should access that past. The direct-cinema documentary, by contrast, is wobbly, a handheld, fast-speed film made with light sound-recording equipment that redefined the notion of screen actuality in the ten years to 1970 through its technical and textual innovation and its desire to shock viewers. One genre locates its authoritativeness in monumentalism, the other in realism. I am attempting here to perform cultural studies on a film and a museum in a way that deals with some of the questions raised in chapters 1, 2, and 5. The approach combines Frederick Wiseman's *Titicut Follies*, recently seen in cinemas after twenty-five years of incarceration; the Fremantle Prison Museum, recently seen on visitor tours after 140 years of incarcerating; and their collective implications for our understanding of ethical zones.

My method is to crosscut between film and museum, following Wiseman's practice of making "an editorial point in the spirit of expository cinema" rather than allowing "events to unfold according to their own rhythm" (Nichols *Representing* 41). This effect also plays on a continuing trope of Australian cultural interpretation and production: the examination of convict themes in literature and cinema to identify the self-society dialectic of exiles' reaction to their carceral introjection from Europe's Industrial Revolution. In terms of governmentality, the public museum embodies a critical shift of focus away from the intramural world of the princely museum. Prior to the Enlightenment, royal collections are meant to express the monarch's grandeur and induce a sense of insignificance in the viewer. But the public site of modernity calls out for identification and a mutual, municipal ownership that hails visitors as participants in the collective exercise of power. And just as the Fremantle Prison Museum is a popular public site, so it has been suggested that more people have seen Wiseman's work than any other body of documentary, apart from World War II newsreels, because he rates well on television (G. Turner *National* 60–62, 74–75, 98; T. Bennett *Birth* 166; B. Grant *Voyages* 7; Bear 62). The irony is that the aura of immediacy, of an urgent address to citizenship, is greater in a 1960s film than in a 1990s site visit.

▶ ───────────────────────────────────────

### Titicut Follies

> *Another observation about the film: it is true.*
> :: "Statement" 3

The first thing to note about *Titicut Follies* is that it was made three decades ago, but became available for public viewing in 1992, the only film in U.S. history to suffer legal restraints on its exhibition for reasons other than

The gatehouse, beautiful but forbidding. Courtesy of Cyril Ayris, from *Fremantle Prison: A Brief History*.

obscenity or national security (Anderson and Benson "Direct" 59). The second thing to note is that the text deals with the occupants of a hospital for the criminally insane. These occupants include doctors, warders, volunteers, filmmakers, and, perhaps least spectacularly, forced residents. Some of the above comments could also be made about Fremantle Prison.

The initial fuss arose because a former social worker read a newspaper report of the film that indicated male genitals were prominently displayed. The fuss developed over the issue of privacy for the inmates and the career hopes of those responsible for them. While this was happening, *Titicut Follies* was judged Best Film at the Mannheim International Filmweek and Best Film Dealing with the Human Condition at Florence's Festival Dei Popoli in 1967 (Zipporah 9). Twenty years later, it was used as evidence to reform the prison it represents—the Massachusetts Correctional Institution at Bridgewater (MCI). And five years after that, it was safe for release.

This is a text of impact. It strikes at the fault lines that mark the uneasy intersection of public and private, where the shrinelike qualities of incarceration meet the forgetfulness of a public that sets aside its sullied linen. As a viewer, you have two opportunities to be offended here—at least two. First, you can be offended because of the depiction of madness, and criminal madness at that. Second, you can be offended because of the depiction of dicks, and criminal dicks at that. I leave it up to you to find other ways to be offended.

*Titicut Follies* is difficult to follow. It moves backward and forward from a revue party of song and dance to interviews between doctors and patients, exercise-yard demagoguery, appeals to release boards, funerals, lady-of-the-manor largesse, cell time, acts of resistance and response, strip searches, nudity, monologues, bath time, and a recurring hallway wander, a leitmotiv of Wiseman's work. Because of this complexity, the spectator to the *Follies* is required to read keenly through an array of sequences that fold back onto one another. The *Follies* is not a horror film; in fact much of it is tame and oblique. But it decidedly deals with the abject, what we'd rather get behind us. This associational narration works by prodding recollection and fear, suggestion through confrontation. Wiseman sees his work as open-ended. It interrogates ideological institutions but offers no options for doing things any other way. That is for the spectator to decide. Viewers are offered not so much a document of policy as an invitation to citizenship.

I am particularly concerned with a notorious sequence in the second reel, usually categorized as part six of the text (shots seventy-four to ninety-seven in the *Theoretical* count by Cunningham, 137–39). After a psychiatrist has told the inmate Mr. Malinowski, "If you don't eat food we are going to feed you with tube," the prisoner is seen in close-up. Then we zoom out to a medium shot of the screws as they apply restraints to his wrists and flank him before cutting to a close-up of the psychiatrist sniffing liquid food. As the naked Malinowski is placed face up on a table, the zoom closes in on the shrink, smoking an endlessly ashing cigarette while he greases appliances and shoves the tube into the patient-prisoner's nose, whose groin and eyes alone are covered. Then this scene is abruptly inter-laced for just two seconds with an extreme close-up of Mr. Malinowski being shaved. His eyes are open. A fly is on his brow and soap on his jaw. Then we are jagged back to the cigarette and its therapist prior to a series of edits between invasion and torpor, until what is clearly the work of a mortician sees cotton buds make their way into Malinowski's eyes. This is followed by parallel movements between psychiatrist and mortician: one finishes with a fed Malinowski, the other with a dead one. The sequence reestablishes an equilibrium of sorts through a lingering view of the door behind which Malinowski's coffin has been slid into a cooler. It is a juxtaposition that invites some normalcy, but in fact is nothing of the sort, as the rapid montage effect might indicate if we think it through in terms of pace rather than image. Instead of a relief, a movement into the quotidian, this is the end of Mr. Malinowski. He is being shaved for his burial.

How might we read this? I will divide the options into the religious, psychoanalytic, cosmetic, exhortatory, voyeuristic, and anthropological. The point I am trying to establish is that we can do a lot more with such a segment than was allowed by the furor in courts of law, that sought, as we shall see, so fixed a meaning for the film (without great success).

### The Religious

Mr. Malinowski has fallen from grace. Attempts to redeem him fail, so *he* must die publicly that *we* might live in normalcy, confirmed in a previously passive distaste for the abjection of madness, a displeasure now rendered active. His passing, a regrettable but necessary corollary of a failure to participate fully in the dietetic economy, signals the way forward for the rest of us: obedience. He starved that we might eat.

### The Psychoanalytic

The psychiatrist has the phallic authority of the Father's law. If his sons disobey him or act independently, they will be symbolically castrated and any right of autonomy over their bodies removed. Punitive, retributive force must be swiftly and overtly exercized in response to such insurrection. Further transgressions will be dealt with by the ultimate sanction. Remember, many of these men are sex offenders (some are not, and some are in prison awaiting trial, a wait of years in some cases). The suggestion is there—confirmed in one instance—that incest is afoot. This fundamental taboo must not be broken, because it distinguishes fathers from others and protects their line from violation and despoliation.

### The Cosmetic

We dress death. The passing of a life, however flawed its performance may have been, is to be noted and respected. Part of that respect involves dressing the body, its face as well as the rest, to restore the normalcy that attended its mythic innocence at birth. The signs of degeneration that designated a failure of lucidity can be allowed no life after death.

### The Exhortatory

Something is rotten in the state of Massachusetts. The medical staff treat people as objects to be manipulated and despised, turned into creatures without a soul. Bridgewater requires investigation urgently; we must know about any similar breaches of humanitarian principles. Punishment and treatment should be distillations from a caring cup of humanness. MCI is aberrant. It departs from correct methods of control, treatment, and re-habilitation, deeming those classified as civically incapable in a way that hypocritically denies civic conscience.

■————————————————————————————————————————

## The Voyeuristic

This process is sick. It's wrong to show people so degraded. The film is deriving pleasure from the pain of others. Why are we looking at this degradation? How do the relatives feel? We should turn away from such nonsense (it's too much fun).

■————————————————————————————————————————

## The Anthropological

Which Malinowski is in shot? (Even Barry Keith Grant, author of the key study on Wiseman's work, seems unsure about Mr. Malinowski, whose name appears spelled differently several times within a single paragraph of his *Voyages of Discovery* [48–49]. ) Consider the following precepts of Bronislaw Malinowski's theoretical work, what he called the "General Axioms of Functionalism":

> Culture is essentially an instrumental apparatus by which man is put in a position the better to cope with the concrete specific problems that face him in his environment in the course of the satisfaction of his needs.
> . . . It is a system of objects, activities, and attitudes in which every part exists as a means to an end. (150)

For Wiseman, the textuality of film must be dedicated to institutions: the public institutions of his first dozen and most recent films, the private institutions of his next few, the international reach of the ones after that, and the impact those institutions have on bodies and their means of sense making. It is for us to determine whether these institutions, which framed and then concluded the life of a Malinowski, are functional, and in whose interests they function.

That depends on who is looking. *Bad Timing: A Sensual Obsession* (Nicolas Roeg, 1980) contains a series of controversial cuts between Milena (Theresa Russell) having her stomach pumped in a hospital and Alex (Art Garfunkel) "ravishing" her body in an apartment. If Roeg hadn't seen *Titicut Follies* or Wiseman's *Hospital* (1970), then I'm one of the unlucky monkeys from the latter's horrifying investigation of animal experimentation, *Primate* (1974). Part of the reason for the controversy surrounding both sequences is the operation of the look. Its controlling power is a re-curring theme in *Titicut Follies*, but not in neat shot-reverse-shot form. The eye-line match is more common, across shots of about half a minute's duration (B. Grant "Point" 57). Looks are exchanged between guards and guards, guards and prisoners, prisoners and prisoners, psychiatrists and prisoners, psychiatrists and psychiatrists, and *all* of the above—but espe-cially the prisoners/inmates/patients—with the camera, and hence with the ultimate disciplinary gaze in cinema, that of the spectator.

As spectators, we are looking at what is locked away, to protect us from physical and psychic darkness. The double effect of the musical revue sequence is to equate madness with the unacceptable side to playfulness, drawing out the implications of a tightly policed but essentially nominalist distinction between madness and entertainment. What is presented is ut-terly mad. The maddest person of the lot is a leeringly unphlegmatic screw, whose delight in tomfoolery is equaled only by his craving for attention. Consider the impact of his singing a duet of "I Want to Go to Chicago Town" with an inmate (black, and of course unable to go fucking any-where) alongside Wiseman's sequence of a few minutes before in which the same guard mocks a black man for his color (Armstrong "Wiseman's Realm" 22, 30).

As Christopher Ricks has argued, "Wiseman's art constitutes an in-vasion of privacy," the privacy of the viewers, their right to be left undis-turbed in any passive denial of the sometimes unsightly grout that holds their social world in a normal grid (161). Not surprisingly, the film has had an unstable career; it moves dramatically along the track of political rectitude. At one moment, *Titicut Follies* is the darling of civil libertari-ans: Wiseman speaks out against the state, offering a voice to those si-lenced by the bonds of prison power. At another, the film is evil, because it invades the privacy of men too abject and incompetent to know the concept or seek to guard it. Some history to the film's career can explain this lineage.

In 1959, Wiseman was teaching a summer seminar in legal medicine at Boston University. His class toured MCI-Bridgewater:

> I took my students on visits to places that, either as prosecutors they might be sending people, or as defence attorneys their clients might end up. [At Bridge-water they saw] . . . [l]onely, isolated men, inadequate medical and psychiatric facilities. Buildings dating from around 1855 [the same decade as Fremantle Prison], poorly heated and totally inadequate for that kind of care. But mainly isolated people without any contact with each other and desolate, wasted faces. (Wiseman quoted in C. Taylor 99)

Six years later, he sought approval from the superintendent to make a documentary. After initial difficulties, permission was given, perhaps because it was thought exposing life at the institution would produce additional resources from a potentially chastened state government. Filming commenced in April 1966, just as the staff and inmates were about to perform their annual revue, the "Titicut Follies." The title derived from the Native American name for the area. Twenty-nine days of shooting, followed by eleven months of editing, saw eighty thousand feet of film compressed into thirty-two thousand, with an eventual running time of eighty-four minutes. During the edit, the institution entered the headlines because of the escape of Albert DeSalvo, "the Boston Strangler." Meanwhile, *Titicut Follies* was being shown in rough-cut form to various representatives of the state of Massachusetts, notably Attorney General Elliot Richardson.

In September 1967, a review of the film was published in advance of its premiere at a New York festival. A former social worker used this review to frame a letter of complaint to various civil liberties luminaries and the governor of Massachusetts about the representation of full-frontal male nudity. The state then claimed the right to censor the film, which was news to Wiseman. It raised some very interesting questions of image ethics: Who owns the ethical subjectivity of nonpersons, people who have relinquished their civil rights? With legal threats afoot, Wiseman engaged Alan Dershowitz as his lawyer. Dershowitz claimed that oral consent from inmates was sufficient, and Wiseman also flourished those written consents he *had* obtained. New York's Channel 13 showed excerpts. An injunction was granted preventing screenings in Massachusetts, but in New York, attempts to prevent a showing at the film festival were unsuccessful. Then the film had a commercial release in the city. Further hearings were under way in Massachusetts, but they were brought into question when it was discovered one of Wiseman's collaborators had recorded and photographed the proceedings. Judge Kalus called the film "a nightmare of ghoulish obscenities." Sensational allegations about the film emerged: a prisoner was masturbating through the pocket of his trousers (who isn't?) and another man's raised hand was parodying the pope (same query) (Kalus quoted in "Statement" 3; C. Taylor 101). A formal case began in November 1967. Wiseman was accused of breaching an oral contract permitting the state right of veto over material; invading the privacy of an inmate, James Bulcock; and misdirecting profits (the state wanted moneys held in trust for the inmates).

Meanwhile, prison guards were conducting their own case against the film. And in 1968, it was banned in Massachusetts over the oral contract and privacy issues. (As Wiseman points out, this is some privacy in an institution that incarcerates people precisely to deny them privacy and invites ten thousand people a year to observe it as part of making them good social work students or functionaries ["Frederick" 69–71].) In appeals, Wiseman gained support from the American Orthopsychiatric Association and the American Sociological Association. The defense was partially successful: *Titicut Follies* could be shown in Massachusetts to qualified therapists. Screenings had to be accompanied by a statement that Bridgewater had been reformed. (Wiseman's fabulously laconic way of complying is to restate the court order twice at the conclusion of the film, once as a quotation and once as his own words, recalling the faux "happy ending" to Hitchcock's *The Wrong Man* [1956]: Henry Fonda's character is acquitted of trumped-up charges, but this righteous denouement does not prevent his wife, played by Vera Miles, from losing her sanity in the face of all that has gone before.)

In 1969, guardians of thirty-five inmates at Bridgewater filed suit against the director. In 1971, screening restraints were diminished, and Wiseman won against the guardians the following year. The Civil Liberties Union of Massachusetts finally supported unrestricted viewing in 1974, when the state of Massachusetts passed new privacy provisions in its General Laws to deal with such invasions as the *Follies*. Three years later, the first public screening in the state was permitted. Then a university student who had appeared in the film in a somewhat different life protested that his privacy had been violated. In 1980, the state again sought to outlaw *Titicut Follies*. The year 1987 found Wiseman once more petitioning for the right to exhibit, with network TV screening segments; reports emerged that five inmates had died in Bridgewater that year, three by their own hands, and Wiseman appeared as an interviewee on an episode of ABC's *Nightline* to discuss the institution. In 1988, the state tried to locate men who had been in the film by placing advertisements in newspapers. Respondents were interviewed by an officer of the court to decide whether they were competent to give consent; the official recommended unrestricted release. The following year, a conference held on the grounds of the hospital included a screening, with Wiseman there for the first time in twenty-three years. The state was no longer opposed to public exhibition, but two inmates were, and the judge presiding decided identities should be facially blurred for any screening. Wiseman successfully appealed (Anderson and Benson "Direct" 80 and *Documentary* 161–73; B. Grant *Voyages* 50). Having established the trace of *Titicut Follies*, I want now to consider the wider implications of Wiseman's work for contemporary citizenship and our understanding of Fremantle Prison.

> *Any documentary, mine or anyone else's, made in no matter*
> *what style, is arbitrary, biased, prejudiced, compressed and*
> *subjective. Like any of its sisterly or brotherly fictional forms*
> *it is born in choice — choice of subject matter, place, people,*
> *camera angles, duration of shooting, sequences to be shot or*
> *omitted, transitional material and cutaways.*
> :: Wiseman "Editing" 4

Wiseman's films investigate how discourses and institutions produce and oversee identity. Again and again, we find him preoccupied with the notion of "looking as the fundamental political activity in modern society." This shifts between the controlling gaze exercized in public institutions, in *Titicut Follies, High School* (1968), *Hospital, Primate,* and *High School II* (1994), and the consuming gaze exercized in private ones, in *Racetrack* (1985), *Model* (1980), and *The Store* (1983). *Canal Zone* (1977), *Sinai Field Mission* (1978), and *Manoeuvre* (1979) explore the American state as an external power, how it looks at what it commands or commandeers. This is the gaze of empire, redisposing systems of surveillance and control from the domestic space (Armstrong "Wiseman" 35, 38–39).

Throughout, we can discern what Dan Armstrong calls "the political relations of *looking* . . . a moral-juridical apparatus that seeks out anomalies, defects, delinquencies, or other deviations from the norm" ("Wiseman's Realm" 20–21). This is an apparatus of judgment between Manichaean fields of the good and its other. Such a division is brought into question at the margin, where the difference between normal and not is policed. Docility and utility are guaranteed by practices of confinement, treatment, and training. Wiseman points to an implicit co-optation: until we identify what is bad, mad, and dangerous to know, we cannot deny those aspects of ourselves and play others up. This interpellation of the hitherto comfortable citizen marks out Wiseman's work. In fact, his metatextual address to the Museum of Television and Radio's *Documentary Films of Frederick Wiseman A to Z* videotape (1993) avows that "the real subject of documentary filmmaking is normalcy" (a remark followed by the force-feeding sequence). He concentrates on human subjects and entities, opening up the significatory space between them to possible action by viewers in their own social formations, as contemporary citizens. As Haskell Wexler puts it, *Titicut Follies* "strips society to the relationships of forces" (quoted in Sullivan 468).

There are few frills: this is 16mm filmmaking, handheld camera, lightweight equipment, and black-and-white stock in a form that tries to get away from conventional representation, *contra* the seamless quilting that makes diegetic space and time singular and encourages spectators to conclude their *experience* of the text at the same time as their viewing of it. Direct cinema eschews a concentration on identifiable filmic characters as guides to the expressive totality of their human achievements or imperfections toward an engagement with the audience's knowledge of history and the social order. In place of ensuring that narratives hold together, it veers away from mainstream documentary techniques such as interviews, which are conventionally mobilized to produce anecdotes with facile audience reactions. Wiseman's work poses difficult questions about what it is to be an ethical subject and, equally, about the abject desire not to know our abject selves. Example: *Primate* details the Yerkes research center. Funded by the U.S. military, the center studies monkeys to develop techniques of behavioral manipulation. When the film was broadcast on public TV in 1974, the New York station screening it was deluged with criticism, a bomb scare, and a threat to kill Wiseman (Armstrong "Wiseman" 40; King "Reconsidering" 228–29; Cunningham "Look" 88–89).

Such a cinema is somewhat different from U.S. cinema verité, with which it is frequently associated. Much North American verité is remorselessly individualistic; it *will* present a tormented individual subject onscreen in full flower. Richard Leacock, D. A. Pennebaker, David and Albert Maysles, and others have been chided for their preoccupation with the famous and the spectacular, the hypernormal above us all. In contrast, the cast of *Titicut Follies* is enormous; no one is selected for character development that dwarfs anybody else. As Wiseman puts it, "The place is always the star rather than individual people." In fact, he calls *American cinema verité* a "bullshit phrase." Rather than notions of a profilmic ontology that he straightforwardly records, the director refers to his work as "reality fictions." As he puts it, "The events . . . are all true, except really they have no meaning except insofar as you impose a form on them, principally through the process of the edit." "A cut is a judgment . . . the only public trace of the private debate" that directors/editors have among themselves and with each other. Wiseman's convention of brief images in montage is homologous to his concentrating on permission to film in place of extensive preliminary study: "The research instead of being on 3-by-5 cards is on film" (Atkins "Wiseman's" 2–3; Wiseman quoted in Bear 20; Wiseman quoted in Armstrong "Wiseman's Realm" 20, 22; Atkins "Preface" vii; Wiseman quoted in J. Graham 35–36; Wiseman "A Nonscholar's" 26; Wiseman quoted in Westlin 48).

We might connect this to Jean Rouch's challenge to the idea of documentation. Here, the camera explores and probes interactively with its environment. Rouch calls this *provocation* (Loisoz 46–47). Cinema verité emerged in Rouch and Edgar Morin's 1960 film *Chronique d'un été* to refer to a new mask the camera's subjects could adopt, halting the everyday flow of life in order to address the intersection of their ordinary world with the process of filmmaking. This is different from the humanistic North American version. Like Rouch, Wiseman is a multiperspectival filmmaker. He wants the material to be "complex and ambiguous," not a singular truth. The aim is to present options for public scrutiny and involvement in reform through a "multiple point of view," not the mechanistically binary device of a "balance" that can supposedly be achieved through a double-sided stance (Wiseman quoted in J. Graham 37, 40; Bear 20). He says:

> If you believe in the idea of the marketplace of ideas, part of that is the idea that in order to do something about anything, you have to understand it. And the more information you have—even information that says it's very complicated—the better chance you have if you're interested in doing anything about it. (Wiseman quoted in Cunningham "Look" 88)

Conventional documentary sets the spectator's gaze up as competent, once it is guided by the knowing hand-eye-technology coordination of the director and editor. But as I have noted, *Titicut Follies* provokes an uncomfortable gaze at the self by the spectator: Where are we at any given moment? Why are we there? What is going on? Am I part of a society that endorses/allows this conduct? There is no closure. The look remains unsatisfied. We are asked to bring into question even our surveillance as viewers. Such an excoriating self-gaze is only to be expected of a man responsible for the following comment about making *Meat* (1976), an account of life and death in a meatpacking plant: "I ate steak every night I was up there, usually something I met earlier in the day." As Wiseman says in his derogation of applied social science, "I'm not a pharmacist" (Cunningham "Look" 89–90; Wiseman quoted in B. Grant "Point" 57; Wiseman quoted in Westlin 56). There are no prescriptions on this row of desolation, just encouragement for engaged viewing to transmogrify into engaged citizenship. Although Wiseman routinely brings the camera tightly in on people's faces, this never emphasizes interiority at the expense of institutional determination (*pace* Arthur 123). And the look back at the citizen has the potential to draw a response of awkward complicity.

Some critics maintain that direct cinema has lost its capacity to shock since the uptake of "alternative" filmmaking signatures by Hollywood and music video. Handheld camera and location shooting no longer signify more than a "documentary feel to a scripted, fictional film." The style has been tamed and redisposed, its vanguard claims to realism now part of commercial technique in the service of seeming spontaneity. And Wiseman himself has moved away from any faith in the sender-message-receiver model of communication. Whereas he may once have seen the *Follies* as a direct conduit to social awareness, his view now is that the documentary form is as much fictive as real, in terms of both its constructedness and its capacity to change socioeconomic conditions. But he still justifies the intrusiveness of this work in terms of the public need to know about the principal institutions of American life (Allen and Gomery 237–38; Wiseman "Editing" 6; B. Grant *Voyages* 29).

Certainly, much controversy continues to surround the invasiveness of these techniques, and not only when applied to prisoners and the mentally outcast/incarcerated. Consider the response to the intense intrusiveness of cinema verité/direct-cinema lenses into British, American, and Australian homes in the TV programs *The Family*, *An American Family*, and *Sylvania Waters*. These series saw lengthy stays in the white heterosexual domestic sphere, with some chaotic effects on the people in view. The complexity of the issues is gone over performatively in the feature fiction film *Real Life* (Albert Brooks, 1979).

The opening, elevated master shot to *Real Life* shows a hall filling with people. Teletext situates what follows in the tradition of *An American Family*: "The motion picture you are about to see is the next step. It documents not only the life of a real family, but of the real people who come to film that family, and the effect they had on each other." The meeting is addressed by Albert Brooks (director of the metatext, star of the text, and director of the text within a text; each character is named "Albert Brooks"). After all are seated, recorded in a long take with only actuality atmospheric sound, the film cuts to a medium shot of a podium speaker, obscured by the out-of-focus head of a participant in the lower-left quadrant of the screen. We are in the genre of documentary assemblage and spontaneity. Brooks is introduced. He promises the townspeople the "motion picture" he is about to make will be about "reality" and asks them to "be yourselves." There is no need for anybody on-camera to "show off": "We don't want a show; or rather, we want the greatest show of all: life!" This is because the everyday offers "the most hilarious comedy, the most gripping drama, the most suspenseful disasters." He sings a song written for the town after this speech, recalling the musical segments from the *Follies*.

That self-seeking commercial discourse goes on throughout the succeeding eighty minutes, leavened by a self-reflexive parody of self-reflexivity. Brooks is shot "antiquing my end table" while waiting for the family under observation to recover from a long flight prior to the filming of their "first supper." As his voice-over explains this, a medium shot of Brooks leaning over the table, brush stroking and wiping it, is accompanied by actuality sound quoting the paint's instructions ("Continuous motion for oldest effect"). Such is *Real Life*'s take on the authenticity of direct cinema. The film fails when the chosen family, having suffered enormous emotional damage from the process, refuses to continue. Following adverse publicity, Brooks is rejected by both his studio and the array of psychologists from the National Institute of Human Behavior enlisted to legitimate his project. He cracks up. The point of the film is that all commercial filmmaking and academic knowledge are liable to pick up on "the public good" and use it for dubious ends.

I have some personal experience of these matters. In 1961, Allen Funt's *Candid Camera* TV series had succeeded his old audio *Candid Mike* in the popular American imagination. I was then a student in a New York nursery school. Parents were asked if they were amenable to having their children filmed. Mine agreed. I was asked what I would do for the camera: "Clean my teeth," I said. Provided with the necessary implements, I was able to respond only by putting a finger in one nostril and turning it around. My parents were advised about this gap of signification. They seemed untroubled.

But other critics see the problem very differently. The argument that Wiseman may be not so much a "subversive freedom fighter against the state" as one more "middle-aged, middle-class authoritarian who demands artistic freedom to create bourgeois art" sets up some savage antinomies (Anderson and Benson "Direct" 82). Brian Winston is perturbed by the director's repeated insistence that objectivity is impossible, alongside claims to social utility. Either Wiseman's work is "mere opinion" or it is something substantive that encourages corrective action, but it is one *or* the other. Anyone unwise enough to accept a necessary linkage of opinion and utility, of observation and participation, of enlistment and problematization, is that espresso drinker par excellence, an escapee into "a postmodernist world of open textuality." Wiseman wants to "have his postmodernist cake and eat it," simultaneously invested in both the authoritativeness of ontology and the artistry of individual vision ("Documentary" 48–49, 55).

Unlike such pomo brats, Winston is happy to have welfare and image ethics institutionalized. He takes previous restraints on the *Follies*—that it be shown only to what he calls "professional audiences" (presumably opposed to paying, amateur ones)—as exemplary for the project of "social value." Welcome to the cultural policy consultants of chapter 2. This sets up a monopsony, a circularity of expertise whereby the therapized subject can be found to be ill or well treated only by the definitional masters of that discourse. It lets citizens off the hook by ceding their authority and responsibility to an elite. I have greater sympathy with some of Winston's other precepts: public figures who elect narcissism as their way of life deserve less privacy than others, identifying and publicizing victims ought to be interrogated for its own rent-seeking conduct, and the power of naming "deviance" should itself be named. Clearly, the economy of information between documentarist and subject is unequal. Direct cinema is much more interested in holding up misery and suffering to the lens than pleasure and power, and it is reasonable to require something of this beyond filmmakers' developing a reputation for caring. Winston asks whether the investigation of social inequality makes a difference to what it surveys, and Cynthia Lucia suggests Wiseman's camera may merge with institutional panoptics because he does not provide an adequate context for effective action by viewers ("Comment" 367–69; Winston "Tradition" 54, 52, 41; Lucia 5). It is certainly disturbing to see the director reflecting on his *Law and Order* (1969) for the *Documentary Films* tape. Wiseman draws attention to a sequence, shot in extreme close-up, of a prostitute being strangled by officers of the vice squad, almost to the point of passing out. He summarizes a binaristic debate about the meaning of this segment, where the options are condemning police brutality or justifying the use of force against criminals, but fails to mention the position of the film crew and what their responsibilities and complicitness were at the scene of this violence.

The sense of a right to privacy is immensely strong in almost everyone involved in theorizing documentary who has enjoyed/endured the individualistic dictates of American public life, where lines are constantly and energetically redrawn from all political perspectives to ensure "we" all think "we" are also "I." Shifts between the singular and the collective are carefully tended, as empiricist forms of knowledge to validate experiential identity and truth that are also desirable political logics. This is well and good as a means of establishing alliances and points of disagreement and convergence, but it is not a guide to the correct means of obtaining consent to be filmed in *Titicut Follies*. The Supreme Court has never clarified that inmates in mental institutions retain privacy rights. People who lose such rights because they have broken the implicit social contract—a contract of which they are unaware in most cases—are unable to draw the attention of their fellow citizens to the fact through conventional channels: their subjectivity is generated from psychiatry and penology rather than politics or economics, and they lack access to the means of communication. Their sense of "privacy" must be unique. Yet Justice Ammi Cutter, speaking on behalf of the Massachusetts Supreme Judicial Court, denounced the *Follies* as "a collective, indecent intrusion into the most private aspects of the lives of these unfortunate persons in the Commonwealth's custody." That court found it "a massive, unrestrained invasion of the intimate lives of these state patients." But as we have seen, by the late 1980s, qualities of artistic achievement, historical archivism, and the public good attributed to the film had leavened such judgments ("Statement" 3; Surette 197).

Legal notions of consent commonly rely on three conditions: no coercive or deceptive means of exchanging information, perfect knowledge of processes and results, and personal ability to agree. The models are essentially economic, founded on the rational, calculating subject who respects property and so retains ownership of the self. This contractual arrangement—unlike the social contract—is perceived as an overt act of choice. Such models do not neatly apply to preproduction of the *Follies*. Prisoners who are mad are not deemed consenting. To repeat, the blueprint does not work for people whose very placement in the institution under review itself denies choice. The ability to consent to being represented as a prisoner in *Titicut Follies* relies on not being a prisoner at MCI.

The film portrays this oxymoron in a formal interview between a prisoner and a board of psychiatrists. The participants engage in "oracular reasoning," whereby a basic premise is reified and all unwelcome evidence discounted or reworked to support it: because he is incarcerated, he is mad. The angrier he becomes in arguing against this, the crazier he seems. Their response is to douse hostility toward them in medication, despite the fact the prisoner has been intelligent and reasonable, beyond the capacity of the board to appreciate (or to replicate). Their hysterical chair calms down only once the prisoner is gone and can be diagnosed in clinical terms (Anderson and Benson "Direct" 59; "Comment" 359, 364; Mehan 166, 170). In short, this is not the prisoner's dilemma of game theory or the Paretian optimality of neoclassical economics. Instead, it is a double bind: as a subject of representation, I need to exercise consent over my role in a text, but the ties that bind me to the main institutional actant of that text preclude my doing so. The text itself might loosen those ties and generate the preconditions for its own demise, for a future irrelevance, for me to be *able* to deny consent to a whole range of practices performed across my body.

▶ _____

**Fremantle Prison**

> Bridgewater was the first institution where I ever felt
> personally in danger. My reaction . . . would border on
> despair every time I went. When I would leave I would
> quickly put the place out of my mind. . . . the film in . . . [a]
> painful way revived the old feelings of depression and . . .

*anger at myself for continuing to ignore the problem. . . .*
*in a small way my reactions are a clue to why [such]*
*institutions . . . exist. There are some things we prefer not to*
*know about . . . not too unlike the Germans who lived near*
*Dachau.*
:: former director of legal medicine in Massachusetts quoted in
*Commonwealth*

So what of Fremantle Prison, now a waltzing museum through "Jailhouse Jive," a "Multicultural Feast" sponsored by the national youth rock station JJJ-FM in November 1992 starring Kanda Bongo Man, Nbungka Dancers, an Italian women's chorus, and the "Aboriginal Bob Dylan," Archie Roach? Irony: Aboriginal Australians made up a disproportionate number of former "residents," and Italian Australians were imprisoned there during World War II without trial (Treweek).

The first time I was aware of the prison was in 1986, prior to its de-commissioning, when I spent a year in Perth. Walking nearby with a friend, I said how beautiful the prison's stonework looked. She averted her eyes and moved away, soon angry and tearful. Her brother had just been released. She had been a regular visitor during his prison term. The stonework did *not* look beautiful to her. Six years later, once more living in Western Australia, I went on a tour of the new museum with another friend, who pointed out closed-off areas. He had tutored maximum-security prisoners there in 1989. They were in chains, separated from their teacher by glass, and constantly under guard. It took him several sessions to find out any pupil's first name: they wanted to be called "Rabbit" and "Fucker." He expressed discomfort at addressing them in this way; why could they only be known by derisive titles? They agreed to tell him their given names, and after a time professed to appreciating the exchange.

I have gone about this in entirely the wrong way. My understanding of the prison fits the chaotic sense Georg Simmel gives us of the modern city. I have not spoken with the managers of the prison, conducted a survey of museum educators and users, or interviewed prison museum guides about their work. I have no idea whether Wiseman has ever heard of what Walter Cronkite calls "the best-kept secret in the world": Fremantle, Western Australia. Instead, I have relied on Simmel's "touch-and-go elements of metropolitan life" (88), merged with a recognition of Jameson's need for a "cognitive map" (*Postmodernism* 51). I am blasé in my research methods, and rationally calculating in my demonstration of the fact. Confession may preempt critique. But this confession seeks not so much a pardon as some degree of interest. For there is method here: the montage effect of Wiseman's film is rather like the impact of a guided tour around a lapsed site of incar-

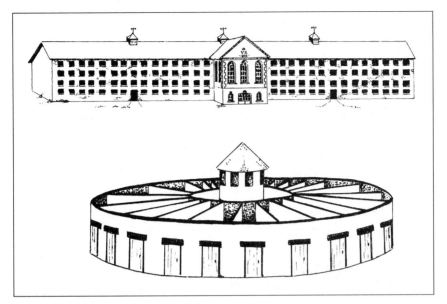

Fremantle Prison with the chapel forming the leg of the "T." "The cage" was a radial exercise yard designed to keep the prisoners separate. The warder was positioned in the middle tower. Courtesy of Cyril Ayris, from *Fremantle Prison: A Brief History*.

ceration, such as Fremantle Prison. The similarity derives from a mosaic of feelings, memories, and mergers of the personal, private, and public. Prison life and its commemoration are not indigenous or sui generis. One way of knowing them is through the *Follies*. The analogy strengthens when we consider Wiseman's account of editing: "a four-way conversation between myself, the sequence being worked on, my memory, and general values and experience" ("Editing" 5). This might be a maxim for the messy shifts from self to collectivity that characterize citizenship.

For a dozen years, until the closure of the prison in November 1991, a small Fremantle Prison Museum existed. Its official mission was "to inform the public of the important part the prison system and prisoners throughout the State have played in the development of Western Australia and to emphasize the contrast between the historical attitudes to prisoners and the present programmes devised to assist and help them" (Policy 23). Already, we can discern the two great wings of museum activity flapping energetically and demonstratively. First, the implied visitor is to be given a proper perspective on the site's history and the visitor's place in it. And second—here, of course, is the rub and the place where history and its public munificence really commence—a prior, non-Enlightenment age of darkness is to be made known and compared unfavorably with the moment such a history is written, that is, now. Put another way, we are to learn of a time when there was no structural homology between crime and its punishment. This time was in our own physical space and is part of our transcended and regrettable heritage. We can learn from it, *but it is definitely over*. Such an understanding, that we now live in a better moment, activates what I call *historical citizenship*. Historical citizenship emerges in the *hic et nunc*, but only in reaction to the past. Unlike *Titicut Follies*'s threatening training in civic conscience, a historical citizenship knows errors lie back there, before we knew better (a similar juxtaposition to the one between previous U.S. policy on El Salvador and today's position on Peru from chapter 5). Fremantle Prison is rendered as a strictly delimited ethical zone, a space in which conduct unbecoming and becoming are divided. This is not criminal conduct; it does not in any sense describe illegal activities that led to imprisonment. This ethical zone is that of the historical citizen, sifting out the good, the bad, and the sublime in past treatment of those prisoners and noting discontinuities and linearities in a movement toward present, enlightened, standards. It seems advisable at this point to look at the history to this ethical technology.

▶

## Museum Truth

> When Millbank Penitentiary opened in 1817, a room festooned with chains, whips and instruments of torture was set aside as a museum. . . . Thus did a new philosophy of punishment committed to the rehabilitation of the offender through the detailed inspection and regulation of behaviour distance itself from an earlier regime of punishment which had aimed to make power manifest by enacting the scene of punishment in public. The same period witnessed a new addition to London's array of exhibitionary institutions. . . . Madame Tussaud set up permanent shop. . . . As the century developed, the dungeons of old castles were opened to public inspection, often as the centrepieces of museums.
> :: T. Bennett *Birth* 153

Two relatively discrete political rationalities inform the museum. The first governs legislative and rhetorical form. The second determines the internal dynamics of a pedagogic site. Certain difficulties emerge from the different dictates of these rationalities. Whereas the genre of the museum calls upon democratic rhetoric associated with access, an open space for the artifactually occasioned site of public *discussion*, the pedagogic site functions in a disciplinary way to forge public *manners*: a contradiction between exchange and narration, reciprocity and imposition. The twin rationalities oppose an opportunity for the public to deliberate on some aspect of cultural history and an opportunity for museum magistrates to give an ethically incomplete citizenry a course of instruction. Of course, this binary can itself be made more subtle. Consider the varied histories that underpin Holocaust memorials in the United States: to remember the dead, to remember the self as survivor or liberator, to draw tourists, to be community centers, to stress religious or ideological affiliations, and to obtain votes. All these decisions are made "in political time, contingent on political realities" (Young 58).

Tony Bennett argues that the early life of museums was predicated on universalisms about "Man" and democracy. The traces of that legacy are in fundamental conflict with the histories of social movements constitutively excluded from singular but totalizing forms of museum narration (the great-white-hunter brand of colonial recollection). Hence the continuous critiques of museums since the rise of these movements. The museum is not so much a space of confinement as a space of education. In both its arrangement of things and its instructions to the public on how to approach collections, the museum hails its audience as respectful trainees. They learn to look and not touch, to walk about calmly and gently, and to distinguish the graceful from the riotous. These are modes of conduct related to behavior in a space, rather than internal reactions to art on a wall or in a display case (T. Bennett *Birth* 1, 7, 90–91, 97, 102–3). (In *Ferris Bueller's Day Off* [John Hughes, 1986], we are given a high-art diegetic insert, as the unruly, fun-loving teens move respectfully around the Chicago Art Institute's impressionist collection, finding themselves to be mature subjects in the process. Something similar is happening when Andreas Huyssen takes his five-year-old son to a museum and the little boy is reprimanded for touching and reclining on artworks. Huyssen reads this symptomatically, as a sign of institutions seeking to reinstate the dissociated organic aura of art [178–79]. I think it's a lesson in manners, part of the museum's mission as an ethical workplace.)

The museum seeks to attract newcomers and to draw reactions that will be taken into the exterior world through a temporary, voluntary enclosure of visitors that combines information and entertainment, instruction and diversion. Museums stop us at the present, pointing out the hectic pace of the modern by freezing its "unceasing dispersal of space and time" in the calibrated space of an archive (Tagg 364). This complex relationship is further complicated by buildings with prior lives. Britain's Imperial War Museum was once Bethlehem Mental Hospital ("Bedlam"), but it now introjects and projects a different form of madness and imposition. Yorkshire's Eden Camp offers visitors a brief stay behind the barbed wire that housed prisoners of war from 1942 to 1948, giving two hundred thousand people a year an exact experience of "the conditions in which prisoners lived." Nazi Germany's *Konzentrationslager* at Dachau is also now a museum (Boniface and Fowler 105). Fremantle Prison Museum achieves a physical unity between its former and current careers, performing successive functions of incarceration/correction and incorporation/education. In this sense it has gone beyond dividing the rowdy from the respectable, in its initial personality, to become an ethical technology for demonstrating that process *and* quietly replicating it as a mimetic space for exercising the mild-mannered gaze. This is the gaze of the decent person, who is being seen and heard as much as she is watching and listening, both at the time of her visit and at later moments that narrativize the visiting experience for others.

It is the task of museums to bring public attention to what has previously been concealed, to take the secrets of an elite into the populace at large. Instead of *obj*ectifying that population, as per the public executions of eighteenth-century Europe, the museum *subj*ectifies people, offering them a position *in* history and a relationship *to* that history. Since its origins in the French Revolutionary administration's designation of the Louvre as a national space, the museum has been associated with virtuous government or elite beneficence disbursed from on high. As I indicated above, its universal address characteristically obliterates difference or, more often, caricatures it through racist and imperialist appropriation and scientism, sexist exclusion or mystification, and class-based narratives of progress. The entire project of "discovery" also infantilizes the visitor, of course. The characteristics of the museum era are very much about mastery, over the physical environment and other countries. These scientific and imperial triumphs target more than the visitor, for they also infantilize those beyond such discourses or subject to them. This rhetoric of universal uplift runs into trouble when it encounters "excellence"-inflected definitions of heritage and the aura of leading museums as prestigious clubs (Duncan 88; T. Bennett *Birth* 97; Jordanova 22, 32; Price 25, 30). These contradictions were made overt at the Whitney Museum of American Art's 1994–95 exhibit "Black Male: Representations of Masculinity in Contemporary Art." Upon exiting the third-floor elevator, visitors faced a wall lined with Fred Wilson's installation *Guarded View* (1991), which presents four headless black male figures dressed in the guard uniforms of the Jewish Museum, the Whitney, the Metropolitan Museum of Art, and the Museum of Modern Art. Of course, the exhibit itself was invigilated primarily by African Americans! An "in your face" confrontation of the distinctions between museum labor and museum delectation was powerfully brought out by Wilson's text, its location, and the power relations of the space, which validated its commentary.

This complex generic heritage places the citizen-addressee at a site such as Fremantle in a complicated position. Consider the Western Australian State Planning Commission's 1988 *Draft Conservation and Management Plan* for the Prison. The *plan* begins by dividing possible futures for the area into the grand binary of citizenship: "opportunity" and "responsibility." The prison is announced as critical to the state's heritage, a "cultural asset [whose] recycling is a major responsibility." Virtually all colonial convict establishments around the world had been decommissioned and destroyed by 1988. In contrast, here was a functioning relic, "possibly the State's most important heritage item." So this zone describes the 1850s (as noted earlier, MCI-Bridgewater and Fremantle Prison are both creatures of that decade). The 1980s idea, following desires expressed by the city of Fremantle, was that the former prison be an *economic* site once the last prisoners had gone, a "city within a city" (Fremantle 1–3). It became a leased profit-making venture reporting to a trust and a state government authority. That public erasure of history—where a disciplining tenet of capitalism becomes a commodity itself and also a site for the controlled functioning of public memory—has corollaries in its historiographic bearings.

I leave it to the reader to unpack the meanings available from an official description of the prison's nineteenth-century architectural significance:

> As part of the changing attitude of Britain toward colonial administration, the Women's Prison indicated the new values attached to the imprisoning of women. It had its own walls, more intricate and delicate ornament, individual yards to cells and generally a less restricting environment. It was later adapted for use as a facility for the "mentally confused." (3.1)

The document continues. We are told more about "evolving policy": incremental increases to exercise space and the development of plans for rehabilitation. This is now a zone of the 1900s. This is the modern. Australia has become a federation of states, recently cast off from its constitutional status as a colony of Great Britain, and well free of the direct association of working people with forced convict immigration. It is now possible to recognize human labor as reusable and capable of ethical improvement. The state is coming to be lovable for its forgiveness and its powers of transmogrification, that special ameliorating capacity to build new persons where once dross alone resided. But we are, significantly, seeing this occur in buildings described as "fine examples of the Royal Engineers' Georgian Style" (3.1).

Of course, something else is going on here, a process with which we are all too familiar from the history of aesthetics. First, a feeling, sensate (perhaps male?) romantic figure locates and luxuriates in the radiance of an object of beauty. This romantic soul goes guarantor of the experience, his "otherworldly" take on the sublime itself in no need of vindication. Second, this transcendence is transferred. No longer the processual quality that derives from the meeting of a will and a text, the transcendence detaches itself from a specific human agent and becomes a quality of the object observed, the text. Now, the aesthetic is an *object* (the text) and no longer a *practice* (the romantic soul *and* the text). *As* an object, it becomes available for redisposal as a method of pedagogic formation. New people are to be formed through the experience of being led to the aesthetic sublime in interaction with this text.

Thirty years ago, most prisons from the convict era in Australia were in disuse or had been transformed for other purposes. Since then, many have become museums, both sites of national significance and local historical-society displays. These two forms serve dual functions: the historicization of Australia and the differentiation of contemporary penology from its uncivilized origins in a developmentalist narrative (T. Bennett *Birth* 154–55). This relates to the sense of filling in place and time in Australian social narratives, the popular argument that "Australia has a blank where its historical consciousness might have been," to use Stephen Bann's telling phrase (103).

And so it is here. The actual use and exchange value of "the Royal Engineers' Georgian Style" as a site of human labor and human incarceration are lost in history. They have attained "Architectural and Technological Significance" (3.1), that is, sign value. But such processes of reification always have targets for humanization, ironically enough. And here, we are told the very architecture is a "*demonstration of a way of life*" (3.2), a central aspect—both material and cultural-cartographic—of Fremantle. The State Planning Commission advises that the prison buildings "represent a well integrated element in the fabric of the city" (3.3). Now, this plan was being promulgated in 1988, the two-hundredth anniversary of English invasion of Australia and the year the prison was "occupied" (a quaint term to describe a reversal of control by people whose lives were contained within the prison), set alight in violent protest at the conditions of everyday life. We find no reference to these conditions in the text, no reference to tiny rooms, pails for shit, or the two open toilets among several hundred men left out in the elements for nine hours a day, each day of the year. I mean, why would you mention that in such a document? It's hardly a question of historical significance, is it, if it fails to provide an opportunity to refer to 1988 as a moment of colonial architecture or applied Enlightenment penology? If we spoke of texts as occupied sites, then the labor that made them might also be reasserted, which would undo the hierarchies that tend architectural history.

We can see more of the same in policies recently adopted by Western Australia's Building Management Authority (James Semple Kerr). The Authority allocates the prison "significance" on the basis of international and national comparisons and a reading of the thirteen reports written about it. This significance is again to do with the prison's location among imperial and colonial public works: its degree of intactness, the symbolism of its development (acknowledging convict labor in an anonymous way), the authorship-functions of its (specified, named) engineers and governors, its artworks, and finally its landscape value (4). Now this document makes concessions to recent prison life, to the complexities of a graffito that reads "Jim Brown is well liked because he is gorgeous," supplemented by "but not as gorgeous as Billy Little." These graffiti come from a guard's watch-tower post (16). And the Authority endorses Aboriginal participation in determining the direction and textuality of the site's heritage (21). But it is ultimately dedicated to a reificatory and nonrelational historicity.

What is implied about the ethical zone of the present? To find out, let's look at the pamphlet thoughtfully provided by the prison manqué and its double interpellation through the first-person plural. The pamphlet calls this place the "most wonderful monument of our history." It says, "We trust that you enjoy your visit." The first "we" ("our history") is the people of Western Australia, historical citizens who securely look back in wonder-ment at the human cruelty and architectural grandeur of their predecessors. These citizens have not been prisoners, of course, although there may be convict lineage somewhere. The second "we" ("We trust") is the managers of the prison now, "many of whom were prison officers." Redundancy be-comes a heritage-inspired line on a curriculum vitae. This is advertised as a splendid continuity, a means to "maintain this most wonderful monument of our history." Between these "we" categories, it becomes possible, within just fifty lines of writing in a pamphlet, to say what I have just quoted *and* to highlight spaces the prison once set aside for flogging and hanging. That's the section of the document ending, "We trust that you enjoy your visit."

The 1992–93 state budget allocated A$2.5 million to continue conser-vation works at the prison. What was being conserved? I think it's an ethical zone dividing the rotten from the good, the past from the present, the op-pressive from the enlightened, the contemporary law abider from the his-toric lawbreaker, and, critically, the museum visitor from the *contemporary citizen*. The zone operates through a strange structural homology, strange in that it might be expected to produce some identification with imprison-ment and a sense of responsibility for the process. But nothing of the sort occurs with many visitors. The homology is what Barbara Kirshenblatt-Gimblett has dubbed the intercalculation of "two different quotidians"

(410). The prisoner's day is redisposed for the tourist, crushed into an hour. It becomes a voluntary sentence, undergone to differentiate the good from the bad in society and its governmental-carceral history.

When I toured the prison, I saw spaces dedicated to mass nudity, strip searching, public showering and shitting, freezing cold, boiling heat, and constant surveillance. I was reassured at every point that this was the past. I was shown murals done by prisoners telling Aboriginal stories, but not told the appalling statistics of the incarceration of Aboriginal Australians, who make up 3 percent of the state's population and 40 percent of its prisoners (although one guide reportedly informs visitors that Aboriginal Australians kill themselves when imprisoned because they are kept from the call of the wild; tell that to the Royal Commission into Black Deaths in Custody that investigated this trend in prisons and police lockups across the country in the late 1980s). I did hear my guide refer to "en suites" in the new prison contained in what she termed "so-called cells," and my fellow trippers saying of the prisoners' art, "*so* talented even though they were in here." This was prior to our being given a technical discussion of systems for murdering people in the prison through capital punishment (which ended in the 1960s). In short, I saw a space that spoke of the history you can see—in a seemingly much older frame—in *Titicut Follies*. But unlike *Titicut Follies*, *this* space spoke entirely of the past: no tasks confronted the contemporary citizen. At Fremantle Prison, and in the domain of punishment now, there is no work to be done. Mistreatment of prisoners is a thing of the past, subject to progressive eradication up to November 1991. Then the *civiliter mortuus* (civilly dead) were transferred to a new-era facility, more thoroughly, electronically, panoptic. Visitors to the museum are, paradoxically, disarticulated from the materiality of what is done to prisoners in their name, unlike the shock of horror and complicity engendered by archival footage from MCI. The museum space has less of the aura of its recent past than does a film that came out the same year—or didn't—as *Sergeant Pepper's*.

Life inside new-era prison facilities is investigated in John Hillcoat's documentary-drama *Ghosts . . . of the Civil Dead* (1989), a remorselessly rugged, massively violent, and quite internal text that imprisons audiences as completely as it does warders and inmates. The film is a fiction based on three years of research into American and Australian prisons. Its Central Industrial Prison is a maximum-security, high-technology site of surveillance where prisoners are drugged, beaten, and sent into a vicious camaraderie. Euphemistically described as a "New Generation Facility," Central Industrial is designed for madness. The narrative concerns events leading up to a "lockdown," when the authorities impose total control over all activity and any sense of the human subject and its differences is lost. *Ghosts* uses the voice-over of a guard and the decay of an inmate to encourage our belief in a conspiracy to deaden resistance through a complex of invigilation, violence, drugs, and sex. The visceral brutality of every character in-shot—apart from the reporter who introduces the text—is all-imposing. The action takes place within the plastic-fluoro world of the prison. Exterior shots showing the building in the complete stillness of the desert develop rather than relieve the claustrophobia engendered by what we see inside. At a time when privately run correctional institutions were first appearing in Australia, the text raised issues connected to contemporary policy (once success in Rio de Janeiro, Montreal, and Berlin gained it a belated local release).

As a visitor to the old Fremantle space, by contrast to the viewer of such films, you don't have to worry. Another ethical zone is upon you that encourages consideration of how people were once "treated" by the state. The prison is like the coda the courts required to the *Follies*, stating, "That was then and something else is now." The zone values the contemporary and will not criticize it. Once we were wrong, which merely serves to confirm that we are now right. And so this might be a useful point to resume the reading options outlined in the discussion of Mr. Malinowski, redisposed from Bridgewater to Fremantle.

---

### The Religious

The prison is a shrine commemorating crime and justice meted out in concert with the revized Judeo-Christian ethic of nineteenth-century England: progressive incarceration. Here, redemption can be earned and granted. It is significant that Father Brian Gore spoke to the question of Aboriginal incarceration when decommissioning the prison.

---

### The Psychoanalytic

The social represses its antisocial side. But this is not merely a suppression of sons who have transgressed the law of the Father-state. It represses guilt-laden reminders to those outside the prison but inside the law. Why else would Western Australia need to lock up so many Aboriginal people who have survived genocide?

### The Cosmetic

Georgian engineering, combined with prison graffiti and heritage histori-
cizing, make for an aesthetic experience. They underwrite the essentially
fetishized nature of the visiting experience, designed to calibrate a social
space that is disarticulated from current penal practice. Instead, it is a *cordon sanitaire*, a cleansed, beatified, and beautified object of architectural
and commemorative interest.

### The Exhortatory

I don't think we can make this category work here, unless one can be ex-
horted to feel nothing about the ramifications of the past for the present
and the consequences of writing teleological history. Jacques Derrida is
quite right to require of a monument that "imposes itself by recalling and
cautioning" that it also "tell us, teach us, or ask us something about its
own possibility" (230). The prison museum authorities, like the many museum officials who call for "pastoral care" and "total immersion experiences" (quoted in Sorensen 66), have not read him.

### The Voyeuristic

It is hard to conceive of a more gruesome voyeurism than *Titicut Follies*.
The gallows experience at Fremantle, with reenacted furnishings, stories of
interstate travel by anonymous hangmen, and the ghoulish delight in alterity expressed by visitors, must approximate.

### The Anthropological

Perhaps all of the above combines in the seamless weave prescribed for cultural theory by the other (Bronislaw) Malinowski, for if there is some truth
in functionalist anthropology — useful positive description among the
blindness to disruption, systemic change, and categorical inequality — it lies
in revealing methods of deploying the past that instantiate the present as a
"good" moment. We can analyze the prison tour as a technology for writing unpleasant history best left behind, unrelated to the responsibilities of
today. As such, its design and life are distant from recent attempts by other

museums to hand back their artifactual past to indigenous peoples or cede authority to explain and display them (one thinks here of the Museum of the American Indian and a range of sites that give Australian Aboriginal peoples control over the museum presentation of their material culture). The "touch and go" of metropolitan life is, assuredly, held up and reordered here by a "cognitive map." But that map describes a cordon between us and the past, a cordon policed by the Fremantle Prison Trust (a quite staggeringly oxymoronic syntagm). The trust rejects "freely accessible" cell blocks because it has its own "plan to develop the interpretation of the prison" (Archibald). The zone and its "trust" guarantee we remain purely historical citizens.

The Fremantle Prison Museum needs to be criticized at both performative and constative levels. It *is* its contents; it performs them. But it also enacts a conceptual argument about respect for the present even as it zones the past as a discontinuous, fetishized prior domain. The museum actively memorializes the mistreatment of potential and actual "bad" visitors at the same time it cuddles the "good" among us with reassurances about improved treatment of others. The curricular mission of museums is conventionally associated with "planning for enlightenment of individuals." But this is now under attack for its passive-aggressive inclinations (Soren 91). Tony Bennett is right to insist that curators decline to organize "a representation claiming the status of knowledge," moving instead toward a view of themselves as holding "a technical competence whose function is to assist groups outside the museum to use its resources to make authored statements about it" ("Political" 51). In 1994, the Film and Television Institute at Fremantle screened a season of cinema thematized around women, prison, and mental illness, in conjunction with the local Arts Centre's *Absence of Evidence* event detailing the history of female prison inmates. This was an innovative mixture of international soap opera, melodrama, and art-house cinema with regional artistic commemoration: local citizenship at work making a counterauthorization of the past, mixing genres, histories, and texts in a technology of public discussion.

The threat of just such contemporary citizenship saw a concerted effort by the state of Massachusetts to hold *Titicut Follies* from public view. That text conspicuously compressed space and time to interpellate its audience, and it continues to do this. The Fremantle Prison Trust has a less transparent modus operandi. It simply translates the citizen through time, while remaining in one place. History can be brought safely up to date, up to November 1991, because it starts and ends in a monument to "Georgian Style," a preemancipatory legacy that moves in a grand narrative of Whiggish historiography. This monument is a zone, disengaged from the present in the name of preserving the past *as the past*. It is resisted by former prisoners, who are renowned for refusing to wear identification stickers when they return as visitors. They are forced back to the official tour whenever they "break away," for what are termed "safety reasons" (Treweek). Like the reserve collection of art museums or library rare-book rooms, these supplemental public sites remind us of the provisionality of open access to the past. They are the unfulfilled promise of museum modernity, the exclusions that define what counts as the public record (Tagg 362). Restrictions on former residents recall the locations where my friend's students had undertaken their shackled and manacled instruction. That in turn draws us back to the anonymous "Comment" on the first *Follies* case published by the *Columbia Law Review* in 1970. In querying the judges' privacy criticisms of the film, it argued that the "only interests clearly protected are the dignity of the Commonwealth and the public image of her agents" (359).

That intertext encourages us to walk away from the conventional binary of museum discourse between populist entertainment and *étatiste* instruction, no longer apt polarities of museum policy and practice. In place of diversion versus elevation, interactivity at the site of the museum should be our underpinning philosophy. This would merge the "resonance" and "wonder" that Greenblatt commends as the way to comprehend museums: a compound that locates us in the present as part of our social formation, even as it asks us to pause and be struck with the singular occasion of our visit ("Resonance" 42).

# Conclusion:
# I Am the Morning DJ on WONK

*As most of you are well aware, just as the personal computer
weakened the supremacy of centralized mainframe data
processors, digital television signals could soon transform the
boob tube into a smart machine, turning couch potatoes into
video programmers who channel-surf through a five-hundred-
channel world. Another bottleneck concern I'm sure I share
with most of you concerns the set-top box of the future. Many
of you are aware of my continued commitment in making the
future HDTV standard as interoperable as possible. The set-
top box for the next frontier in the open-system discussion is
perhaps amongst the most important of all issues.*

::   Representative Edward Markey, Democrat-Massachusetts,
    speaking to the "Telecommunications Issues" conference of
    *Broadcasting and Cable* magazine, 9 November 1993, broadcast
    on C-SPAN

*During my 15 years in the Commons, I have witnessed a . . .
decrease in the acceptance of personal responsibility. The
flaccid language of entitlements, the idea that there is no
truth, that everything is just an opinion, are the words which
should be written on this generation's collective tombstone.*

*    The absence of fathers and the disintegration of the family
have also played their part. Across a broad swathe of society,
children are now growing up without father figures. Whole
communities lack the moral presence which fathers should
apply.*

::   Member of the House of Commons David Alton, Liberal Democrat-
    Liverpool, in an article explaining his campaign to restrict the
    distribution of horror-genre videos among children (171–72)

Is there something wrong with these statements? In the first, does the mixing of metaphors (boob, smart, couch, potato, surf, bottleneck, frontier)

confuse and conflate issues? Or, if we subject the logic to a synchronic and diachronic analysis, does it open up contradictory linguistic heritages, allowing us to see how certain anti-popular culture themes return? Perhaps it also indicates the risks of separating communications and cultural policy. In the second, is it the misogyny of objections to flaccidity and untrammeled mothering, a distaste for the popular ooze that makes its way from the screen into the playpen through women's playful irresponsibility? Or does this exemplify the costs and benefits to experiential narration of the collapse of the modern into the postmodern, where labor and certainty are displaced by welfare and indeterminacy? We could quickly dismiss Alton's position as a yearning after the premodern, an era when, as Britain's chief censor proudly announced in 1937, "there is not a single film showing in London today which deals with any of the burning questions of the day" (quoted in "Child-Minders" 79).

Representative Edward Markey continued:

> We could create an informational apartheid, a nation of information-haves and information-have-nots. When I was in grade school, we would gather every Monday morning in the schoolyard and compare notes about the TV shows we'd watched the night before, the guests on *The Ed Sullivan Show*, or the adventures of the Cartwrights on *Bonanza*. Television and the schoolyard were great equalizers, bringing everyone together: rich and poor, Irish and Italian, Jewish and African American, and giving them some common ground. Television helped create a unified national self-image, a shared, common heritage.

Markey spoke in his then-capacity as chair of the House Telecommunications and Finance Subcommittee. His speech pointed to dangers facing those without cable TV: citizens who would be unprepared for the global information economy both as a market and as a public good, because of the coming competition for industries and employment with people all over the world (a new international division of cultural labor). Then Markey displayed his credentials as an opponent of violence, calling for parents to be endowed with the capacity to prevent their children from viewing television through warnings about the degree of violence in upcoming programs and the requirement that all new sets carry a V (for violence)-chip to block the reception of certain texts by parental choice. He cited evidence given before the subcommittee by the American Medical Association, the National Institute for Mental Health, the Centers for Disease Control, the surgeon general, and social science effects research. The consensus of these authorities was that children who watch violence on television become violent because they cannot distinguish fantasy from reality or comprehend the state's monopoly on legitimate violence. Markey then set up a choice as to whether a twelve-year-old boy would prefer access to digital technology or access to weapons technology: back to his totalizing theme. Multiple channels and information had the potential for *"elevating* the culture of our society . . . [and] the potential to *vulgarize* our society." As channels proliferate, ratings drop. Temptations increase for producers to sensationalize programs and make them violent. There must be some protection of the citizenry. Of course, that was also Alton's argument, but in his case, dedicated not so much to preparing young people for the NICL as allowing them "to grow up as innocents" (172).

Consider now Ervin Duggan, speaking on the future of multiple channels at the same conference as Markey. He was then a Federal Communications commissioner, moving on to become head of PBS:

> I would like to believe the more utopian visions about content on the information superhighway. It has been my observation that when a new technology or delivery system comes on-stream—I think first of 900 numbers—there seems to be a business built and a market created at the lowest common denominator of taste and I don't see much to suggest that we're all going to become policy wonks and education freaks on the information superhighway, or that there will be a giant burst of creativity, home commuting, that sort of thing. I think that the American people are going to see the "vast wasteland" become vaster. The range of choice on the wasteland will become greater. I don't want to seem cynical, but I do feel a certain pessimism. I think that the danger of the American people entertaining themselves literally to death over an infinity of channels is great, and that the technology is brilliant but our ability to keep up with it in sort of moral and cultural terms does not equal the brilliance of the technology.

There are connections between such anxieties and the "Baltimore Truth Declaration" of 1913 mentioned in my introduction—back to history. Think of Ben Hecht's prologue to *Nothing Sacred* (William Wellman, 1937), which matches a montage sequence of New York, "Skyscraper Champion of the World," with the following remark on commodity fetishism: "Truth, crushed to earth, rises again more phony than a glass eye." When Rudolf Arnheim wrote a "Forecast of Television" in 1935, he imagined something more splendid than later laments for TV would suggest, but with the same antinomies we encounter today. Arnheim predicted a global simultaneity of visual expression and experience through the transmission of railway disasters, professorial addresses, town meetings, boxing title fights, dance bands, carnivals, and aerial mountain views; an instantaneous montage of Broadway and Vesuvius. A common world of vision would produce transcendental meaning, surpassing linguistic competence and interpretation. An end to "the describing word" of radio would see "the wide world itself enter . . . our room." It would terminate the previously inevitable lapse in time common to all modes of communicative transla- tion, inducing a new modesty: "We are located as one among many." But this was no naive welcome. Arnheim warned, "Television is a new, hard test of our wisdom." The very ease of knowledge that was its grand offer- ing suggested either enrichment or dormancy: an informed public, vibrant and active, or an indolent audience, domesticated and private (160–63).

Nor was Hollywood silent on the matter. In *Murder by Television* (Clifford Sanforth, 1935), every conceivable large media corporation is keen to obtain the new technology, but each one is confounded by its in- ventor, Professor Houghland, who wishes to keep television free of corpo- rate despoliation. He refuses to obtain a patent, so keen is he to cordon TV off from conventional notions of property in order that it can become "something more than another form of entertainment." As per Arnheim's forecast, a grand demonstration joins people across the United States "with- out the use of relays." Then the professor takes us live to Paris, London, and an unnamed Asian city. But at the moment of triumph, when TV seems set to assure "the preservation of humanity" and to "make of this earth a paradise," Houghland is killed onscreen. A doctor secretly involved with "foreign governments" (a cable to him in code is signed "J.V.S.") uses the sound of a telephone ringing back in his office to radiate waves that merge with those from the TV to create what Bela Lugosi later informs us is "an interstellar frequency, which is a death ray." The invention incorporates the best and the worst of human thought and guile, and the mystery of the modern: great spirals emanate periodically from the television set, suggest- ing a trancelike condition that never quite departs the film. Writing five years earlier, in the *Daily Worker* of 1930, Samuel Brody drew this divide in political economic rather than psychological-citizenship terms. TV was one moment in the multiplicity of war-directed capitalist inventions. Its po- litical uses would be presidential campaigning and the installation of quies- cence in its audience, through "the same authentic lies" as those found in documentary cinema and the fiction film. Conversely, the Soviet Union would be aided by television in its efforts to "build socialism and a better world for the laboring masses" (106).

What is so extraordinary about the testimony of these men—over six decades—is their touching separation of commerce from culture and their shared commitment to freedom and lack of faith in the sensitivity of people who have it. Olivier Mongin's treatise on the terror of the televisual void, its emptiness of materiality that so affronts democrats, poses a similar query: "À quelles conditions la citoyenneté est-elle encore possible? La morale et l'économie n'ont-elles pas dévoré le politique, cet art fragile du vivre-ensemble? [Under what conditions is citizenship still possible? Haven't moralism and the economy devoured the political, that fragile art of living together?]" (12). Of course, they have. This very Aristotelian understanding has been overdetermined by the unhelpful antinomies of consumption versus ethics in many theories of citizenship. For Richard Merelman, cultural-capitalist states frustrate the possibilities of democracy because the popular provides "partial visions" of the possible. Popular culture may focus on key aspects of liberalism, such as public-private relations and connections between the individual and the collectivity, but that concentration does not produce an animated, conceptually realized participation in politics, for it is mired in the temporary purchasing power of the consumer.

Clearly, these rather negative pursuits of the popular are a little pessimistic for my taste. But there are also difficulties in the way cultural studies deals with the issue. Consider Noel King's provocation on this score:

> I always wondered what [a] polemical siding with "the people" would make of the phenomenon of the "spot special." When I'm told that if I rush to a corner of the supermarket immediately, bottles of mineral water will be half price for a few minutes, what do I do as a desiring-to-be-resistive-and-empowered subject? As the song asks, do I go or do I stay? Would I be more empowered and resistive to refuse the injunction of the spot special even though submitting to this particular "hailing" will save me money? ("'Play'" 9)

As Frow argues in "The Concept of the Popular," the political animation behind cultural studies derives from an attempt to shatter conventional hierarchies of artistic value and connect left intellectuals to "the people." But this articulation is always imbued with a particular series of definitional legacies. The first is derived from neoclassical economics. Unfettered expressions of the desire and capacity to pay for services stimulate the provision of entertainment and hence—when the product is publicly accepted—generate the popular. This is a processual and quantitative measure, as opposed to the directional and qualitative definitions that seek out originary, organic sites of the popular in the people themselves (folk culture). Then there is a Marxist meaning. In this formulation, popular culture exists in opposition to dominant culture. As with neoclassical economics, there is no necessary aesthetic value attached to particular texts. In the reactionary model, value is assigned through supply and demand. In the radical alternative, it is found in contingent occasions of internal and external difference from and struggle with dominant symbols.

These discourses specify the what, when, where, and how of analysis, without revealing the identity of the subject at hand: Who *are* "the people"? As with the audience, I think the answer lies in textuality: "the people" exists as a representational effect, in the output of the popular, and as a knowledge effect, in its investigation and regulation. And this textuality is political.

Institutionalist understandings of politics locate it within the apparatus of the state: the paraphernalia of making and administering legislation and spending taxpayers' money. This generates what Jürgen Habermas calls "a Janus-faced public that takes the form of a public of citizens at the entrance to the state and a public of clients at its exit" (65). The people learn to vote, lobby, and receive benefits before commencing the cycle again. The state takes the citizenry—a political entity—to be isomorphic with the population—a social entity—and hence the primary object of governance (Foucault "Subject" 790). Here are "the people." Recall the three folds of governmentality: the economy, where the population could be productive; the polity, where it could be loyal and healthy; and justice, where it could be rejuvenated. These spheres infuse sovereignty with demography. They operate in popular culture through three human sciences. Aesthetics, the psy-complexes, and economics divide up the popular as genres, audiences/nations, and modernity/postmodernity. Throughout, the popular is figured in homology with "the people": forms of life that must be domesticated and controlled by both corporations and governments.

It is not enough for the state to have its existence legitimated and its actions ratified by a public of citizens acting as an electorate. That sense of the public also signifies a population, which can pose problems. It falls sick, becomes irascible, breaks laws, requires knowledge, and acts selfishly, shortsightedly, and foolishly. In short, this population loses it, which presents a special set of problems when dealing with the popular. The public has to be conceived and engaged with as a reader of dirty books (chapter 3), a spectator to foreign television (chapter 4), a viewer of foreign policy and domestic state violence (chapter 5), or a visitor to prison museums (chapter 6).

Dealing with a variegated population is very different from dealing with its comparatively homogeneous equivalent, the disembodied citizenry of conventional political theory or psephology. Although the citizenry can be figured as a voting creature that acts infrequently, but at the same moment and with very similar effect, the population is figured as sane, mad, healthy, ill, employed, unemployed, racial, gendered, aging, youthful, and so on. In short, in order to administer a diverse group of people, it is necessary to carve it up, shattering the illusion of unity so vital for the myth of constitutional government. Hence the messy contradictoriness of a design for unanimity that must engage with differentiation. Cultural citizenship becomes the integrative forum, through processes of governmentality inextricably intertwined with tracking the popular. Renato Rosaldo is wrong: cultural citizenship is not oxymoronic in its blend of "the right to be different" with "the right to belong" ("Cultural" 402); an efficiently functioning postindustrial capitalist state could not have it any other way inside the new international division of cultural labor. Hence the brief given to Australia's Great Southern Films to adapt a Scandinavian toothpaste commercial for broadcast in Thailand. Following the requisite computer animation, the Southeast Asian version was exported back to its Northern European place of origin, brightening the Old World's smile as space, time, and decay were simultaneously obliterated by capital (Strickland). This is the right to be different, to belong, to have healthy gums, and to organize your workforce as you wish.

The state and business act and are acted upon not merely through self-professedly political or commercial institutions, but across a broad band of knowledge: health, social work, auditing, censorship, subvention, accountancy, and other sites of human modulation. So dispersed a set of actions allows for the expression of difference. The very *act* of government here involves problematizing and slicing to render social issues smaller, creating more and more difficulties in need of resolution. Living, breathing subjects who act in the everyday become objects of contemplation and intervention. This makes the space for politics to occur through the work of social movements, for a reference to "politics" always already "means that there is something to institute," some aspect of change through prescription to make the social world conform to its supposedly true nature. The notion of truth decides the direction of reforms. This *can* be a profoundly antidemocratic sentiment, when it embodies the powermongering expertise of an intellectual elite, whether advisers to government or talk-show hosts. We can achieve a disarticulation of this expertise if policy prescriptions are ratified not through abstract "truth," but through consultation and evaluation involving those affected (Rose and P. Miller 174–75, 180–81; Barron 109, 116–17; Lyotard in Lyotard and Thébaud 22–24): the future of Fremantle Prison Museum needs to be decided by former inmates as much as by historians of architecture. Social movements that have emerged in the past thirty years replicate divisions of the population attended to and figured by the practice of government: you could compare the categories of subject from the census and governmental programs with those of contemporary identity politics and uncover a remarkable similarity. African Americans and women are targets of the state and advertisers, so they target institutions from these demographic subject positions, not as universalist voters. Of course, this occurs against a geopolitical background of international affairs (notably the detritus of the Vietnam War) and economic change (the requirement for women to join the paid workforce in order for conventional nuclear families to survive). Politics is not just what governments do (manage the population) but what populations do (deal with government). This relationship has increasingly taken place over issues of representation. And again, the meaning of *that* awkward term has shifted. *The politics of representation* once referred to the means by which the public was spoken for in Congress by elected persons. Now it also refers to the look and speech of figures in popular and state culture and their relationship to segments of that population. Much of this terrain is concerned with the problematic nature of truth and normalcy, thanks to the efforts of social movements to highlight questions of who speaks for whom, and on what authority. In short, the nature of the popular and populations promotes the impossibility of any singular, correct model of representativeness *or* representation. On the cultural front, that does not mean representation and interpretation are unchartably chaotic. Such practices are always partial, and they come *from* somewhere, as we can see from the two examples below.

They come from a 1968 manual introducing studio photographers to airbrushing, both a technical and an ethical innovation. The manual's author, Alexander Shafran, suggests using the airbrush for correction and creation. Corrective uses are called for when technical errors, such as the presence of a flash in-shot, mar a print. Creative uses, by contrast, are about retrospective composition. Such applications are called for when professionals "produce a good photograph, either pictorially or commercially, which, although adequate, seems to be ordinary and unexceptional." Shafran pauses briefly to pose the authenticity question ("Is this ethical?"), answering himself by moving into the domains of historical precedent and professional practice ("Retouching has always been a part of photography") and assuring readers there are no rules prohibiting photographers from seeking "the best possible result" (provided they master airbrushing as part of their trade, rather than subcontracting the work but taking the credit). His six-line detour completed, Shafran emphasizes, "It is not our province to settle this controversy" in such a volume; the key is instruction, not ethics (8).

The book's examples range from archival records and studio portraits through to "happy-snappies" of the white nuclear family. Two before-and-after images are of particular concern. The first reproduces ash clouds emanating from Mount Vesuvius in 1944, eliding the sky and the billows and looking overexposed. In the revised version, the background is darkened and the contours of the ash are highlighted (65). A second instance is of a man in U.S. military uniform standing on the deck in front of a house. An automobile is in the background. Here, airbrushing transforms the car into foliage. Shafran likes the new version because the vehicle "dates the picture"

(114–15). These revisions reference specific notions of truth. A correspondence model reforms Vesuvius: light and shade diminish the reproduced power of the volcano, so they must be redisposed in order to offer an accurate record—not of what was recorded, but of what a volcanic eruption is expected to resemble. The initial representation of the soldier fails a coherence test, his contemporaneity diminished by the mise-en-scène. The car seems to prejudice the matching of signs: modernity requires old autos to be replaced, for the mechanical is a datable signifier.

But each of these truth systems is itself historically contingent and awkwardly interlaced. Correspondence theories aim to present rather than represent information, with no mediation between knowledge and knowing subject; their means of being "in the true" is external corroboration. Coherence theories assume the implausibility of a perfect match between truth and understanding, depending instead on a consistent and transparent intellectual method: their means of being "in the true" is replication. But the two systems bleed into one another. What is the referent of the Vesuvius pictures: a memory of the moment, geological expertise, popular understandings of the mountain's history, or conventions of photographic realism? These are all questions of knowledge. And how can the soldier's portrait function in an up-to-date fashion when fashions in clothing themselves shift? Today, such photographic realism is problematized quite overtly. Even in news pictures, there may be a license for multiperspectivalism. Murdo MacLeod of the London *Observer* uses a double exposure to depict a litigious cancer sufferer asleep on the couch, with his wife in two positions: both sitting alongside him, her chin in her hands, and leaning down from above to touch him. The presumption of pure documentation that used to characterize the news photo has been enriched.

Other popular expressions of truth require some different methods if they are to be understood. Yale University Press's *Literature & Literary Criticism* catalog for 1994 offers toll-free orders through the number 1-800-YUP-READ (truly). Page 24 of the catalog contains information about "Literature & Religion." Nestling against *Mark and Luke in Poststructuralist Perspective*, Yale announces a new translation of the First Gospel, with commentary. The scholar responsible for this translation is described in biographical notes as follows: "J. Enoch Powell was professor of Greek in the University of Sydney, New South Wales." Well he was—in the late 1930s, his only period living in that country. Enoch Powell is rather better known for his 1960s "Rivers of Blood" speech, part of fifty years in British political life devoted—inter alia—to alerting white Britons to the perils of "colored immigration." Did Yale University Press lie, or stick to information relevant to the authorship of its new volume? It deployed one generic mode of classification rather than another, related to potential readership. In correspondence terms, it certainly offered accurate information, and in accordance with coherent rules of publicizing authorship.

The production of truth has been a central concern of every society on record. The labor of religion, storytelling, science, and speculative and analytic philosophy is to explain things, from the nature and history of existence to means of establishing falsehood. The spread of electronic popular culture has rendered this production an overproduction, with the dividing lines between genres of truth comprehensively problematized, democratized, and compromised. Some of this we might welcome, notably assaults on certain castes of person monopolizing truth and power. Other aspects, such as the lack of a coherent vocabulary of civil, economic, and cultural rights, we must query.

I want this volume to stand in vigorous opposition to any singular systems or certainties of truth. It gives voice to this position in an applied way that is largely performative; hence the synecdochic mosaic of the first part of this conclusion. So it seems useful to conclude in a more constative mode that endeavors to make this procedure transparent, to specify how the technologies of truth argument can be run. My aim has been to show empirically the risks of metaphysical pronouncements on the popular that ground themselves in a solid-state subject or assume the power of pure reason. Such positions seek to condition the competent mind in the direction of competent citizenship. This ideal of philosophical training clearly assumes an objective state of being in the world that can be represented by and to human subjects in terms that may then be evaluated. The next move places its faith in rational deliberation. The Foucauldian history of truth, where power is exercised over bodies through the use of knowledge, is challenged by a utopic promise of truth that can emerge from "the public sphere of open argumentative debate" rather than dogmatic and arbitrary authority (Norris 289). But on what ground and by what rules might such discursive formations come into play? As Foucault rightly argues, the purism of the ultimately open and impressionable figure in search of dictionary meanings (or ideal speech-act situations) is fatally compromised. Before words there were phrases, utterances predated vocabulary, and mutterings came prior to syllabic cordons. Meaning is never clearly morphological, semantic, or referential, but is created as an event, a specific moment that is also always citational (*Sept* 23, 30): "Des discours pris dans les scènes, dans les luttes, dans le jeu incessant des appétits et des violences, forment peu à peu ce grand bruit répétitif qui est le mot [Discourse lives in a setting, in a struggle, in the incessant play of appetite and violence, forming little by little the grand repetitive noise that is the word]" (*Sept* 34). Any utopics of communication needs to unpack language into theoretical strands, but also reassemble it as a working technology of truth. I am indebted here to Horst Ruthrof's attempt in *Pandora and Occam* to describe the oscillation between tightly codified, denotative notions of language and more poly-vocal, connotatively aware positions. Ruthrof argues convincingly for a nec-essarily opaque quality to communication, where communicative acts are generated by and engage in vastly variant sign systems. This does not make them purely ludic and open to all and any readings, but constitutively cita-tional and cross-referential. Hence the tension between the restrictiveness of Occam and the openness of Pandora.

I am particularly interested in his theorization of semiotic corrobora-tion. Ruthrof argues that "what we call reality is the product of the inter-action of at least two different sign systems" (102). If I pick something up thinking it is a heavy rock (or a book by a contemporary classicist), but discover it to be a rubber film prop (or a book by an outmoded racist), my methods of reading confound one another. If I leap from a wall thinking it is a foot above ground, but land an inch below, pain tells me I made a mis-take, but not how to correct my procedures next time. That relies on my reinterpreting the event through an admixture of sign systems: the memory of how I "saw" the height, the vision of the distance from below and above, and the physical sensation of restaging the event by placing one leg at ground level and one at the point of takeoff. The more corroborations of and explanations for my referent (injury through stupidity) I have, the more truth I produce. The relationship of correspondence and reference is not an empiricist one, between meaning and experience, or words and objects. Rather, this referentiality is achieved by confirmation across sign systems (114–15).

The overarching interpretative semiotic authority of language makes it "our dominant sign system." Language can pronounce on indexicality in a metatextual way, adjudicating—or at least signifying the differences between—sign systems that contradict one another. An example might be the occasion of a John Waters film in which the spectator, instructed to "scratch and sniff" some cardboard provided as part of admission to the theater, rubs the wrong section of paper, breathes in odors designed to cor-roborate a different section of the sound-image track, and is told of this through other odors in the room and her own linguistic understanding of the "correct" function. As Ruthrof phrases it, "Linguistic construals of re-ality gather meaning according to the rate of corroboration by non-linguistic signs" (103). This does not mean these systems are always subservient to language, but they are less capable of abstraction. Such forms of corrobo-ration also achieve a complex intermingling of individuality and sociability in establishing and countering meaning. Interpretation is a function of membership of a variety of semiotic communities (119). Ruthrof offers a "ladder of discourses" to categorize these systems, commencing at the highest rung with the most "saturated social discourse" and descending to more technical or limited discourses. There are nine levels on the ladder, but their specific identities and operations are arbitrarily selected and could be varied (134). I shall briefly outline these stages, redesignating the ladder to suit this book and my attempt at a *combinatoire* and revision of the trinitarian human sciences model of the popular that utilizes aesthetics, the psy-complexes, and economics.

Ruthrof places "literary discourse" at the top of the ladder because it can activate all the processes at work in different forms of language, through referentiality in other systems and an awareness of internal presentational norms produced in its readers. Put another way, this is about establishing a diegetic world, the extratextual domain to which it refers, and the means by which this is done (134–35). My aim has been to offer a similar form of cultural studies that shows how certain worlds are created in discourse through the emphasis of sameness and the obliteration of difference in the relationship of power and subjectivity, pointing out the referentiality of particular systems of meaning and indicating how this can be charted. An instance is the montage effects proposed in chapter 6's unruly connections of museums and cinema verité. This is an overt foregrounding of the moment and motivation underpinning control of the means of communication, where correspondence and coherence are held up as production and reception protocols. Consider the sequence when a handcuffed Jody asks his captor Fergus to help him urinate in *The Crying Game* (Neil Jordan, 1992), exclaiming, "It's just a piece of meat." Susan Bordo explains this as the cosmically mutable anxiety evoked by the penis, that it changes too much to embody the stable authority of the phallus (696–97). The form is constitutively inconstant, unruly in its unremittingly temporal status as an organ with a recurring yet unpredictable history: both a simple "piece of meat" and a symbol of the ready and the unready. Jody calls up this motile quality when he asks for Fergus's hand after saying to him "You're the handsome one." This is a complex occasion. Jody is a black British soldier kidnapped during a sexual encounter with a white woman, Jude. He represents certain colonized and sexualized motifs. Fergus, his captor, is a white Irish revolutionary whose lover entrapped Jody and who must now decide whether to hold his penis. Clearly, this is a multiply ironic moment, in terms of the knowledges that audiences bring to the text about sex, color, and colonialism; doubly engaging in a mainstream release that uses art-cinema techniques in this early phase of the film, concentrating on dialogue between the men interspersed with fantasy sequences to set up their connection, in ways quite detached from the use of coincidence in classical Hollywood. Extratextual ideas are called up alongside quasi-modernist protocols of intersubjective intensity and framing through a shooting style that has the camera looking through doorways and windows to foreground the film's constructedness. And later on, the question of the penis as a store of textual information becomes stronger yet, when Fergus gags after discovering he has been fellated by a man.

Ruthrof's second rung is "mythical language." By this he means the erasure of process and the situatedness of enunciation that favor an "authoritative-authoritarian" world, a singular account brooking no interrogation (134, 143). The homology here would be with the struggles over representations of the Shining Path described in chapter 5. We can also find connections to anxieties over the power of the popular, particularly photographic images, to distort truth and its audience. Consider again the penile materials assembled in chapter 3. The *Harvard Law Review* glossed the 1936 Camel cigarettes trial to come to terms with what it described as "a representation which denies itself." The judgment said that because the ridicule of the rider was accidental and clearly "an optical illusion," it could not be read as a "representation of fact." Put another way, there was no sense in which this photograph represented the man at its center, *even though* he was libeled by the very "incongruity of the jest." So a claim to truthfulness would be no defense ("Libel" 841). The image leads to derision of its subject in the eye of the court—regardless of the fact that he is constitutively and inadvertently *not* represented. This is how language can be used to "resolve" *différends*. A *différend* arises when certain modes of speech are so comprehensively incommensurate with one another that no universal means of deciding between them can do so without violating their own codes of communication (Lyotard *Differend* xi). The magical denial of this irreconcilability is the ultimate force of myth. Myths ignore their own conditions of existence to pronounce on, or force to cohere, fundamentally opposed genres of speech, as per a representation that harms a person depicted as part of it (and whose parts partially constitute it) even though no one thinks he is represented by it.

Ruthrof's next category is "historiography." This refers to the extent to which historical narrative is determined by evidence. Ruthrof finds a double-world, as per literary discourse: a picture of the past and a speaking subject, a simulacrum and a point of enunciation. Both become apparent to the reader (134, 143, 145). Chapter 6 tries to force open a space of speech and responsibility tying present to past in the conduct of imprisonment. Here, the essence of mythic speech, that it refuse the contingency of is emergence, floating free of metatextual signification, is done in by the groundedness of telling a story, a process that sees the moment of making history as overt and determining. We might return here to the uptake of *Schindler's List*. Ten years before the film—when the novel was first released—critic Les White pushed his father, a "Schindler Jew," to reminisce about the experience, opening up what had been unsayable in the family. So when Spielberg praises his scriptwriter for "inordinate restraint," White is taken back to the rage he felt growing up not knowing about his father's past: "Cut the bullshit," he asks. Armed with a new parental account, White takes the film to task for mitigating the horror of the real: his grandmother and aunt shot, his grandfather and one uncle gassed, and another uncle hanged, "*indiscriminately*." This is the key adverb for White, and he claims it is absent from the Spielberg version. The film's suggestion that the Nazis targeted inefficient or resistant workers ascribes reason to what was much more a matter of chance and willfullness. And the Hollywood account places an unrepresentative "emphasis on hope" and the prospect of survival. At the same time, White recognizes that this has opened up dialogue: far distant now from familial reticence, his father is transformed into a public lecturer in schools and movie theaters (L. White 3–5).

This raises the contingency of historical representation, in keeping with Ruthrof's protocols: the film renews public discussion of the past, gives an object against which a father's recollection can be enunciated, and foregrounds distinctions between experiential and Hollywood narration. By contrast, the museum logic of Fremantle Prison seeks to shut down critical discussion by keeping two different strategies from clashing. The first strategy claims the site is beholden to its objects, a replicant mirror that lacks agency but is resplendently authentic (the deictic register that says, "This is the old way"). The second strategy asserts it is beholden to the nation as a historical metonym that provides an expressive key to the totality of the past (the deictic register that says, "You are the bearers of progress"). If we move into a historiographic mode, contradictions can be pointed out between these classificatory systems, opening up the opportunity for contemporary citizenship through debate, as per the design of France's ecomuseums (Tagg 362; Poulot).

Ruthrof continues with "juridical language." This discourse walks the line dividing "the letter and the spirit of the law." It mingles interpretations of the past with prescriptions for the future in a contradictory mixture of case-law precedents and contemporary values (134, 147). We can see similar forms of life at play in the Ettingshausen case discussed in chapter 3 and the first Rodney King trial, addressed in chapter 5. It is significant that both involve the use of photographic images and bring together sex and violence: in ET's life as model, role model, and footballer, and in Mr. King's treatment by the police and the sexual associations of large, looming "blackness" in racist discourse about him. A good example of such intermingling comes in the discussion of Hollywood's "voluntary" censorship by its archbureaucrat, Jack Valenti (head of the Motion Picture Association of America):

> Violence is harder to catalog than sensuality. There either is copulation or there isn't. There is writhing or there isn't. But it's hard to measure gradations of violence. John Wayne hitting the beaches at Iwo Jima and mowing down 2,000 people—how do you equate that with a fellow being fellated? It's pretty difficult. (quoted in Svetkey 32)

Jack is right. It is difficult. But the daily execution of administrative decisions equates—however implicitly—incommensurate acts. In other words, organizational power produces equivalencies by the rough-and-ready intermingling of logical precedent and unargued fiat. Juridical language is inordinately difficult for conventional cultural studies to engage, because much of our work likes to keep a distance between the supposed antinomies of freedom and surveillance, expressiveness and order, government and autonomy. The possibilities thrown up by engaging this arbitrariness are beautifully brought out in Carrie Mae Weems's *Commemorating* series of decorative souvenir plates in honor of prominent African American men (1991). It tropes a high-European elitist dining mode, but displaces the usual subjects; on one of the plates, poignant political tribute is paid to "Thurgood Marshall and the NAACP Defense Team for their deep commitment to justice being more than mere precedence." This complex multiple signification opens up the many tracks of power that inscribe the law as both "letter and spirit."

Ruthrof's next stage is "everyday speech," traditionally the stuff of cultural studies' claim to political currency, with modality rather than formal propositionality critical to understanding the workings of power (134, 149). Consider the intersection of the everyday with the generic/industrial dictates of advertising. Scott Sanders provided literally hundreds of voice-overs to congressional campaigns in 1994. His aim was to insinuate criticisms of opposing candidates through speech tone, sounding like an angry everyday person rather than an orator. A low pitch, with diaphragmatic breathing, was the physical key. But the usual techniques of irony—pauses, elisions, and stretched syllables—take up space in a thirty-second commercial. Digital editing came to the aid of the party by removing breaths and compressing words ("Man"). We can also discern here shifts between private and public, audience member and citizen, that have long characterized radio: the casual medium, its simple reception a naturalizing mode for moving across such categories. At the same time, the everyday is also a site for encountering linguistic "accidents" that derive from the modal as much as the propositional. We might instance Clinton's remark to Helmut Kohl that the German chancellor was increasingly resembling a sumo wrestler. Clinton may have intended this as a jocular expression of friendliness. It called up, however, racist caricatures of an artistic and highly technical sport, an implied critique of Kohl's body shape, and a slice of shared German-Japanese history that embarrassed everyone concerned. The everyday casualness of this encounter in fact comprised multiple histories and forms of communication, overdetermined by Clinton's failure to observe the equally everyday protocols of state visits. Again, when Jane Fonda shows Yves Montand a photograph of a hand stroking a penis in *Tout va Bien* (Jean-Luc Godard, 1972) this seems quite shocking; it is rare in cinema to have a subsidiary diegesis that shows the actants observing a genital. But what follows is equally destabilizing. The scene is resumed to the quotidian space that is the ordinary fate of the penis, for as the camera lingers on the image, Fonda's voice from offscreen jerks us into the mundanity of the moment: "Admit that this image satisfies you less than it did three years ago." The penis has resumed "touch" to the everyday.

Ruthrof's sixth rung is "technical language," instructional signs such as labeling on cans or the classification of museum exhibits. This supposedly nonideological form of address is necessarily connected to obsolescence, waste disposal, and public health (134, 154, 156). The technicist appeal of cultural policy studies activists detailed in chapter 2 and the multisided, productive complexities of Foucault's concept of governmentality apply here. It is easy to be caught in the logic of the terms one is using without contemplating the historically bounded nature of what counts as technical. For instance, Thomas Malthus, whose demography helped to mold governmentality, was a true revisionist of his time. In Europe the late eighteenth century was a period of lamentation over the modern, but in ways that appear odd today. We are used to tears being shed for dissociated personalities or divided workers who suffer from "psychic crowding." But that era saw something much more interesting: a debate over the capacity to populate and its allegorical significance for politics. A century of anxiety over the question of population amounted to a competition between contemporary England and "the ancient world." The civic virtue of a society was routinely judged by its birthrate, and it was feared the old city-state of Athens outdid the brisk capital of London on this score. So when Malthus announced *over*population as the trend, and said this was a bad thing, his stand was doubly upsetting. Not only did he argue there would soon be major overpopulation, but he made this into a problem rather than a sign of plenitude and happiness, reversing both correspondence and coherence grounds of truth (F. Ferguson 106, 111). This new way of thinking about the public also ushered in methods of calculation that were to characterize the nineteenth century's interest in government. What had been acceptable as technical discourse—modern life was flawed because it produced fewer bodies than its predecessors—was doubly overturned, revised by new mathematical ratios in place of speculation and the concept of overpopulation.

Ruthrof's next category is "scientific statements" (134, 156). These attempt to establish agreed systems of falsification/verification, as per efforts to construct a chain of cause and effect between violence and audiovisual culture, discussed in chapter 1 and again here. Bruno Latour's sociology of science concentrates on cross-categorical difficulties, the spaces and practices that elude taxonomic neatness and Popperian method. Latour uses interdisciplinary translations and networks to make nature and culture equally subject to orders of discourse that center events, structures, and agents. He rejects discussion of things, populations, or discourses in themselves, exemplifying his preferred alternatives by looking at the sociology of science: the internal guidance systems of missiles must always be understood as a technology of death as well as logic; the informational career of articles in science journals illustrates capitalist industry and academic method as much as it illuminates molecular truth; the history of inventors covers the space between internal mental workings and global transformations; and "the domestication of microbes" has political significance for society, textuality, and biology. "Rhetoric, textual strategies, writing, staging, semiotics—all these are really at stake, but in a new form that has a simultaneous impact on the nature of things and on the social context. . . . it is not reducible to the one or the other" (3–5).

On the surface, the falsifiability systems of science seem to counter my arguments about the plenitude of truths, their efflorescence with the spread of the popular; the weight of Popperian methodology is surely to disprove through nonreplication. But the unending processes of such testing, with successive accounts established as accurate and then compromised, in addition to the centrality of correlated phenomena rather than biochemical or physical experimentation and etiology, suggest that science produces as much as it reduces.

Science figures consistently in popular culture. Ronald Thomas has demonstrated the interpenetration of science with popular fiction and the work of government in his analysis of methods for identifying criminality in 1890s Britain. Sherlock Holmes told stories against the grain, transforming experiential narratives into alibis and verifying the evidentiary status of inanimate objects inductively and deductively. These systems of interpretation instantiated the idea that "persons were given their true and legitimate identities by someone else." At the same time, criminology was emerging to classify criminal personality types, frequently by race, and to identify traces of their presence, such as fingerprints. Between them, these discourses popularized counterindicative reasoning (Thomas 656, 659).

Consider the technicist chill given to the African American Impossible Mission Force member, how it makes whiteness safe by disciplining and desexualizing black masculinity through the delegation of science. This is brought out in another work by Weems. Her gelatin silver print *Jim, If You Choose to Accept, the Mission Is to Land on Your Own Two Feet* (1990) shows a black man seated at a table. The lighting and mise-en-scène match a film noir setting, unlike the high-key look of *M:I*. The man has his head turned in a rather doubting way toward a cassette player. Elsewhere on the table are a phone, wine bottle, glass, and ashtray. He is directly beneath an old-fashioned, low-slung lampshade. We could look at this as moralizing welfarism, urging the therapized subject to look inside himself in search of the strength to build a new life. Science is a color-blind field of knowledge; like sports and music, it presents as a meritocratic site that brooks no prejudice. Alternatively, we could read the text as a cry for self-reliance away from the world of white authorization, beyond obedience to a disembodied voice that instructs the black man to function as per technocratic rationality. And the subject in-shot has just the uncertainty and sense of questioning unacceptable in IMF work and the depoliticized myths of falsification/ verification.

The last rung on Ruthrof's scale is the digital (161). The digital is a binarized metalanguage. We have seen its categories deployed in the positive/ negative evaluation of the internationalization of screen culture, in chapter 4, and the multiple-choice, true-false statements about terrorism elaborated in chapter 5. It breaks up some of the correspondence-coherence materials beloved of debates over authentic versus artificial screen culture. Consider the scene in *Clear and Present Danger* (Phillip Noyce, 1994) in which Harrison Ford drives up to the White House gates. His identification established, the camera pans up to the White House in a single, unedited move. Or does it? In fact, the government prohibited shooting inside White House grounds, so a motion-control shot was constructed digitally. The White House gates were photographed with a computerized camera that recorded the information that would have been in a shot from the character's (absent) car up to the entrance and digitally matched that with footage of the real car pulled up at a full-size model of the gates in a parking lot. An identical process was used elsewhere in the film to pan down from the White House to Ford going out through the checkpoint (Weiner 10).

With the assistance of Ruthrof's ladder, we can now return to Representative Markey's bewildering array of mixed-metaphor policy making and schoolyard narrativization. His statement is "wrong" because of the congressman's paradoxical failure to examine the intersemiotic corroborations involved in his migration from populist journalism to folksy experience. The multiple technologies of truth he draws on are typical of the pursuit of the popular to discipline the citizen. Significantly, those forms of knowledge he lists as influences on his views about violence and television are stolidly scientistic, without reference to textuality and political economy. In other words, there are no radical ideas at play here. And this should not surprise us, as the critical study of television is mired in a division of political economy from textual and active-audience work that effectively leaves the field open to the psy-complexes (Murdock "Visualizing"). *But*, Representative Markey's very mode of address and deployment of personal recollection reference the space of familiarity, of everydayness, of narrative—in short, of the popular. Cultural studies can offer something to this form of debate, if it reasserts its nexus at the meeting point of the humanities and the social sciences. Then we can help to recast public discourse on popular culture by mobilizing enough of the rungs on Ruthrof's ladder of meaning to make an impact beyond the seminar.

This multiple set of associations can also apply to an individual engaged in a specific communicative occasion. Foucault gives the example of a treatise on mathematics. It contains a prefatory metasentence that accounts for the existence of what follows. Here, the authors of the text are clearly also the subjects of its enunciation. A less specific subject is encountered as the treatise proceeds to show how equations work by drawing upon knowledge meant to exist without the determining agency of the speaking subject. Yet a return to the metastatement that is also unique to the treatise (Foucault's example is "'We have already shown that . . .") reinstates a high degree of specificity to speech and its enunciator, simultaneously referencing a prefatory metastatement about overall intent and objective knowledge, what *has* already been shown. Clearly, this is a masssively rent subject, divided between its status as the subject of action and the subject of speech, between being an agent and a reporter—rather like Representative Markey (*Archaeology* 93–95).

What of those formative notions of genre, audience, and the modern/postmodern with which we began? The internationally integrated telecommunications industry produces new, mixed, and localized genres, forming audiences around the world that are also audiences inside nations. As communicative forms converge and diverge industrially and textually, truth becomes an endlessly producible commodity. This merging makes the audience a target for both consumption and citizenship. It is formed as a buyer and a populace, with desires and responsibilities to purchase and serve, a suitable object for both seduction and treatment. As Cunningham puts it, the key question for cultural studies in the remainder of the decade is "the citizenship question": how audiences/consumers are served by "deregulated and increasingly convergent communications forms"—a question best posed by an analysis of the distributional *and* textual politics of information ("Cultural" 35).

Returning for a moment to Ruthrof's last category, we can see how the new utopia of the digital references old anxieties. It is heralded both as the ultimate refinement of television—its second chance, the one that makes the medium "a good cultural object"—and its destruction (Boddy 116, 107). Clinton's science adviser, John H. Gibbons, claims, "Information superhighways will revolutionize the way Americans work, learn, shop, and live." Al Gore goes a little further; in his version, the National Information Infrastructure will "educate, promote democracy, and save lives" (quoted in Gomery "In" 9). In short, it is a new governmentality, but inflected with the phenomenological awe of the precocious child who can be returned to the Edenic condition proposed by Alton's desire for a revival of innocence. Redeemed television will heal the wounds of the modern, binding back together private and public, labor and leisure, commerce and culture, individuality and collectivity. While the new "digital individual" has his or her persona defined through computerized forms that provide freedom of representation inside screen space, those forms also subject the person to intense surveillance and definition through governmental and corporate identification, while operating in a privatized way financially restricted to the upper social echelon. Conventional broadcast television will remain what it has been for many years, "a consolation prize" (Agre 73; Gomery "In" 17; Gitlin "Flat" 48).

It seems appropriate to return to Tony Bennett's work, as his shift from Gramsci to Foucault references the problems and opportunities associated with the changes to cultural studies I am proposing. Bennett now perceives culture as constitutively governmental: a human aesthetic interior is constructed to engage in transactions with improving works of art, at the same time the population is configured through statistical surveys. So culture is both a logic of artistic training, concerned with the appreciation of textual norms, and a system for distributing cultural competence. Each is meant to influence the conduct of citizens (T. Bennett "Multiplication"). What would an analysis derived from this understanding look like?

In "A Defence of Detective Stories," G. K. Chesterton argues that the genre is "a perfectly legitimate form of art, . . . an agent of the public weal." Chesterton finds "the poetry of modern life" in crime fiction through the everyday greatness of cities, the "romance of detail in civilization" on show in the "flints and tiles" of urban existence. Like most popular art, crime fiction is concerned with intersubjectivity. As such, it emphasizes the complexity of contemporary morality, the way in which "police management" represents a radical departure from the chaos of the primordial world, crime's social Darwinism (227–29). Bennett's last work of textual criticism was the notable *Bond and Beyond* book with Janet Woollacott. We might now recall, in a new light, telling lessons in the management of nuclearity from the film version of *Goldfinger* (Guy Hamilton, 1964). Bennett and Woollacott regard this as a moment when their hero is "comically reduced" (236), but something more significant is going on. Toward the climax of the text, the hand of a nameless, speechless bureaucrat brushes confidently past 007's clammy paws to disarm the bomb that threatens both them and Fort Knox. Smooth and direct, entirely free of the panic revealed on Bond's face through a series of edits from ticking timer to sweating spy, this sober administrative intellectual simply cuts off the device. Rather than succumbing to the desire to track the florid ideological sensuality of a man licensed to kill with charm and Her Majesty's permission, we would do well to prize technique and government as objects of critical study as much as looks and excitement (as per Chesterton).

Clearly, I welcome the valorization of the popular, provided we reject conventional aesthetics, psychology, and neoclassical economics as ways of understanding it. And some reconstitution of cultural-governmental relations, as per cultural policy studies, is due. But the lesson we should draw is the equally Foucauldian one: there *is* power, it *is* productive, and it works through the production and dissemination of truth, disciplining the citizen through a pursuit of the popular. We should not travesty Foucault's careful conceptualization of the administrative domain by using it to justify an uncritical embrace of government. As he put it, "Leave it to our bureaucrats and our police to see that our papers are put in order" (*Archaeology* 17).

If we are to open discussion of the cultural citizen beyond the spread of governmentality, consuming and renominating the popular, it should be with as much critical attention to everyday managerial power as textual interpretation. We can use governmentality and nationalism by working with the knowledge that these most contradictory of concepts and prospects are mired in the same kinds of ambiguity as the very processes of communication. Governmentality is forever trying to create a united populace under the idea of sovereignty, but to be practical about this it must divide that nominally unitary group into separate problems and powers. Its apparent ideological running mate, national identity, is increasingly troubled by this very problem: "we" need to be more unified because of the effects of globalization on both demographics and representation, so "we" need to call on a shared heritage. But that heritage is invented, again and again, in reaction to these contemporary difficulties.

Citizenship and communication both manage difference, sometimes obliterating it, at other times co-opting or being changed by it. If correspondence and coherence theories of truth are up against contradictory as well as confirmatory sign systems, then the mythic originary social contract and its associated codes of civility, as well as the mythic founding consensus underpinning intersubjective discourse, are in trouble. Both these myths assume a unity that transcends specific disagreements. This ineradicable consensus binds sovereign states together despite internal divisions, as well as being the source of a linguistic charity to ensure that speakers and listeners communicate effectively. It enables the very possibility of people knowing they are in dispute, through shared procedures of recognition. We should disarticulate citizenship from idealist(ic) communicative hermeneutics, accepting the necessity for shared understandings as a base to all discussion while disputing that this produces, models, or mirrors social consensus. In other words, many discursive formations operate on agreed/understood grounds of internal dissent, providing a vocabulary of potential (and sometimes essential) dispute that is the necessary *preliminary* to any linguistic exchange, and often constitutes the major outcome of such encounters. This can derive from participants in communication functioning on different rungs of Ruthrof's ladder of discourse, constituting different truths in their engagements with popular culture.

Foucault's efforts to understand madness as a binary machine for Western thought to develop reason can be commuted by the popular. He regarded madness as "the Absence of Work." Similarly, the popular is routinely conceived as intellectual, bodily, and ethical indolence, a site for projecting undesirable sides of contemporary life: "*at a distance* from madness but *within distance* of it" ("Madness" 292). The popular is a new madness, its excesses equally the bounty of capital *and* its sovereign threat. Just as Foucault saw the new publicness of medicine under capitalism bringing the body out into secular, social life, so today's pursuit of the popular administers this body into correct forms of individuation and collectivity ("Histoire" 15). The "grey morning of tolerance" that seemed to be dawning for diverse sexual practice in the 1970s could never be wholly welcomed. It was necessarily marked by anxieties over sudden change and the inevitability of cheapened commodification: Foucault's "movement of growth-consumption-tolerance" ("Grey" 73–74).

The best riposte by intellectuals to commodified electronic culture seems to be working through textual criticism and organizational innovation to change it from within, or regulating it through government. The European Parliament's formative 1982 resolution underpinning intervention in radio and television programs and commercials refers to "protecting young people," and ten separate items of legislation before the U.S. Congress in 1994 proposed to regulate video content. The opposing poles are both complicit, one with the industry's project of the commodity and the other with the state's project of control. But if we look at, for example, the spread of popular fiction through nineteenth-century Britain, we are forced to adopt a much messier, less binarized view. Moral panics associated with perverting the minds of young men and arguments holding urban dross and the rise of the secular responsible for the "penny dreadful" are congenial explanations. But the erasure of Britain's tax on knowledge, the appearance of the railway terminus, new penny postal services, and the spread of public training in literacy—governmental initiatives all—are equally responsible for the emergence of publishing entrepreneurs interested in young working men as readers and in the *development* of London as a site of urban anomie (Parliament quoted in Wedell 320; "Violent"; Springhall 567–69).

Adam Gopnik accuses radicals in the United States of being overcommitted to abstract intellection and the assumption that "consciousness produces reality," such that the "energy on the American left is in cultural studies, not health care" (96). Now, the failure of medical insurance reform in 1994 had more to do with the effective lobbying of capital than with the concentration of university humanities theorists on cultural studies, but even so, the burden of my labors here has been to indicate that the discipline should look at actionable policy as its lodestone and direction finder. In recognition of this, cultural studies must turn its gaze onto shifts in public discourse between self-governance and external governance and make the political technology of truth its principal axis. This means recalling Foucault's provocation that the modern has as much to do with the governmentalization of the state as of the social, and looking at the piecemeal ordinariness of both sides to this analysis. That will give us something to say about the institutional control of culture and the democratic potential of everyday life, pointing out erasures in the former and the potential of the latter to show how multiple and contradictory truths do their work of power. Then we might be able to follow the lead of sports journalist Jenny Kellner. Confronted by naked New York Jet Mark Gastineau in a locker room, she countered his "What does this look like?" with "Like a penis, only smaller" (quoted in Postman and Stone 223).

# Bibliography

"ABC, Par TV to Resurrect 'Impossible.'" *Variety* 20 July 1988: 23.

Abelove, Henry, Michèle Aina Barale, and David M. Halperin, eds. *The Lesbian and Gay Studies Reader*. New York: Routledge, 1993.

Abelmann, Nancy, and John Lie. *Blue Dreams: Korean Americans and the Los Angeles Riots*. Cambridge: Harvard University Press, 1995.

Ackerman, Mark D., John P. D'Attilio, Michael H. Antoni, Robert K. Rhamy, David Weinstein, and Victor A. Politano. "Patient-Reported Erectile Dysfunction: A Cross-Validation Study." *Archives of Sexual Behavior* 22, no. 6 (1993): 603–18.

Adams, Phillip. "Aaron's Okay . . . Just Not Our Way." *Weekend Australian* 25–26 November 1989: 12.

Adler, Amy M. "Why Art Is on Trial." *Journal of Arts Management, Law and Society* 22, no. 4 (1993): 322–34.

Adorno, Theodor W. "Culture Industry Reconsidered." *Culture and Society: Contemporary Debates*. Ed. Jeffrey C. Alexander and Steven Seidman. Cambridge: Cambridge University Press, 1991. 275–82.

Adorno, Theodor W., and Max Horkheimer. "The Culture Industry: Enlightenment as Mass Deception." *Mass Communication and Society*. Ed. James Curran, Michael Gurevitch, and Janet Woollacott. London: Edward Arnold, 1977. 349–83.

Agre, Philip E. "Understanding the Digital Individual." *Information Society* 10, no. 2 (1994): 73–76.

Agresto, John. "Legitimate Restrictions on Federal Arts Funding." *Journal of Arts Management and Law* 21, no. 4 (1992): 333–37.

Akinasso, F. Niyi. "Linguistic Unification and Language Rights." *Applied Linguistics* 15, no. 2 (1994): 139–68.

Alasuutari, Pertti. *Researching Culture: Qualitative Method and Cultural Studies*. London: Sage, 1995.

Alderson, Evan. "Introduction." *Reflections on Cultural Policy: Past, Present and Future*. Ed. Evan Alderson, Robin Blaser, and Harold Coward. Waterloo: Wilfrid Laurier University Press, 1993. 1–16.

Alexander, Elizabeth. "'Can You be BLACK and Look at This?': Reading the Rodney King Video(s)." *Public Culture* 7, no. 1 (1994): 77–94.

Alexander, Jeffrey C., and Philip Smith. "The Discourse of American Civil Society: A New Proposal for Cultural Studies." *Theory and Society* 22, no. 2 (1993): 151–207.

Allan, Blaine. "The State of the State of the Art on TV." *Queen's Quarterly* 95, no. 2 (1988): 318–29.

Allen, Robert C. *Horrible Prettiness: Burlesque and American Culture*. Chapel Hill: University of North Carolina Press, 1991.

Allen, Robert C., and Douglas Gomery. *Film History: Theory and Practice*. New York: McGraw-Hill, 1985.

Allor, Martin, and Michelle Gagnon. *L'État de culture: Généalogie discursive des politiques culturelles Québécoises*. Montreal: Concordia University/University of Montreal, 1994.

Alomes, Stephen, and Dirk den Hartog, eds. *Post Pop: Popular Culture, Nationalism and Postmodernism*. Melbourne: Footprint, 1991.

Alsop, Neil. "Mission Status." *Primetime* no. 14 (Winter 1988–89): 17–25.

Altman, Rick. "Film Studies, Inc.: Lessons from the Past about the Current Institutionalization of Film Studies." *Film Criticism* 17, nos. 2–3 (1993): 22–30.

Alton, David. "Our Video Culture." *Contemporary Review* 264, no. 1539 (1994): 169–72.

Amad, Patricia, and Philippa Hawker. "The Delinquents." *Cinema Papers* no. 74 (July 1989): 3–7.

Amirault, Chris. "Posing the Subject of Early Medical Photography." *Discourse* 16, no. 2 (1993–94): 51–76.

Ammon, Ulrich. "Editor's Preface." *International Journal of the Sociology of Language* no. 95 (1992): 5–9.

Amy, Douglas J. "Why Policy Analysis and Ethics Are Incompatible." *Journal of Policy Analysis and Management* 3, no. 4 (1984): 573–91.

Anderson, Benedict. *Imagined Communities: Reflections on the Origins and Spread of Nationalism.* London: Verso, 1983.

Anderson, Carolyn, and Thomas W. Benson. "Direct Cinema and the Myth of Informed Consent: The Case of Titicut Follies." *Image Ethics: The Moral Rights of Subjects in Photographs, Film, and Television.* Ed. Larry Gross, John Stuart Katz, and Jay Ruby. New York: Oxford University Press, 1988. 58–90.

———. *Documentary Dilemmas: Frederick Wiseman's Titicut Follies.* Carbondale: Southern Illinois University Press, 1991.

Andrews, Nigel. "Nightmares and Nasties." *The Video Nasties: Freedom and Censorship in the Media.* Ed. Martin Barker. London: Pluto, 1984. 39–47.

Ang, Ien. *Desperately Seeking the Audience.* London: Routledge, 1991.

Appleton, Gillian. *How Australia Sees Itself: The Role of Commercial Television.* Australian Content Inquiry Discussion Paper. Canberra: Australian Broadcasting Tribunal, 1988.

Archibald, Jenny. "Promising Prison." *Fremantle Herald* 21 October 1992: n.p.

Armstrong, Dan. "Wiseman and the Politics of Looking: Manoeuvre in the Documentary Project." *Quarterly Review of Film and Video* 11, no. 4 (1990): 35–50.

———. "Wiseman's Realm of Transgression: Titicut Follies, the Symbolic Father, and the Spectacle of Confinement." *Cinema Journal* 29, no. 1 (1989): 20–35.

Arnheim, Rudolf. *Film as Art.* London: Faber and Faber, 1969.

Arroyo, José. "Mission: Sublime." *Sight and Sound* 6, no. 7 (1996): 18–21.

Arthur, Paul. "Jargons of Authenticity (Three American Moments)." *Theorizing Documentary.* Ed. Michael Renov. New York: Routledge, 1993. 108–34.

Asch, Timothy, John Marshall, and Peter Spier. "Ethnographic Film: Structure and Function." *Annual Review of Anthropology* no. 2 (1973): 179–87.

"Asia/Pacific as Space of Cultural Production." *boundary 2* 21, no. 1 (1994).

Astley, Thea. "Being a Queenslander: A Form of Literary and Geographical Conceit." *Southerly* 36, no. 3 (1976): 252–64.

Atkins, Thomas R. "Preface." *Frederick Wiseman.* Ed. Thomas R. Atkins. New York: Simon & Schuster, 1976. vii–x.

———. "Wiseman's America: Titicut Follies to Primate." *Frederick Wiseman.* Ed. Thomas R. Atkins. New York: Simon & Schuster, 1976. 1–29.

Atkinson, J. Maxwell, and Paul Drew. *Order in Court: The Organization of Interaction in Judicial Settings.* Atlantic Highlands, N.J.: Humanities Press, 1979.

Attali, Jacques, and Yves Stourdze. "The Birth of the Telephone and Economic Crisis: The Slow Death of Monologue in French Society." *The Social Impact of the Telephone.* Ed. Ithiel de Sola Pool. Cambridge: MIT Press, 1977. 97–111.

Augustine. *Concerning the City of God against the Pagans.* Ed. David Knowles. Trans. Henry Bettenson. Harmondsworth: Penguin, 1976.

———. *Confessions.* Trans. R. S. Pine-Coffin. Harmondsworth: Penguin, 1961.

Aumont, Jacques, Alain Bergala, Michel Marie, and Marc Vernet. *Aesthetics of Film.* Ed. and Trans. Richard Neupert. Austin: University of Texas Press, 1992.

"Australia: Preserving Paradise: A Survey." *Economist* 311, no. 7601 (1990): 60–66.

Australian Broadcasting Tribunal. *Amounts of Time Occupied by Different Program Categories.* Australian Content Inquiry Discussion Paper. Canberra, 1988.

———. *Broadcasting in Australia: The Fourth Annual Review of the Industry by the Australian Broadcasting Tribunal.* Sydney, 1992.

Australian Film Commission. "ABT Australian Content Inquiry." *AFC News* no. 74 (July 1989): 2–3.

Axtmann, Roland. "Society, Globalization and the Comparative Method." *History of the Human Sciences* 6, no. 2 (1993): 53–74.

Baggaley, Jon, and Steve Duck. *Dynamics of Television.* Westmead: Saxon House, 1978.

Bailey, Julie James. "A Queensland Film Industry. What Is It? Who Needs It?" *Culture and Policy* no. 5 (1993): 81–102.

Baker, Houston A., Jr. *Black Studies, Rap, and the Academy.* Chicago: University of Chicago Press, 1993.

———. "Scene . . . Not Heard." *Reading Rodney King/Reading Urban Uprising.* Ed. Robert Gooding-Williams. New York: Routledge, 1993. 38–48.

Baker, Houston A., Jr., Manthia Diawara, and Ruth H. Lindeborg, eds. *Black British Cultural Studies: A Reader.* Chicago: University of Chicago Press, 1996.

Bann, Stephen. "On Living in a New Country." *The New Museology*. Ed. Peter Vergo. London: Reaktion, 1991. 99–118.

Barber, Susanna. *News Cameras in the Courtroom: A Free Press-Fair Trial Debate*. Norwood, N.J.: Ablex, 1987.

Barham, Susan Baggett. "The Phallus and the Man: An Analysis of Male Striptease." *Australian Ways: Anthropological Studies of an Industrialised Society*. Ed. Lenore Manderson. Sydney: Allen & Unwin, 1985. 51–65.

Barker, Ernest. *National Character and the Factors in Its Formation*. London: Methuen, 1927.

Barker, Martin. "Sex, Violence, and Videotape." *Sight and Sound* 3, no. 5 (1993): 10–12.

Barker, Martin, and Anne Breezer, eds. *Reading into Cultural Studies*. London: Routledge, 1992.

Barnouw, Erik. *The Sponsor: Notes on a Modern Potentate*. New York: Oxford University Press, 1978.

Baron-Cohen, Simon, Angel Riviere, Masato Fukushima, Davina French, Julie Hadwin, Pippa Cross, Catherine Bryant, and Maria Sotillo. "Reading the Mind in the Face: A Cross-Cultural and Developmental Study." *Visual Cognition* 3, no. 1 (1996): 39–59.

Barron, Anne. "Legal Discourse and the Colonisation of the Self in the Modern State." *Post-Modern Law: Enlightenment, Revolution and the Death of Man*. Ed. Anthony Carty. Edinburgh: Edinburgh University Press, 1990. 107–25.

Barry, Brian. "Abuses of Literacy." *New Statesman and Society* no. 8379 (17 November 1995): 36–37.

Barthes, Roland. *Mythologies*. Trans. Annette Lavers. St. Albans: Paladin, 1973.

Barwise, Patrick, and Andrew Ehrenberg. *Television and Its Audience*. London: Sage, 1990.

Batra, Ashok, and Tom F. Lue. "Physiology and Pathology of Penile Erection." *Annual Review of Sex Research* no. 1 (1990): 251–63.

Baughman, James L. *The Republic of Mass Culture: Journalism, Filmmaking, and Broadcasting in America since 1941*. Baltimore: Johns Hopkins University Press, 1992.

Bear, Liza. "Veteran Wiseman Discusses Unique Documentary Style." *Film Journal* 97, no. 9 (1994): 20, 62.

Beatie, Bruce A. "The Myth of the Hero: From Mission: Impossible to Magdalenian Caves." *The Hero in Transition*. Ed. Ray B. Browne and Marshall W. Fishwick. Bowling Green, Ohio: Bowling Green University Popular Press, 1983. 46–65.

Beauchamp, Tom L. "Ethical Issues in Funding and Monitoring University Research." *Business and Professional Ethics Journal* 11, no. 1 (1992): 5–16.

Beaverstock, J. V. "Subcontracting the Accountant! Professional Labour Markets, Migration, and Organisational Networks in the Global Accountancy Industry." *Environment and Planning A* 28, no. 2 (1996): 303–26.

Beck, Marilyn. "'Mission' Checks In." *Daily News* 17 January 1990: 34.

Becker, Gary. "Nobel Lecture: The Economic Way of Looking at Behavior." *Journal of Political Economy* 101, no. 3 (1993): 385–409.

Becker, Howard S., and Michal M. McCall, eds. *Symbolic Interaction and Cultural Studies*. Chicago: University of Chicago Press, 1990.

Beemyn, Brett, and Mickey Eliason, eds. *Queer Studies: A Lesbian, Gay, Bisexual, and Transgender Anthology*. New York: New York University Press, 1996.

Bell, Philip, and Roger Bell. *Implicated: The United States in Australia*. Melbourne: Oxford University Press, 1993.

Bell, Philip, and Theo van Leeuwen. *The Media Interview: Confession, Contest, Conversation*. Sydney: University of New South Wales Press, 1994.

Bennett, David. "PC Panic, the Press and the Academy." *Cultural Studies: Pluralism and Theory*. Ed. David Bennett. Melbourne: Melbourne University, Department of English, 1993. 197–210.

Bennett, Philip. "The Fractious Making of a WGBH Film." *Boston Globe* 10 January 1993: B25, B30.

Bennett, Tony. *The Birth of the Museum: History, Theory, and Politics*. London: Routledge, 1995.

———. "Culture: Theory and Policy." *Culture and Policy* 1, no. 1 (1989): 5–8.

———. *Formalism and Marxism*. London: Methuen, 1979.

———. "The Multiplication of Culture's Utility." *Critical Inquiry* 21, no. 4 (1995): 861–89.

———. "Out in the Open: Reflections on the History and Practice of Cultural Studies." *Cultural Studies* 10, no. 1 (1996): 133–53.

———. *Outside Literature*. London: Routledge, 1990.

———. "The Political Rationality of the Museum." *Continuum* 3, no. 1 (1990): 35–55.

———. "Putting Policy into Cultural Studies." *Cultural Studies*. Ed. Lawrence Grossberg, Cary Nelson, and Paula A. Treichler. New York: Routledge, 1992. 23–37.

———. "Useful Culture." *Relocating Cultural Studies: Developments in Theory and Research*. Ed. Valda Blundell, John Shepherd, and Ian Taylor. London: Routledge, 1993. 67–85.

Bennett, Tony, Jennifer Craik, Ian Hunter, Colin Mercer, and Dugald Williamson. "Series Editors' Preface." *Rock and Popular Music: Politics, Policies, Institutions*. Ed. Tony Bennett, Simon Frith, Lawrence Grossberg, John Shepherd, and Graeme Turner. London: Routledge, 1993. x–xi.

Bennett Tony, Graeme Turner, and Michael Volkerling. "Introduction: Post-Colonial Formations." *Culture and Policy* 6, no. 1 (1994): 1–5.

Bennett, Tony, and Janet Woollacott. *Bond and Beyond: The Political Career of a Popular Hero*. London: Macmillan, 1987.

Bennett, W. Lance, and Martha S. Feldman. *Reconstructing Reality in the Courtroom: Justice and Judgment in American Culture*. New Brunswick, N.J.: Rutgers University Press, 1981.

Benson, Jim. "Firstrun-Syndie, Cable 'Mission' Possible." *Variety* 9 May 1988: 76.

Berger, Arthur Asa. *The TV-Guided American*. New York: Walker, 1976.

Bergery, Benjamin. "Imaging the Impossible." *American Cinematographer* 77, no. 6 (1996): 42–50.

Berman, Nathaniel. "Nationalism Legal and Linguistic: The Teachings of European Jurisprudence." *New York University Journal of International Law and Politics* 24, no. 4 (1992): 1515–78.

Berry, Chris. "Australian TV Content and Its Discontents." *Overland* no. 135 (Winter 1994): 11–16.

Bersani, Leo. "Is the Rectum a Grave?" *October* no. 43 (Winter 1987): 197–222.

Bertrand, Ina. *Film Censorship in Australia*. St. Lucia: University of Queensland Press, 1978.

Bianchini, Franco, and Michael Parkinson, eds. *Cultural Policy and Urban Regeneration: The West European Experience*. Manchester: Manchester University Press, 1993.

Bier. "Mission: Impossible." *Variety*: 56.

"Black Men and the Criminal Justice System." *Society* 33, no. 5 (1996): 3–4.

Bloch, Maurice. *From Blessing to Violence: History and Ideology in the Circumcision Ritual of the Merina of Madagascar*. Cambridge: Cambridge University Press, 1986.

Blundell, Valda, John Shepherd, and Ian Taylor, eds. *Relocating Cultural Studies: Developments in Theory and Research*. London: Routledge, 1993.

Boddy, William. "Archaeologies of Electronic Vision and the Gendered Spectator." *Screen* 35, no. 2 (1994): 105–22.

Bogle, Donald. *Blacks in American Films and Television: An Illustrated Encyclopedia*. New York: Fireside, 1989.

Bolton, Kingsley, and Christopher Hutton. "Bad and Banned Language: Triad Secret Societies, the Censorship of the Cantonese Vernacular, and Colonial Language Policy in Hong Kong." *Language in Society* 24, no. 2 (1995): 159–86.

Boniface, Priscilla, and Peter J. Fowler. *Heritage and Tourism in "the Global Village."* London: Routledge, 1993.

Boone, Joseph A. "Vacation Cruises; or, The Homoerotics of Orientalism." *PMLA* 110, no. 1 (1995): 89–107.

Bordo, Susan. "Reading the Male Body." *Michigan Quarterly Review* 32, no. 4 (1993): 696–737.

Borham, Susan. "Archibald Shower Scene Is Water off a Duck's Back." *Sydney Morning Herald* 11 March 1993: 2.

Bourdieu, Pierre. "How Can One Be a Sports Fan?" Trans. Richard Nice. *The Cultural Studies Reader*. Ed. Simon During. New York: Routledge, 1993. 339–56.

———. *In Other Words: Essays toward a Reflexive Sociology*. Trans. Matthew Adamson. Stanford: Stanford University Press, 1990.

———. "The Peculiar History of Scientific Reason." Trans. Channa Newman and Loïc J. D. Wacquant. *Sociological Forum* 6, no. 1 (1991): 3–26.

———. "Rethinking the State: Genesis and Structure of the Bureaucratic Field." Trans. Loïc J. D. Wacquant and Samar Farage. *Sociological Theory* 12, no. 1 (1994): 1–18.

Bowie, Norman E. "The Clash between Academic Values and Business Values." *Business and Professional Ethics Journal* 12, no. 4 (1993): 3–19.

Boyarin, Jonathan, and Daniel Boyarin, eds. *Jews and Other Differences: The New Jewish Cultural Studies*. Minneapolis: University of Minnesota Press, 1996.

Boylen, Louise. "Nine Still the Giant of the TV Arena." *Australian Financial Review* 27 June 1989: 5.

Bradley, Michael. "The Lesson of Rodney King." *Why L.A. Happened: Implications of the '92 Los Angeles Rebellion*. Ed. Haki R. Madhubuti. Chicago: Third World Press, 1993. 212–20.

Bragg, Billy. "Looking for a New England." *New Statesman and Society* no. 8344 (17 March 1995): 14.

Brannigan, Augustine, and Michael Lynch. "On Bearing False Witness: Credibility as an Interactional Accomplishment." *Journal of Contemporary Ethnography* 16, no. 2 (1987): 115–46.

Brantlinger, Patrick. *Crusoe's Footprints: Cultural Studies in Britain and America*. New York: Routledge, 1990.

Brill, Steven. Remarks to seminar *Cameras in Court*. Center for Communication, Inc. New York, 23 February 1994.

Briller, Bert R. "The Globalization of American TV." *Television Quarterly* 24, no. 3 (1990): 71–79.

Brodie, John. "Sex! Controversy! PR!" *Variety* 29 August–4 September 1994: 7–8.

Brody, Samuel. "Television: A New Weapon for the New Imperialist War." *Jump Cut* no. 33 (June 1988): 105–6. Reprinted from *Daily Worker*, 1930.

Brooks, Peter. "Frighted with False Fire: Misunderstandings of the Culture Wars." *Times Literary Supplement* 26 May 1995: 10–11.

Browett, J. and R. Leaver. "Shifts in the Global Capitalist Economy and the National Economic Domain." *Australian Geographical Studies* 27, no. 1 (1989): 31–46.

Brown, Les. *Television: The Business behind the Box*. New York: Harcourt Brace Jovanovich, 1971.

Buck, Elizabeth B. "Asia and the Global Film Industry." *East-West Film Journal* 6, no. 2 (1992): 116–33.

Burke, Kenneth. "Literature as Equipment for Living." *Contemporary Literary Criticism: Literary and Cultural Studies*, 2d ed. Ed. Robert Con Davis and Ronald Schleifer. New York: Longman, 1989. 76–81.

Burns, Rob, ed. *German Cultural Studies: An Introduction*. Oxford: Oxford University Press, 1996.

Burrows, A. R. *The Story of Broadcasting*. London: Cassell, 1924.

*Burton v. Crowell Pub. Co.* 82 *Federal Reporter* 2d Series 154. 1936.

Buvat, J., M. Buvat-Herbaut, A. Lemaire, G. Marcolin, and E. Quittelier. "Recent Developments in the Clinical Assessment and Diagnosis of Erectile Dysfunction." *Annual Review of Sex Research* no. 1 (1990): 265–308.

Buxton, David. *From* The Avengers *to* Miami Vice: *Form and Ideology in Television Series*. Manchester: Manchester University Press, 1990.

Calder, Angus. Review of *Cultural Policy and Urban Regeneration*. *Political Quarterly* 65, no. 4 (1994): 453–55.

"California TV Crews Tape Police Beating." *New York Times* 2 April 1996: A14.

Cameron, Deborah. "Naming of Parts: Gender, Culture, and Terms for the Penis among American College Students." *Feminist Cultural Studies*, vol. 2. Ed. Terry Lovell. Aldershot, England: Elgar, 1995. 271–86.

Carey, James. "The Mass Media and Democracy: Between the Modern and the Postmodern." *Journal of International Affairs* 47, no. 1 (1993): 1–21.

———. "Political Correctness and Cultural Studies." *Journal of Communication* 42, no. 2 (1992): 56–72.

Carr, C. "What Is to Be Done?" *Village Voice* 22 August 1995: 36.

Catley, Bob. "Australia and the Great Powers 1933-83." *Australian Outlook* 37, no. 3 (1983): 143–49.

Caughie, John. "Adorno's Reproach: Repetition, Difference and Television Genre." *Screen* 32, no. 2 (1991): 127–53.

Chadwick, Bruce. "In New 'Mission,' Son Also Rises." *Daily News* 16 May 1989: 35.

Chambers, Iain. *Urban Rhythms: Pop Music and Popular Culture*. Basingstoke: Macmillan, 1986.

Chance, Sandra F. "Considering Cameras in the Courtroom." *Journal of Broadcasting and Electronic Media* 39, no. 4 (1995): 555–61.

Chaney, David. *The Cultural Turn: Scene-Setting Essays on Contemporary History*. London: Routledge, 1994.

Chanticleer. "Report Views TV Industry as a Tarnished Eldorado." *Australian Financial Review* 26 May 1989: 88.

Chartrand, Harry Hillman. "International Cultural Affairs: A Fourteen Country Survey." *Journal of Arts Management, Law and Society* 22, no. 2 (1992): 134–54.

———. "Subjectivity in an Era of Scientific Imperialism: Shadows in an Age of Reason." *Journal of Arts Management and Law* 18, no. 3 (1988): 5–29.

Chatterjee, Partha. *The Nation and Its Fragments: Colonial and Postcolonial Histories*. Princeton, N.J.: Princeton University Press, 1993.

Chen, Kuan-Hsing, and David Morley, eds. *Stuart Hall: Critical Dialogues in Cultural Studies*. London: Routledge, 1996.

Chesterton, G. K. "A Defence of Detective Stories." *Essays of To-Day: An Anthology*. Ed. F. H. Pritchard. London: George G. Harrap, 1932. 226–29.

"Child-Minders." *Economist* 332, no. 7876 (1994): 78–79.

Chomsky, Noam. *Aspects of the Theory of Syntax*. Cambridge: MIT Press, 1965.

Chow, Rey. *Writing Diaspora: Tactics of Intervention in Contemporary Cultural Studies*. Bloomington: Indiana University Press, 1993.

Christie, James. "Ad More Than Magazine Will Bare: Adidas Pulls Business from Canadian Edition of Sports Illustrated." *Globe and Mail* 29 June 1993: B1–B2.

———. "Uninhibited Soccer Team Finds Itself without a League." *Globe and Mail* 13 July 1993: A12.

Christopherson, Susan, and Michael Storper. "The City as Studio; the World as Back Lot: The Impact of Vertical Disintegration on the Location of the Motion Picture Industry." *Environment and Planning D: Society and Space* 4, no. 3 (1986): 305–20.

Church Gibson, Pamela, and Roma Gibson, eds. *Dirty Looks: Women, Pornography, Power*. London: British Film Institute, 1993.

*Cinema Papers*. no. 71 (January 1989): 75.

Clark, Kenneth. *The Nude: A Study in Ideal Form*. New York: Pantheon, 1956.

Clark, Peter. "Mission Impossible? Not in Queensland! Anything Hollywood Can Do, We Can Do Better." *Industrial and Commercial Photography* May–June 1989: 55–57.

Clément, Étienne. "A View from UNESCO." *African Arts* 28, no. 4 (1995): 58.

Clendinen, Dudley. "Theater; Of Old South Violence Only Yesterday." *New York Times* 4 February 1996: 5.

Clifton, Brad. "Ettingshausen Claim 'Storm in a Tea Cup.'" *Australian* 10 February 1993: 9.

Clover, Carol J. "Introduction." *Dirty Looks: Women, Pornography, Power*. Ed. Pamela Church Gibson and Roma Gibson. London: British Film Institute, 1993. 1–21.

Cohen, Bob. "Circumcision: Should We Cut It Out?" *Living Marxism* no. 90 (May 1996): 10–12.

Cohen, Robin. *Contested Domains: Debates in International Labour Studies*. London: Zed, 1991.

Colebatch, H. K., and P. Degeling. "Talking and Doing in the Work of Administration." *Public Administration and Development* 6 (1986): 339–56.

Coleman, Wil. "Doing Masculinity/Doing Theory." *Men, Masculinities and Social Theory*. Ed. Jeff Hearn and David Morgan. London: Unwin Hyman, 1990. 186–99.

Collini, Stefan. "Escape from DWEMsville: Is Culture Too Important to Be Left to Cultural Studies?" *Times Literary Supplement* 27 May 1994: 3–4.

Collins, Hugh. "Political Ideology in Australia: The Distinctiveness of a Benthamite Society." *Daedalus* 114, no. 1 (1985): 147–69.

Collins, Jim. "Television and Postmodernism." *Channels of Discourse, Reassembled: Television and Contemporary Criticism*, 2d ed. Ed. Robert C. Allen. Chapel Hill: University of North Carolina Press, 1992. 327–53.

Collins, Richard. *Television: Policy and Culture*. London: Unwin Hyman, 1990.

Comfort, Alex, ed. *The Joy of Sex: A Gourmet Guide to Lovemaking*. Adelaide: Rigby, 1978.

Commager, Henry Steele. *The American Mind: An Interpretation of American Thought and Character since the 1880's*. New Haven, Conn.: Yale University Press, 1974.

"Comment: The 'Titicut Follies' Case: Limiting the Public Interest Privilege." *Columbia Law Review* no. 70 (1970): 359–71.

*Commonwealth and Others v. Frederick Wiseman and Others*. 356 Mass. 1969.

Comstock, George. "Violence." *International Encyclopedia of Communications*, vol. 4. Ed. Erik Barnouw, George Gerbner, Larry Gross, Wilbur Schramm, and Tobia L. Worth. New York: Oxford University Press, 1989. 289–94.

Condon, Turi. "Film Studio Expansion Loan." *Australian Financial Review* 7 November 1989: 37.

Connell, R. W. *Masculinities*. Berkeley: University of California Press, 1995.

Connolly, Bob, and Robin Anderson. *First Contact: New Guinea's Highlanders Encounter with the Outside World*. Sydney: Penguin, 1988.

Connor, Tom, and Jim Downey. *Martha Stuart's Better than You at Entertaining*. New York: Harper-Perennial, 1996.

Coombe, Rosemary J. *Cultural Appropriations: Authorship, Alterity, and the Law*. Unpublished manuscript.

Corliss, Richard. "What's Old Is Gold: A Triumph for Indy 3." *Time Australia* 4, no. 22 (1989): 68–70.

Corner, John. "Presumption as Theory: 'Realism' in Television Studies." *Screen* 33, no. 1 (1992): 97–102.

Corporation for Public Broadcasting. *1993 Annenberg/CPB Collection Video Series*. N.p., n.d.

Craik, Jennifer. "Cashing in on Cultural Studies: Future Fortunes." *Culture and Policy* 6, no. 2 (1994): 23–43.

———. "Mapping the Links between Cultural Studies and Cultural Policy." *Southern Review* 28, no. 2 (1995): 190–207.

Craven, Peter. "Writers Lose in Cultural Sweepstakes." *Australian* 26 October 1994: 34.

Crawford, Robert. "Male Infertility." *London Review of Books* 17, no. 16 (24 August 1995): 22.

Crenshaw, Kimberlé, and Gary Peller. "Reel Time/Real Justice." *Reading Rodney King/Reading Urban Uprising*. Ed. Robert Gooding-Williams. New York: Routledge, 1993. 56–70.

Crofts, Stephen. "Re-Imaging Australia: Crocodile Dundee Overseas." *Continuum* 2, no. 2 (1989): 129–42.

Crump, James. "The Kinsey Institute Archive: A Taxonomy of Erotic Photography." *History of Photography* 18, no. 1 (1994): 1–12.

"Cultural Studies." *Critical Matrix* 7, no. 2 (1993).

"Cultural Studies." *Critical Studies in Mass Communication* 6, no. 4 (1989).

"Cultural Studies in the Asia Pacific." *Southeast Asian Journal of Social Science* vol. 22 (1994).

"Cultural Studies in Canada." *University of Toronto Quarterly* 64, no. 4 (1995).

"Cultural Studies: Crossing Boundaries." *Critical Studies* 3, no. 1 (1991).

"Cultural Studies: Disciplinarity and Divergence." *University of Toronto Quarterly* 65, no. 2 (1996).

"Cultural Studies/Les Études culturelles." *Canadian Review of Comparative Literature/Revue Canadienne de littérature comparée* 22, no. 1 (1995).

Cumings, Bruce. *War and Television*. London: Verso, 1992.

Cummings, Milton C., Jr., and Richard S. Katz. "Government and the Arts: An Overview." *The Patron State: Government and the Arts in Europe, North America, and Japan*. Ed. Milton C. Cummings, Jr., and Richard S. Katz. New York: Oxford University Press, 1987. 3–16.

Cunningham, Stuart. "Cultural Criticism and Policy." *Arena Magazine* no. 7 (October–November 1993): 33–35.

———. *Framing Culture: Criticism and Policy in Australia.* Sydney: Allen & Unwin, 1992.

———. "The Look and Its Revocation: Wiseman's Primate." *Australian Journal of Screen Theory* nos. 11–12 (1982): 86–95.

———. "Nascent Innovation: Notes on Some Australian Features of the 1950s." *Continuum* 1, no. 1 (1987): 93–99.

———. *A Theoretical Critique of "Direct" Documentary: The Case of Frederick Wiseman.* Unpublished master's thesis. McGill University, 1979.

Cunningham, Stuart, and Elizabeth Jacka. *Australian Television and International Mediascapes.* Cambridge: Cambridge University Press, 1996.

Cunningham, Stuart, and Toby Miller, with David Rowe. *Contemporary Australian Television.* Sydney: University of New South Wales Press, 1994.

Curran, James. "The New Revisionism in Mass Communication Research: A Reappraisal." *European Journal of Communication* 5, nos. 2–3 (1990): 135–64.

Curran, James, David Morley, and Valerie Walkerdine, eds. *Cultural Studies and Communications.* London: Edward Arnold, 1996.

Cvetkovich, Ann, and Douglas Kellner, eds. *Articulating the Global and the Local: Globalization and Cultural Studies.* Boulder, Colo.: Westview, 1997.

Czaplicka, John, Andreas Huyssen, and Anson Rabinach. "Introduction: Cultural History and Cultural Studies: Reflections on a Symposium." *New German Critique* 22, no. 2 (1995): 3–17.

Czitrom, Daniel. *Media and the American Mind: From Morse to McLuhan.* Chapel Hill: University of North Carolina Press, 1982.

Danan, Martine. "Marketing the Hollywood Blockbuster in France." *Journal of Popular Film and Television* 23, no. 3 (1995): 131–40.

Dane, Francis C., and Lawrence S. Wrightsman. "Effects of Defendants' and Victims' Characteristics on Jurors' Verdicts." *The Psychology of the Courtroom.* Ed. Norbert L. Kerr and Robert M. Bray. New York: Academic Press, 1982. 83–115.

Danto, Arthur C. *Beyond the Brillo Box: The Visual Arts in Post-Historical Perspective.* New York: Noonday, 1993.

Danziger, Marie. "Policy Analysis Postmodernized: Some Political and Pedagogical Ramifications." *Policy Studies Journal* 23, no. 3 (1995): 435–50.

Darnton, Robert. "Censorship, a Comparative View: France, 1789–East Germany, 1989." *Representations* no. 49 (Winter 1995): 40–60.

Davidson, Cathy N. "Introduction: Toward a History of Books and Readers." *Reading in America: Literature and Social History.* Ed. Cathy N. Davidson. Baltimore: Johns Hopkins University Press, 1989. 1–26.

Davidson, John. "Does Penis Size Really Matter? One Guy Gets Honest." *Cleo* October 1992: 68–70.

Davies, Anne. "Film Workers Push for More Local TV Content." *Australian Financial Review* 30 November 1988: 56.

Davies, Ioan. "Cultural Theory in Britain: Narrative and Episteme." *Theory, Culture & Society* 10, no. 3 (1993): 115–54.

Davis, Michael. "Conflict of Interest Revisited." *Business and Professional Ethics Journal* 12, no. 4 (1993): 21–41.

Dawson, Jonathan. "BIFF! The Making of an International Film Festival." *Culture and Policy* no. 5 (1993): 67–80.

Dawtrey, Adam. "Eurobucks Back Megapix." *Variety* 7–13 March 1994: 1, 75.

Day, J. Laurence. "United States News Coverage of Latin America: A Short Historical Perspective." *Studies in Latin American Popular Culture* no. 6 (1987): 301–9.

Dean, Carolyn. "The Great War, Pornography, and the Transformation of Modern Male Subjectivity." *Modernism/Modernity* 3, no. 2 (1996): 59–72.

———. "Pornography, Literature, and the Redemption of Virility in France, 1880–1930." *differences* 5, no. 2 (1993): 62–91.

Dean, Peter. "Mission: Spot the Location." *Courier-Mail* 3 August 1989: 20.

De Bens, Els, Mary Kelly, and Marit Bakke. "Television Content: Dallasification of Culture?" *Dynamics of Media Politics: Broadcast and Electronic Media in Western Europe.* Ed. Karen Siune and Wolfgang Truetzschler. London: Sage, 1992. 75–100.

Deem, Melissa D. "From Bobbitt to SCUM: Re-Memberment, Scatological Rhetorics, and Feminist Strategies in the Contemporary United States." *Public Culture* 8, no. 3 (1996): 511–37.

DeGrane, Lloyd. *Tuned In: Television in American Life.* Urbana: University of Illinois Press, 1991.

Dehon, Pierre-Jacques. "La Conception Antique de l'Originalité et le Cinéma Américain Contemporain." *Mosaic* 27, no. 3 (1994): 1–18.

deLeon, Peter. "Democratic Values and the Policy Sciences." *American Journal of Political Science* 39, no. 4 (1995): 886–905.

Deleuze, Gilles, and Félix Guattari. *Qu'est-ce que la philosophie?* Paris: Les Éditions de Minuit, 1991.

DeLillo, Don. *End Zone*. Harmondsworth: Penguin, 1987.

Denby, David. "Documenting America." *Nonfiction Film Theory and Criticism*. Ed. Richard Meran Barsam. New York: E. P. Dutton, 1976. 310–14.

Dennis, Kelly. "'Leave It to Beaver': The Object of Pornography." *Strategies* no. 6 (February 1991): 122–67.

Dent, Gina, ed. *Black Popular Culture: A Project by Michele Wallace*. Seattle: Bay, 1992.

Dermody, Susan, and Elizabeth Jacka. *The Screening of Australia*, vol. 1, *Anatomy of a Film Industry*. Sydney: Currency, 1987.

———. *The Screening of Australia*, vol. 2, *Anatomy of a National Cinema*. Sydney: Currency, 1988.

de Roche, Constance, and John de Roche. "Black and White: Racial Construction in Television Police Dramas." *Canadian Ethnic Studies/Études ethniques au Canada* 23, no. 3 (1991): 69–91.

Derrida, Jacques. "'To Do Justice to Freud': The History of Madness in the Age of Psychoanalysis." Trans. Pascale-Anne Brault and Michael Naas. *Critical Inquiry* 20, no. 2 (1994): 227–66.

Dervin, Daniel. "The Bobbitt Case and the Quest for a Good-Enough Penis." *Psychoanalytic Review* 82, no. 2 (1995): 249–56.

de Sola Pool, Ithiel, Craig Decker, Stephen Dizard, Kay Israel, Pamela Rubin, and Barry Weinstein. "Foresight and Hindsight: The Case of the Telephone." *The Social Impact of the Telephone*. Ed. Ithiel de Sola Pool. Cambridge: MIT Press, 1977. 127–57.

Diamond, Jared M. "Variation in Human Testis Size." *Nature* 320, no. 6061 (1986): 488–89.

Diawara, Manthia. *African Cinema*. New York: Routledge, 1992.

———. "Black Studies, Cultural Studies, Performative Acts." *Race, Identity and Representation in Education*. Ed. Cameron McCarthy and Warren Crichlow. New York: Routledge, 1994. 262–67.

DiMaggio, Paul J. "Can Culture Survive the Marketplace?" *Journal of Arts Management and Law* 13, no. 1 (1983): 61–87.

———. "Classification in Art." *American Sociological Review* 52, no. 4 (1987): 440–55.

———. "Cultural Policy Studies: What They Are and Why We Need Them." *Journal of Arts Management and Law* 13, no. 1 (1983): 241–48.

———. "Decentralization of Arts Funding from the Federal Government to the States." *Public Money and the Muse: Essays on Government Funding for the Arts*. Ed. Stephen Benedict. New York: Norton, 1991. 216–52.

———. "The Nonprofit Instrument and the Influence of the Marketplace." *The Arts and Public Policy in the United States*. Ed. W. McNeil Lowry. Englewood Cliffs, N.J.: Prentice Hall, 1984. 57–99.

———. "State Expansion and Organizational Fields." *Organizational Theory and Public Policy*. Ed. Richard H. Hall and Robert E. Quinn. Beverly Hills: Sage, 1983. 147–62.

———, ed. *Nonprofit Enterprise in the Arts*. New York: Oxford University Press, 1986.

DiMaggio, Paul J., and Paula Brown. *Audience Studies of the Performing Arts and Museums: A Critical Review*. National Endowment for the Arts, Research Division Report No. 9, 1978.

DiMaggio, Paul J., and Walter W. Powell. "The Iron Cage Revisited: Institutional Isomorphism and Collective Rationality in Organizational Fields." *American Sociological Review* 48, no. 2 (1983): 147–60.

———, eds. *The New Institutionalism in Organizational Analysis*. Chicago: University of Chicago Press, 1991.

DiMaggio, Paul J., and Michael Useem. "Cultural Democracy in a Period of Cultural Expansion." *Performers and Performances*. Ed. Jack B. Kamerman and Rosanne Martarella. South Hadley, Mass.: Bergin & Garvey, 1983.

DiMaggio, Paul J., and Sharon Zukin, eds. *Structures of Capital: The Social Organization of Economic Life*. New York: Cambridge University Press, 1990.

Dirks, Nicholas B., Geoff Eley, and Sherry B. Ortner, eds. *Culture/Power/History: A Reader in Contemporary Social Theory*. Princeton, N.J.: Princeton University Press, 1994.

Disch, Lisa, and Mary Jo Kane. "When a Looker Is Really a Bitch: Lisa Olson, Sport, and the Heterosexual Matrix." *Signs* 21, no. 2 (1996): 278–308.

Donald, James. "Review Article on Channels of Discourse and Television Culture." *Screen* 31, no. 1 (1990): 113–18.

Dryzek, John S. *Discursive Democracy: Politics, Policy, and Political Science*. Cambridge: Cambridge University Press, 1994.

Dubrow, Heather. *Genre*. London: Methuen, 1982.

Dumm, Thomas L. "The New Enclosures: Racism in the Normalized Community." *Reading Rodney King/Reading Urban Uprising*. Ed. Robert Gooding-Williams. New York: Routledge, 1993. 178–95.

Duncan, Carol. "Art Museums and the Ritual of Citizenship." *Exhibiting Cultures: The Poetics and Politics of Museum Display*. Ed. Ivan Karp and Steven C. Lavine. Washington, D.C.: Smithsonian Institution Press, 1991. 88–103.

Dunn, Robert G. "Science, Technology and Bureaucratic Domination: Television and the Ideology of Scientism." *Media, Culture & Society* 1, no. 4 (1979): 343–54.

During, Simon, ed. *The Cultural Studies Reader*. New York: Routledge, 1993.

Durkheim, Émile. "The Division of Labour in Society." Trans. G. Simpson. *Sociological Perspectives: Selected Readings*. Ed. Kenneth Thompson and Jeremy Tunstall. New York: Penguin, 1976. 94–105.

Durkheim, Émile, and Marcel Mauss. *Primitive Classification*. Ed. and Trans. Rodney Needham. London: Cohen and West, 1970.

Dyer, Richard. "Coming to Terms." *Jump Cut* no. 30 (June 1985): 27–29.

———. "Idol Thoughts: Orgasm and Self-Reflexivity in Gay Pornography." *Critical Quarterly* 36, no. 1 (1994): 49–62.

———. *Only Entertainment*. London: Routledge, 1992.

Eagleton, Terry. "Where Do Postmodernists Come From?" *Monthly Review* 47, no. 3 (1995): 59–70.

Easthope, Antony. *Literary into Cultural Studies*. London: Routledge, 1991.

———. *What a Man's Gotta Do: The Masculine Myth in Popular Culture*. London: Paladin, 1986.

Eco, Umberto. *The Role of the Reader: Explorations in the Semiotics of Texts*. London: Hutchinson, 1981.

———. "Stefano Rosso. A Correspondence with Umberto Eco Genova-Bologna-Binghamton-Bloomington August–September, 1982, March–April, 1983." Trans. Carolyn Springer. *boundary 2* 12, no. 1 (1983): 1–13.

———. "Towards a Semiotic Inquiry into the Television Message." Trans. Paola Splendore. *Working Papers in Cultural Studies* no. 3 (1972): 103–21.

———. *Travels in Hyperreality*. Trans. William Weaver. London: Picador, 1987.

Egeberg, Morten. "Bureaucrats as Public Policy-Makers and Their Self-Interests." *Journal of Theoretical Politics* 7, no. 2 (1995): 157–67.

Eisner, Michael. "Planetized Entertainment." *New Perspectives Quarterly* 12, no. 4 (1995): 8–10.

Elias, Norbert. "An Essay on Sport and Violence." *Quest for Excitement: Sport and Leisure in the Civilizing Process*. Norbert Elias and Eric Dunning. Oxford: Basil Blackwell, 1986. 150–74.

Elliott, Stuart. "Advertising." *New York Times* 8 November 1995: D10.

Ellis, Bob. "Star-Crossed Love and the Unhousetrained Visitor from Space." *National Times* 28 June–4 July 1985: 36.

*Encore* 7, no. 2 (1989).

Erens, Patricia. "The Times of Harvey Milk: An Interview with Robert Epstein." *Cineaste* 14, no. 3 (1986): 26–27.

*Ettingshausen v. Australian Consolidated Press Ltd*. 12807 of 1991. Supreme Court of New South Wales Common Law Division.

Evans, David T. *Sexual Citizenship: The Material Construction of Sexualities*. London: Routledge, 1993.

Evans, Peter. *Dependent Development: The Alliance of Multinational, State, and Local Capital in Brazil*. Princeton, N.J.: Princeton University Press, 1979.

Falk, Pasi. *The Consuming Body*. London: Sage, 1994.

Faludi, Susan. "The Money Shot." *New Yorker* 71, no. 34 (1995): 64–87.

Falvey, Jennifer. "ET Damages Jury 'Over the Top.'" *Australian* 4 October 1993: 3.

Fanon, Frantz. *Black Skin, White Masks*. Trans. Charles Lam Markmann. London: Pluto, 1986.

Favez, Jean-Claude, with Genevieve Billetur. *Une mission impossible? Le CICR, les déportations et les camps de concentration Nazis*. Lausanne: Payot, 1988.

Ferguson, Frances. "Malthus, Godwin, Wordsworth, and the Spirit of Solitude." *Literature and the Body: Essays on Populations and Persons*. Ed. Elaine Scarry. Baltimore: Johns Hopkins University Press, 1990. 106–24.

Ferguson, Kathy E. *The Man Question: Visions of Subjectivity in Feminist Theory*. Berkeley: University of California Press, 1993.

Ferguson, Marjorie, and Peter Golding, eds. *Cultural Studies in Question*. London: Sage, 1997.

ffytche, Matt. "Virtual Banality." *Modern Review* 1, no. 16 (1994): 27.

Fife-Yeomans, Janet. "RL Star's Damages Payout Cut by $250,000." *Australian* 2 February 1995: 2.

"Film Victoria's *Mission Impossible*." *Cinema Papers* no. 74 (July 1989): 2.

Fisher, John H. "A Language Policy for Lancastrian England." *PMLA* 107, no. 5 (1992): 1168–80.

Fiske, John. "Audiencing: A Cultural Studies Approach." *Poetics* 21, no. 4 (1992): 345–59.

———. *Power Plays, Power Works*. London: Verso, 1993.

———. *Television Culture*. New York: Routledge, 1988.

Fitzgerald, Kate. "The Truth Comes Out: Trend Is Clear as Marketers Place 'True' Faith in Ad Themes, Product Names." *Advertising Age* 65, no. 43 (1994): 3.

Flannery, Tim. "Sports and the Courts: Several Issues Should Be Considered before Starting Drug-Testing Program." *Interscholastic Athletic Administration* 22, no. 3 (1996): 8–12.

Fogel, Aaron. "The Prose of Populations and the Magic of Demography." *Western Humanities Review* 47, no. 4 (1993): 312–37.

Fogel, Danil Mark. "'Schindler's List' in Novel and Film: Exponential Conversion." *Historical Journal of Film, Radio and Television* 14, no. 3 (1994): 315–20.

Forbes, Jill, and Michael Kelly, eds. *French Cultural Studies: An Introduction.* Oxford: Oxford University Press, 1996.

Forgacs, David, and Robert Lumley, eds. *Italian Cultural Studies: An Introduction.* Oxford: Oxford University Press, 1996.

Foss, Paul. "Mapplethorpe Aglance." *Photofile* 3, no. 3 (1985): 8–10.

Foucault, Michel. *The Archaeology of Knowledge.* Trans. A. M. Sheridan Smith. London: Tavistock, 1974.

———. "Conversation with Michel Foucault." *Threepenny Review* (Winter/Spring 1980): 4–5.

———. "The End of the Monarchy of Sex." Trans. Dudley M. Marchi. *Foucault Live (Interviews, 1966–84).* Ed. Sylvère Lotringer. New York: Semiotext(e), 1989. 137–55.

———. "An Ethics of Pleasure." Trans. John Johnston. *Foucault Live (Interviews, 1966–84).* Ed. Sylvère Lotringer. New York: Semiotext(e), 1989. 257–77.

———. "Governmentality." Trans. Pasquale Pasquino. *The Foucault Effect: Studies in Governmentality.* Ed. Graham Burchell, Colin Gordon, and Peter Miller. London: Harvester Wheatsheaf, 1991. 87–104.

———. "Grey Mornings of Tolerance." Trans. Danielle Kormos. *Stanford Italian Review* 2, no. 2 (1982): 72–74.

———. "Histoire de la Médicalisation." *Masses et politique.* Ed. Dominique Wolton. Paris: Éditions du Centre National de la Recherche Scientifique, 1988. 13–29.

———. *The History of Sexuality: An Introduction.* Trans. Robert Hurley. Harmondsworth: Penguin, 1984.

———. "Interview with Lucette Finas." Trans. Paul Foss and Meaghan Morris. *Michel Foucault: Power, Truth, Strategy.* Ed. Meaghan Morris and Paul Patton. Sydney: Feral, 1979. 67–75.

———. "Madness, the Absence of Work." Trans. Peter Stastny and Deniz Sengel. *Critical Inquiry* 21, no. 2 (1995): 290–98.

———. "Politics and the Study of Discourse." Trans. Anthony M. Nazzaro. Rev. Colin Gordon. *Ideology and Consciousness* no. 3 (Spring 1978): 7–26.

———. "Problematics: Excerpts from Conversations." *Crash: Nostalgia for the Absence of Cyberspace.* Ed. Robert Reynolds and Thomas Zummer. New York: Third Waxing Space, 1994. 121–27.

———. *Remarks on Marx: Discussions with Duccio Trombadori.* Trans. R. James Goldstein and James Cascaito. New York: Semiotext(e), 1991.

———. *Sept Propos sur le septième ange.* N.p.: Éditions Fata Morgana, 1986.

———. "The Subject and Power." Trans. Leslie Sawyer. *Critical Inquiry* 8, no. 4 (1982): 777–95.

———. "Truth and Power." Trans. Colin Gordon. *Power/Knowledge: Selected Interviews and Other Writings 1972–77.* Michel Foucault. Ed. Colin Gordon. New York: Pantheon, 1980. 109–33.

———. "La Volonté de savoir: 1970–71." *Résumé des cours 1970–1982: Conférences, essais et leçons du Collège de France.* Paris: Julliard, 1989. 9–16.

Foucault, Michel, and Richard Sennett. "Sexuality and Solitude." *Humanities in Review* 1 (1982): 3–21.

Francoeur, Robert T., ed. *The Complete Dictionary of Sexology,* rev. ed. New York: Continuum, 1995.

Franklin, Sarah, Celia Lury, and Jackie Stacey, eds. *Off-Centre: Feminism and Cultural Studies.* London: Hutchinson, 1991.

Fraser, Jane. "Mission: Ridiculous." *Australian Magazine* 12–13 August 1989: 8–13.

Fraser, Nancy. "Rethinking the Public Sphere: A Contribution to the Critique of Actually Existing Democracy." *Social Text* 8, no. 3–9, no. 1 (1990): 56–80.

Freadman, Anne. "Untitled (On Genre)." *Cultural Studies* 2, no. 1 (1988): 67–99.

Freedman, Warren. *Press and Media Access to the Criminal Courtroom.* New York: Quorum, 1988.

Fremantle Prison Management Committee. *Fremantle Prison Draft Conservation and Management Plan.* Perth: State Planning Commission, 1988.

Frith, Simon. "Contemporary Culture and the Academy: Notes Towards a Research Strategy." *Critical Quarterly* 35, no. 1 (1993): 1–7.

———. "Knowing One's Place: The Culture of Cultural Industries." *Cultural Studies Birmingham* no. 1 (1991): 134–55.

———. "Youth/Music/Television." *Sound and Vision: The Music Video Reader.* Ed. Simon Frith, Andrew Goodwin, and Lawrence Grossberg. London: Routledge, 1993. 67–83.

Fröbel, Folker, Jürgen Heinrichs, and Otto Kreye. *The New International Division of Labour: Structural Unemployment in Industrialised Countries and Industrialisation in Developing Countries.* Trans. Pete Burgess. Cambridge: Cambridge University Press, 1980.

"From Cultural Studies to Cultural Policy." *Culture and Policy* 6, no. 2 (1994).

Frow, John. "The Concept of the Popular." *New Formations* no. 18 (Winter 1993): 25–38.

———. "Cultural Markets and the Shape of Culture." *Continental Shift: Globalisation and Culture.* Ed. Elizabeth Jacka. Sydney: Local Consumption, 1992. 7–24.

———. *Cultural Studies and Cultural Value.* Oxford: Clarendon, 1995.

Frow, John, and Meaghan Morris. "Introduction." *Australian Cultural Studies: A Reader.* Ed. John Frow and Meaghan Morris. Sydney: Allen & Unwin, 1993. vii–xxxii.

————, eds. *Australian Cultural Studies: A Reader*. Sydney: Allen & Unwin, 1993.

Fujimori, Alberto. "Saving the State in Peru." *New Perspectives Quarterly* 10, no. 4 (1993): 10–12.

Fukurai, Hiroshi, Edgar W. Butler, and Richard Krooth. *Race and the Jury: Racial Disenfranchisement and the Search for Justice*. New York: Plenum, 1993.

Fuller, Linda K. "Reporters' Rights to the Locker Room." *Feminist Issues* 12, no. 1 (1992): 39–45.

Fung, Richard. "Looking for My Penis: The Eroticized Asian in Gay Video Porn." *How Do I Look? Queer Film and Video*. Ed. Bad Object-Choices. Seattle: Bay, 1991. 145–68.

Fussell, Sam. "Bodybuilder Americanus." *Michigan Quarterly Review* 32, no. 4 (1993): 577–96.

"The Future of the Field—Between Fragmentation and Cohesion." *Journal of Communication* 43, no. 3 (1993).

Gaines, Jane M. *Contested Culture: The Image, the Voice, and the Law*. Chapel Hill: University of North Carolina Press, 1991.

Gans, Herbert J. *Popular Culture and High Culture: An Analysis and Evaluation of Taste*. New York: Basic Books, 1974.

————. "Reopening the Black Box: Toward a Limited Effects Theory." *Journal of Communication* 43, no. 4 (1993): 29–35.

Garber, Marjorie. *Vested Interests: Cross-Dressing and Cultural Anxiety*. New York: HarperPerennial, 1993.

Gardella, Kay. "CBS' Mission: Impossible Warmed Up for Next Year." *Daily News* 14 February 1970: n.p.

Garfinkel, Harold. *Studies in Ethnomethodology*. Cambridge: Polity, 1992.

Garnham, Nicholas. "Concepts of Culture: Public Policy and the Cultural Industries." *Cultural Studies* 1, no. 1 (1987): 23–37.

————. "Political Economy and Cultural Studies: Reconciliation or Divorce?" *Critical Studies in Mass Communication* 12, no. 1 (1995): 62–71.

Gates, Henry Louis, Jr. "A Big Brother from Another Planet." *New York Times* 12 September 1993: 51.

Gelfand, Steve. *Television Theme Recordings: An Illustrated Discography, 1951–1994*. Ann Arbor, Mich.: Popular Culture, Ink, 1994.

Gellately, Robert. "Between Exploitation, Rescue, and Annihilation: Reviewing Schindler's List." *Central European History* 26, no. 4 (1993): 475–89.

Gellner, Ernest. "Nationalism." *Theory and Society* 10, no. 6 (1981): 753–76.

Gerbner, George. "Cameras on Trial: The 'O. J. Show' Turns the Tide." *Journal of Broadcasting and Electronic Media* 39, no. 4 (1995): 562–68.

————. "The Politics of Media Violence: Some Reflections." *Mass Communication Research: On Problems and Policies: The Art of Asking the Right Questions. In Honor of James D. Halloran*. Ed. Cees J. Hamelink and Olga Linné. Norwood, N.J.: Ablex, 1994. 133–45.

Gerhart, Mary. *Genre Choices, Gender Questions*. Norman: University of Oklahoma Press, 1992.

Gever, Martha. Review of *The Male Nude in Contemporary Photography*. *Discourse* 16, no. 2 (1993–94): 175–79.

Gibson, Ronnie. "Good and Bad in the Mission." *TV Scene* 2 July 1989: 10.

Gibson, Ross. *South of the West: Postcolonialism and the Narrative Construction of Australia*. Bloomington: Indiana University Press, 1992.

Gilpin, Robert. "The Political Economy of the Multinational Corporation: Three Contrasting Perspectives." *American Political Science Review* 70, no. 1 (1976): 184–91.

Girard, René. *Violence and the Sacred*. Trans. Patrick Gregory. Baltimore: Johns Hopkins University Press, 1992.

Gitlin, Todd. "Flat and Happy." *Wilson Quarterly* 17, no. 4 (1993): 47–55.

————. "Who Communicates What to Whom, in What Voice and Why, about the Study of Mass Communication?" *Critical Studies in Mass Communication* 7, no. 2 (1990): 185–96.

Given, Jock. "Researching Film and Television: The Role of the Australian Film Commission." *Media Information Australia* no. 73 (August 1994): 11–15.

Gleiberman, Owen. "Terms of Attachment." *Entertainment Weekly* no. 248 (1994): 86–87.

"Global Smarming: America's Pop Influence." *New York Times* 30 January 1994: H31.

Goethals, Gregor T. *The TV Ritual: Worship at the Video Altar*. Boston: Beacon, 1981.

Gollaher, David L. "From Ritual to Science: The Medical Transformation of Circumcision in America." *Journal of Social History* 28, no. 1 (1994): 5–36.

Gomery, Douglas. "In Search of the Cybermarket." *Wilson Quarterly* 18, no. 3 (1994): 9–17.

————. "Media Economics: Terms of Analysis." *Critical Studies in Mass Communication* 6, no. 1 (1989): 43–60.

Good, Mary-Jo Delvecchio. "Cultural Studies of Biomedicine: An Agenda for Research." *Social Science and Medicine* 41, no. 4 (1995): 461–73.

Gooding-Williams, Robert. "'Look, a Negro!'" *Reading Rodney King/Reading Urban Uprising*. Ed. Robert Gooding-Williams. New York: Routledge, 1993. 157–77.

Goodwin, Charles. "Professional Vision." *American Anthropologist* 96, no. 3 (1994): 606–33.

Gopnik, Adam. "Read All about It." *New Yorker* 70, no. 41 (1994): 84–102.

Gordon, David Frederick. "Testicular Cancer and Masculinity." *Men's Health and Illness: Gender, Power, and the Body*. Ed. Donald Sabo and David Frederick Gordon. Thousand Oaks, Calif.: Sage, 1995. 246–65.

Grabiner, Gene, and Virginia E. Grabiner. "The First 'Rodney King Trial.'" *Humanity and Society* 19, no. 2 (1995): 89–96.

Grace, Helen. "Eating the Curate's Egg: Cultural Studies for the Nineties." *West* 3, no. 1 (1991): 46–49.

Graham, Helen, and Jo Labanyi, eds. *Spanish Cultural Studies: An Introduction: The Struggle for Modernity*. Oxford: Oxford University Press, 1996.

Graham, Hugh Davis. "The Stunted Career of Policy History: A Critique and an Agenda." *Public Historian* 15, no. 2 (1993): 15–37.

Graham, John. "'There Are No Simple Solutions': Wiseman on Film Making and Viewing." *Frederick Wiseman*. Ed. Thomas R. Atkins. New York: Simon & Schuster, 1976. 33–45.

Grant, Alan. "The Videotaping of Police Interrogations in Canada." *The Media and Criminal Justice Policy: Recent Research and Social Effects*. Ed. Ray Surette. Springfield, Ill.: Charles C Thomas, 1990. 265–76.

Grant, Barry Keith. "Point of View and Spectator Position in Wiseman's Primate and Meat." *Wide Angle* 13, no. 2 (1991): 56–67.

———. *Voyages of Discovery: The Cinema of Frederick Wiseman*. Urbana: University of Illinois Press, 1992.

Grant-Taylor, Tony. "Studio Stores in the Village." *Sydney Morning Herald* 22 November 1995: 33.

Gray, Ann, and Jim McGuigan. "Introduction." *Studying Culture: An Introductory Reader*. Ed. Ann Gray and Jim McGuigan. London: Edward Arnold, 1993. vii–xi.

———, eds. *Studying Culture: An Introductory Reader*. London: Edward Arnold, 1993.

Gray, Jerry. "Fuss over Skater's Nude Video Echoes in New Jersey Assembly." *New York Times* 20 February 1994: 44.

Greenberg, Joel. "A Tape Shows Israeli Police Beating Arabs." *New York Times* 20 November 1996: A8.

Greenblatt, Stephen. *Learning to Curse: Essays in Early Modern Culture*. New York: Routledge, 1990.

———. "Resonance and Wonder." *Exhibiting Cultures: The Poetics and Politics of Museum Display*. Ed. Ivan Karp and Steven C. Lavine. Washington, D.C.: Smithsonian Institution Press, 1991. 42–56.

Greenhouse, Steven. "The North Carolinian Has Enemies, but No One Calls Him Vague." *New York Times* 27 November 1994: E7.

Gross, Larry, John Stuart Katz, and Jay Ruby. "Introduction: A Moral Pause." *Image Ethics: The Moral Rights of Subjects in Photographs, Film, and Television*. Ed. Larry Gross, John Stuart Katz, and Jay Ruby. New York: Oxford University Press, 1988. 3–33.

Grossberg, Lawrence. "Can Cultural Studies Find True Happiness in Communication?" *Journal of Communication* 43, no. 4 (1993): 89–97.

———. "Cultural Studies vs. Political Economy: Is Anybody Else Bored with This Debate?" *Critical Studies in Mass Communication* 12, no. 1 (1995): 72–81.

———. "The Formations of Cultural Studies: An American in Birmingham." *Relocating Cultural Studies: Developments in Theory and Research*. Ed. Valda Blundell, John Shepherd, and Ian Taylor. London: Routledge, 1993. 21–66.

———. "Introduction: Bringin' It All Back Home—Pedagogy and Cultural Studies." *Between Borders: Pedagogy and the Politics of Cultural Studies*. Ed. Henry A. Giroux and Peter McLaren. New York: Routledge, 1994. 1–25.

———. *We Gotta Get Out of This Place: Popular Conservatism and Postmodern Culture*. New York: Routledge, 1992.

Grossberg, Lawrence, Cary Nelson, and Paula A. Treichler, eds. *Cultural Studies*. New York: Routledge, 1992.

Groves, Don. "Arts Center Exchange Urged." *Variety* 2–8 May 1994: 70.

———. "Aussie Showbiz on Upswing." *Variety* 2–8 May 1994: 45, 72.

———. "B.O. Looking UP for Exhibs Down Under." *Variety* 2–8 May 1994: 54, 56.

———. "Pix: The Blizzard of Oz." *Variety* 24–30 October 1994: 46, 48.

———. "Roadshow Looks to High-Tech Future." *Variety* 7–13 March 1994: 55.

Groves, Ernest R., Gladys Hoagland Groves, and Catherine Groves. *Sex Fulfillment in Marriage*. New York: Emerson, 1945.

Guattari, Félix. "Becoming-Woman." *Semiotext(e)* 4, no. 1 (1981): 86–88.

Gubernick, Lisa, and Joel Millman. "El Sur Is the Promised Land." *Forbes* 153, no. 7 (1994): 94–95.

Gunew, Sneja, and Fazal Rizvi, eds. *Culture, Difference and the Arts*. Sydney: Allen & Unwin, 1994.

Guttmann, Allen. *Sports Spectators*. New York: Columbia University Press, 1986.

Haberman, Clyde. "NYC; Firebombing: Putting Blame on Prozac." *New York Times* 6 February 1996: B1.

Habermas, Jürgen. "The New Obscurity: The Crisis of the Welfare State and the Exhaustion of Utopian

Energies." *The New Conservatism: Cultural Criticism and the Historians' Debate*. Ed. and Trans. Shierry Weber Nicholsen. Cambridge: MIT Press, 1989. 48–70.

Hall, Sandra. "A Class of His Own." *Australian Magazine* 10–11 July 1993: 8–12, 14.

Hall, Stuart. "Deviance, Politics, and the Media." *The Lesbian and Gay Studies Reader*. Ed. Henry Abelove, Michèle Aina Barale, and David M. Halperin. New York: Routledge, 1993. 62–90.

————. "Minimal Selves." *Studying Culture: An Introductory Reader*. Ed. Ann Gray and Jim McGuigan. London: Edward Arnold, 1993. 134–38.

Halliwell, Leslie. *Halliwell's Teleguide*. London: Granada, 1979.

Hamamoto, Darrell Y. *Monitored Peril: Asian Americans and the Politics of TV Representation*. Minneapolis: University of Minnesota Press, 1994.

Hamburger, Estelle. *It's a Woman's Business*. New York: Vanguard, 1939.

Hamermesh, Daniel S., and Jeff E. Biddle. "Beauty and the Labor Market." *American Economic Review* 84, no. 5 (1994): 1174–94.

Hamilton, Peter, and Sue Mathews. *American Dreams: Australian Movies*. Sydney: Currency, 1986.

Hammack, David. "Think Tanks and the Invention of Policy Studies." *Nonprofit and Voluntary Service Quarterly* 24, no. 2 (1995): 173–81.

Hammond, Jane. "Video Justice." *Australian* 20 November 1992: 15.

Hannerz, Ulf. "Cosmopolitans and Locals in World Culture." *Theory, Culture & Society* 7, nos. 2–3 (1990): 237–51.

Hansen, Miriam Bratu. "Schindler's List Is Not Shoah: The Second Commandment, Popular Modernism, and Public Memory." *Critical Inquiry* 22, no. 2 (1996): 292–312.

Hanson, Barbara Gail. "The Potential of Videotape Data: Emotional Correlates of Senile Dementia in Families as a Case in Point." *Quality and Quantity* 28, no. 3 (1994): 219–32.

Harari, Fiona. "The Crotch of the Matter." *Australian* 11 February 1993: 11.

————. "The New Face of Beauty." *Australian* 18 June 1993: 15.

Harris, Daniel. "The Current Crisis in Men's Lingerie: Notes on the Belated Commercialization of a Noncommercial Product." *Salmagundi* no. 100 (Fall 1993): 130–39.

Harris, David. *From Class Struggle to the Politics of Pleasure: The Effects of Gramscianism on Cultural Studies*. London: Routledge, 1992.

Harris, Mike. "TV Travelling Well to Europe." *Variety* 31 October–6 November 1994: 76, 82.

Harris, Thomas J. *Courtroom's Finest Hour in American Cinema*. Metuchen, N.J.: Scarecrow, 1987.

Hartley, John. *The Politics of Pictures: The Creation of the Public in the Age of Popular Media*. London: Routledge, 1992.

————. "Popular Reality: A (Hair)Brush with Cultural Studies." *Continuum* 4, no. 2 (1991): 5–18.

————. *Tele-ology: Studies in Television*. London: Routledge, 1992.

Hartman, Geoffrey. "The Cinema Animal: On Spielberg's Schindler's List." *Salmagundi* nos. 106–7 (Summer 1995): 127–45.

Harvey, Sylvia. Review of *Framing Culture*. *Media, Culture & Society* 16, no. 1 (1994): 170–73.

Haskell, Molly. "In 'The Birth of a Nation,' the Birth of Serious Film." *New York Times* 20 November 1995: D5.

Hatt, Michael. "Exposure Time." *Oxford Art Journal* 17, no. 2 (1994): 132–37.

Haug, W. F. *Critique of Commodity Aesthetics: Appearance, Sexuality and Advertising in Capitalist Society*. Trans. Robert Bock. Cambridge: Polity, 1986.

Hay, David. "Down and Out in Beverly Hills." *Sydney Morning Herald* 9 July 1988: 76.

Hayward, Malcolm. "Genre Recognition of History and Fiction." *Poetics* 22, no. 5 (1994): 409–21.

Hayward, Susan. "State, Culture and the Cinema: Jack Lang's Strategies for the French Industry 1981–93." *Screen* 34, no. 4 (1993): 382–91.

Hearn, Jeff. *Men in the Public Eye: The Construction and Deconstruction of Public Men and Public Patriarchies*. London: Routledge, 1992.

Hegel, Georg Wilhelm Friedrich. *Lectures on the Philosophy of World History. Introduction: Reason in History*. Trans. H. B. Nisbet. Cambridge: Cambridge University Press, 1988.

Heilemann, John. "A Survey of Television: Feeling for the Future." *Economist* 330, no. 7850 (1994): Survey 1–18.

Heins, Marjorie. *Sex, Sin, and Blasphemy: A Guide to America's Censorship Wars*. New York: New Press, 1993.

Heller, Agnes. *Everyday Life*. Trans. G. L. Campbell. London: Routledge and Kegan Paul, 1984.

Hendon, William S., James L. Shanahan, and Alice J. MacDonald. "Preface." *Economic Policy for the Arts*. Ed. William S. Hendon, James L. Shanahan, and Alice J. MacDonald. Cambridge, Mass.: Abt, 1980. ix–xiii.

Herbert, Steve. "The Trials of Laurence Powell: Law, Space, and a 'Big Time Use of Force.'" *Environment and Planning D: Society and Space* 13, no. 2 (1995): 185–99.

Herodotus. *The Histories*. Trans. Aubrey de Sélincourt. Harmondsworth: Penguin, 1974.

Herr, Cheryl Temple. *Critical Regionalism and Cultural Studies: From Ireland to the American Midwest.* Miami: University of Florida Press, 1996.

"Hi Ho, Remake." *Economist* 310, no. 7591 (1989): 103.

Hickie, Kathleen. "Editor 'Careless' in Printing ET's Photo." *Sydney Morning Herald* 5 February 1993: n.p.

———. "ET Case a Storm in a Teacup: QC." *Sydney Morning Herald* 10 February 1993: 5.

———. "Judge Defends Payout to ET." *Sydney Morning Herald* 13 February 1993: 7.

———. "Nudity Not on for ET the 'Sex Symbol.'" *Sydney Morning Herald* 3 February 1993: n.p.

———. "Photographer Says 'No Denying' ET Exposure." *Sydney Morning Herald* 10 February 1993: n.p.

———. "Rugby League Star 'Repulsed' by ET's Nude Shower Shot." *Sydney Morning Herald* 4 February 1993: n.p.

Hill, George H., and Sylvia Savenson Hill. *Blacks on Television.* Metuchen, N.J.: Scarecrow, 1985.

Hitchcock, Alfred. "Film Production." *Hitchcock on Hitchcock: Selected Writings and Interviews.* Ed. Sidney Gottlieb. Berkeley: University of California Press, 1995. 210–26.

Hobsbawm, Eric. "Introduction: Inventing Tradition." *The Invention of Tradition.* Ed. Eric Hobsbawm and Terence Ranger. Cambridge: Cambridge University Press, 1989. 1–14.

Hodge, Bob, and Vijay Mishra. "Anthropology and/or/as 'Cultural Studies'? A Response to Trigger." *Anthropological Forum* 6, no. 4 (1993): 614–18.

Hodge, Bob, and David Tripp. *Children and Television.* Cambridge: Polity, 1986.

Hodge, Robert. *Literature as Discourse: Textual Strategies in English and History.* Cambridge: Polity, 1990.

Hodge, Robert, and Gunther Kress. "Functional Semiotics: Key Concepts for the Analysis of Media, Culture and Society." *Australian Journal of Cultural Studies* 1, no. 1 (1983): 1–17.

Hofstede, Geert. "Cultural Dimensions in People Management: The Socialization Perspective." *Globalizing Management: Creating and Leading the Competitive Organization.* Ed. Vladimir Pucik, Noel M. Tichy, and Carole K. Barnett. New York: John Wiley, 1993. 139–58.

Hoggart, Richard. *Speaking to Each Other,* Vol. 1, *About Society.* Harmondsworth: Penguin, 1973.

Holden, Stephen. "Mission Accepted: Tom Cruise as Superhero." *New York Times* 22 May 1996: C13, C16.

Holland, Bernard. "'Harvey Milk,' a Gay Opera as a Grand Coming-Out Party." *New York Times* 6 April 1995: C17.

Holland, Norman N. "Film Response from Eye to I: The Kuleshov Experiment." *Classical Hollywood Narrative: The Paradigm Wars.* Ed. Jane Gaines. Durham, N.C.: Duke University Press, 1992. 79–106.

Hong Kong Cultural Policy Study Group. *In Search of Cultural Policy '93.* Hong Kong: Zuni Icosahedron, 1994.

Hoover, Deborah A. "Developing a Cultural Policy in the Gambia: Problems and Progress." *Journal of Arts Management and Law* 18, no. 3 (1988): 31–39.

Horvitz, Philip. "Don't Cry for Me Academia." *Jimmy and Lucy's House of K* no. 2 (August 1985): 78–80.

Hoskins, Colin, and Stuart McFadyen. "The U.S. Competitive Advantage in the Global Television Market: Is It Sustainable in the New Broadcasting Environment?" *Canadian Journal of Communication* 16, no. 2 (1991): 207–24.

Hoskins, Colin, and Roger Mirus. "Reasons for the US Dominance of the International Trade in Television Programmes." *Media, Culture & Society* 10, no. 4 (1988): 499–515.

Hoskins, Colin, Roger Mirus, and W. Rozeboom. "US Television Programs in the International Market: Unfair Pricing?" *Journal of Communication* 39, no. 2 (1989): 55–75.

Houston, Penelope. "007." *Sight and Sound* 34, no. 1 (1964-65): 14–16.

Hunt, David J. Judgment in 12807 of 1991—*Ettingshausen v. Australian Consolidated Press Ltd.*

Hunter, Ian. "Accounting for the Humanities." *Meanjin* 48, no. 3 (1989): 438–48.

———. *Culture and Government: The Emergence of Literary Education.* London: Macmillan, 1988.

———. "The Humanities without Humanism." *Meanjin* 51, no. 3 (1992): 479–90.

———. "Providence and Profit: Speculations in the Genre Market." *Southern Review* 22, no. 3 (1988): 211–23.

———. *Rethinking the School: Subjectivity, Bureaucracy, Criticism.* Sydney: Allen and Unwin, 1994.

———. "Setting Limits to Culture." *New Formations* no. 4 (Spring 1988): 103–23.

Hunter, Ian, David Saunders, and Dugald Williamson. *On Pornography: Literature, Sexuality and Obscenity Law.* London: Macmillan, 1993.

Huyssen, Andreas. *After the Great Divide: Modernism, Mass Culture and Postmodernism.* London: Macmillan, 1988.

Hyam, Ronald. *Empire and Sexuality: The British Experience.* Manchester: Manchester University Press, 1990.

Indiana, Gary. "A Day at the Sex Factory." *Village Voice* 38, no. 34 (1993): 26–28, 30, 33–37.

Inglis, Fred. *Cultural Studies.* Oxford: Basil Blackwell, 1993.

"Injected Drug for Impotence Is Found Effective." *New York Times* 4 April 1996: A14.

Innis, Harold A. *The Bias of Communication*. Toronto: University of Toronto Press, 1991.

"Invited Reviews." *Journal of Research in Personality* 23, no. 1 (1989): 1–54.

"Ireland and Irish Cultural Studies." *South Atlantic Quarterly* 95, no. 1 (1996).

Jacka, Elizabeth. "Australian Cinema: An Anachronism in the '80s?" *The Imaginary Industry: Australian Film in the Late '80s*. Ed. Susan Dermody and Elizabeth Jacka. Sydney: Australian Film, Television and Radio School, 1988. 117–30.

———. "Financing Australian Films." *The Imaginary Industry: Australian Film in the Late '80s*. Ed. Susan Dermody and Elizabeth Jacka. Sydney: Australian Film, Television and Radio School, 1988. 7–21.

———. "Introduction." *Continental Shift: Globalisation and Culture*. Ed. Elizabeth Jacka. Sydney: Local Consumption, 1992. 1–6.

———. "Overseas Links." *The Imaginary Industry: Australian Film in the Late '80s*. Ed. Susan Dermody and Elizabeth Jacka. Sydney: Australian Film, Television and Radio School, 1988. 50–64.

Jacka, Elizabeth, and Stuart Cunningham. "Australian Television: An International Player?" *Media Information Australia* no. 70 (November 1993): 17–27.

Jacobs, Ronald N. "Civil Society and Crisis: Culture, Discourse, and the Rodney King Beating." *American Journal of Sociology* 101, no. 5 (1996): 1238–72.

Jacobsen, Kurt. "WGBH Makes History." *Bulletin of Concerned Asian Scholars* 25, no. 2 (1993): 46–49.

Jagose, Annamarie. "Way Out: The Category 'Lesbian' and the Fantasy of the Utopic Space." *Journal of the History of Sexuality* 4, no. 2 (1993): 264–87.

Jameson, Fredric. "On 'Cultural Studies.'" *Social Text* 11, no. 1 (1993): 17–52.

———. *Postmodernism, or, The Cultural Logic of Late Capitalism*. London: Verso, 1991.

Jayyusi, Lena. "The Reflexive Nexus: Photo-Practice and Natural History." *Continuum* 6, no. 2 (1993): 25–52.

Jenks, Chris, ed. *Cultural Reproduction*. London: Routledge, 1993.

Jianying Zha. "Yellow Peril." *TriQuarterly* no. 93 (Spring-Summer 1995): 238–64.

Jobert, Bruno. "The Normative Frameworks of Public Policy." *Political Studies* 37, no. 3 (1989): 376–86.

Johnson, Constance. "More Courts Are Tuning in to TV Hearings." *Wall Street Journal* 1 September 1995: B1, B5.

Johnson, Richard. "The Story So Far: And Further Transformations?" *Introduction to Contemporary Cultural Studies*. Ed. David Punter. London: Longman, 1986. 277–313.

Jordan, Glenn, and Chris Weedon. *Cultural Politics: Class, Gender, Race and the Postmodern World*. Oxford: Basil Blackwell, 1995.

Jordanova, Ludmilla. "Objects of Knowledge: A Historical Perspective on Museums." *The New Museology*. Ed. Peter Vergo. London: Reaktion, 1991. 22–40.

Joseph, May. "Diaspora, New Hybrid Identities, and the Performance of Citizenship." *Women and Performance* 7, no. 2–8, no. 1 (1995): 3–13.

Joyce, James. *A Portrait of the Artist as a Young Man*. New York: Viking, 1982.

"Judge Attacks Media Reports on E.T. Case." *West Australian* 13 February 1993: 24.

"Judge Slams Reporting of Ettingshausen Case." *Weekend Australian* 13–14 February 1993: 7.

Kaminski, Edmund P., and Gerald R. Miller. "How Jurors Respond to Videotaped Witnesses." *Journal of Communication* 34, no. 1 (1984): 88–102.

Kaplan, E. Ann. "Introduction to Special Issue of *American Imago* on 'Psychoanalysis and Cinema.'" *American Imago* 50, no. 4 (1993): 393–99.

Katsh, M. Ethan. *The Electronic Media and the Transformation of Law*. New York: Oxford University Press, 1989.

Katzman, Lisa. "The Women of Porn: They're Not in It for the Money Shot." *Village Voice* 38, no. 34 (1993): 31–33.

Kellehear, Allan. *The Unobtrusive Researcher: A Guide to Methods*. Sydney: Allen & Unwin, 1993.

Kellner, Douglas. *Media Culture: Cultural Studies, Identity and Politics between the Modern and the Postmodern*. London: Routledge, 1995.

———. *Television and the Crisis of Democracy*. Boulder, Colo.: Westview, 1990.

Keneally, Thomas. *Schindler's List*. New York: Simon & Schuster, 1982.

Kerr, James. "Hunks." *HQ* no. 17 (April 1991): 94–99.

Kerr, James Semple. *Fremantle Prison: A Policy for Its Conservation*. Perth: Building Management Authority of Western Australia, 1992.

Keuls, Eva C. *The Reign of the Phallus: Sexual Politics in Ancient Athens*. New York: Harper & Row, 1985.

Keynes, John Maynard. *The General Theory of Employment Interest and Money*. London: Macmillan, 1957.

Kim, Albert. "Cyber Spice." *Entertainment Weekly* no. 252 (1994): 11.

Kimball, Roger. "'Diversity,' 'Cultural Studies' and Other Mistakes." *New Criterion* 14, no. 9 (1996): 4–9.

Kimmel, Michael S. "Consuming Manhood: The Feminization of American Culture and the Recreation of the Male Body, 1832–1920." *Michigan Quarterly Review* 33, no. 1 (1994): 7–36.

King, Noel. "From 'Play' to 'Players.'" *Filmnews* 22, no. 8 (1992): 8–9, 14.

———. "Reconsidering the Film-Politics Relation." *Radio — Sound and Film Culture*. Ed. Toby Miller. Perth: Continuum, 1992. 228–35.

King, Noel, and Colin MacCabe. "'That Was Then, This Is Now': An Interview with Colin MacCabe, British Film Institute, 3 September 1992." *Southern Review* 26, no. 3 (1993): 157–69.

Kingston, Margo. "How Violence Shapes Our Viewing." *Sydney Morning Herald*. 28 June 1989: 9.

Kirshenblatt-Gimblett, Barbara. "Objects of Ethnography." *Exhibiting Cultures: The Poetics and Politics of Museum Display*. Ed. Ivan Karp and Steven C. Lavine. Washington, D.C.: Smithsonian Institution Press, 1991. 386–443.

Kobré, Ken. "Nudity and News: How Would You Play It?" *Visual Communication Quarterly* 4, no. 2 (1997): 13–14.

Koch, Gertrude. "The Body's Shadow Realm." Trans. Jan-Christopher Horak and Joyce Rheuban. *Dirty Looks: Women, Pornography, Power*. Ed. Pamela Church Gibson and Roma Gibson. London: British Film Institute, 1993. 22–45.

Kohn, Hans. *The Idea of Nationalism: A Study in Its Origins and Background*. New York: Macmillan, 1945.

Konaré, Alpha Oumar. "Toward More Efficient International Collaboration." *African Arts* 28, no. 4 (1995): 27.

Koon, Stacey C., with Robert Deitz. *Presumed Guilty: The Tragedy of the Rodney King Affair*. Washington, D.C.: Regnery Gateway, 1992.

Kristeva, Julia. *Desire in Language: A Semiotic Approach to Literature and Art*. Ed. Leon S. Roudiez. Trans. Thomas Gora, Alice Jardine, and Leon S. Roudiez. New York: Columbia University Press, 1980.

Kuhn, Annette. *Cinema, Censorship and Sexuality 1909–1925*. London: Routledge, 1988.

Kunstler, William. "Dramatic Evidence." *Entertainment Weekly* no. 254 (1994): 75.

Lake, Marilyn. "Mission Impossible: How Men Gave Birth to the Australian Nation — Nationalism, Gender and Other Seminal Acts." *Gender and History* 4, no. 3 (1992): 305–22.

Lang, Andrew. *Letters to Dead Authors*. London: Longman Green, 1892.

Lang, Tim, and Colin Hines. *The New Protectionism: Protecting the Future against Free Trade*. New York: New Press, 1993.

La Planche, Shirley. "Studio to Bring Jobs, Money and Fame." *Australian* 23 June 1989: Special Report Gold Coast 8.

Lassiter, G. Daniel, and Audrey A. Irvine. "Videotaped Confessions: The Impact of Camera Point of View on Judgments of Coercion." *Journal of Applied Social Psychology* 16, no. 3 (1986): 268–76.

Latour, Bruno. *We Have Never Been Modern*. Trans. Catherine Porter. Cambridge: Harvard University Press, 1993.

Lattas, Andrew. "Aborigines and Contemporary Australian Nationalism: Primordiality and the Cultural Politics of Otherness." *Writing Australian Culture: Text, Society, and National Identity*. Ed. Julie Marcus. Adelaide: Social Analysis, 1990. 50–69.

Lawson, Ronald. "Towards Demythologizing the 'Australian Legend': Turner's Frontier Thesis and the Australian Experience." *Journal of Social History* 13, no. 4 (1980): 577–87.

Lawson, Sylvia. "General Editor's Preface." *Images and Industry: Television Drama Production in Australia*. Albert Moran. Sydney: Currency, 1985. 5–6.

Lazarsfeld, Paul F. *On Social Research and Its Language*. Ed. Raymond Boudon. Chicago: University of Chicago Press, 1993.

Lears, T. J. Jackson. "From Salvation to Self-Realization: Advertising and the Therapeutic Roots of the Consumer Culture, 1880–1930." *The Culture of Consumption: Critical Essays in American History, 1880–1980*. Ed. Richard Wightman Fox and T. J. Jackson Lears. New York: Pantheon, 1983. 1–38.

Lee, Paul S. N., and Georgette Wang. "Satellite TV in Asia: Forming a New Ecology." *Telecommunications Policy* 19, no. 2 (1995): 135–49.

Leech, Graeme. "Voyager Pulls Off Mission Impossible." *Weekend Australian* 26–27 August 1989: 1.

Le Hir, Marie-Pierre. "Defining French Cultural Studies." *Journal of the Midwest Modern Language Association* 29, no. 1 (1996): 76–86.

Lehman, Peter. "Penis-Size Jokes and Their Relation to Hollywood's Unconscious." *Comedy/Cinema/ Theory*. Ed. Andrew S. Horton. Berkeley: University of California Press, 1991. 43–59.

Leonard, Elmore. *City Primeval: High Noon in Detroit*. Boston: G. K. Hall, 1986.

———. *Split Images*. Boston: G. K. Hall, 1986.

Leonard, Jerry D., ed. *Legal Studies as Cultural Studies: A Reader in (Post) Modern Critical Theory*. Albany: State University of New York Press, 1995.

Leong, Laurence Wei-Teng. "Cultural Resistance: The Cultural Terrorism of British Male Working-Class Youth." *Current Perspectives in Social Theory* no. 12 (1992): 29–58.

Lever, Janet, and Stanton Wheeler. "Mass Media and the Experience of Sport." *Communication Research* 20, no. 1 (1993):125–43.

Levy, Bronwen. "Ruffling the Feathers of the Cultural Polity." *Meanjin* 51, no. 3 (1992): 552–55.

Lewis, Berwyn. "Writers' Block Spoils the Script." *Weekend Australian* 2–3 July 1988: Magazine 6.

Lewis, Jon. *The Road to Romance and Ruin: Teen Films and Youth Culture*. New York: Routledge, 1992.

Lewis, P. "Men on Pedestals." *Ten-8* no. 17 (1985): 22–29.

Lewis, Richard Warren. "Is This Mission Possible? The IM Force Struggles to Overcome Cast Changes, Power Plays, Hollywood Intrigue." *TV Guide* 17, no. 42 (1969): 30–39.

"Libel and Slander—Liability for Publishing Photograph Which Created Optical Illusion Concerning Plaintiff." *Harvard Law Review* 49 (1936): 840–42.

Liebes, Tamar, and Elihu Katz. *The Export of Meaning: Cross-Cultural Readings of Dallas*. New York: Oxford University Press, 1990.

Lindblom, Charles E. *The Policy-Making Process*, 2d ed. Englewood Cliffs, N.J.: Prentice Hall, 1980.

Lissit, Robert. "Gotcha!" *American Journalism Review* March 1995: 16–21.

Loisoz, Peter. *Innovations in Ethnographic Film: From Innocence to Self-Consciousness 1955–1985*. Chicago: University of Chicago Press, 1993.

Lovell, Terry, ed. *Feminist Cultural Studies*, vols. 1–2. Aldershot, England: Elgar, 1995.

Lowry, Cynthia. "Phelps' New Mission Has a Lot More Possibilities." *New York Post* 25 August 1970: n.p.

Lucia, Cynthia. "Revisiting High School: An Interview with Frederick Wiseman." *Cineaste* 20, no. 4 (1994): 5–11.

Luhmann, Niklas. *Love as Passion: The Codification of Intimacy*. Trans. Jeremy Gaines and Doris L. Jones. Cambridge: Polity, 1986.

Lull, James. *Media, Communication, Culture: A Global Approach*. New York: Columbia University Press, 1995.

Lunenfeld, Peter. "Genre-Alizations: Genre Theory in Film Studies." *Spectator* 12, no. 2 (1992): 6–15.

Lutz, Catherine A., and Jane L. Collins. *Reading* National Geographic. Chicago: University of Chicago Press, 1993.

Lynch, Michael, and David Bogen. *The Spectacle of History: Speech, Text, and Memory at the Iran-Contra Hearings*. Durham, N.C.: Duke University Press, 1996.

Lynch, Paul. "Brisbane Turned Off Police State." *Australian* 23 June 1989: 5.

Lyotard, Jean-François. *La Condition postmoderne: Rapport sur le savoir*. Paris: Les Éditions de Minuit, 1988.

———. *The Differend: Phrases in Dispute*. Trans. Georges Van Den Abbeele. Minneapolis: University of Minnesota Press, 1988.

Lyotard, Jean-François, and Jean-Loup Thébaud. *Just Gaming*. Trans. Wlad Godzich. Minneapolis: University of Minnesota Press, 1985.

MacCabe, Colin. "Cultural Studies and English." *Critical Quarterly* 34, no. 3 (1992): 25–34.

Macdonald, Dwight. "A Theory of Mass Culture." *Culture and Mass Culture*. Ed. Peter Davison, Rolf Meyersohn, and Edward Shils. Cambridge: Chadwyck-Healy, 1978. 167–83.

MacDonald, J. Fred. *Blacks and White TV: Afro-Americans in Television since 1948*. Chicago: Nelson-Hall, 1983.

———. *Television and the Red Menace: The Video Road to Vietnam*. New York: Praeger, 1985.

MacDougall, David. "Ethnographic Film: Failure and Promise." *Annual Review of Anthropology* no. 7 (1978): 405–23.

MacInnes, Judy, Jr. "Small Penis Poems." *Room of One's Own* 19, no. 1 (1996): 30.

MacLeod, Murdo. Photograph. *Observer* 18 September 1994: 7.

Madalengoitia, Laura. "Paradoxes in the Relations between the United States and Perú." *International Journal of Political Economy* 21, no. 2 (1991): 26–45.

"Made in Oz: Mission Impossible." *TV Scene* 30 July 1989: 16.

"Made in Oz: Mission Impossible." *TV Scene* 3 September 1989: 12.

"Made in Oz: Mission Impossible." *TV Scene* 17 September 1989: 17.

Magid, Ron. "Peering behind Cameron's New Curtain." *American Cinematographer* 75, no. 12 (1994): 64–76.

Maguire, Joseph. "Bodies, Sportscultures and Societies: A Critical Review of Some Theories in the Sociology of the Body." *International Review for the Sociology of Sport* 28, no. 1 (1993): 33–52.

———. "Preliminary Observations on Globalisation and the Migration of Sport Labour." *Sociological Review* 42, no. 3 (1994): 452–80.

Malinowski, Bronislaw. *A Scientific Theory of Culture and Other Essays*. London: Oxford University Press, 1969.

Maloney, Frank. *Australian Drama on Commercial Television*. Australian Content Inquiry Discussion Paper. Canberra: Australian Broadcasting Tribunal, 1988.

Malpas, Jeff. "Retrieving Truth: Modernism, Post-Modernism and the Problem of Truth." *Soundings* 75, nos. 2–3 (1992): 288–306.

"The Man behind the Voice behind the 1994 Elections." *New Yorker* 70, no. 39 (1994): 49–50.

Manchel, Frank. "A Reel Witness: Steven Spielberg's Representation of the Holocaust in Schindler's List." *Journal of Modern History* 67, no. 1 (1995): 83–100.

Mankiewicz, Frank, and Joel Swerdlow. *Remote Control: Television and the Manipulation of American Life*. New York: Times, 1978.

Mann, Michael. "Nation-States in Europe and Other Continents: Diversifying, Developing, Not Dying." *Daedalus* 122, no. 3 (1993): 115–40.

Manning, Maria. "Futile Attraction." *New Statesman and Society* 3, no. 122 (1990): 12–13.

Marc, David. "Mission: Impossible Special Unintelligence." *Village Voice* 15 November 1988: 47–48.

Marconi, Guglielmo. "Foreword." *The Story of Broadcasting*. A. R. Burrows. London: Cassell, 1924. vii.

Marcus, George E., and Fred R. Myers, eds. *The Traffic in Culture: Refiguring Art and Anthropology*. Berkeley: University of California Press, 1995.

Margolick, David. "Does Mrs. Bobbitt Count as Another Battered Wife?" *New York Times* 16 January 1994: E5.

Markoff, John. "If Medium Is the Message, the Message Is the Web." *New York Times* 20 November 1995: A1, D5.

———. "The Rise and Swift Fall of Cyber Literacy." *New York Times* 13 March 1994: E1, E5.

Markoff, John, and Veronica Montecinos. "The Ubiquitous Rise of Economists." *Journal of Public Policy* 13, no. 1 (1993): 37–68.

Markusen, James R. "The Boundaries of Multinational Enterprises and the Theory of International Trade." *Journal of Economic Perspectives* 9, no. 2 (1995): 169–89.

Marriott, David. "Bordering on the Black Penis." *Textual Practice* 10, no. 1 (1996): 9–28.

Martin, Richard. "'Feel Like a Million!': The Propitious Epoch in Men's Underwear Imagery, 1939–1952." *Journal of American Culture* 18, no. 4 (1995): 51–58.

Marvasti, A. "International Trade in Cultural Goods: A Cross-Sectional Analysis." *Journal of Cultural Economics* 18, no. 2 (1994): 135–48.

Mashon, Mike. "Losing Control: Popular Reception(s) of the Rodney King Video." *Wide Angle* 15, no. 2 (1993): 7–18.

Mason, Bobbie Ann. *In Country*. London: Fontana, 1987.

Massey, Murray. "Toad Invasion Adds to State of Confusion." *Australian Financial Review* 28 July 1989: 4.

Masters, Kim. "Sex, Lies, and an 8-Inch Carving Knife." *Vanity Fair* 56, no. 11 (1993): 168–72, 207–12.

Matabane, Paula W., and Oscar H. Gandy Jr. "Through the Prism of Race and Controversy: Did Viewers Learn Anything from *The Africans*?" *Journal of Black Studies* 19, no. 1 (1988): 3–16.

Mattelart, Armand. *Advertising International: The Privatisation of Public Space*. Trans. Michael Chanan. London: Routledge, 1991.

Mattelart, Armand, Xavier Delcourt, and Michèle Mattelart. "International Image Markets." *Global Television*. Ed. Cynthia Schneider and Brian Wallis. New York: Wedge, 1988. 13–33.

Mattelart, Armand, and Michèle Mattelart. *Rethinking Media Theory: Signposts and New Directions*. Trans. James A. Cohen and Marina Urquidi. Minneapolis: University of Minnesota Press, 1992.

Maurer, Richard. Interview with Judith Vecchione. WGBH series feature, 1992.

May, Anthony. "The Magnetics of Policy: Stuart Cunningham's Framing Culture." *New Researcher* nos. 1–2 (1992): 116–21.

Mazama, Ama. "An Afrocentric Approach to Language Planning." *Journal of Black Studies* 25, no. 1 (1994): 3–19.

Mazrui, Ali A. *Cultural Forces in World Politics*. London: James Currey, 1990.

McAnany, Emile G. "Television and Cultural Discourses: Latin American and United States Comparisons." *Studies in Latin American Popular Culture* no. 8 (1989): 1–21.

McAnulty, Richard D., and Henry E. Adams. "Validity and Ethics of Penile Circumference Measures of Sexual Arousal: A Reply to McConaghy." *Archives of Sexual Behavior* 21, no. 2 (1992): 177–86.

McAsey, Jennifer. "The Cult of Biffo." *Australian* 18 June 1993: 15.

McChesney, Robert W. "Is There Any Hope for Cultural Studies?" *Monthly Review* 47, no. 10 (1996): 1–18.

McConaghy, Nathaniel. "Validity and Ethics of Penile Circumference Measures of Sexual Arousal: A Critical Review." *Archives of Sexual Behavior* 18, no. 4 (1989): 357–69.

McGillick, Paul. "Hollywood May Bail Out Australian Films." *Australian Financial Review* 10 August 1988: 12.

McGuigan, Jim. *Cultural Populism*. London: Routledge, 1992.

McHoul, Alec. *Semiotic Investigations: Towards an Effective Semiotics*. Lincoln: University of Nebraska Press, 1996.

McHoul, Alec, and Tom O'Regan. "Towards a Paralogics of Textual Technologies: Batman, Glasnost and Relativism in Cultural Studies." *Southern Review* 25, no. 1 (1992): 5–26.

McKay, Jim, Geoffrey Lawrence, Toby Miller, and David Rowe. "Globalization and Australian Sport." *Sport Science Review* 2, no. 1 (1993): 10–28.

McKimmie, Jackie. Letter on Behalf of Australian Writers Guild to Mike Ahern 26 February 1988. *Queensland Film and Television Industries: Current Problems and Future Options*. Sue Pavasaris. Brisbane: Queensland Media Network, 1988. 41–43.

McLean, Sandra. "Hotline." *TV Scene* 5 November 1989: 3.

McLeod, Douglas M. Review. *Journal of Broadcasting and Electronic Media* 39, no. 4 (1995): 569–74.

McLuhan, Marshall. *Understanding Media: The Extensions of Man*. London: Abacus, 1974.

McMahon, Barrie, and Robyn Quin. "Genre Study and Australian Film." *Metro Media and Education Magazine* no. 78 (Summer 1988–89): 4–9.

McNaughton, Patrick R. "Malian Antiquities and Contemporary Desire." *African Arts* 28, no. 4 (1995): 22–27.

McQuail, Denis. "Media Policy Research: Conditions for Progress." *Mass Communication Research: On Problems and Policies: The Art of Asking the Right Questions. In Honor of James D. Halloran*. Ed. Cees J. Hamelink and Olga Linné. Norwood, N.J.: Ablex, 1994. 39–51.

McQueen, Humphrey. "Queensland: A State of Mind." *Meanjin* 38, no. 1 (1979): 41–51.

McRobbie, Angela. "All the World's a Stage, Screen or Magazine: When Culture Is the Logic of Late Capitalism." *Media, Culture & Society* 18, no. 3 (1996): 335–42.

McWilliams, Wilson Carey. "The Arts and the American Political Tradition." *Art, Ideology, and Politics*. Ed. Judith H. Balfe and Margaret Jane Wyszomirski. New York: Praeger, 1985. 15–57.

*Meat: How Men Look, Act, Walk, Talk, Dress, Undress, Taste and Smell: True Homosexual Experiences from S.T.H.* San Francisco: Gay Sunshine, 1981.

Medhurst, Andy. "Can Chaps Be Pin-Ups? The British Male Film Star of the 1950s." *Ten-8* no. 17 (1985): 3–8.

Mehan, Hugh. "Oracular Reasoning in a Psychiatric Exam: The Resolution of Conflict in Language." *Conflict Talk: Sociolinguistic Investigations of Arguments in Conversations*. Ed. Allen D. Grimshaw. Cambridge: Cambridge University Press, 1990. 160–77.

Meisler, Andy. "Lucy Sure Didn't Start It, But She Has Stuck to It." *New York Times* 20 November 1995: D5.

Mellor, Adrian. "Discipline and Punish? Cultural Studies at the Crossroads." *Media, Culture & Society* 14, no. 4 (1992): 663–70.

Mercer, Colin. "Cultural Policy: Research and the Governmental Imperative." *Media Information Australia* no. 73 (August 1994): 16–22.

Mercer, Kobena. "Dark and Lovely Too: Black Gay Men in Independent Film." *Queer Looks: Perspectives on Lesbian and Gay Film and Video*. Ed. Martha Gever, John Greyson, and Pratibha Parmar. New York: Routledge, 1993. 238–56.

Merelman, Richard M. *Partial Visions: Culture and Politics in Britain, Canada, and the United States*. Madison: University of Wisconsin Press, 1991.

Metz, Christian. *Film Language: A Semiotics of the Cinema*. Trans. Michael Taylor. New York: Oxford University Press, 1974.

Meyers, Richard. *TV Detectives*. San Diego, Calif.: A. S. Barnes, 1981.

Michaels, Eric. "A Model of Teleported Texts (with Reference to Aboriginal Television)." *Continuum* 3, no. 2 (1990): 8–31.

Michelson, Annette. Statement Prepared for the Society of Cinema Studies on the occasion of the announcement of her honorary membership, 1994.

Michnik, Adam. "Nationalism." Trans. Elzbieta Matynia. *Social Research* 58, no. 4 (1991): 757–63.

Miège, Bernard. *The Capitalization of Cultural Production*. Trans. Josiane Hay, Nicholas Garnham, and UNESCO. New York: International General, 1989.

Miller, D. A. "Bringing out Roland Barthes." *Raritan* 11, no. 4 (1992): 38–49.

Miller, Gerald R., and Norman E. Fontes. *Videotape on Trial: A View from the Jury Box*. Beverly Hills: Sage, 1979.

Miller, Gerald R., and James B. Stiff. *Deceptive Communication*. Newbury Park, Calif.: Sage, 1993.

Miller, Peter, and Ted O'Leary. "Accounting, 'Economic Citizenship' and the Spatial Reordering of Manufacture." *Accounting, Organizations and Society* 19, no. 1 (1993): 15–43.

Miller, Toby. "Beyond the Ur-Text of Radicalism." *Australian Journal of Communication* 17, no. 3 (1990): 174–84.

———. "Film and Media Citizenship." *Filmnews* 20, no. 1 (1990): 5.

———. *The Well-Tempered Self: Citizenship, Culture, and the Postmodern Subject*. Baltimore: Johns Hopkins University Press, 1993.

Miller, Toby, Tony Bennett, Gillian Swanson, and Gordon Tait. "Youth Cultures and Arts Policies." *Culture and Policy* 2, no. 2–3, no. 1 (1990–91): 135–56.

Minogue, Kenneth. "Philosophy." *Times Literary Supplement* 25 November 1994: 27–28.

"Mission Impossible." *Economist* 312, no. 7618 (1990): 15.

"Mission Impossible." *TV Scene* 16 July 1989: 10.

"Mission Impossible." *TV Scene* 3 September 1989: 25.

"Mission Impossible." *TV Scene* 17 September 1989: 28.

"Mission Impossible: Australia's Central Bank—the One-Armed Juggler." *Australian Financial Review* 19 July 1989: 1.

"Mission Impossible—Keeping Roger Down." *Weekend Australian* 5–6 August 1989: 20.

Mitchell, J. M. *International Cultural Relations*. London: Allen and Unwin, 1986.

Modleski, Tania. *Feminism without Women: Culture and Criticism in a "Postfeminist" Age*. New York: Routledge, 1991.

Mokia, Rosemary Ntumnyuy. "Publishers, United States Foreign Policy and the Third World, 1960–1967." *Publishing Research Quarterly* 11, no. 2 (1995): 36–51.

Molloy, Bruce. "Film in Queensland: An Overview." *Cinema Papers* no. 96 (December 1993): 4–8.

———. "Screensland: The Construction of Queensland in Feature Films." *Queensland Images in Film and Television*. Ed. Jonathan Dawson and Bruce Molloy. St. Lucia: University of Queensland Press, 1990. 66–77.

Molloy, Simon, and Barry Burgan. *The Economics of Film and Television in Australia*. Sydney: Australian Film Commission, 1993.

Monaghan, David. "Drama in Reel Life: Hollywood Invades Australia's Film Industry." *Good Weekend* 2 December 1989: 12–20.

Mongin, Olivier. *La Peur du vide: Essai sur les passions démocratiques*. Paris: Éditions du Seuil, 1991.

Montgomery, Scott L. "What Kind of Memory? Reflections on Images of the Holocaust." *Contention* 5, no. 1 (1995): 79–103.

Moran, Albert. "Foreign Exchange: Reflections on the Grundy Buy-Out." *Media International Australia* no. 83 (February 1997): 123–34.

Morris, Meaghan. *Ecstasy and Economics: American Essays for John Forbes*. Sydney: EM, 1992.

———. "A Gadfly Bites Back." *Meanjin* 51, no. 3 (1992): 545–51.

———. *The Pirate's Fiancée: Feminism, Reading, Postmodernism*. London: Verso, 1988.

Morris, Meaghan, and Paul Patton. "Preface." *Michel Foucault: Power, Truth, Strategy*. Ed. Meaghan Morris and Paul Patton. Sydney: Feral, 1979. 7–10.

Morrison, Blake. "Children of Circumstance: What Influences Could Compel Two Young Boys to Kill a Third? A City and a Country Are Left to Wonder." *New Yorker* 69, no. 50 (1994): 48–60.

Morrow, Raymond A. "The Challenge of Cultural Studies." *Canadian Review of Comparative Literature/ Revue Canadienne de littérature comparée* 22, no. 1 (1995): 1–20.

Morse, Margaret. "Sport on Television: Replay and Display." *Regarding Television: Critical Approaches—An Anthology*. Ed. E. Ann Kaplan. Los Angeles: American Film Institute, 1983. 44–66.

Moss, Howard B., George L. Panzak, and Ralph E. Tarter. "Sexual Functioning of Male Anabolic Steroid Abusers." *Archives of Sexual Behavior* 22, no. 1 (1993): 1–12.

"A Movie Career Next for Thaao?" *TV Scene* 16 July 1989: 24.

"Moviemakers Fear US Drain on Investment." *Sunday Mail* 21 May 1989: 35.

Muecke, Stephen. "Fashioning Stories: Cultural Criticism and the Yves Saint Laurent Show." *Age Monthly Review* October 1987: 15–18.

Mulhern, Francis. "The Politics of Cultural Studies." *Monthly Review* 47, no. 3 (1995): 31–40.

Murdock, Graham. "Across the Great Divide: Cultural Analysis and the Condition of Democracy." *Critical Studies in Mass Communication* 12, no. 1 (1995): 89–95.

———. "Cultural Studies at the Crossroads." *Australian Journal of Communication* no. 16 (December 1989): 37–49.

———. "Figuring Out the Arguments." *The Video Nasties: Freedom and Censorship in the Media*. Ed. Martin Barker. London: Pluto, 1984. 56–67.

———. "Visualizing Violence: Television and the Discourse of Disorder." *Mass Communication Research: On Problems and Policies: The Art of Asking the Right Questions. In Honor of James D. Halloran*. Ed. Cees J. Hamelink and Olga Linné. Norwood, N.J.: Ablex, 1994. 171–87.

Murphy, D. J. "Queensland's Image and Australian Nationalism." *Australian Quarterly* 50, no. 2 (1978): 77–92.

Murphy, John W., and Jung Min Choi. "Imagocentrism and the Rodney King Affair." *Et Cetera* 49, no. 4 (1992–93): 478–84.

Myers, Fred R. *Pintupi Country, Pintupi Self: Sentiment, Place, and Politics among Western Desert Aborigines*. Berkeley: University of California Press, 1991.

Myers, James. "Nonmainstream Body Modification: Genital Piercing, Branding, Burning, and Cutting." *Journal of Contemporary Ethnography* 21, no. 3 (1992): 267–306.

Nairn, Tom. "Internationalism and the Second Coming." *Daedalus* 122, no. 3 (1993): 155–70.

National Foundation on the Arts and the Humanities Act of 1965.

Nelson, Cary, and Dilip Goankar, eds. *Disciplinarity and Dissent in Cultural Studies*. New York: Routledge, 1996.

Nespor, Jan. "Strategies of Discourse and Knowledge Use in the Practice of Bureaucratic Research." *Human Organization* 48, no. 4 (1989): 325–32.

Neuman, W. Russell. *The Future of the Mass Audience*. Cambridge: Cambridge University Press, 1993.

"New Void, Old Series." *New York Times* 14 July 1988: C28.

Nichols, Bill. *Blurred Boundaries: Questions of Meaning in Contemporary Culture*. Bloomington: Indiana University Press, 1994.

———. *Representing Reality: Issues and Concepts in Documentary*. Bloomington: Indiana University Press, 1991.

Niney, Francois. "Shoah and Schindler's List." *Dox* no. 2 (Summer 1994): 27.

Nisbet, Robert A. "Project Camelot: An Autopsy." *On Intellectuals: Theoretical Studies. Case Studies.* Ed. Philip Rieff. New York: Anchor, 1970. 307–39.

Niven, William J. "The Reception of Steven Spielberg's Schindler's List in the German Media." *Journal of European Studies* 25, no. 98 (1995): 165–89.

Noble, Kenneth B. "The Nation; The Endless Rodney King Case." *New York Times* 4 February 1996: 5.

Nolan, David. "Sperm: Out for the Count?" *Living Marxism* no. 90 (May 1996): 18–20.

Norris, Christopher. *The Truth about Postmodernism*. Oxford: Basil Blackwell, 1993.

"Objectivity and Militancy: A Debate." *Current Anthropology* 36, no. 3 (1995): 399–440.

O'Connor, Alan. "The Problem of American Cultural Studies." *Critical Studies in Mass Communication* 6, no. 4 (1989): 405–13.

O'Connor, Barbara, and Raymond Boyle. "Dallas with Balls: Televized Sport, Soap Opera and Male and Female Pleasures." *Leisure Sciences* 12, no. 2 (1993): 107–19.

O'Heffernan, Patrick. "The L.A. Riots: A Story Made for and by TV." *Television Quarterly* 26, no. 1 (1992): 5–11.

Okantah, Mwatabu S. "America's Poem, or, 81 Seconds and 56 Blows." *Why L.A. Happened: Implications of the '92 Los Angeles Rebellion*. Ed. Haki R. Madhubuti. Chicago: Third World Press, 1993. 136–40.

"On the Third Realm—Aesthetics and National Standards for the Arts." *Journal of Aesthetic Education* 29, no. 2 (1995): 1–6.

O'Neill, Anne-Marie. "Public Exposure." *Courier-Mail* 13 February 1993: 8.

O'Regan, Tom. "(Mis)taking Policy: Notes on the Cultural Policy Debate." *Australian Cultural Studies: A Reader*. Ed. John Frow and Meaghan Morris. Sydney: Allen & Unwin, 1993. 192–206.

Ormsby, Mary. "What's the Bare Facts behind SI's Decision to Ban Naked Players?" *Toronto Star* 3 July 1993: B6.

Orr, Bernadette M., with Bárbara Cruz. *Americas Study Guide*. New York: Oxford University Press, 1993.

Osborne, Thomas. "Bureaucracy as Vocation: Governmentality and Administration in Nineteenth-Century Britain." *Journal of Historical Sociology* 7, no. 3 (1994): 289–313.

O'Shea, Peter. "Out on the Field." *Advocate* no. 691 (1995): 54–57.

Oshima, Nagisa. *Cinema, Censorship, and the State: The Writings of Nagisa Oshima, 1956–1978*. Ed. Annette Michelson. Trans. Dawn Lawson. Cambridge: MIT Press, 1992.

Ouellette, Laurie. "Will the Revolution Be Televised? Camcorders, Activism, and Alternative Television in the 1990s." *Transmission: Toward a Post-Television Culture*, 2d ed. Ed. Peter d'Agostino and David Tafler. Thousand Oaks, Calif.: Sage, 1995. 165–85.

Pacific Film and Television Commission. "Heaven." *Variety* 2–8 May 1994: 47.

Packard, Vance. *The Hidden Persuaders*. Harmondsworth: Penguin, 1960.

"Panel Discussion." *Journal of Arts Management and Law* 21, no. 4 (1992): 349–54.

"Paramount Triggers Fight to Death in Media Takeover Epic." *Sunday Times*. Reprinted in *Australian* 13 June 1989: 15–16.

Pareles, Jon. "A Theme That Never Failed to Accomplish Its Mission." *New York Times* 16 June 1996: 32.

Parsons, Talcott. *Societies: Evolutionary and Comparative Perspectives*. Englewood, Cliffs, N.J.: Prentice Hall, 1966.

Patton, Cindy. "Hegemony and Orgasm—or the Instability of Heterosexual Pornography." *Screen* 30, nos. 1–2 (1989): 100–12.

Pavasaris, Sue. *Queensland Film and Television Industries: Current Problems and Future Options*. Brisbane: Queensland Media Network, 1988.

———. "Warner Roadshow Studios, Qld." *Filmnews* 20, no. 10 (1990): 20.

Pearce, Melissa, and Bronwyn Campbell. "Breaking the Rules." *B and T* 43, no. 1928 (1993): 18–19.

Peckham, Morse. *Art and Pornography: An Experiment in Explanation*. New York: Harper & Row, 1971.

Pendleton, Jennifer. "World Wise." *Emmy* 16, no. 1 (1994): 24–30.

Pener, Degen. "Egos and Ids: He Ain't Heavy, He's My Co-Star." *New York Times* 29 August 1993: 4v.

Peters, Roy. *Television Coverage of Sport*. Stenciled Paper 1. Birmingham: Centre for Contemporary Cultural Studies, 1976.

Peterson, Richard A. "Foreword: Beyond the Production of Culture." *Art, Ideology, and Politics*. Ed. Judith H. Balfe and Margaret Jane Wyszomirski. New York: Praeger, 1985. iii–v.

———. "The Production of Cultural Change: The Case of Contemporary Country Music." *Social Research* 45, no. 2 (1978): 292–314.

Phelan, Peggy. *Unmarked: The Politics of Performance*. London: Routledge, 1993.

Phillips, Dennis. *Ambivalent Allies: Myth and Reality in the Australian-American Relationship*. Ringwood, Australia: Penguin, 1988.

Phillipson, Robert. "English Language Spread Policy." *International Journal of the Sociology of Language* no. 107 (1994): 7–24.

Pike, Andrew, and Ross Cooper. *Australian Film 1900–1977: A Guide to Feature Film Production.* Melbourne: Oxford University Press, 1981.

Pingree, Suzanne, and Robert Hawkins. "US Programs on Australian Television: The Cultivation Effect." *Journal of Communication* 31, no. 1 (1981): 97–105.

Policy Planning and Review, Western Australia Prisons Department. *The Western Australian Prison System.* Perth, 1985.

Poole, Deborah, and Gerardo Rénique. *Peru: Time of Fear.* London: Latin America Bureau, 1992.

Porter, Roy. "History of the Body." *New Perspectives on Historical Writing.* Ed. Peter Burke. Cambridge: Polity, 1991. 206–32.

Porter, Roy, and Lesley Hall. *The Facts of Life: The Creation of Sexual Knowledge in Britain, 1650–1950.* New Haven, Conn.: Yale University Press, 1995.

Postman, A., and L. Stone. *The Ultimate Book of Sports Quotes.* New York: Bantam.

Poulot, Dominique. "Identity as Self-Discovery: The Ecomuseum in France." Trans. Marc Roudebush. *Museum Culture: Histories, Discourses, Spectacles.* Ed. Daniel J. Sherman and Irit Rogoff. Minneapolis: University of Minnesota Press, 1994. 66–84.

Preston, Joan M., and Shirley A. Clair. "Selective Viewing: Cognition, Personality and Television Genres." *British Journal of Social Psychology* 33, no. 3 (1994): 273–88.

Price, Clement Alexander. *Many Voices, Many Opportunities: Cultural Pluralism and American Arts Policy.* New York: American Council for the Arts/Allworth, 1994.

Prince, Stephen, and Wayne E. Hensley. "The Kuleshov Effect: Recreating the Classic Experiment." *Cinema Journal* 31, no. 2 (1992): 59–75.

Pronger, Brian. *The Arena of Masculinity: Sports, Homosexuality, and the Meaning of Sex.* New York: St. Martin's Press, 1990.

"Public Relations Ethics." *Public Relations Review* 20, no. 3 (1994).

"Publisher Told to Pay ET's Costs." *West Australian* 3 March 1993: 12.

Pudovkin, V. I. *Film Technique and Film Acting.* Ed. and Trans. Ivor Montagu. New York: Grove, 1978.

Pullan, Robert. "Payout's All a Matter of Size for Jury." *Australian* 2 February 1995: 2.

Punter, David, ed. *Introduction to Contemporary Cultural Studies.* New York: Longman, 1986.

Puplick, Christopher, and Tony Bennett. "'Arts National' Programme on Museums: A Discussion with Christopher Puplick and Tony Bennett Held Following the Delivery of 'Thanks for the Memories,' August 1989." *Culture and Policy* 1, no. 2 (1990): 67–74.

Pye, Lucian W. "Introduction: Political Culture and Political Development." *Political Culture and Political Development.* Ed. Lucian W. Pye and Sidney Verba. Princeton, N.J.: Princeton University Press, 1965. 3–26.

Quartermaine, Peter. *Thomas Keneally.* London: Edward Arnold, 1991.

Queensland Film Development Office. *Queensland Australia: A Producer's Paradise.* Brisbane, n.d.

Quester, George H. *The International Politics of Television.* Lexington, Mass.: D. C. Heath, 1990.

Rabinowitz, Paula. *They Must Be Represented: The Politics of Documentary.* London: Verso, 1994.

Rafferty, Terrence. "The Illusionist." *New Yorker* 72, no. 14 (1996): 85–87.

Rakow, Lana F. "Feminist Studies: The Next Stage." *Critical Studies in Mass Communication* 6, no. 2 (1989): 209–15.

Ray, Robert B. "Film Studies/Crisis/Experimentation." *Film Criticism* 17, nos. 2–3 (1993): 56–78.

"Real-Life Father/Son TV Drama: Mission:Possible." *Ebony* 44, no. 8 (1989): 70, 72, 74.

Redhead, Steve. *Unpopular Cultures: The Birth of Law and Popular Culture.* Manchester: Manchester University Press, 1995.

Reed, Katherine. "Post-Rodney King: The Reciprocal Gaze." *Images That Injure: Pictorial Stereotypes in the Media.* Ed. Paul Martin Lester. Westport, Conn.: Praeger, 1996. 173–78.

Reeves, Geoffrey. *Communications and the "Third World."* London: Routledge, 1993.

Reiss, Marie. "Police Action 'Out of Mission Impossible.'" *Australian* 25 August 1989: 2.

Renov, Michael. "Introduction: The Truth about Non-Fiction." *Theorizing Documentary.* Ed. Michael Renov. New York: Routledge, 1993. 1–11.

"Rethinking Black (Cultural) Studies." *Callaloo* 19, no. 1 (1996).

"Review Forum on Cultural Studies." *Victorian Studies* 36, no. 4 (1993): 455–72.

Rich, B. Ruby. "Dissed and Disconnected: Notes on Present Ills and Future Dreams." *Transition* no. 62 (1993): 27–47.

Ricks, Christopher. "Wiseman's Witness." *Grand Street* 8, no. 2 (1989): 160–71.

Riddell, Elizabeth. "Entertainment." *Ten Years of Television.* Ed. Mungo MacCallum. Melbourne: Sun, 1968. 27–43.

Ridley, F. F. "Cultural Economics and the Culture of Economists." *Journal of Cultural Economics* 7, no. 1 (1983): 1–17.

Rieff, Philip. "The Case of Dr. Oppenheimer." *On Intellectuals: Theoretical Studies. Case Studies.* Ed. Philip Rieff. New York: Anchor, 1970. 341–69.

Ries, Ivor. "Video Shows Recruit Man Trying to Bribe." *Australian Financial Review* 3 November 1988: 21.

Rigby, Mark T. "Ozone Objective: To Save the Earth: Mission Impossible." *Courier-Mail* 11 July 1989: 20.

Riggs, Karen E. "The Case of the Mysterious Ritual: Murder Dramas and Older Women Viewers." *Critical Studies in Mass Communication* 13, no. 4 (1996): 309–23.

Roberts, Sam. "Alone in the Vast Wasteland." *New York Times* 24 December 1995: n.p.

Roddick, Nick. "A Hard Sell: The State of Documentary Film Marketing." *Dox* no. 2 (Summer 1994): 30–32.

Rogers, James M. "Social Science Disciplines and Policy Research: The Case of Political Science." *Policy Studies Review* 9, no. 1 (1989): 13–28.

Ronell, Avital. "Video/Television/Rodney King: Twelve Steps beyond the Pleasure Principle." *differences* 4, no. 2 (1992): 1–15.

Rorty, Richard. "Intellectuals in Politics." *Dissent* 38, no. 4 (1991): 483–90.

———. "Richard Rorty Replies." *Dissent* 39, no. 2 (1992): 265–67.

Rosaldo, Renato. "Cultural Citizenship and Educational Democracy." *Cultural Anthropology* 9, no. 3 (1994): 402–11.

———. "Whose Cultural Studies?" *American Anthropologist* 96, no. 3 (1994): 524–29.

Rose, Nikolas, and Peter Miller. "Political Power beyond the State: Problematics of Government." *British Journal of Sociology* 43, no. 2 (1992): 173–205.

Rosen, James S. "Dan the Man." *City* 1, no. 3 (1994): 23–24.

Rosenberg, Warren. "Making Manhood Visible." *masculinities* 2, no. 3 (1994): 71–79.

Ross, Andrew. "Ballots, Bullets, or Batmen: Can Cultural Studies Do the Right Thing?" *Screen* 31, no. 1 (1990): 26–44.

———. "On Intellectuals in Politics." *Dissent* 39, no. 2 (1992): 263–65.

Rosteck, Thomas. "Cultural Studies and Rhetorical Studies." *Quarterly Journal of Speech* 81, no. 3 (1995): 386–403.

Routt, William D. "The Truth of Documentary." *Continuum* 5, no. 1 (1991): 60-75.

Rovin, Jeff. *The Great Television Series.* South Brunswick: A. S. Barnes, 1977.

Rowe, David. *Popular Cultures: Rock Music, Sport and the Politics of Pleasure.* London: Sage, 1995.

Rowe, David, and Peter Brown. "Promoting Women's Sport: Theory, Policy and Practice." *Leisure Studies* 13, no. 2 (1994): 97–110.

Rowell, John. "The Politics of Cultural Appropriation." *Journal of Value Inquiry* 29, no. 1 (1995): 137–42.

Ruscio, Kenneth P. "Policy Cultures: The Case of Science Policy in the United States." *Science, Technology, and Human Values* 19, no. 2 (1994): 205–22.

Rushton, J. Philippe, and Anthony F. Bogaert. "Race Differences in Sexual Behavior: Testing an Evolutionary Hypothesis." *Journal of Research in Personality* 21, no. 4 (1987): 529–51.

Russo, Vito. *The Celluloid Closet: Homosexuality in the Movies,* rev. ed. New York: Harper & Row, 1987.

Ruthrof, Horst. *Pandora and Occam: On the Limits of Language and Literature.* Bloomington: Indiana University Press, 1992.

Ryan, Colleen. "Studio Profit Forecasts a Mystery." *Sydney Morning Herald* 22 November 1995: 8.

Ryan, Rosemary. "Undie Revolution Led by Sexy Men." *Ad News* 4 June 1993: 6.

Sacks, Harvey. *Lectures on Conversation,* vol. 2. Ed. Gail Jefferson. Oxford: Basil Blackwell, 1992.

———. "Notes on Police Assessment of Moral Character." *Studies in Social Interaction.* Ed. David Sudnow. New York: Free Press, 1972. 280–93.

Safire, William. "On Language: The Horny Dilemma." *New York Times* 6 February 1994: Magazine 10.

Salzman, Jack. "Editor's Note." *Prospects: An Annual Journal of American Cultural Studies* no. 1 (1975): iii.

Saunders, David. *Legal Decisions and Cultural Theory.* Cultural Policy Studies Occasional Paper No. 6. Brisbane: Institute for Cultural Policy Studies, 1989.

Savan, Leslie. *The Sponsored Life: Ads, TV, and American Culture.* Philadelphia: Temple University Press, 1994.

Sayer, Andrew. "Cultural Studies and 'the Economy, Stupid.'" *Environment and Planning D: Society and Space* 12, no. 6 (1994): 635–37.

Scarry, Elaine. *The Body in Pain: The Making and Unmaking of the World.* New York: Oxford University Press, 1985.

*Scene on TV.* Advertisement. *Sunday Mail* 28 May 1989: 18.

"Seedy CDs." *Economist* 315, no. 7656 (1990): 73.

Schaefer, George. "The Independent Producer." *The Meaning of Commercial Television: The Texas-Stanford Seminar, 1966.* Ed. Stanley T. Donner. Austin: University of Texas Press, 1968. 21–25.

Schiller, Herbert I. *Culture, Inc.: The Corporate Takeover of Public Expression.* New York: Oxford University Press, 1989.

———. "Transnational Media: Creating Consumers Worldwide." *Journal of International Affairs* 47, no. 1 (1993): 47–58.

Schivelbusch, Wolfgang. *The Railway Journey: The Industrialization of Time and Space in the 19th Century*. Trans. Anselm Hollo. Berkeley: University of California Press, 1977.

Schlesinger, Philip. *Media, State and Nation: Political Violence and Collective Identities*. London: Sage, 1991.

———. "On National Identity: Some Conceptions and Misconceptions Criticized." *Social Science Information* 26, no. 2 (1987): 219–64.

Schlesinger, Philip, R. Emerson Dobash, Russell P. Dobash, and C. Kay Weaver. *Women Viewing Violence*. London: British Film Institute, 1992.

Schøu, Soren. "Postwar Americanisation and the Revitalisation of European Culture." *Media Cultures: Reappraising Transnational Media*. Ed. Michael Skovmand and Kim Christian Schroder. London: Routledge, 1992. 142–58.

Schwab, Shelly. "Television in the 90's: Revolution or Confusion?" *Tenth Joseph I. Lubin Memorial Lecture*. New York University, New York, 1 March 1994.

Schwarz, K. Robert. "Classical Music; A Brash Opera Holds a Mirror to Gay Life in America." *New York Times* 2 April 1995: 33.

Schwichtenberg, Cathy. "Feminist Cultural Studies." *Critical Studies in Mass Communication* 6, no. 2 (1989): 202–8.

Sechrest, Dale K., William Liquori, and Jim Perry. "Using Video Technology in Police Patrol." *The Media and Criminal Justice Policy: Recent Research and Social Effects*. Ed. Ray Surette. Springfield, Ill.: Charles C Thomas, 1990. 255–64.

Sewell, James P. "UNESCO: Pluralism Rampant." *The Anatomy of Influence: Decision Making in International Organization*. Ed. Robert W. Cox and Harold K. Jacobson. New Haven, Conn.: Yale University Press, 1974. 139–74.

Shafran, Alexander. *Airbrush Photo Retouching Manual: The Techniques of Airbrush Retouching Positive Prints and Negatives*. Philadelphia: Chilton, 1968.

Shannon, Patrick, and Henry A. Giroux. "Editor's Comments." *Review of Education/Pedagogy/Cultural Studies* 16, no. 1 (1994): v.

Shapiro, Michael J. *Reading "Adam Smith": Desire, History, and Value*. Newbury Park, Calif.: Sage, 1993.

———. *Reading the Postmodern: Political Theory as Textual Practice*. Minneapolis: University of Minnesota Press, 1992.

Sharkey, Betsey. "Summer Sequels." *American Film* 14, no. 8 (1989): 40–41.

Sheehan, Neil. "The Last Battle." *New Yorker* 71, no. 9 (1995): 78–87.

Sherwood, Steven Jay, Philip Smith, and Jeffrey C. Alexander. "The British are Coming . . . Again! The Hidden Agenda of 'Cultural Studies.'" *Contemporary Sociology* 22, no. 3 (1993): 370–75.

Shilling, Chris. Review of *Body Matters*. *Sociological Review* 42, no. 1 (1994): 143–45.

Shils, Edward. "Mass Society and Its Culture." *Reader in Public Opinion and Communication*, 2d ed. Ed. Bernard Berelson and Morris Janowitz. New York: Free Press, 1966. 505–28.

Shoebridge, Neil. "League's New Tack Wins Converts." *Business Review Weekly* 11, no. 40 (1989): 164, 167.

———. "Networks Shape Up for the Ratings Battle." *Business Review Weekly* 11, no. 24 (1989): 81.

———. "No One Rushes to Be in Pictures." *Business Review Weekly* 11, no. 24 (1989): 135–38.

Sholle, David. "Resisting Disciplines: Repositioning Media Studies in the University." *Communication Theory* 5, no. 2 (1995): 130–43.

Sider, Daphne. "Dressing Room Is Still Boys Only." *Sydney Morning Herald* 12 November 1993: 2.

Sikes, Gini. "The Real People's Court." *TV Guide* 20 January 1994: 30–35.

Silber, John R. "Television: A Personal View." *The Meaning of Commercial Television: The Texas-Stanford Seminar, 1966*. Ed. Stanley T. Donner. Austin: University of Texas Press, 1968. 113–39.

Sills, Judith. "Prime Time Passion." *Sunday Mail* 3 September 1989: 44.

Silverstone, Roger. "Television: Text or Discourse?" *Science as Culture* 6 (1989): 104–23.

Simmel, Georg. "The Metropolis and Mental Life." Trans. Kurt H. Wolff. *Sociological Perspectives: Selected Readings*. Ed. Kenneth Thompson and Jeremy Tunstall. Harmondsworth: Penguin, 1976. 82–93.

Simmons, Charles E. "The Los Angeles Rebellion: Class, Race and Misinformation." *Why L.A. Happened: Implications of the '92 Los Angeles Rebellion*. Ed. Haki R. Madhubuti. Chicago: Third World Press, 1993. 141–55.

Simon, Art. *Dangerous Knowledge: The JFK Assassination in Art and Film*. Philadelphia: Temple University Press, 1996.

Simpson, Christopher. *Science of Coercion: Communication Research and Psychological Warfare 1945–1960*. New York: Oxford University Press, 1994.

Simpson, Mark. *Male Impersonators: Men Performing Masculinity*. London: Routledge, 1994.

Skolnick, Jerome H., and James J. Fyfe. *Above the Law: Police and the Excessive Use of Force.* New York: Free Press, 1993.

Smith, Adam. *The Wealth of Nations,* books 1–3. Ed. Andrew Skinner. Harmondsworth: Penguin, 1970.

Smith, Anna Deveare. *Twilight: Los Angeles, 1992.* New York: Doubleday, 1994.

Smith, Margaret. "Milk Is Metaphor for Values in Conflict." *Australian Financial Review* 21 June 1985: 39.

Smith, Paul. "A Memory of Marxism." *Polygraph* nos. 6-7 (1993): 98–105.

Smith, Todd D. "Gay Male Pornography and the East: Re-Orienting the Orient." *History of Photography* 18, no. 1 (1994): 13–21.

Society of Cinema Studies. *General Business Meeting.* 1992.

Sofoulis, Zoë. "Position-Envy and the Subsumption of Feminism: Some Hypotheses." *Cultural Studies: Pluralism and Theory.* Ed. David Bennett. Melbourne: Melbourne University Department of English, 1993. 213–20.

Solomon, William S. "Framing Violence: Press Coverage of the L.A.P.D./Rodney King Beating and First Trial." *New Political Science* no. 27 (Winter 1993): 85–104.

Solomon-Godeau, Abigail. *Photography at the Dock: Essays on Photographic History, Institutions, and Practices.* Minneapolis: University of Minnesota Press, 1991.

Sonenstein, Raphael J. *Politics in Black and White: Race and Power in Los Angeles.* Princeton, N.J.: Princeton University Press, 1993.

Soren, Barbara. "The Museum as Curricular Site." *Journal of Aesthetic Education* 26, no. 3 (1992): 91–101.

Sorensen, Colin. "Theme Parks and Time Machines." *The New Museology.* Ed. Peter Vergo. London: Reaktion, 1991. 60–73.

Speckens, Anne E. M., Michiel W. Hengeveld, Guus Lycklama à Nijeholt, Albert M. van Hemert, and Keith E. Hawton. "Psychosexual Functioning of Partners of Men with Presumed Non-Organic Erectile Dysfunction: Cause or Consequence of the Disorder?" *Archives of Sexual Behavior* 24, no. 2 (1995): 157–72.

Springhall, John. "'Disseminating Impure Literature': The 'Penny Dreadful' Publishing Business since 1860." *Economic History Review* 47, no. 3 (1994): 567–84.

Stahler, Gerald J., and William R. Tash. "Centers and Institutes in the Research University: Issues, Problems, and Prospects." *Journal of Higher Education* 65, no. 5 (1994): 540–54.

Stam, Robert. *Subversive Pleasures: Bakhtin, Cultural Criticism, and Film.* Baltimore: Johns Hopkins University Press, 1989.

Stark, Andrew. "'Political-Discourse' Analysis and the Debate over Canada's Lobbying Legislation." *Canadian Journal of Political Science* 25, no. 3 (1992): 513–34.

Starke, J. G. "Showing to Jury of Videotape of Examination de bene esse." *Australian Law Journal* 62, no. 9 (1988): 727–28.

"Statement of the Case." *Commonwealth v. Frederick Wiseman.* Superior Court Civil Action no. 87583. 1989.

Stavans, Ilan. "Two Peruvians: How a Novelist and a Terrorist Came to Represent Peru's Divided Soul." *Transition* no. 61 (1993): 18–39.

Stein, Elliott. "Mothers and Milk." *Film Comment* 20, no. 6 (1984): 64, 68–71.

Stevens, John D. "Sex as Education: A Note on the Pre-1930 Social Hygiene Films." *Film and History* 13, no. 4 (1983): 84–87.

Stevenson, Richard W. "Lights! Camera! Europe!" *New York Times* 6 February 1994: 1, 6.

Stokes, Walter R. *Modern Pattern for Marriage: The Newer Understanding of Married Love.* New York: Rinehart, 1948.

Stoltenberg, John. *Refusing to Be a Man.* Glasgow: Fontana/Collins, 1990.

Storey, John. *An Introductory Guide to Cultural Theory and Popular Culture.* Athens: University of Georgia Press, 1993.

Straayer, Chris. *Deviant Eyes, Deviant Bodies: Sexual Re-Orientations in Film and Video.* New York: Columbia University Press, 1996.

———. "The Seduction of Boundaries: Feminist Fluidity in Annie Sprinkle's Art/Education/Sex." *Dirty Looks: Women, Pornography, Power.* Ed. Pamela Church Gibson and Roma Gibson. London: British Film Institute, 1993. 156–75.

Strange, Susan. "The Limits of Politics." *Government and Opposition* 30, no. 3 (1995): 291–311.

———. "States, Firms and Diplomacy." *International Affairs* 68, no. 1 (1992): 1–15.

Stratton, David. *The Avocado Plantation: Boom and Bust in the Australian Film Industry.* Sydney: Macmillan, 1990.

Stratton, Jon. "Australia—This Sporting Life." *Power Play: Essays in the Sociology of Australian Sport.* Ed. Geoffrey Lawrence and David Rowe. Sydney: Hale and Iremonger, 1986. 85–114.

Straw, Will. "Shifting Boundaries, Lines of Descent: Cultural Studies and Institutional Realignments." *Relocating Cultural Studies: Developments in Theory and Research.* Ed. Valda Blundell, John Shepherd, and Ian Taylor. London: Routledge, 1993. 86–102.

Streeter, Thomas. *Selling the Air: A Critique of the Policy of Commercial Broadcasting in the United States*. Chicago: University of Chicago Press, 1996.

Strickland, Katrina. "Moving Pictures." *Australian* 16 January 1995: 30.

Sturken, Marita. *Tangled Memories: The Vietnam War, the AIDS Epidemic, and the Politics of Remembering*. Berkeley: University of California Press, 1997.

Sullivan, Patrick J. "'What's All the Cryin' About?' The Films of Frederick Wiseman." *Massachusetts Review* 13, no. 3 (1972): 452–68.

Surette, Ray. *Media, Crime, and Criminal Justice: Images and Realities*. Belmont, Calif.: Wadsworth, 1992.

Surette, Ray, and W. Clinton Terry. "Media Technology and the Courts: The Case of Closed Circuit Video Arraignments in Miami, Florida." *The Media and Criminal Justice Policy: Recent Research and Social Effects*. Ed. Ray Surette. Springfield, Ill.: Charles C Thomas, 1990. 243–53.

Svetkey, Benjamin. "Why Movie Ratings Don't Work." *Entertainment Weekly* no. 250 (1994): 26–33.

Swenson, Jill Dianne. "Rodney King, Reginald Denny, and TV News: Cultural (Re)Construction of Racism." *Journal of Communication Inquiry* 19, no. 1 (1995): 75–88.

Synnott, Anthony. *The Body Social: Symbolism, Self and Society*. London: Routledge, 1993.

Syvet, Paul. "DEL Starts Over Again." *Australian Business* 8, no. 29 (1988): 32-33.

Tagg, John. "A Discourse (with Shape of Reason Missing)." *Art History* 15, no. 3 (1992): 351–73.

Tarazona-Sevillano, Gabriela, with John B. Reuter. *Sendero Luminoso and the Threat of Narcoterrorism*. New York: Praeger, 1990.

Taylor, Charles. "Titicut Follies." *Sight and Sound* 57, no. 2 (1988): 98–103.

Taylor, Lewis. "Peru's 'Time of Cholera': Economic Decline and Civil War, 1985–1990." *Third World Quarterly* 14, no. 1 (1993): 173–79.

"Teach America's History." *American Quarterly* 46, no. 3 (1994).

Terrace, Vincent. *The Complete Encyclopedia of Television Programs 1947–76*, Vol. 2, L–Z. South Brunswick: A. S. Barnes, 1976.

Thaler, Paul. *The Watchful Eye: American Justice in the Age of the Television Trial*. Westport, Conn.: Praeger, 1994.

Thelen, David. "History after the Enola Gay Controversy: An Introduction." *Journal of American History* 82, no. 3 (1995): 1029–35.

"Theme: Culture and Urban Regeneration: Some European Examples." *Built Environment* 18, no. 2 (1992).

Thomas, Ronald R. "The Fingerprint of the Foreigner: Colonizing the Criminal Body in 1890s Detective Fiction and Criminal Anthropology." *ELH* 61, no. 3 (1994): 655–83.

Thorp, Diana. "League Star Hurt by Photo, Says Wife." *Australian* 4 February 1993: 3.

Throsby, C. D., and G. A. Withers. *The Economics of the Performing Arts*. New York: St. Martin's Press, 1979.

Thwaites, Tony, Lloyd Davis, and Warwick Mules. *Tools for Cultural Studies: An Introduction*. Melbourne: Macmillan, 1994.

Tiefer, Leonore. "In Pursuit of the Perfect Penis." *American Behavioral Scientist* 29, no. 5 (1986): 579–99.

Todorov, Tzvetan. *Genres in Discourse*. Trans. Catherine Porter. Cambridge: Cambridge University Press, 1990.

"Top 100 All-Time Domestic Grossers." *Variety* 17–23 October 1994: M-60.

Towse, Ruth, and Mark Crain. "Editorial: The Culture of Cultural Economics." *Journal of Cultural Economics* 18, no. 1 (1994): 1–2.

Treweek, Ann. "Ex-Prisoners Flock to Visit Fremantle Jail: Bleak, Bucket-Toilet Cells Shock Most Jail Visitors." *Sunday Times* 6 December 1992: n.p.

Trigger, David S. "Australian Cultural Studies: Radical Critique or Vacuous Posturing?" *Anthropological Forum* 6, no. 4 (1993): 607–13.

Triggs, Teal. "Framing Masculinity: Herb Ritts, Bruce Weber and the Body Perfect." *Chic Thrills: A Fashion Reader*. Ed. Juliet Ash and Elizabeth Wilson. Berkeley: University of California Press, 1993. 25–29.

Tulloch, John, and Marian Tulloch. "Understanding TV Violence: A Multifaceted Cultural Analysis." *Nation, Culture, Text: Australian Cultural and Media Studies*. Ed. Graeme Turner. London: Routledge, 1993. 211–45.

Turim, Maureen. *Flashbacks in Film: History and Memory*. New York: Routledge, 1989.

Turner, Graeme. *British Cultural Studies: An Introduction*. Boston: Unwin Hyman, 1990.

———. "Cultural Policy and National Culture." *Nation, Culture, Text: Australian Cultural and Media Studies*. Ed. Graeme Turner. London: Routledge, 1993. 67–71.

———. "Dilemmas of a Cultural Critic: Australian Cultural Studies Today." *Australian Journal of Communication* no. 16 (December 1989): 1–12.

———. *Making It National: Nationalism and Australian Popular Culture*. Sydney: Allen & Unwin, 1994.

———. *National Fictions: Literature, Film and the Construction of Australian Narrative*, 2d ed. Sydney: Allen & Unwin, 1993.

————, ed. *Nation, Culture, Text: Australian Cultural and Media Studies*. London: Routledge, 1993.

Turner, Patricia A. *I Heard It through the Grapevine: Rumor in African-American Culture*. Berkeley: University of California Press, 1993.

Udovitch, Mim. "The Cutting Edge." *Village Voice* 20 November 1993: 16.

Urban, Andrew. "Coote Does Hollywood." *Bulletin* 29 August 1989: 102–3.

Urla, Jacqueline. "Cultural Politics in an Age of Statistics: Numbers, Nations, and the Making of Identity." *American Ethnologist* 20, no. 4 (1993): 818–43.

Vahimagi, Tise. "Mission: Impossible CBS, 1966-73." *Primetime* no. 9 (Winter 1984–85): 13.

Vargas Llosa, Alvaro. *The Madness of Things Peruvian: Democracy under Siege*. New Brunswick, N.J.: Transaction, 1994.

Veitch, Carol. "Hollywood on Our Doorstep." *Sunday Mail* 5 February 1989: 9.

"Violent Reactions." *Economist* 332, no. 7876 (1994): 18.

Volkerling, Michael. "Death or Transfiguration: The Future for Cultural Policy in New Zealand." *Culture and Policy* 6, no. 1 (1994): 7–28.

Walkowitz, Rebecca L. "Reproducing Reality: Murphy Brown and Illegitimate Politics." *Media Spectacles*. Ed. Marjorie Garber, Jann Matlock, and Rebecca L. Walkowitz. New York: Routledge, 1993. 40–56.

Wallerstein, Edward. *Circumcision: An American Health Fallacy*. New York: Springer, 1980.

Warner Village Roadshow Studios. Promotional material, n.d.

Washington, Paul. "'Being Post-Colonial': Culture, Policy and Government." *Southern Review* 28, no. 3 (1995): 273–82.

Wasko, Janet. *Hollywood in the Information Age: Beyond the Silver Screen*. Cambridge: Polity, 1994.

Wasser, Frederick. "Is Hollywood America? The Trans-Nationalization of the American Film Industry." *Critical Studies in Mass Communication* 12, no. 4 (1995): 423–37.

Waters, John. "Out on the Edge." *Index on Censorship* 24, no. 6 (1995): 10–19.

————. *Trash Trio — Three Screenplays: Pink Flamingos, Desperate Living, Flamingos Forever*. New York: Vintage, 1988.

Watkins, Peter. "Media Repression: A Personal Statement." *Explorations in Film Theory: Selected Essays from Ciné-Tracts*. Ed. Ron Burnett. Bloomington: Indiana University Press, 1991. 221–28.

Waugh, Thomas. "Gay vs. Straight." *Jump Cut* no. 30 (June 1985): 30–32.

————. "Lesbian and Gay Documentary: Minority Self-Imaging, Oppositional Film Practice, and the Question of Image Ethics." *Image Ethics: The Moral Rights of Subjects in Photographs, Film, and Television*. Ed. Larry Gross, John Stuart Katz, and Jay Ruby. New York: Oxford University Press, 1988. 248–72.

Waye, Vicki. "Video Tape Recording of Custodial Interrogation." *Adelaide Law Review* 12, no. 2 (1989): 230–42.

Weber, Max. *General Economic History*. Trans. Frank H. Knight. New York: Collier, 1961.

Wedell, George. "Prospects for Television in Europe." *Government and Opposition* 29, no. 3 (1994): 315–31.

Weiner, Rex. "Special F/X: Hollywood Splices Mother Nature." *Variety* 29 August–4 September 1994: 7, 10.

Weissman, Gary. "A Fantasy of Witnessing." *Media, Culture & Society* 17, no. 2 (1995): 293–307.

Welch, Lawrence S., and Reijo Luostarinen. "Internationalization: Evolution of a Concept." *Journal of General Management* 14, no. 2 (1988): 34–55.

Wells, Jeff. "A Slavering Ambush If I Should Dare to Catch It!" *Australian* 6 February 1989: 22.

West, Candace, and Sarah Fenstermaker. "Doing Difference." *Gender & Society* 9, no. 1 (1995): 8–37.

West, Candace, and Don H. Zimmerman. "Doing Gender." *Gender & Society* 1, no. 2 (1987): 125–51.

Westlin, Alan. "'You Start Off with a Bromide': Wiseman on Film and Civil Liberties." *Frederick Wiseman*. Ed. Thomas R. Atkins. New York: Simon & Schuster, 1976. 47–66.

WGBH. *Americas Biographical Notes*. Boston, 1992.

————. *Americas Fact Sheet/Listings*. Boston, 1992.

————. *Americas Series Backgrounder*. "Discovering AMERICAS: A Look behind the Scenes." Boston, 1992.

————. *Americas Series Press Release*. Boston, n.d.

White, Geoffrey M. "Culture Talk in the 90s." *Culture and Policy* 6, no. 2 (1994): 5–22.

White, Hayden. *The Content of the Form: Narrative Discourse and Historical Representation*. Baltimore: Johns Hopkins University Press, 1992.

White, Les. "My Father Is a Schindler Jew." *Jump Cut* no. 39 (June 1994): 3–6.

White, Patrick J. *The Complete* Mission: Impossible *Dossier*. New York: Avon, 1991.

Whitlock, Gillian. "Queensland: The State of the Art on 'the Last Frontier.'" *Westerly* 29, no. 2 (1984): 85–90.

Whitt, J. Allen, and Allen J. Share. "The Performing Arts as an Urban Development Strategy: Transforming the Central City." *Research in Politics and Society* no. 3 (1988): 155–72.

Wicke, Jennifer. *Advertising Fictions: Literature, Advertisement, and Social Reading*. New York: Columbia University Press, 1988.

Wicking, Christopher, and Tise Vahimagi. *The American Vein: Directors and Directions in Television*. New York: E. P. Dutton, 1979.

Wicks, Paul. "Nine Sticks with Winning Series." *Courier-Mail* 3 August 1989: 20.

Wilcox, Michael. *Part Indigenous Drama Co-Productions*. Australian Content Inquiry Discussion Paper. Canberra: Australian Broadcasting Tribunal, 1988.

Wildt, Michael. "The Invented and the Real: Historiographical Notes on Schindler's List." Trans. Pamela Selwyn. *History Workshop Journal* no. 41 (Spring 1996): 240–49.

Williams, Linda. "Fetishism and the Visual Pleasure of Hard Core: Marx, Freud, and the 'Money Shot.'" *Quarterly Review of Film and Video* 11, no. 2 (1989): 23–42.

Williams, Patricia J. "The Rules of the Game." *Reading Rodney King/Reading Urban Uprising*. Ed. Robert Gooding-Williams. New York: Routledge, 1993. 51–55.

Williams, Patrick, and Laura Chrisman, eds. *Colonial Discourse and Post-Colonial Theory: A Reader*. New York: Columbia University Press, 1994.

Williams, Raymond. *The Long Revolution*. Harmondsworth: Pelican, 1975.

———. *Marxism and Literature*. Oxford: Oxford University Press, 1977.

———. *The Politics of Modernism: Against the New Conformists*. Ed. Tony Pinkney. London: Verso, 1989.

Winkelman, Michael. "Cultural Factors in Criminal Defense Proceedings." *Human Organization* 55, no. 2 (1996): 154–59.

Winn, Peter. *Americas: The Changing Face of Latin America and the Caribbean*. New York: Pantheon, 1992.

———. *Americas Telecourse Faculty Guide*. New York: Oxford University Press, 1993.

———. Introductory remarks to conference on *The Americas*. Center for Media, Culture, and History, New York University, New York, 29–30 October 1993.

Winston, Brian. *Claiming the Real: The Documentary Film Revisited*. London: British Film Institute, 1995.

———. "The Tradition of the Victim in Griersonian Documentary." *Image Ethics: The Moral Rights of Subjects in Photographs, Film, and Television*. Ed. Larry Gross, John Stuart Katz, and Jay Ruby. New York: Oxford University Press, 1988. 34–57.

Winterson, Jeanette. *Sexing the Cherry*. London: Vintage, 1989.

Wiseman, Frederick. "Editing as a Four-Way Conversation." *Dox* no. 1 (Spring 1994): 4–6.

———. "Frederick Wiseman Replies." *Frederick Wiseman*. Ed. Thomas R. Atkins. New York: Simon & Schuster, 1976. 69–73.

———. "A Nonscholar's Approach to Monologue." *Threepenny Review* no. 68 (Winter 1997): 26–29.

Wittgenstein, Ludwig. *The Blue and Brown Books: Preliminary Studies for the "Philosophical Investigations."* New York: Harper Torchbooks, 1958.

———. *Tractatus Logico-Philosophicus*. Trans. D. F. Pears and B. F. McGuinness. London: Routledge and Kegan Paul, 1981.

Wolf, Thomas. "The Role of Research in Developing Cultural Policy." *Journal of Arts Management and Law* 13, no. 1 (1983): 184–86.

Wolfe, Alan. "The Culture of Cultural Studies." *Partisan Review* 53, no. 3 (1996): 485–92.

Worssam, Adrian. "Handsome Myth." *XY: Men, Sex, Politics* 3, no. 2 (1993): 3–4.

Wright, Handel Kashope. "Take Birmingham to the Curb, Here Comes African Cultural Studies: An Exercise in Revisionist Historiography." *University of Toronto Quarterly* 65, no. 2 (1996): 355–65.

Wright, Lawrence. "Silent Sperm." *New Yorker* 71, no. 44 (1996): 42–48.

Wyszomirski, Margaret Jane. "Federal Cultural Support: Toward a New Paradigm?" *Journal of Arts Management, Law and Society* 25, no. 1 (1995): 69–83.

Young, James E. "Holocaust Memorials in America: Public Art as Process." *Critical Issues in Public Art: Content, Context, and Controversy*. Ed. Harriet F. Senie and Sally Webster. New York: Iconeditions, 1992. 57–70.

Yúdice, George. "Civil Society, Consumption, and Governmentality in an Age of Global Restructuring: An Introduction." *Social Text* 13, no. 4 (1995): 1–25.

Zimmerman, Diane Leenheer. "False Light Invasion of Privacy: The Light That Failed." *New York University Law Review* 64, no. 2 (1989): 364–453.

Zipporah Films. *Award Winning Documentaries by Frederick Wiseman*, Fall 1991/92. Cambridge, Mass., 1991.

Zolberg, Vera L. "Museum Culture and the Threat to National Identity in the Age of the GATT." *Journal of Arts Management, Law and Society* 25, no. 1 (1995): 5–16.

# Index

Bragg, Billy, 28
Brambilla, Marco, 190; *Demolition Man*, 190
Brando, Marlon, 38–39, 120
Brecht, Bertolt, 61
Brill, Steven, 191
Briseno, Ted, 187
Brody, Samuel, 248
Brooks, Albert, 228–29; *Real Life*, 228–29
Brooks, Peter, 83
Brown, Jim, 239
Bulcock, James, 223
Bulger, James, 62, 199–200, 209
Burke, Kenneth, 38
Burns, Ken, 210; *Baseball*, 210
Burrows, A. R., 27
Burton, Crawford, 112–13, 140
Burton, Tim, 57; *Batman*, 57
*Burton v. Crowell Pub. Co.*, 112–13, 257
Bush, George, 213
Buxton, David, 160

Calder, Angus, 97
Caldwell, Ben, 78
Cale, John, 108
*California v. Powell, Wind, Briseno, and Koon*, 186–92
Callinan, Ian, 110, 139
Cameron, Deborah, 129
Cameron, James, 184; *True Lies*, 184
Campos, Yezid, 206–07
*Candid Camera*, 229
*Candid Mike*, 229
Carey, James, 82
Cartland, Barbara, 33
Cassidy, David, 56
*Cathy Come Home*, 207
Chatterjee, Partha, 55
Chauvel, Charles, 145; *Sons of Matthew*, 145
Chesterton, G. K., 265
Chomsky, Noam, 96
Chow, Rey, 46
Citizenship, 4, 70, 72, 74, 77, 79, 134, 151, 154–55, 182–83, 208–15, 219, 227, 233–41, 246–52, 254, 258, 263–66
Clark, Kenneth, 133
Cleland, John, 60; *Fanny Hill; or, Memoirs of a Woman of Pleasure*, 60
Clinton, Bill, 38, 83, 131, 213, 260
Cobb, Portia, 190; *No Justice, No Peace*, 190
Coburn, James, 180
Cochrane, Brett M., 111–12
Coleman, Wil, 138–39
Collini, Stefan, 64
*Columbo*, 143
*Commonwealth and Others v. Frederick Wiseman and Others*, 216
Comstock, George, 60–61
Connally, John, 194
Connell, R. W., 137–38
Conner, Bruce, 192; *Report*, 192
Connery, Sean, 174
Connop, Cynthia, 132; *Sacred Sex*, 132
Cooke, Sam, 89

Coote, Greg, 170, 176
Copeland, Alan, 162
Cornell, John, 181; *Crocodile Dundee II*, 181
Costner, Kevin, 171, 174; *Dances with Wolves*, 174
Craik, Jennifer, 88
Cronkite, Walter, 232
Cukor, George, 51; *Gaslight*, 51
Cultural imperialism, 51–52, 142, 145–51, 174–75
Cultural policy studies, 71–90, 265
Cultural studies, 40–58, 64, 69–71, 73, 78–80, 82, 89–92, 156, 258–59, 263–64, 267
Cunningham, Stuart, 68–70, 81, 89, 96, 264
Curran, James, 41, 49
Curtiz, Michael, 159, 180; *Casablanca*, 159; *Dodge City*, 180
Cutter, Ammi, 230

*Dallas*, 25, 149
Daguerrotrope, 5, 32, 34, 59, 134
Dahl, John, 119; *The Last Seduction*, 119
*Danger Man*, 160
Danto, Arthur, 57
D'Arcy, Les, 142
Daves, Delmer, 51; *Dark Passage*, 51
Davidson, John, 130
*DEA*, 19
Dead Kennedys, 205
Dean, Carolyn, 131
de Beaufort, Marc, 206–7, 211
Debord, Guy, 38
*Def 2*, 162
Defoe, Daniel, *Life and Strange Surprising Adventures of Robinson Crusoe, The*, 35
DeGrane, Lloyd, 211; *Tuned In: Television in American Life*, 211
de Laurentiis, Dino, 143, 154, 173
Deleuze, Gilles, 38
DeLillo, Don, 129; *End Zone*, 129
DeLorean, John, 199
Demme, Jonathan, 197; *Philadelphia*, 197
De Palma, Brian, 160, 181, 192; *Blow Out*, 192; *Mission: Impossible*, 160, 181
Dermody, Susan, 153
Derrida, Jacques, 242
Dershowitz, Alan, 223
Dervin, Daniel, 127
DeSalvo, Albert, 223
Dethridge, Joseph, 195–96
Deveson, Anne, 110
*Devil and Miss Jones, Part 3, The*, 118
Diawara, Manthia, 43–44
DiMaggio, Paul, 87–88
Divine, 137
Doc Box, 162
Documentary, 121–22, 183–84, 201, 203, 207, 217, 225–31
*Documentary Films of Frederick Wiseman A to Z*, 225, 230
Donald, James, 181
Douglas, Roger, 161
*Dragnet*, 201
Dryzek, John, 86
Du, Soon Ja, 195

Latour, Bruno, 261
Lavarch, Michael, 110
Lawrence, D. H., 137; *Lady Chatterley's Lover*, 91
Lawson, Sylvia, 153
Leacock, Richard, 226
*Leave It to Beaver*, 66, 143
Leavis, F. R., 66, 87, 89
Lee, Christopher, 169
Lee, Peggy, 137
Lee, Spike, 57–58, 190; *Do the Right Thing*, 57; *Malcolm X*, 58, 174–75, 190
Lehman, Peter, 119
Leonard, Elmore, 129; *City Primeval*, 129; *Split Images*, 129
Lesbian Avengers, 162
Liebes, Tamar, 146, 149
Limbaugh, Rush, 191
Lindblom, Charles, 77
Little, Billy, 239
Little River Band, 65
Loftis, Elizabeth, 188
*Lois & Clark: The New Adventures of Superman*, 39
*Lonesome Dove*, 142
Lovell, Terry, 41
Lowy, Frank, 142
Lucia, Cynthia, 230
Lue, Tom F., 123
Lugosi, Bela, 51, 248
Luhmann, Niklas, 130
Lukács, György, 72
Lull, James, 186
Lumière, Auguste, 7
Lumière, Louis, 7; *L'Arrivée d'un Train en Gare*, 7
Lury, Celia, 41
Lynch, David, 19, 162; *Wild at Heart*, 162; *Twin Peaks*, 19
Lyotard, Jean-François, 96

MacCabe, Colin, 89
Macdonald, Dwight, 32
MacFadden, Bernarr, 124
Machiavelli, Niccolò, 14
MacInnes, Judy, 119
Mackey, Allan, 105
MacLeod, Murdo, 253
*Mad Mission, 3*, 161
Madonna, 89
Magnay, Jacqueline, 136
Maguire, Joseph, 104, 140
Malinowski, Bronislaw, 221, 242
Malinowski, Mr., 219–21, 241
Malthus, Thomas, 24, 75, 260–61
Manet, Edouard, 133
*Man from U.N.C.L.E., The*, 160
Mankiewicz, Joseph L., 38; *Julius Caesar*, 38
Mann, Emily, 205; *Execution of Justice*, 205
Mann, Michael, 149, 151
*Mannix*, 169
Mapplethorpe, Robert, 133
Marc, David, 141
Marconi, Guglielmo, 27
Marcus, George E., 57

Markey, Edward, 245–48, 263
Markwell, Terry, 145
Marky Mark, 105
Marriott, David, 116
Marsalis, Branford, 190
Marshall, E. G., 37
Marshall, Thurgood, 188, 259
Martinson, Leslie H., 38; *PT 109*, 38
Martyn, Shona, 111–12, 134
Marxism, 50–51, 55, 72, 76, 79, 102, 208
Mason, Bobbie Ann, 177
Matsubara, Hiroshi, 199
Mattelart, Armand, 150, 179
Mattelart, Michèle, 150, 179
May, Anthony, 90
Maysles, Albert, 226
Maysles, David, 226
Mazrui, Ali A., 208; *The Africans: A Triple Heritage*, 208
McDuffie, Arthur, 195
McGuigan, Jim, 41
McHoul, Alec, 43, 52–53, 138
McKimmie, Jackie, 145, 167; *Australian Daze*, 145
McQuail, Denis, 82
McRobbie, Angela, 67, 81
Meninga, Malcolm, 108
Menzies, Robert, 179
Mercer, Colin, 79, 85
Mercer, Kobena, 44
Mercurio, Paul, 101
Merelman, Richard, 249
Metz, Christian, 19, 38
*Miami Vice*, 165
Michaels, Eric, 22
Michelangelo, 131
Michelson, Annette, 82
Michnik, Adam, 30
Midnight Oil, 65
Miles, Vera, 224
Milestone, Lewis, 167; *Kangaroo*, 167, 169
Milk, Harvey, 182, 185, 201–6
*Miller v. California*, 122
Miller, D. A., 204
Miller, George, 119, 181; *Mad Max*, 181; *The Witches of Eastwick*, 119
Miller, Gerald R., 201
Millman, Joel, 147
Minogue, Kenneth, 48
*Miranda v. Arizona*, 198
Mishra, Vijay, 47
*Mission: Impossible*, 141, 143–45, 152, 155–70, 174, 176, 179, 181, 262. *See also* De Palma, Brian
Modernity, 31–36, 102, 118, 121, 137, 147–48, 161, 181, 183, 216–17, 235, 237, 244, 246, 248, 253, 260, 263–64
Modleski, Tania, 118
*Mod Squad*, 157
Mongin, Olivier, 248–49
Montand, Yves, 119, 260
*Moonlighting*, 165
Moore, Michael, 141; *Roger & Me*, 141

Ronell, Avital, 193
Ronstadt, Linda, 38
Rorty, Richard, 95
Rosaldo, Renato, 251
Ross, Andrew, 95
Rothwax, Harold, 197
Rouch, Jean, 43, 226–27; *Chronique d'un été*, 227
Routt, William D., 184
Royalle, Candida, 118–19
Rush, Richard, 121; *Color of Night*, 121
Rushdie, Salman, 58
Rushton, J. Philippe, 115–16
Russell, Theresa, 221
Ruthrof, Horst, 255–64, 266; *Pandora and Occam*, 255

Sacks, Harvey, 57, 189
Safire, William, 126
Salmon, Edward, 7
Sanders, Scott, 259
Sanforth, Clifford, 248; *Murder by Television*, 248
Schepisi, Fred, 131; *Six Degrees of Separation*, 131
Schifrin, Lalo, 162
Schiller, Friedrich, 75
Schiller, Herbert, 51–52, 55
Schlesinger, Philip, 29
Schultz, Carl, 145; *Goodbye Paradise*, 145
Schwichtenberg, Cathy, 78
Scott, Ridley, 54; *Blade Runner*, 54
Scott, Tony, 184; *Top Gun*, 184
*Seaquest*, 39
*See It Now*, 34
Sehn, James, 126
Serious, Yahoo, 142, 145; *Young Einstein*, 145
Shafran, Alexander, 252
Shapiro, Michael J., 15
Shils, Edward, 32–33
Siegel, Don, 37; *Dirty Harry*, 37
Silverstone, Roger, 33
Simmel, Georg, 232
Simon, Art, 192
Simpson, Nicole Brown, 184
Simpson, O. J., 183, 190
*Simpsons, The*, 142–43
Sinatra, Frank, 147
Singleton, John, 119, 188; *Poetic Justice*, 119
Skase, Christopher, 142
Smith, Adam, 15, 171
Smith, Anna Deveare, 205; *Twilight: Los Angeles, 1992*, 205
Smith, Desmond, 195–96
Smith, Paul, 93
Smith, William Kennedy, 137, 200
Sofoulis, Zoë, 81
Solanas, Valerie, 126
Sonenstein, Raphael, 182, 200
Spicer, Bryan, 144; *Mighty Morphin Power Rangers*, 144
Spielberg, Steven, 9–10, 39, 258; *Schindler's List*, 9–10, 62, 92, 258
Spock, Benjamin, 123
Springsteen, Bruce, 161

Sprinkle, Annie, 57, 60, 132
Stacey, Jackie, 41
Stallone, Sylvester, 149
*Star Trek*, 39, 157
Stavans, Ilan, 208
Stein, Elliott, 203
Stein, Gertrude, 162
Steinberg, Leo, 197
Stern, Howard, 126
Stewart, Martha, 127
Stiff, James B., 201
Stillwell, Richard, 208
Stokes, Walter R., 124
Stone, Michael, 188
Stone, Oliver, 37–38, 200; *JFK*, 38, 200
Straayer, Chris, 102
Stratton, Jon, 103
Streeter, Thomas, 46, 86
Sturken, Marita, 189
St. Vincent, Julia, 122; *Exhausted*, 122
*Sylvania Waters*, 35, 228
Sylvester, Arthur, 158
Synnott, Anthony, 8

Talalay, Rachel, 119; *Tank Girl*, 119
Taylor, Ashley, 112
Taylor, Damian, 106
Technology, 4, 59, 263
Television, 3, 22–26, 34, 38, 58, 60–61, 107, 155, 175–77, 179–80, 245–49, 264
Thackeray, William, 31
Thomas, Ronald, 261
Thompson, E. P., 38, 89
Thompson, Ernest, 161; *1969*, 161
Thompson, Robert, 199–200
Thring, Frank, 165
Tisdale, Danny, 186; *The Rodney King Police Beating Disaster Series*, 186
Todorov, Tzvetan, 19
Toklas, Alice B., 162
Torr, Diane, 138–39
*Tour of Duty*, 62, 178
Treichler, Paula, 39
Triffin, Robert, 85
Trigger, David, 47
Triggs, Teal, 105
Truth, 4–5, 59, 62–63, 183–85, 193–200, 208–9, 216–17, 245, 251–64
Turner, Graeme, 46, 181
Turner, Patricia, 116–17
Turner, Tina, 107
*21 Beacon Street*, 159
*20/20*, 126

*Uhl v. Columbia Broadcasting System*, 194
Updike, John, 108

Vahimagi, Tise, 156
Valenti, Jack, 259
Vecchione, Judith, 211
Venables, Jon, 199–200
Violence, 59–62, 95, 199–200, 209, 212, 245–47, 263

**TOBY MILLER** is associate professor of cinema studies at New York University. He formerly taught at Murdoch and Griffith Universities and the University of New South Wales, in addition to working for the Australian Broadcasting Corporation and in public and private enterprise. He is the author of *The Well-Tempered Self: Citizenship, Culture, and the Postmodern Subject* (1993), *Contemporary Australian Television* (with Stuart Cunningham) (1994), and *The Avengers* (1997). Editor of the *Journal of Sport & Social Issues* since 1996 and coeditor of *Social Text* since 1997, he has also served on the editorial boards of *Continuum*, *Media International Australia*, *Culture and Policy*, and the *International Journal of Cultural Studies*. He recently edited a special issue of *Social Text* on sport (1997).